The Challenge of Same-Sex Marriage

The Challenge of Same-Sex Marriage

Federalist Principles and Constitutional Protections

MARK STRASSER

PRAEGER

Westport, Connecticut
London

Library of Congress Cataloging-in-Publication Data

Strasser, Mark Philip, 1955–
The challenge of same-sex marriage : federalist principles and constitutional protections / Mark Strasser.
p. cm.
Includes bibliographical references (p.) and index.
ISBN 0–275–96624–0 (alk. paper)
1. Same-sex marriage—Law and legislation—United States.
I. Title.
KF539.S768 1999
346.7301'6—dc21 99–21589

British Library Cataloguing in Publication Data is available.

Library of Congress Catalog Card Number: 99–21589
ISBN: 0–275–96624–0

First published in 1999

Praeger Publishers, 88 Post Road West, Westport, CT 06881
An imprint of Greenwood Publishing Group, Inc.
www.praeger.com

Printed in the United States of America

The paper used in this book complies with the Permanent Paper Standard issued by the National Information Standards Organization (Z39.48–1984).

10 9 8 7 6 5 4 3 2 1

To Vincent Samar,
whose dedication to teaching and
research is a source of inspiration

Contents

Acknowledgments

I have discussed some of these subjects in various law reviews:

"*Baker* and Some Recipes for Disaster: On DOMA, Covenant Marriages, and Full Faith and Credit Jurisprudence," 64 *Brooklyn Law Review* 307–351 (1998).

"Constitutional Limitations and *Baehr* Possibilities: On Retroactive Legislation, Reasonable Expectations, and Manifest Injustice," 29 *Rutgers Law Journal* 271–314 (1998).

"DOMA and the Two Faces of Federalism," 32 *Creighton Law Review* 457–475 (1998).

"Ex Post Facto Laws, Bills of Attainder, and the Definition of Punishment: On DOMA, the Hawaii Amendment, and Federal Constitutional Constraints," 48 *Syracuse Law Review* 227–259 (1998).

"For Whom *Bell* Tolls: On Subsequent Domiciles' Refusing to Recognize Same-Sex Marriages," 66 *University of Cincinnati Law Review* 339–383 (1998).

"The Future of Same-Sex Marriage," 19 *University of Hawaii Law Review* (1998).

"Natural Law and Same-Sex Marriage," 48 *DePaul Law Review* 51–81 (1998).

"Sodomy, Adultery, and Same-Sex Marriage: On Legal Analysis and Fundamental Interests," 8 *University of California at Los Angeles Women's Law Journal* 313–339 (1998).

"Statutory Construction, Equal Protection, and the Amendment Process: On *Romer*, *Hunter*, and Efforts to Tame *Baehr*," 45 *Buffalo Law Review* 739–777 (1997).

I thank each of these law reviews, without whose help this book would not have been possible. I also wish to thank Heather Staines of Praeger Publishers and George Cronheim for their help in seeing this project through to completion.

Introduction

In 1993, a plurality of the Hawaii Supreme Court held that the state's same-sex marriage ban implicated equal protection concerns and remanded the case to give the state an opportunity to show that it had compelling interests in maintaining such a ban. In 1996, a Hawaii circuit court held that the state had not met its burden and that the state's reserving marriage for opposite-sex couples was prohibited by the state constitution, although the court stayed that ruling pending review by the state supreme court. In February, 1998, an Alaska trial court held that the state's same-sex marriage ban violated the state constitution's due process guarantees. In November, 1998, the Hawaii and Alaska electorates voted to modify their state constitutions, effectively nullifying the court holdings on this issue, since the constitutions upon which those opinions had been based had themselves changed. This book examines the legal ramifications of the amendments to the Hawaii and Alaska Constitutions, both for those states and for the nation, and also explores what will likely happen as soon as Hawaii, Alaska, or some other state recognizes same-sex marriages.

Marriage promotes a variety of individual and state interests, whether the marital couple is composed of individuals of the same or opposite sex. Arguably, state legislatures should pass legislation to extend legal recognition to same-sex unions as a matter of good public policy, although that seems unlikely in the near future. In the short term, same-sex marriage rights will most likely be accorded as a result of a court's recognizing that they are protected by state or federal constitutional guarantees.

Same-sex marriage opponents offer a variety of specious arguments in their attempts to establish that there is no constitutional right to marry a same-sex partner. For example, some commentators argue that if a state is constitutionally required to recognize same-sex marriages, then that state would also be constitutionally required to recognize incestuous and polygamous marriages and, further, would be constitutionally precluded from passing adultery and sodomy laws. Yet, these claims are specious. The harms that are implicated in incestuous and polygamous marriages simply are not present in same-sex marriages, which involve only two individuals who are not members of the same family. Adulterous relationships and same-sex unions are disanalogous in a constitutionally significant respect, since the protection of the former would tend to undermine families while the recognition of the latter would tend to strengthen them. Those arguing that sodomy laws would somehow be invalidated if same-sex marriages were recognized seem to forget that most sodomy laws are not restricted to same-sex sodomy. Just as there is a marital exception to sodomy laws for opposite-sex married couples, there would be a marital exception to such laws for same-sex married couples. Were same-sex unions legally recognized, the couples would be protected by an existing exception and thus the invalidation of all sodomy laws would not be required. Although sodomy laws are probably unconstitutional because they violate the Due Process Clause of the Fourteenth Amendment of the United States Constitution, that is so whether or not same-sex marriages are recognized. Thus, a court's recognizing that same-sex marriage rights are constitutionally protected simply would not entail the claimed proliferation of rights.

Before the Hawaii Constitution was amended, the Hawaii Supreme Court was expected to hold that the state's same-sex marriage ban violated the Equal Protection Clause of the state constitution, both facially and as applied. Because the law permitted men to marry women but not men and women to marry men but not women, a plurality of the court had already held that the ban implicated equal protection guarantees. The only question that had remained for the court to decide had been whether the asserted state interests justified such a ban. Assuming that the referendum did not itself violate constitutional guarantees, the Hawaii Supreme Court will no longer have to address the state constitutional question which had been posed.

An important difference between the Hawaii Constitution's Equal Protection Clause and the United States Constitution's Equal Protection Clause is that the former imposes a heavier burden of justification on the state when statutes employing sex-based classifications are at issue. Thus, suppose that the same law were challenged on federal and state constitutional grounds. A court might suggest that the law meets the constitutional requirements imposed by the federal but not by the state constitution and that the statute would be unconstitutional in Hawaii but not anywhere else where this heavier burden was not imposed. However, merely because a statute could *conceivably* pass the federal but not the state test does not establish that a same-sex marriage ban would in fact pass the weaker test imposed by the United States Constitution.

If indeed same-sex marriage bans implicate federal equal protection guarantees, then it seems likely that those bans will not survive federal scrutiny. Further, there is reason to think that federal guarantees are implicated by such bans, since an important similarity between the Hawaii and United States Constitutions has not received adequate attention, namely, the test determining whether a statute implicates the Equal Protection Clause is the *same* under the Hawaii and federal constitutions. Thus, if a plurality of the Hawaii Supreme Court was convinced that the statute at issue implicated state equal protection guarantees, the plurality should also be convinced that the statute implicates federal equal protection guarantees. By the same token, the Alaska trial court believed that equal protection issues were implicated by the state's same-sex marriage ban without implying that the state constitutional protections were any broader in scope than are the federal protections.

Realizing that the state supreme courts might hold that the state bans violated state constitutional guarantees, same-sex marriage opponents succeeded in having issues placed on the ballot in November, 1998, which would amend the state constitutions to prohibit same-sex marriage or to permit the legislature to reserve marriage for opposite-sex couples. Those issues passed. Because the state constitutions have been changed, it does not matter that the same-sex marriage bans might have violated the former constitutions. For state constitutional purposes, the relevant question before the courts will be whether the statute violates the *current* state constitution. Because the state constitution now specifically authorizes the Hawaii Legislature to reserve marriages for opposite-sex couples, the legislature's doing so would obviously not violate that constitution. Because the Alaska Constitution now prohibits same-sex marriage, the state statute to that effect obviously does not violate that constitution's guarantees.

Yet, it should not be thought that the referenda themselves will be without constitutional difficulty. The United States Supreme Court has held other state amendments unconstitutional because they were designed to disadvantage identifiable minorities. Given the purpose of these amendments, there is good reason to believe that they, themselves, will be held unconstitutional.

Suppose that the amendments are challenged in court and their constitutionality is upheld, past precedent notwithstanding. The approved amendments do not make the same-sex marriage bans non-sex-based, but merely amend the state constitutions to permit this sex-based distinction. Passage of the amendment notwithstanding, the Hawaii Supreme Court will likely hold that the state's same-sex marriage ban offends federal constitutional guarantees. The Alaska Supreme Court may do so as well, although the issue of whether such bans in fact violate federal guarantees will eventually have to be resolved by the United States Supreme Court.

Suppose that the Hawaii Supreme Court had struck down the same-sex marriage ban under the former state constitution but, several months later, had also upheld the permissibility of reserving marriages for opposite-sex couples under the new constitution. The court might have had to determine the validity of those same-sex marriages which had been celebrated in the interim. Even if a state could enact a same-sex marriage ban without offending constitutional guarantees, that would not also entitle the legislature to void those marriages that had already been celebrated. While this issue is not presented in the Hawaii or Alaska cases in particular, it may be raised if an analogous state constitutional amendment is passed in a different state after that state supreme court has held that the previously existing constitution required the recognition of same-sex marriages.

Suppose that same-sex marriages are recognized in Hawaii and Alaska, perhaps because the referenda themselves are found to violate constitutional guarantees. A separate question will be whether other states will have to recognize those unions validly celebrated in Hawaii and Alaska. The Full Faith and Credit Clause requires that *judgments* issued in any state be given full faith and credit in all of the states, as long as certain jurisdictional requirements have been met. For example, a divorce secured in one state must be given full faith and credit in all of the states, absent fraud or lack of jurisdiction. However, because as a general matter marriages are not reduced to judgment, it might seem that the Constitution would not require that same-sex marriages celebrated in one state would have to be recognized by any other state, although that is false, since there are other reasons that states are not free to refuse to recognize marriages valid in the states of celebration and domicile at the time of the marriage.

A question related to but different from whether full faith and credit must be given to another state's judgment involves which state's law should be applied to a transaction or occurrence when more than one state's law is potentially applicable. The general rule for marriages is that only the laws of the states of celebration or domicile at the time of the marriage are even *potentially* applicable. That rule further specifies that the law of the state of celebration will be applied unless the marriage violates an important public policy of the domicile at the time of the marriage.

Suppose that Smith and Jones live in one state, and marry and honeymoon in another. As long as their marriage is valid where they in fact celebrate the marriage and as long as their home state does not treat their marriage as void, the general rule is that their marriage will be valid in *all* states. No other state's law would be used to determine the validity of that marriage. Suppose further that two years into their marriage the couple decides to move to a new state to take advantage of a job opportunity. The general rule is that their new home state would have to recognize the marriage, even if that state had a law making such marriages void.

The Defense of Marriage Act (DOMA) *may* have changed the rules for the validity of same-sex marriages, although the very brevity of the Act makes it difficult to interpret. Arguably, nothing has changed with respect to when marriages should be recognized. Indeed, the proponents of the Act claim that it does not change existing law, which means that the rule described above would also apply to same-sex marriages. However, on a different interpretation of the Act, any state could refuse to recognize the validity of a same-sex marriage, even if the couple had never been domiciled there and even if the couple had been married for twenty years in a different state.

The Defense of Marriage Act violates a number of constitutional guarantees such as those provided by the Due Process Clause, the Equal Protection Clause, the Privileges and Immunities Clause, and the Bill of Attainder Clause. Protestations to the contrary notwithstanding, the Congress has not prevented a particular group from enjoying "special rights," but has instead picked out a distinct minority and subjected them to unique disabilities. The United States Supreme Court has already suggested that this kind of selective, adverse treatment is unconstitutional, although that did not stop the Congress from pandering to particular constitutencies. Indeed, the very obviousness of the pandering provides additional support for the claim that the Congress has acted unconstitutionally. Further, some of these same federal constitutional guarantees would preclude states from refusing of their own accord to recognize validly celebrated same-sex marriages.

As a separate matter, the Defense of Marriage Act is very unwise legislation. It undermines the goals of other legislation that Congress has passed and permits individuals to avoid their marital obligations. Further, by even attempting to enact this legislation, Congress has issued an open invitation for groups to pressure it to make other exceptions to the Full Faith and Credit Clause, thereby promoting disharmony and disunity among the states.

When Congress passed this Act, it claimed to be promoting federalism. However, there are two faces to federalism. Federalism involves respecting state sovereignty over certain protected matters as part of a *bargain* in which the states surrendered some of their sovereignty to become part of the United States rather than remain a loose collection of independent states. The Congress has tried to change the basic structure of the system, thereby throwing off the balance which federalist principles had already achieved. By giving in to particular groups who want to force a disfavored minority to undergo hardships which no other group must undergo, the Congress has both lent credence to arguments that ignore constitutional guarantees and, in addition, has further jeopardized the federalist balance which is growing increasingly difficult to maintain. When Congress passed DOMA, it *undermined* rather than strengthened our system of federalism. Congress is supposed to promote the interests of the country as a whole while respecting constitutional guarantees. When it passed DOMA, it did neither.

Chapter 1 suggests that same-sex marriages would promote the same individual and state interests that opposite-sex marriages already promote. The chapter further suggests that polygamous, adulterous, and incestuous unions are distinguishable from same-sex marriages in legally significant ways and thus that the latter being protected by the Constitution would not also entail that the former must be protected as well. Although same-sex marriage rights will likely be recognized because of equal protection guarantees, this chapter demonstrates that even were that recognition based on due process guarantees, the holding would not have the implications that some same-sex marriage opponents claim.

Chapter 2 discusses the view expressed by a plurality of the Hawaii Supreme Court and by the Alaska trial court that same-sex marriage bans implicate equal protection guarantees. Notwithstanding the great attention that has been given to that aspect of the Hawaii holding which entails that such a ban must receive the utmost scrutiny, the more important aspect of the holding may be that such bans implicate equal protection guarantees. Because the United States Constitution prevents states from discriminating on the basis of sex absent an exceedingly persuasive reason for doing so, the suggestion by these courts that same-sex marriage bans trigger those protections may have much more significant implications than currently seems to be appreciated.

Chapter 3 discusses the November, 1998, referenda in which the Hawaii and Alaska electorates decided to amend their state constitutions. Various United States Supreme Court decisions suggest that even though the amendments passed, federal constitutional guarantees might prevent their implementation. Because the amendments were clearly designed to impose a special burden on an identifiable class, their constitutionality is quite doubtful.

Suppose that the supreme courts of Hawaii and Alaska had held that the (former) constitutions required that same-sex marriages be recognized and that some same-sex couples had indeed taken their vows and been legally recognized as married. Suppose further that the constitutionality of the referenda had been upheld. Chapter 4 discusses whether those same-sex marriages that had already been celebrated could be retroactively nullified and whether the state legislatures could simply have dissolved all those same-sex unions that had already been celebrated, concluding that the United States Constitution would bar such an action. This chapter has import both because the hypothesized scenario may well occur in a different state and because the chapter helps to establish why certain states would be precluded from refusing to recognize some same-sex marriages that had been validly celebrated in sister states.

Chapter 5 discusses the Full Faith and Credit Clause, which requires states to give full faith and credit to sister state judgments. While lesser obligations are imposed with respect to sister states' laws and records, states nonetheless traditionally recognize those marriages valid in the domicile at the time of the marriage, even if contrary to their own law. Further, the faith and credit due other state courts' judgments *may* force states to recognize same-sex marriages validly celebrated elsewhere, although not for the reasons or in the circumstances commonly discussed.

Chapter 6 discusses whether subsequent domiciles will be allowed to refuse to recognize marriages valid in the states of celebration and domicile at the time of the marriage. While there are exceptions to the general rule requiring subsequent domiciles to recognize marriages validly celebrated in sister domiciliary states, those exceptions do not apply in this case. Indeed, many states would seem required by their *own* laws to recognize such marriages under those circumstances.

Chapter 7 discusses the natural law critique of same-sex marriage. That critique is unpersuasive both because many of the arguments seem as readily to support as to undermine same-sex marriage and because those arguments that allegedly establish the impermissibility of same-sex marriage would also seem to establish the impermissibility of a variety of practices that are currently permitted by law. Theorists who claim that their analyses are reflected in the existing law either misrepresent or misunderstand current domestic relations law.

Chapter 8 discusses the Defense of Marriage Act, which not only violates several constitutional guarantees but involves Congress's having exceeded its authority under the Full Faith and Credit Clause. If the constitutionality of this Act of Congress is upheld, the stage will have been set not only for the gutting of a variety of constitutional protections for individuals but also for a return to the days when this country was more like a loose confederation of independent sovereignties than a collection of states that are integral parts of a single nation.

The Challenge of Same-Sex Marriage

1

Marriage Rights

In 1996, a Hawaii court held the state's same-sex marriage ban unconstitutional. The Hawaii Supreme Court was expected to affirm that decision until the state constitution was amended by referendum in November, 1998. Such a decision would have forced the rest of the states to confront a variety of issues, not the least of which would have been whether their own prohibitions violate state or federal constitutional guarantees. In order for a same-sex marriage ban to be constitutional, there must be legitimate reasons supporting such a statute rather than, for example, a mere desire to disadvantage a disfavored group.

While the United States Supreme Court has held that legislation is unconstitutional if it seems inexplicable by anything but animus toward the class that it affects,[1] the Court has also made clear that reasonable regulations, including reasonable marital regulations, are constitutionally permissible. Further, a marital regulation may be reasonable even if it permanently bars some individuals from marrying other individuals. For example, various courts have suggested that statutes barring incest and polygamy do not violate constitutional guarantees. One issue that must be addressed is whether same-sex marriages serve the same individual and state interests that other marriages do or whether, instead, they are analogous to polygamous or incestuous unions and hence arguably subject to state regulation.

Even if same-sex marriages are not analogous to those unions, a related issue that would have to be addressed by any court considering the constitutionality of a same-sex marriage ban is whether striking down that statute would somehow imply that all statutes limiting the right to marry are also constitutionally offensive. Some commentators suggest that if same-sex marriage bans are unconstitutional, then all marriage bans are unconstitutional, including bans on polygamous, adulterous, or incestuous unions. Yet, the fallacy of such a claim is clear when the costs and benefits of each type of ban are considered. Same-sex marriage would promote many of the same interests that other marriages do[2] and are disanalogous to polygamous, adulterous, and incestuous unions in legally significant ways.

THE STATE INTERESTS IN MARRIAGE

Any analysis of the constitutionality of a same-sex marriage ban must begin with the recognition that the state has a variety of interests in promoting marriage, since marriage promotes stability for adults and children and helps individuals lead happier and more productive lives. The state has an interest in providing a setting for the production and raising of the next generation,[3] which would be *promoted* by recognizing same-sex unions, since same-sex couples also have and raise children. Regrettably, the state's interest in the next generation is easily misunderstood and has been mischaracterized in a way which purportedly establishes that individuals should not be permitted to marry a same-sex partner.

The state has an interest in having parents raise their biological children because, at least in part, it is presumed that such parents will care for their children and will provide an environment in which those children will thrive. However, the state has an interest in having healthy and flourishing children produced and raised, even if those children are *not* raised by both of their biological parents. As long as the child will be happy and well-adjusted,[4] it should not matter to the state that the child's parents include only one adult who is biologically related to that child or even whether the two parents are of the same or of the opposite sex. Indeed, even where the child is raised by two adults, neither of whom has any biological connection to the child, the state's interests in the next generation are promoted as long as the child is well cared for.[5]

The state has an interest in *both* the production *and* the raising of children. Even if lesbians and gays were producing *no* children and were "merely" providing homes in which the children might thrive, the state's interest in the next generation would still be promoted by allowing same-sex partners to marry and to provide homes in which the children might be raised to grow up to be happy and productive members of society. Thus, claims to the contrary notwithstanding, the state's compelling interest in fostering procreation and in providing status and stability to the environment in which children are raised supports rather than undermines the state's recognizing same-sex marriages.[6]

Courts and commentators who discuss why same-sex couples should not be allowed to marry imply that the interest of the state in the creation and care of the next generation can only be served if the children are produced "through the union" of the couple.[7] But that is not the state's interest, as is clear from the state's policies on adoption, foster care, etc. Indeed, given current demographics concerning the surprisingly small percentage of children in households with both of their biological parents, it is at the very least surprising that this kind of argument would be offered.[8] That this argument is not offered to prevent sterile opposite-sex couples from marrying or to make it more difficult for single individuals to adopt children but is only offered in the context of trying to invent some justification for prohibiting same-sex couples from marrying suggests that the rationale is pretextual and not offered in good faith.[9] While it is of course not argued here that sterile opposite-sex couples should be prevented from marrying or that adopting children should be made more difficult, it is argued that selective use of the "through the union" rationale makes the argument even less plausible.

Marriage provides stability for adults as well as for children. Stability benefits the individuals themselves and society as a whole. It is in *society's* interest that individuals have homes that are a source of strength and stability, at least in part because the individuals will then be more productive members of society.

The state has a financial interest in promoting marriage because, for example, the marital partners will provide care for each other, should the need arise, so that the state will not have to do so.[10] Thus, should someone become ill[11] or temporarily in need of financial support because of unfortunate circumstances,[12] society has an interest in the marital partner's helping out rather than having the state be required to do so. By promoting marriage for same-sex couples, the state will be promoting individuals to take care of their (marital) partners in times of need.

Given the incidence of divorce in this country,[13] it is likely that some same-sex couples will seek a divorce, should they be allowed to marry. Yet, society also has an interest in assuring that break-ups occur in an organized way,[14] that property is divided equitably, and that the custodial arrangements for children promote their best interests.[15]

Commentators sometimes discuss the "civilizing" influence of marriage.[16] Especially in the context of whether same-sex couples should be allowed to marry, however, it is quite clear that different individuals have very different things in mind when discussing this issue. While they all have in mind something about the possible effects on attitudes or actions of permitting same-sex individuals to marry, the kinds of attitudes and actions that are included within the "civilizing" category are sufficiently dissimilar that grouping them together may be confusing. Two different claims about the "civilizing" effect of marriage are discussed below: (1) that marriage reduces promiscuity, and (2) that marriage co-opts individuals into adopting traditional roles.

Some commentators suggest that same-sex marriage cannot have the desirable civilizing or "domesticating" effect,[17] since individuals who seek to marry their same-sex partners are allegedly promiscuous[18] and, in addition, incapable of not being so.[19] Yet, such an argument is unpersuasive for at least two reasons. First, the initial claims are inaccurate, since the promiscuity is at the very least exaggerated.[20] Second, the implication that gays are subject to uncontrollable urges is clearly false,[21] since the AIDS crisis has brought about a change in sexual behavior.[22]

Consider the suggestion that marriage would not civilize gay men because "the great tendency of homosexual males to be promiscuous"[23] would not be tamed by marriage. Given that there is no reason to believe that only gay males would have such a trait, the claim is presumably that males in general have this trait.[24] Yet, if heterosexual males can be domesticated through marriage, notwithstanding this alleged tendency to be promiscuous, some reason must be offered to explain why gay males would not also be changed by marriage. The further argument offered is that only women can domesticate men.[25] Since males would be marrying other males, there would be no one to stop them from their wandering ways.

Yet, there is reason to doubt these characterizations of men and women.[26] Further, insofar as these characterizations involve stereotypes and these stereotypes are providing a specious basis for enacting a law barring same-sex marriages, the statute at issue may violate the Equal Protection Clause of the Fourteenth Amendment of the United States Constitution.

It seems plausible to suggest that recognizing same-sex marriage would promote but not guarantee long-term, monogamous, same-sex relationships, just as the recognition of opposite-sex marriage promotes but does not guarantee long-term, monogamous, opposite-sex relationships.[27] Insofar as marriage might lessen promiscuity and insofar as promiscuity is viewed as bad,[28] one would expect this to be a reason to allow such marriages. One would certainly not expect commentators to claim that because it has not yet been *established* that "marriage would have the same, domesticating effect on homosexual members as it has on heterosexuals,"[29] same-sex couples should not be allowed to marry, as if this would have to be something that was proven *before* one could take the chance of allowing same-sex partners to marry.

When trying to defend its antimiscegenation law, the state of Virginia argued that because science had not yet established whether there was a rational basis for a state's treating interracial marriages differently from other marriages, the United States Supreme Court should defer to the wisdom of the Virginia Legislature, which after due deliberation had decided to adopt a policy of discouraging interracial marriages.[30] The Court rejected the state's analysis, recognizing the invidious nature of the argument offered,[31] notwithstanding the state's claims about the alleged scientific uncertainties associated with recognizing the marriage at issue. So, too, a court hearing an argument concerning the alleged scientific uncertainties with respect to marriage's civilizing effect on same-sex couples should recognize the invidious nature of the state's argument and treat it accordingly.

The point here should not be misunderstood. It is reasonable to believe that some who marry their same-sex partners will not be monogamous. Yet, it is quite clear that not all heterosexuals who marry are faithful,[32] and no one is (yet) suggesting that they therefore be prohibited from marrying.

There is yet another reason to believe that accusations of incurable promiscuity are not only false but made in bad faith. Accusations of promiscuity are often made against traditionally disfavored groups. For example, some have claimed that racial minorities are more promiscuous than whites,[33] perhaps as a kind of justification for a reduction in public support of "those" people.[34] Sometimes, single welfare mothers are accused of being promiscuous, at least in part, in an attempt to offer some rationale to help "justify" compulsory sterilization of them.[35] Accusations of promiscuity are often made as a way of allegedly justifying a deprivation of rights that cannot otherwise be justified.[36]

Sometimes, commentators discussing the civilizing effects of marriage are not discussing the sexual habits of the parties but, instead, whether allowing same-sex couples to marry would somehow co-opt them into adopting traditional roles and becoming more mainstream.[37] Of course, some same- sex couples are already mainstream, and others are not and will consciously choose to reject traditional roles even if allowed to marry.[38] It is simply too difficult to predict how allowing individuals to marry would affect the roles they adopt, although it seems plausible to believe that many couples would not adopt significantly different roles than they have already adopted in their long-term, not-yet-legally-recognized relationships.[39] In any event, these simply are not the bases upon which the same-sex marriage issue should be decided.

Suppose that the issue was whether interracial couples should be allowed to marry. Individuals would presumably be embarrassed to argue that the recognition of such marriages should depend either upon whether the union would have a civilizing influence upon the would-be marital partners or upon whether there were assurances that the individuals who entered into such marriages would not be co-opted into adopting particular roles or values. The discussion about the civilizing effect would rightly be viewed as insulting and invidious and the discussion about being co-opted would rightly be viewed as imposing a political litmus test on a fundamental right. Individuals should be allowed to allocate marital duties in the way they feel appropriate, without having their right to marry hang in the balance.

INDIVIDUAL INTERESTS IN MARRIAGE

The Supreme Court has recognized that the right to marry is of fundamental importance for all individuals.[40] Yet, if indeed it is of fundamental importance for *all* individuals, then that must mean that it is of fundamental importance for lesbians and gays, too. Further, it would strain credulity to claim that lesbians and gays have the fundamental right to marry, but they simply do not have the right to marry a same-sex partner.[41] One can imagine the response that would be offered were a state to reserve marriage for same-sex couples and then claim that those who wished to marry opposite-sex partners of course had the fundamental right to marry, just not someone of the opposite sex.

The Supreme Court has articulated the numerous and significant individual interests that are implicated in marriage—marriages are expressions of emotional support and public commitment,[42] marriages may involve an expression of religious faith or personal dedication[43] and, further, marriage is often a precondition to the receipt of government benefits.[44] All of these would apply to same-sex as well as opposite-sex couples.[45] Same-sex couples also wish to manifest their commitment both privately and publicly. Some religions will sanctify same-sex unions, lack of accompanying legal recognition notwithstanding. Thus, when one examines the articulated, significant interests that are implicated in marriage for opposite-sex couples, one finds that those same interests are implicated in marriage for same-sex couples.

LIMITATIONS ON STATE POWER

Historically, states had, and to some extent still have, great discretion with respect to the content of their marital statutes. States set the age of consent for marriage[46] and the conditions under which individuals who have not yet attained that age may nonetheless marry—for example, if a pregnancy is involved[47] or if parental permission has been obtained.[48] Further, states may set the conditions under which individuals will be allowed to divorce, which will affect when and if individuals will be permitted to remarry. Since no state allows individuals to enter into a polygamous marriage, an individual's being unable to divorce would of course preclude that person from marrying someone else.

Until fairly recently, states would set their own policies with respect to whether interracial couples would be allowed to marry.[49] It was not until 1967 in *Loving v. Virginia*[50] that the Supreme Court held that interracial bans violated the Equal Protection Clause of the Fourteenth Amendment to the United States Constitution.

Perhaps it would seem surprising that it would take about 100 years after the passage of the Civil War Amendments for the Court to find that such laws were unconstitutional.[51] Certainly, one would think, someone must have realized that the Fourteenth Amendment might prohibit such bans. In fact, bans on interracial marriage did not go unchallenged. However, courts almost universally upheld the state marital laws against the Fourteenth Amendment challenge,[52] holding that the state's right to make its own marriage laws was a matter of state sovereignty.[53] Indeed, before the United State Supreme Court struck down interracial marriage bans on federal constitutional grounds, some states had provisions within their own state constitutions which prohibited such unions.[54]

Perhaps it would seem that interracial marriage is a special case and thus the Court's having struck down state antimiscegenation laws does not reflect anything about the right to marry as such. However, the Supreme Court made very clear in *Loving v. Virginia* that although the statute at hand was invidious because of its clear white supremacist overtones,[55] the statute was also invidious because it denied the freedom to marry, which had long been recognized as one of the vital personal rights essential to the orderly pursuit of happiness.[56] Further, the Supreme Court has struck down other state laws limiting the right to marry, even when race was not implicated. For example, the Court has held that states may be precluded from preventing indigents or prisoners from marrying.[57] Because the right to marry is a fundamental right which all citizens may enjoy, statutes which significantly interfere with that right will only be upheld if the state has important state interests at stake and if the marriage legislation is closely tailored to promote only those interests.[58]

Many individuals either do not understand or do not appreciate the importance of the above requirement. It simply will not suffice to say that because this is a democracy, the issue of who may marry whom should be determined by a popular vote. This is a *constitutional* democracy, where the will of the majority is constrained by the protections that have been guaranteed by federal and state constitutions. The Supreme Court has made clear that fundamental rights may not be submitted to a vote and do not depend on the outcome of particular elections.[59]

It simply is not a plausible reading of our constitutional history to believe that something as fundamental as who should be allowed to marry whom should simply be left up to a popular vote. Were that the test for the constitutionality of marital statutes, the Supreme Court presumably should not have struck down Virginia's antimiscegenation law, since there was ample support for laws barring interracial marriage at the time.

Suppose one were to ask individuals who were already married whether they would be willing to put to a popular vote whether the state should continue to recognize their marriages. Perhaps some would be willing, confident that the populace would vote to continue state recognition of their union. Yet, presumably, many would not think this the appropriate way to determine whether the state should recognize their marriages, even if in fact they were confident that the majority would vote the "correct" way.

Disfavored minorities might be especially uneasy about subjecting their right to marry to popular vote, since there is ample historical precedent to justify the belief that such rights may not be adequately protected. Before the Civil War, slave marriages were not recognized as legal marriages,[60] ostensibly because slaves were not able to give consent.[61] Even if the masters "consented" for the slaves, the marriages still were not legally recognized,[62] although these marriages were recognized as having moral force.[63]

When courts discussed the moral force to be given to slave marriages, they presumably believed that God recognized such marriages, since those discussing morality often believed it inextricably connected to God's Will. Thus, the courts would be claiming that while God might recognize the slave marriages, the state would not.

Certainly, many would claim that the laws of the civil state need not mirror religious dictates, both because of the differences in religious belief (and nonbelief) in this country and because some religious dictates are aspirational rather than obligatory in any event. Yet, there is reason to believe that the state's failure to recognize unions that God recognized was not due to a respect for religious pluralism but instead a rejection of the content of that particular view. For example, when it was claimed that God recognized interracial marriages, God's view was thought irrelevant insofar as the issue was whether the state should recognize such unions. However, when it was claimed that God would not recognize interracial marriages, that was viewed as a reason that the state should not do so either.[64]

Some commentators currently argue that the state should not recognize same-sex unions because, allegedly, God does not recognize them. However, such commentators are strangely silent when it is pointed out that others believe that God does recognize such marriages and that some religions recognize same-sex unions.

TESTS FOR FUNDAMENTAL RIGHTS

An examination of American history will suggest why minority rights should not be left up to popular vote.[65] It will also suggest the wrongheadedness of some of the tests sometimes proposed or used to determine which rights are fundamental for constitutional purposes. Consider the approach of Justice Scalia, who has suggested that a particular practice or activity is not protected if "(1) the Constitution says absolutely nothing about it, and (2) the longstanding traditions of American society have permitted it to be legally proscribed."[66] Given that the Constitution says nothing about interracial marriage or marriage at all for that matter,[67] such an approach would seem to imply that *Loving v. Virginia* was wrongly decided and that interracial marriage bans do not violate constitutional guarantees.[68]

Justice Scalia has denied that his approach would yield such a result, arguing that the tradition which would require upholding interracial marriage bans "was contradicted by a text—an Equal Protection Clause that explicitly establishes racial equality as a constitutional value."[69] Yet, there is reason to believe Justice Scalia's response disingenuous. First, the Equal Protection Clause reads in relevant part, "No State shall . . . deny to any person within the jurisdiction the equal protection of the laws."[70] While this text of course precludes discrimination on the basis of race, it also precludes discrimination on a variety of other grounds, since *no* person shall be denied the equal protection of the laws. Indeed, the text does not explicitly single out race, Justice Scalia's comments notwithstanding. Further, it is quite clear that

Justice Scalia believes that this clause should only apply to certain groups, explicit text lacking such a qualification notwithstanding.[71]

To suggest that Justice Scalia's test is inappropriate does not establish which test is correct. Perhaps it will be thought unnecessary to establish that because it is thought unnecessary to have *any* test. Yet, there ought to be some test, since judges often have to decide whether contested statutes unfairly burden fundamental rights.

Perhaps it would seem that no *uniform* test is necessary. When a judge is confronted with a claim that a particular statute burdens a fundamental right, she might simply decide to use that test which seems most likely to yield a particular result. Thus, a judge who believed that the number of fundamental interests should be increased might, all else equal, favor a relatively unrestrictive test while a judge who believed that the number of fundamental interests should not be increased or, perhaps, should be decreased might favor a relatively restrictive test. However, the test to determine which rights are fundamental should not simply be based on an individual judge's preferences with respect to whether the number of fundamental rights should be increased, decreased, or remain constant, since such an approach would at best be unprincipled. At the very least, the test to be employed should account for those fundamental interests that have already been recognized and those that have not. Regrettably, Justice Scalia's approach fails in this regard as well. While his approach can explain why particular activities were *not* recognized as implicating fundamental interests—they were not mentioned in the Constitution and there were long-standing traditions permitting the legal proscription of those activities—his approach can neither explain nor account for why a number of activities have in fact been recognized as involving fundamental interests. For example, on his account, no fundamental interests would be implicated in laws prohibiting contraception, abortion, or interracial marriage, Supreme Court rulings to the contrary notwithstanding.[72]

An alternative approach to determining which rights are fundamental has been discussed and employed by the courts—namely, looking to see whether the right at issue is "so rooted in the traditions and collective conscience of our people that failure to recognize it would violate the fundamental principles of liberty and justice that lie at the base of all our civil and political institutions."[73] Yet, this approach is open to the same kinds of criticisms as is Justice Scalia's, since historically disfavored groups will *of course* not be protected if that test is used. Indeed, since something that is deeply rooted in the traditions and collective conscience of our people would presumably not be something that the long-standing traditions of American society would permit to be legally proscribed, it seems unlikely that many interests would be recognized as fundamental in the collective conscience approach that would not also be recognized using Justice Scalia's approach. Certainly, the collective conscience approach would not have prevented contraception, abortion, or interracial marriage from being legally proscribed.

It is at best ironic that the traditions and collective conscience test is currently interpreted to mean that an activity or practice will not be thought to involve a fundamental interest unless that activity is *already* deeply rooted in the collective conscience of the people, given the interpretation that this standard was given in *Rochin v. California*.[74] In *Rochin*, the Court viewed the traditions and collective conscience test as a kind of *compromise* between two unacceptable approaches: (a) an approach in which judges would draw on their merely personal and private notions, and (b) an approach in which judges would think of the list of fundamental rights as final and fixed.[75] However, if one ignores the *Rochin* Court's warning and interprets the traditions and conscience test such that it cannot be met unless the Framers would have recognized the interest at issue as protected, the test freezes the list of fundamental rights and does exactly what the *Rochin* Court warned must not be done.[76] A better approach for determining which activities are protected by the right to privacy involves reasoned judgment in light of the developing constitutional jurisprudence[77] rather than the traditions and conscience test; indeed, Justice Scalia admits that the latter test is not in fact the test that the Court uses to determine which rights are fundamental.[78]

The Supreme Court has already recognized that the right to marry is fundamental. Arguably, that right includes the right to marry a same-sex partner,[79] although most courts have refused to recognize that this right extends to same-sex couples.[80]

Even were the right to marry a same-sex partner fundamental, that would not preclude the state from prohibiting such marriages if the state had sufficiently compelling reasons to do so. The Constitution permits states to impose *reasonable* limitations on who can marry whom.[81] For example, some limitations on the rights of minors to marry are permissible, in part because minors may not be able to make an informed, deliberate decision and in part because their not being allowed to marry might only delay the union rather than preclude it entirely, since they presumably can marry once they reach majority.[82]

Neither of the rationales supporting the permissibility of regulating the marriages of minors supports the permissibility of the state's preventing same-sex couples from marrying. Insofar as the same-sex individuals are adults, it cannot be claimed that the decisions of these individuals will be any less informed or deliberate than the decisions of any other adults who wish to marry. Further, insofar as a state *ban* on same-sex marriage is at issue, it cannot be claimed that the prohibition would simply involve a delay, since it would entirely preclude the individuals from marrying.

INCEST

Precisely because minors may not yet be mature enough to make the appropriate decisions and precisely because their being precluded from marrying may merely mean that they have to wait until they both have reached majority, the state's ability to regulate minor marriages may not seem to have much import for whether the state can ban same-sex marriages. A better example might seem to involve a prohibition that involves a permanent ban on two adults marrying—for example, a state's ban on incestuous relations.

States have some latitude in defining incest in the way in which they believe appropriate, thereby specifying how closely related individuals may be before they will be precluded from marrying. Some states regard sexual relations between first cousins as incestuous while others do not;[83] some states regard sexual relations between adoptive parents and their adopted children as incestuous while others do not;[84] and some states regard sexual relations between stepparents and stepchildren as incestuous while others do not.[85]

When commentators discuss why it is allegedly permissible for states to preclude same-sex marriages, they point to laws prohibiting incest. Basically, the suggestion is that if same-sex unions are allowed, then everything must be allowed, including fathers marrying their daughters.[86] Yet, there is no reason to believe this, as should be clear when one considers what would be involved in each kind of union.

There are obvious differences between same-sex marriages on the one hand and incestuous marriages on the other. Incestuous marriages involve two individuals who marry despite being too closely related by blood. Permitting same-sex marriages would mean that the individual could marry *one* person of the same sex who was *not* a sibling, parent, etc. Even some of the existing laws allowing same-sex couples to register as same-sex partners have incest limitations.[87]

Allowing two men to marry or two women to marry would no more allow the man to marry his brother or the woman her sister than would allowing two individuals of different sexes to marry entitle a man to marry his sister or a woman her brother. The state interests implicated in preventing incest do not suddenly disappear merely because two individuals of the same sex might be involved in the union.

Certainly, it is not a new phenomenon for courts or commentators to refuse to consider the actual state interests supporting a marital ban and instead to claim that striking down one existing marital prohibition will necessitate striking them all down. The Supreme Court of Tennessee held that an interracial couple, validly married in Mississippi, could not live together as lawful husband and wife in the state of Tennessee, explaining that were the state to recognize the marriage of two such individuals, "we might have in Tennessee the father living with his daughter, the son with the mother, the brother with the sister."[88] Just as there was no foundation to the claim that the recognition of interracial marriages would lead to the recognition of incestuous marriages, there is no foundation to the analogous claim with respect to same-sex marriages.

Numerous reasons have been offered to establish why incestuous unions should not be permitted. When a child has incestuous relations with her parent, she may suffer severe emotional and psychological harm.[89] Further, the existence and extent of such harms may not come to light until after the child has become an adult,[90] at which point the harms may be quite severe.[91]

Even if a child has reached adulthood before the incest occurs, having sexual relations with her father might be quite harmful.[92] Further, despite both individuals being adults, the sexual relations still might not be fully voluntary.[93] Thus, the potential for exploitation and domination might well provide the rationale for prohibiting incestuous relationships even if both parties have attained majority,[94] although it is clear that courts are more worried about incestuous relations between a child and an adult than between two adults.[95]

Courts and commentators have suggested that an additional reason to prohibit incest is to encourage individuals to go outside of the family for mates[96] and, further, to encourage the maintenance of safe, sex-free zones within the family.[97] As a Georgia appellate judge explained, "It is the violation of familial relationships and the trust and emotional attachments that stem from those relationships that are, in addition to sexual relations, proscribed by the incest statute."[98] Yet, there is no reason to think that same-sex marriages will involve a violation of familial relationships and the trust and emotional attachments stemming from such relationships.

Different states assign very different weights to the possible interests that are implicated when family members have sexual relations with each other. For example, some states seem to worry most about the possible genetic difficulties which might result,[99] while others emphasize very different concerns. As might be expected given these very different emphases, some states regard sexual relations between adoptive parents and their adopted children as incestuous while others do not,[100] and some states regard sexual relations between stepparents and stepchildren as incestuous while others do not.[101] Thus, those states primarily worried about genetic difficulties tend to have more "liberal" marital policies when family members not related by blood wish to marry.

The point here should not be misunderstood. Whenever an adult has sexual relations with a child, there will be an issue of statutory rape, but that is a separate question that does not speak to the incest regulation.[102] The point here is that one state's emphasizing genetics may yield one kind of incest classification while a different state's emphasizing trust and safety might yield a different kind of classification.

Suppose that two individuals who are first cousins wish to marry each other. Suppose further that the state legislature is worried about the possible genetic difficulties that might arise from first-cousin marriages and has decided to prohibit such unions. If two first cousins of the same sex wish to marry, there will be no worries about the possible genetic difficulties that might result from their union and thus it might seem that if same-sex marriages are permitted, states will be forced to change their incest laws.

Yet, in the scenario above, the state would not be changing its incest law but merely applying it for the purposes for which it had been intended. Currently, several states permit first cousins to marry only if the parties can establish that they are *unable* to have a child through their union.[103] The same-sex couple would be like one of these couples. Just as opposite-sex first cousins unable to have children through their union might be allowed to marry, same-sex first cousins unable to have children through their union might be allowed to marry.

Merely because a state allows first cousins to marry if they cannot reproduce does not entail that the state will therefore be forced to allow siblings to marry if they cannot reproduce, since there are other interests implicated when siblings wish to marry. Indeed, merely because some states allow first cousins to marry if they cannot reproduce does not mean that other states must do the same.[104] Thus, it is simply false that permitting same-sex couples to marry will necessitate a change in the incest laws. If opposite-sex first cousins who are unable to reproduce through their union are nonetheless precluded from marrying, the same will be true of same-sex first cousins. The same will be true if same-sex siblings wish to marry, if an adoptive parent wishes to marry a same-sex child, etc.

An examination of the incest statutes of different states will reveal that the states try to tailor their statutes to the interests they believe important—an emphasis on genetic concerns will yield one type of law and an emphasis on safety and trust within the family will yield another. The kinds of state interests that are implicated when incest statutes are at issue are much different from those cited to justify same-sex marriage bans and thus permitting the latter kind of marriage would hardly require that all incest laws be scrapped.

POLYGAMOUS MARRIAGES

Commentators sometimes suggest that if same-sex marriages must be permitted, then polygamous marriages must also be permitted. Yet, it is difficult to understand why permitting same-sex couples to marry would somehow entail that polygamous marriages would also have to be permitted. Those seeking to marry *a* same-sex partner are not asking to marry *many* same-sex partners at the same time.[105] Further, when the reasons supporting polygamous marriage bans are examined, it becomes even clearer that recognizing same-sex marriages would not require that polygamous marriages also be recognized. Those claiming that the recognition of same-sex marriages requires recognition of polygamous marriages are in error, as are those making the same claim with respect to incestuous marriages, precisely because they refuse to take seriously the differing reasons for banning the respective marriages.

Certainly, it is not difficult to understand why some of the reasons offered to support polygamy bans are not taken seriously, since they are simply specious and do not deserve careful consideration. For example, over one hundred years ago, the Supreme Court suggested that it was permissible to prohibit polygamous marriages because only Asian or African peoples had a practice of recognizing such marriages.[106] Yet, marital unions should not be prohibited merely because European countries do not permit them.[107] When something as important as marriage is at issue, the justifications for a marriage ban should indicate with some specificity the harms that will thereby be prevented.[108] Further, when allegations of harm are made, it will not suffice to allude to the evil consequences that flow from plural marriages[109] without explaining what those consequences are. If indeed, allowing polygamy would have horrendous results and would be or cause a return to barbarism,[110] then these terrible effects should be spelled out.

The Court has sometimes been more willing to articulate its reasons for believing that polygamous marriages may be prohibited without offending the Constitution. For example, the Supreme Court suggested that polygamous unions "tend to destroy the purity of the marriage relation, to disturb the peace of families, to degrade woman, and to debase man."[111] Certainly, it would not be difficult to see how a polygamous marriage might be problematic if, for example, a first wife did not approve of her husband's marrying someone else and, in fact, eventually secured a divorce because her husband had taken another wife without her consent.[112]

Suppose that it could credibly be established that all parties were willing to allow the husband to have more than one legal spouse. There might be additional reasons to believe that polygamy would be destructive to the family, for example, because such an arrangement might encourage competition for scarce resources.[113] Thus, different "families" might be competing for time, financial resources, etc., thereby promoting feelings of insecurity, jealousy, etc.[114]

Some have suggested that polygamous marriages that involve one husband and more than one wife impose great burdens on women[115] or are patriarchal.[116] If one considers Mormon practices in the past, however, it is unclear that the burdens on Mormon women were as onerous as supposed—it has been suggested that, historically, Mormon women who were practicing polygamy were allowed to do things, such as run their own businesses, that other women were not allowed to do at the time.[117]

Suppose that it were true that Mormon women were given more autonomy than were other women at the time. A separate question would be whether that historical fact would have any bearing on whether polygamous marriages should be allowed *now*, especially if there are other reasons to preclude such marriages.[118] For example, some commentators argue that the practice of polygamy is incompatible with democracy[119] and, further, that this is the only legitimate basis upon which to outlaw such a practice.[120]

Just as it is now suggested that recognizing same-sex marriages would require recognizing polygamous marriages, it was once suggested that recognizing interracial marriages would require recognizing polygamous marriages. The Supreme Court of Tennessee worried that if a validly celebrated interracial marriage were to be recognized in Tennessee, the "Turk or Mohammedan, with his numerous wives . . . [could] establish his harem at the doors of the capitol, and we [would be] . . . without remedy."[121] Just as the claim was false with respect to the implications of recognizing interracial marriages, the claim is false with respect to the implications of recognizing same-sex marriages.

Numerous reasons are offered to justify prohibiting polygamous marriages,[122] ranging from claims that such marriages will be destructive to the family to claims that such marriages will result in the state's having to support individuals who may become public charges[123] to charges that such arrangements are incompatible with democracy. None of these reasons has anything to do with the reasons offered to justify same-sex marriages bans and thus the recognition of the latter would imply nothing about whether the former unions should be recognized.

ADULTERY

Same-sex marriage opponents suggest that if there is a constitutional right to marry a same-sex partner, then there is also a constitutional right to do many things including committing adultery.[124] But, it might be argued, since it is absurd to believe that the Constitution protects adulterous relations, it is also absurd to believe that the Constitution protects the right to marry a same-sex partner. Yet, even if the right to commit adultery is not protected by the Constitution, this hardly establishes that the right to marry a same-sex partner is also not protected, since recognition of the latter right would promote marriage and family whereas recognition of the former arguably would not.

The Supreme Court has recognized that "freedom of personal choice in matters of family life" is a fundamental interest protected by the Fourteenth Amendment.[125] If the "freedom of personal choice in matters of family life" is broadly construed, then it might be argued that the freedom to have an adulterous affair is included within those fundamental interests protected by the Constitution. Indeed, a variety of plaintiffs have argued that the right to privacy includes the right to commit adultery.[126] However, no court has accepted that argument, at least not without having been overturned by a higher court.[127] Most courts addressing the matter have concluded that adultery is antithetical to marriage and family and thus cannot plausibly be included within the right to privacy.[128]

The Supreme Court of Texas has pointed out that adultery often injures third persons, such as spouses and children, and has suggested that adultery undermines marriages and often rips families apart.[129] If the relevant standard for protecting an interest is whether it promotes marriage and family,[130] adultery and same-sex marriage are dissimilar in an important respect. Extending legal recognition and protection to same-sex unions would *promote* marriage and family, whereas extending legal protection to adulterous unions would tend to have the opposite effect.[131]

Some commentators claim that recognizing same-sex marriages will somehow dilute the worth of traditional opposite-sex marriages. Yet, unlike adulterous relations, same-sex marriages are not a threat to opposite-sex marriages, since adulterous relations would undermine feelings of marital love and trust and same-sex marriages would not.[132] It would be most surprising if married couples would seek divorces because same-sex couples had married, whereas it would not be at all surprising for couples to divorce as a result of one of the members of the couple having committed adultery.

Even if couples would not seek divorces because same-sex couples had been allowed to marry, there might nonetheless be some who felt that their own marriages would somehow be devalued by such marriages and that this provided sufficient justification for the state to refuse to accord such unions recognition. But the same argument could have been made about recognizing interracial or interreligious marriages (i.e., that marriage between members of the same race or religion would, at least in the eyes of some, somehow be devalued if marriages between members of different races or religions were recognized and that this allegedly provided sufficient justification for the state to refuse to accord legal recognition to the latter marriages).[133] However, no one would seriously maintain that such a justification would suffice to establish the constitutional permissibility of a state's refusing to recognize such marriages.

The claim that the Constitution's protecting same-sex marriages entails the Constitution's protecting adulterous relationships is false. For example, the United States Supreme Court recently articulated a conservative test to determine whether something is protected by the right to privacy, namely, whether it promotes marriage and family.[134] Same-sex marriages and adulterous unions are relevantly dissimilar in light of this test, since the former promote marriage and family and the latter do not. A separate question is whether states should criminalize adultery[135] or, perhaps, whether a more inclusive right to privacy would include both adulterous relations and same-sex marriages. Nonetheless, the point remains that same-sex marriages and adulterous relations are distinguishable in a way that may well be constitutionally significant.

SODOMY

Yet another claim is sometimes offered to establish that the recognition of same-sex marriages would have "dire" consequences—namely, that such a recognition would imply that sodomy statutes were unconstitutional. Because the United States Supreme Court has already recognized that such statutes are constitutionally permissible,[136] it might seem that same-sex unions cannot be constitutionally protected.[137] Thus, it might be argued that because the state has a legitimate interest in regulating sodomy and because same-sex couples would presumably be having sodomitical relations, the state would allegedly have a legitimate interest in preventing their marrying. Indeed, it might seem absurd to allow same-sex couples to marry, since they might be breaking the law every time that they had sexual relations.

At one time, this argument would have been more persuasive (e.g., when more states criminalized sodomy and when it was believed that sodomy within the marital context was not protected by the Constitution).[138] However, the majority of states do not currently criminalize sodomy[139] and there is good reason to believe that in the minority of states that have such laws sodomitical relations within the marital context are indeed constitutionally protected.[140] Just as the constitutionality of laws criminalizing opposite-sex sodomy is not undermined merely because opposite-sex marital sodomy is protected, the constitutionality of laws criminalizing same-sex sodomy would not be undermined merely because same-sex marital sodomy was protected. While sodomy laws are probably unconstitutional, that is true whether or not same-sex marriages are legally recognized.

Ironically, the more pressing issue involving marital sodomy has not been whether it was protected but whether *forcible* marital sodomy fell outside of this protected marital sphere. For example, it was only in 1986 that an Alabama appellate court held that forcible marital sodomy was not protected by the marital exemption.[141] Perhaps even more surprising is that in 1984 the Supreme Court of Kansas held that a married individual could *not* be convicted of aggravated sodomy.[142] The Kansas Supreme Court did not see any constitutional difficulties in the state's criminalizing sexual acts between persons of the same sex but not criminalizing those same acts when engaged in by persons of the opposite sex[143] or in the state's criminalizing an individual's forcibly sodomizing a nonspouse but not in criminalizing an individual's forcibly sodomizing a spouse.[144]

The Montana Supreme Court struck down that state's sodomy law, reasoning that it was hard to imagine any activity that adults would consider more fundamental, more private, and more deserving of protection from governmental interference than noncommercial, consensual, adult sexual activity.[145] Chief Justice Turnage would have decided the case on different grounds, arguing that a statutory scheme which criminalizes sexual acts between persons of the same sex but decriminalizes the same sexual conduct engaged in by persons of the opposite sex violates both the federal and the state constitutions.[146]

Arguably, adult, consensual, noncommercial sodomy is protected by the United States Constitution. While it is true that the Supreme Court held otherwise in *Bowers v. Hardwick*,[147] some suggest that the vitality of *Bowers* is in doubt after *Romer v. Evans*.[148] Further, as suggested by Chief Justice Turnage, there is an additional reason to believe that statutes criminalizing same-sex but not opposite-sex sodomy are unconstitutional—namely, that they violate the Equal Protection Clause, an issue that the *Bowers* Court explicitly refused to address.[149] Yet, the argument here is not predicated on sodomy's being protected by either the Due Process or the Equal Protection Clause of the Fourteenth Amendment, especially when one considers the reasoning in *Bowers* and in various decisions that have dealt with sodomy.[150]

The *Bowers* Court upheld the Georgia sodomy statute because no connection between sodomy and marriage, family, or procreation had been established.[151] The Court further worried that its striking down a sodomy law would make it difficult to uphold laws against adultery.[152] Even if one ignores that sodomy and adultery laws are easily distinguishable,[153] it should be clear that the reasons allegedly justifying upholding the sodomy law would hardly apply to a law banning same-sex marriage. Thus, it would be difficult for the Court to credibly claim that no connection could be established between same-sex marriage on the one hand and marriage, family, or procreation on the other.

Commentators argue speciously when they suggest that were the Court to recognize a right to same-sex marriage, the right to privacy would have been expanded to include so much that a whole host of laws would be at risk—for example, laws prohibiting polygamy, incest, adultery, or sodomy. Were one to look at the criteria that the United States Supreme Court has used in the past to determine which rights were fundamental and which were not, one would see that the latter laws are quite compatible with a holding that same-sex marriage is a fundamental right. It is of course a separate question whether the latter statutes are wise or even constitutional. Those analyses can be made through the use of reasoned judgment in light of the developing right to privacy jurisprudence. However, it "would be a stultification of the responsibility which the course of constitutional history has cast upon . . . [the] Court"[154] were it to refuse to recognize the fundamental right to same-sex marriage because of the specious claim that adultery statutes would also therefore be unconstitutional. The disingenuousness of such an analysis might indeed "shock the conscience."[155]

The claims of this chapter are rather modest. First, same-sex marriages promote many of the state and individual interests that opposite-sex marriages do. Second, same-sex marriages are different from polygamous, adulterous, and incestuous unions in legally significant ways, and constitutional recognition of the former would not require constitutional recognition of the latter. These points notwithstanding, the Hawaii same-sex marriage case was neither predicated on a recognition of the fundamental right to marry a same-sex partner nor on the significant legal differences between same-sex unions and some of the other unions discussed above. Rather, it was based on an equal protection argument, which will be discussed in the next chapter.

NOTES

1. *Romer v. Evans*, 517 U.S. 620, 632 (1996).
2. See generally David L. Chambers, "What If? The Legal Consequences of Marriage and the Legal Needs of Lesbian and Gay Male Couples," 95 *Mich. L. Rev.* 447 (1996).
3. See *Adams v. Howerton*, 486 F. Supp. 1119, 1124 (C.D. Cal. 1980), aff'd, 673 F.2d 1036 (9th Cir.), cert. denied, 458 U.S. 1111 (1982).
4. Lesbian and gay couples are raising happy and well-adjusted children. See generally Mark Strasser, "Legislative Presumptions and Judicial Assumptions: On Parenting, Adoption, and the Best Interest of the Child," 45 *U. Kan. L. Rev.* 49, 66–88 (1996).
5. G. Keith Nedrow, "Polygamy and the Right to Marry: New Life for an Old Lifestyle," 11 *Mem. St. U. L. Rev.* 303, 338 (1981) ("The key to a happy, well-adjusted child seems to be parental love, concern and respect, rather than the lifestyle in which one is raised").
6. See Mark Strasser, "Domestic Relations Jurisprudence and the Great, Slumbering *Baehr*: On Definitional Preclusion, Equal Protection, and Fundamental Interests," 64 *Fordham L. Rev.* 921, 959 (1995).
7. See *Singer v. Hara*, 522 P.2d 1187, 1195 (Wash. Ct. App. 1974); *Adams*, 486 F. Supp. at 1124–1125. See also Lynne Marie Kohm, "A Reply to 'Principles and Prejudice': Marriage and the Realization That Principles Win over Political Will," 22 *J. Contemp. L.* 293, 322 (1996).
8. Craig W. Christensen, "Legal Ordering of Family Values: The Case of Gay and Lesbian Families," 18 *Cardozo L. Rev.* 1299, 1311 (1997) (by 1990, barely one in every four households was home to a nuclear family composed of a married couple and their biological children).
9. See Strasser, "Domestic Relations Jurisprudence," 64 *Fordham L. Rev.* at 959.
10. See Jonathan Rauch, "For Better or Worse," in Andrew Sullivan ed., *Same-Sex Marriage: Pro and Con: A Reader*, 169, 179 (New York: Vintage Books, 1997).
11. See id. at 179 (discussing admirable devotion of many gays and lesbians to partners who are ill).
12. See The Editors, "Let Them Wed," in Sullivan ed., *Same-Sex Marriage: Pro and Con*, 181, 183 (discussing marriage as providing an "economic bulwark" in times of need).
13. See Christensen, "Legal Ordering of Family Values," 18 *Cardozo L. Rev.* at 1311 (about 50 percent of first marriages end in divorce, and about 60 percent of

second marriages end in divorce). See also Wendy Koch, "Americans Quick to Marry—Quick to Divorce, Too. Great Expectations: 'Perhaps Other Cultures Are More Tolerant of Difficulties,' " *S. F. Examiner*, Mar. 17, 1996 at A2 (half of American marriages end in divorce).

14. See Mark Strasser, "Family, Definitions, and the Constitution: On the Antimiscegenation Analogy," 25 *Suffolk U. L. Rev.* 981, 991 (1991) (the state has an interest in limiting the social costs that are involved in the disorganized breakdown of relations).

15. If a same-sex couple breaks up, the adult who had the most contact with the children and did the most in raising them might not only not get custody but might not even be allowed to see them. See generally Strasser, "Legislative Presumptions and Judicial Assumptions," 45 *U. Kansas L. Rev.* at 90–110 (discussing various situations including those in which same-sex couples are raising children, the relationship between the adults ends, and the primary caretaker is denied visitation).

16. See William N. Eskridge, Jr., *The Case for Same-Sex Marriage: From Sexual Liberty to Civilized Commitment*, 8–10 (New York: The Free Press, 1996); The Editors, "Let Them Wed," in Sullivan ed., *Same-Sex Marriage: Pro and Con* at 183.

17. See James Q. Wilson, "Against Homosexual Marriage," in Sullivan ed., *Same-Sex Marriage: Pro and Con*, 159, 163.

18. See id. at 167. Suzanne B. Goldberg, "Gay Rights Through the Looking Glass: Politics, Morality and the Trial of Colorado's Amendment 2," 21 *Fordham Urban L.J.* 1057, 1078 (1994) (discussing claim by the Director of Cultural Research Studies at the Family Research Council that "most gay people are generally promiscuous").

19. See Dennis Prager, "Homosexuality, the Bible, and Us—A Jewish Perspective," in Sullivan ed., *Same-Sex Marriage: Pro and Con*, 61, 66 ("Male nature, not the inability to marry, compels gay men to wander from man to man").

20. See Stephen Macedo, "Homosexuality and the Conservative Mind," 84 *Geo. L.J.* 261, 284 (1995) (discussing sweeping generalizations that falsely depict all gays as promiscuous); Marc A. Fajer, "Can Two Real Men Eat Quiche Together? Storytelling, Gender-Role Stereotypes, and Legal Protection for Lesbians and Gay Men," 46 *U. Miami L. Rev.* 511, 537 (1992) (discussing beliefs held by some that gay men and lesbians are "promiscuous, predatory, and obsessed with sex"); William E. Adams, Jr., "Whose Family Is It Anyway? The Continuing Struggle for Lesbians and Gay Men Seeking to Adopt Children," 30 *New. Eng. L. Rev.* 579, 594 (1996) (discussing claims about promiscuity, which are often either overstated or simply false); William N. Eskridge, Jr., Essay, "Gaylegal Narratives," 46 *Stan. L. Rev.* 607, 625 (1994) (discussing "the stereotype that gay men are 'promiscuous' "); Devjani Mishra, "The Road to Concord: Resolving the Conflict of Law over Adoption by Gays and Lesbians," 30 *Colum. J. L. & Soc. Probs.* 91, 93 (1996) (discussing the unfounded myth and stereotype that gays and lesbians are more promiscuous than heterosexuals); Judith Lillian Dillon, Note, "A Proposal to Ban Sexual Orientation Discrimination in Private Employment in Vermont," 15 *Vt. L. Rev.* 435, 479 (1991) (discussing the myth that lesbians and gay men lead promiscuous lifestyles). Cf. *Campbell v. Sundquist*, 926 S.W.2d 250, 263 (Tenn. App. 1996) (suggesting that there is insufficient evidence to prove that homosexual relationships are short-lived and shallow).

21. See Thomas R. Mendicino, Note, "Characterization and Disease: Homosex-

uals and the Threat of AIDS," 66 *N.C. L. Rev.* 226, 245 (1987) (discussing the false view of gays as having uncontrollable sexual urges).

22. See id. at 233, 245.

23. See Wilson, "Against Homosexual Marriage," in Sullivan ed., *Same-Sex Marriage: Pro and Con* at 167.

24. See Prager, "Homosexuality, the Bible, and Us," in Sullivan ed., *Same-Sex Marriage: Pro and Con* at 66 (discussing the "male tendency to promiscuity"). See also Daniel Maguire, "The Morality of Homosexual Marriage," in Robert M. Baird & Stuart E. Rosenbaum eds., *Same-Sex Marriage: The Moral and Legal Debate*, 57, 66 (New York: Prometheus Books, 1997) (suggesting that there is no reason to think gay men any more likely to be promiscuous than straight men would be if given equal opportunity).

25. See Prager, "Homosexuality, the Bible, and Us," in Sullivan ed., *Same-Sex Marriage: Pro and Con* at 66. ("It is women who keep most heterosexual men monogamous, or at least less likely to cruise, but gay men have no such brake on their cruising natures").

26. See Linda C. McClain, " 'Irresponsible' Reproduction," 47 *Hastings L.J.* 339, 422 (1996) (discussing feminist critiques suggesting that these claims about the nature of men are cultural excuses that allow men to escape the consequences of their actions).

27. See Richard A. Posner, *Sex and Reason*, 302 (Cambridge, MA: Harvard University Press, 1992) (suggesting that gays are more promiscuous because they cannot marry); Macedo, "Homosexuality and the Conservative Mind," 84 *Geo. L.J.* at 290–91; Dwight J. Penas, "Bless the Tie That Binds: A Puritan-Covenant Case for Same-Sex Marriage," in Baird & Rosenbaum eds., *Same-Sex Marriage: The Moral and Legal Debate*, 146, 154 ("Same-sex marriage would foster commitment, loyalty, and intimacy, just as does heterosexual marriage").

28. But cf. Darren Rosenblum, "Queer Intersectionality and the Failure of Recent Lesbian and Gay 'Victories'," 4 *L. & Sex.* 83, 112 (1994) (suggesting that some "practice promiscuity as sexual revolution").

29. See Wilson, "Against Homosexual Marriage," in Sullivan ed., *Same-Sex Marriage: Pro and Con* at 163.

30. *Loving v. Virginia*, 388 U.S. 1, 8 (1967).

31. Id. at 11.

32. See Caryn James, "TV Mirrors the '90s View of Adultery," *San Diego Union & Trib.*, Aug. 17, 1997 at E13 (discussing broad range of estimates of the percentage of those who have had marital affairs). See also Nedrow, "Polygamy and the Right to Marry," 11 *Mem. St. U. L. Rev.* at 307 (discussing the "propensity for breaking the monogamous mold through divorce and adultery even in the face of severe social and legal sanctions").

33. See Darren Lenard Hutchison, "Out Yet Unseen: A Racial Critique of Gay and Lesbian Legal Theory and Political Discourse," 29 *Conn. L. Rev.* 561, 608 (1997) ("under racial hierarchy, blacks are considered sexually deviant—promiscuous and predatory").

34. See Beverly Horsburgh, "Schrdegreesodinger's Cat, Eugenics, and the Compulsory Sterilization of Welfare Mothers: Deconstructing the Old/New Rhetoric and Constructing the Reproductive Right to Natality for Low-Income Women of Color," 17 *Cardozo L. Rev.* 531, 561 (1996) (discussing theorists who argue that blacks are

more promiscuous than whites and individuals who use such theories to support their view that public funding should be cut).

35. Id. at 574 (discussing charge and increased likelihood that these women will lose even more of their reproductive rights).

36. See David A. J. Richards, *Women, Gays, and the Constitution: The Grounds for Feminism and Gay Rights in Culture and Law*, 248–49 (Chicago: University of Chicago Press, 1998) (discussing claim that male slaves should not be allowed to marry because of their alleged inability to be faithful to their spouses).

37. See Paula L. Ettelbrick, "Since When Is Marriage a Path to Liberation," in Baird & Rosenbaum eds., *Same-Sex Marriage: The Moral and Legal Debate*, 164, 165 (suggesting that permitting same-sex marriage would have an undesirable mainstreaming effect). See also Craig W. Christensen, "If Not Marriage: On Securing Gay and Lesbian Family Values by a 'Simulacrum of Marriage,' " 65 *Fordham L. Rev.* 1699, 1709–11 (1998) (discussing commentators critical of attempts to acquire marriage rights for same-sex couples).

38. See Barbara Cox, "A (Personal) Essay on Same-Sex Marriage," in Baird & Rosenbaum eds., *Same-Sex Marriage: The Moral and Legal Debate*, 27, 28 (suggesting that the author's same-sex union was not a mere "aping" of traditional marriages).

39. See Chambers, "What If?" 95 *Mich. L. Rev.* at 449 ("A large proportion of American adults who identify themselves as lesbian or gay live with another person of the same sex and regard that person as their life partner").

40. *Zablocki v. Redhail*, 434 U.S. 374, 384 (1978).

41. Some commentators see nothing untoward in making such a claim. See Kohm, "A Reply to 'Principles and Prejudice,' " 22 *J. Contemp. L.* at 302.

42. *Turner v. Safley*, 482 U.S. 78, 95 (1987).

43. Id. at 96.

44. Id.

45. The passage of the Defense of Marriage Act, Pub. L. No. 104–199, 110 Stat. 2419 (1996) may mean that same-sex couples will not be entitled to federal benefits, assuming its constitutionality is upheld. For reasons to doubt that the Act passes constitutional muster, see generally Mark Strasser, "*Loving* the *Romer* Out for *Baehr*: On Acts in Defense of Marriage and the Constitution," 58 *U. Pitt. L. Rev.* 279 (1997).

46. See Cal. Fam. Code § 301 (West 1994) (at least 18).

47. See Ga. Code Ann. § 19–3-2 (1991) (pregnancy exception); Iowa Code Ann. § 595.2 (West 1996) ("Pregnancy alone does not establish that the proposed marriage is in the best interest of the underaged party or parties"); N.C. Gen. Stat. § 51–3 (1984) (pregnancy exception); Okla. Stat. Ann. tit. 43 § 3 (West 1990) (same); S.C. Code Ann. § 20–1-300 (Law Co-op 1985) (spelling out conditions under which underage individuals can marry if the female is pregnant).

48. See Ariz. Rev. Stat. Ann. § 25–102 (West 1991) (some underage individuals can marry with parental permission); Fla. Stat. Ann. § 741.0405 (West 1997) (same); Idaho Code § 32–202 (1996) (same); 750 Ill. Comp. Stat. Ann. 5/301 (West 1993) (same).

49. Before 1967, Virginia prohibited interracial marriages whereas New Jersey permitted them. See *Calma v. Calma*, 128 S.E.2d 440 (Va. 1962) (case involving

whether interracial marriage validly celebrated in New Jersey would be recognized in Virginia).

50. 388 U.S. 1 (1967).

51. The Fourteenth Amendment was approved in 1868.

52. See *State v. Gibson*, 36 Ind. 389 (1871) (rejecting Fourteenth Amendment challenge to the state's antimiscegenation law). See also *State v. Kennedy*, 76 N.C. 251 (1877) (enforcing state's antimiscegenation law). The Supreme Court of Alabama struck down the state antimiscegenation statute. See *Burns v. State*, 48 Ala. 195 (Ala. 1872). However, the court overruled that decision five years later in *Green v. State*, 58 Ala. 190 (Ala. 1877).

53. See *Gibson*, 36 Ind. at 403 ("The right, in the states, to regulate and control, to guard, protect, and preserve this God-given, civilizing, and Christianizing institution is of inestimable importance, and cannot be surrendered, nor can the states suffer or permit any interference therewith").

54. See Ala. Const. Art. 4, § 102 ("The legislature shall never pass any law to authorize or legalize any marriage between any white person and a negro, or descendant of a negro"); Fla. Const. Art. 16, § 24 ("All marriages between a white person and a negro, or between a white person and a person of negro descent to the fourth generation, inclusive, are hereby forever prohibited"); Miss. Const. Art. 14, § 263 ("The marriage of a white person with a negro or mulatto, or person who shall have one-eighth or more of negro blood, shall be unlawful and void"); N.C. Const. Art. XIV, § 8 ("All marriages between a white person and a negro, or between a white person and a person of negro descent to the third generation, inclusive, are hereby forever prohibited"); S.C. Const. Art. III, § 33 ("The marriage of a white person and a negro or mulatto, or person who shall have one-eighth or more of negro blood, shall be unlawful and void."); Tenn. Const. Art. XI, § 15 ("The intermarriage of white persons with negroes, mulattoes, or persons of mixed blood, descended from a negro to the third generation inclusive or their living together as man and wife in this State is prohibited").

55. See *Loving*, 388 U.S. at 11.

56. Id. at 12.

57. See *Zablocki v. Redhail*, 434 U.S. 374 (1978) (individual cannot be precluded from marrying despite inability to meet current support obligations); *Turner v. Safley*, 482 U.S. 78 (1987) (prison marriages).

58. See *Zablocki*, 434 U.S. at 388.

59. See *West Virginia State Bd. of Educ. v. Barnette*, 319 U.S. 624, 638 (1943).

60. See *Hall v. United States*, 92 U.S. 27, 30 (1875); *Patterson v. Bingham*, 101 Va. 372, 375 (1903); *Cantelou v. Doe, ex dem. Hood*, 56 Ala. 519, 520–21 (1876). See also Michael L. Closen & Carol R. Heise, "HIV-AIDS and the Non-Traditional Family: The Argument for State and Federal Judicial Recognition of Danish Same-Sex Marriages," 16 *Nova L. Rev.* 809, 820 (1992) (slave marriages were without legal effect and masters could split up couples at will).

61. *Johnson v. Shepherd*, 143 Ala. 325, 327 (1904); *Washington v. Washington*, 69 Ala. 281, 285 (1881).

62. *Washington*, 69 Ala. at 284; *Francis v. Tazewell*, 120 Va. 319, 321 (1917).

63. See *Woods v. Moten*, 129 Ala. 228, 230–31 (1900); *Scott v. Raub*, 88 Va. 721, 723 (1892).

64. See *Loving*, 388 U.S. at 3 (discussing lower court's view that God did not intend for the races to mix).

65. See generally Richards, *Women, Gays, and the Constitution.*

66. *Planned Parenthood of Southeastern Pennsylvania v. Casey*, 505 U.S. 833, 980 (1992) (plurality opinion) (Scalia, J., concurring in part and dissenting in part).

67. See *Roe v. Wade*, 410 U.S. 113, 168 (1973) (Stewart, J., concurring) ("The Constitution nowhere mentions a specific right of personal choice in matters of marriage and family life").

68. See *Planned Parenthood*, 505 U.S. at 847–48 ("Marriage is mentioned nowhere in the Bill of Rights and interracial marriage was illegal in most States in the 19th century, but the Court was no doubt correct in finding it an aspect of liberty protected against state interference by the substantive component of the Due Process Clause in *Loving v. Virginia*").

69. See id. at 2874 n.1 (Scalia, J., concurring and dissenting).

70. U.S. Const., amend. XIV, § 1.

71. See *Romer*, 517 U.S. at 636 (Scalia, J., dissenting) (implying that orientation bias is somehow permissible).

72. In *Griswold v. Connecticut*, 381 U.S. 479 (1965) and *Eisenstadt v. Baird*, 405 U.S. 438 (1972), the Court recognized that contraception involves a fundamental interest. In *Loving v. Virginia*, 388 U.S. 1 (1967), the Court recognized that marriage, including interracial marriage, involved a fundamental interest. In *Roe v. Wade*, 410 U.S. 113 (1973), the Court recognized that abortion involves a fundamental interest.

73. See *Baehr v. Lewin*, 852 P.2d 44, 57 (Haw.) (plurality opinion), reconsideration granted in part, 875 P.2d 225 (Haw. 1993).

74. 342 U.S. 165 (1952).

75. Id. at 170.

76. Cf. *Lucas v. South Carolina Coastal Council*, 505 U.S. 1003, 1068 (1992) (Stevens, J., dissenting) (criticizing the majority opinion because the "Court's holding today effectively freezes the State's common law").

77. See *Planned Parenthood*, 505 U.S. at 849.

78. See *United States v. Virginia*, 518 U.S. 515, 567–68 (1996) (Scalia, J., dissenting) ("It is my position that the term 'fundamental rights' should be limited to 'interest[s] traditionally protected by our society', but the Court has not accepted that view . . .") (citing *Michael H. v. Gerald D.*, 491 U.S. 110, 122 (1989) (plurality opinion)).

79. See Mark Strasser, *Legally Wed: Same-Sex Marriage and the Constitution*, Chap. 3 (Ithaca, N.Y.: Cornell University Press, 1997).

80. In *Brause v. Bureau of Vital Statistics*, 1998 WL 88743 (Alaska Super.), a trial court in Alaska recognized a fundamental right to choose a same-sex partner under the Alaska Constitution. That constitution has since been amended.

81. See *Zablocki*, 434 U.S. at 386 ("reasonable regulations that do not significantly interfere with decisions to enter into the marital relationship may legitimately be imposed").

82. See *Moe v. Dinkins*, 669 F.2d 67 (2nd Cir.), cert. denied, 459 U.S. 827 (1982).

83. Compare Ky. Rev. Stat. Ann. § 402.010 (Banks-Baldwin 1993) (persons

nearer of kin than second cousins not permitted to marry) with Cal. Fam. Code §2200 (West 1994) (first cousins may marry).

84. Compare *Bagnardi v. Hartnett*, 366 N.Y.S.2d 89 (1975) (adoptive father permitted to marry adopted daughter) with *Edmondson v. State*, 464 S.E.2d 839, 842 (Ga. App. 1995) (adoptive father stands on same footing as biological father—having sexual relations with adoptive daughter would be incest).

85. Compare *State v. McQuiston*, 922 P.2d 519, 525 (Mont. 1996) (suggesting that sexual relations between stepparent and adult stepchild are not forbidden if consensual) with *State v. Buck*, 757 P.2d 861, 864 (Or. App. 1988) (sexual relations incestuous if between individual and child of individual's spouse).

86. William Bennett, "Leave Marriage Alone," in Sullivan ed., *Same-Sex Marriage: Pro and Con*, 274, 275; Hadley Arkes, "The Closet Straight," in Sullivan ed., *Same-Sex Marriage: Pro and Con*, 154, 158.

87. Craig A. Bowman & Blake M. Cornish, Note, "A More Perfect Union: A Legal and Social Analysis of Domestic Partnership Ordinances," 92 *Colum. L. Rev.* 1164, 1192 (1992) (discussing imposition of traditional incest limitations on those who wish to register as domestic partners).

88. *State v. Bell*, 66 Tenn. 9, 11 (1872). See also *Perez v. Lippold*, 198 P.2d 17, 46 (Cal. 1948) (Shenk, J., dissenting) ("The underlying factors that constitute justification for laws against miscegenation closely parallel those which sustain the validity of prohibitions against incest and incestuous marriages").

89. See *Byrne v. Bercker*, 501 N.W.2d 402, 403 (Wis. 1993); *Tyson v. Tyson*, 727 P.2d 226, 227 (Wash. 1986) (en banc).

90. Melissa G. Salten, "Statutes of Limitations in Civil Incest Suits: Preserving the Victim's Remedy," 7 *Harv. Women's L.J.* 189, 200–201 (1984).

91. *Tyson*, 727 P.2d at 234 (Pearson, J., dissenting); Jocelyn B. Lamm, Note, "Easing Access to the Courts for Incest Victims: Toward an Equitable Application of the Delayed Discovery Rule," 100 *Yale L.J.* 2189, 2194 (1991).

92. Usually, parent-child incest cases involve relationships between father and daughter. See Marc Elovitz, "Adoption by Lesbian and Gay People: The Use and Mis-use of Social Science Research," 2 *Duke J. Gender, L. & Pol.* 207, 217 (1995); Steve Susoeff, Comment, "Assessing Children's Best Interests When a Parent Is Gay or Lesbian: Toward a Rational Custody Standard," 32 *UCLA L. Rev.* 852, 881 (1985).

93. See Kenneth Karst, "The Freedom of Intimate Association," 89 *Yale L.J.* 624, 672 (1980) ("incest laws forbidding parent-child marriage are arguably sustainable even when the child is mature, on the theory that parental authority established during one's childhood may have a lasting impact, dominating what would otherwise be the child's freedom of choice"). See also Jed Rubenfeld, "The Right of Privacy," 102 *Harv. L. Rev.* 737, 757 (1989) (discussing an argument against adult incestuous relations as involving the claim "that consent to incestuous sex is always suspect because of the peculiar, mysterious pressures at work within the nuclear family").

94. Christopher J. Keller, "Divining the Priest: A Case Comment on *Baehr v. Lewin*," 12 *L. & Inequality* 483, 506 (1994) ("It is the potential for domination and exploitation in incestuous relationships which undermines consent to the extent that the value of the liberty interest is grossly outweighed by its potential for harm").

95. *In re Estate of Robert D.B. (Cheryl D. v. Estate of Robert D.B.)*, 559 N.W.2d

272, 275 (Wis. App. 1996) ("Allegations of incest between adults trivialize the truly genuine and unquestionably tragic cases of child or minor sexual abuse").

96. *Benton v. State*, 461 S.E.2d 202, 205 (Ga. 1995) (Sears, J., concurring) ("the restriction forces family members to go outside their families to find sexual partners").

97. See *In re Estate of Loughmiller*, 629 P.2d 156, 158 (Kan. 1981) (incestuous marriages should be prohibited to "prevent the sociological consequences of competition for sexual companionship among family members"); *In re Enderle Marriage License*, 1 Pa. D. & C.2d 114, 120 (1954) (a purpose in forbidding incestuous marriages is "to maintain the sanctity of the home and prevent the disastrous consequences of competition for sexual companionship between members of the same household or family"); *Benton*, 461 S.E.2d at 203 ("The prohibition against incest is rationally related to a legitimate governmental interest—the protection of children and of the family unit"); id. at 205 (Sears, J., concurring) ("A second purpose of the [incest] taboo . . . is maintaining the stability of the family hierarchy by protecting young family members from exploitation by older family members in positions of authority, and by reducing competition and jealous friction among family members"); Margaret M. Mahoney, "A Legal Definition of the Stepfamily: The Example of Incest Regulation," 8 *BYU J. Pub. L.* 21, 29 (1993) (discussing the theory suggesting that "the incest ban strengthens and stabilizes family relationships by removing the potential for sexual unions and jealousy within the family household"); Bowman & Cornish, "A More Perfect Union," 92 *Colum. L. Rev.* at 1182–83 ("The prohibition on incest . . . may find support in a concern for promoting social integration by encouraging marriage across family lines and by a concern for preserving nonsexual intimacy within the family").

98. *Edmonson*, 464 S.E.2d at 843 (Ruffin, J., concurring specially).

99. J. Harvie Wilkinson III & G. Edward White, "Constitutional Protection for Personal Lifestyles," 62 *Cornell L. Rev.* 563, 570 (1977) (genetic deformities). See also *Loughmiller*, 629 P.2d at 158 (same); *Enderle Marriage License*, 1 Pa. D. & C.2d at 120 (incestuous marriage forbidden "for eugenic reasons, to preserve and strengthen the general racial and physical qualities of its citizens by preventing inbreeding"). But see *Bucca v. State*, 128 A.2d 506, 510 (N.J. Super. Ct. Ch. Div. 1957) ("Geneticists agree generally that the only effect upon offspring would be an increased chance of transmitting any disease or weakness which already existed in the blood line. Such incestuous relationship may be treated not as biologically harmful but only as sociologically improper").

100. Compare *Bagnardi v. Hartnett*, 366 N.Y.S.2d 89 (1975) (adoptive father permitted to marry adopted daughter) with *Edmondson*, 464 S.E.2d at 842 (adoptive father stands on same footing as biological father—having sexual relations with adoptive daughter would be incest).

101. Compare *McQuiston*, 922 P.2d at 525 (suggesting that sexual relations between stepparent and adult stepchild are not forbidden if consensual) with *Buck*, 757 P.2d at 864 (sexual relations incestuous if between individual and child of individual's spouse).

102. See *Jackson v. State*, 682 N.E.2d 564, 568 (Ind. App. 1997) (Kirsch, J., dissenting) ("A parent of an adopted child or stepchild stands in the same shoes under the current incest statute as does any adult stranger to the child victim; while

such a person may be convicted of some other crime, e.g., child molestation, he may not be convicted of incest").

103. See Ariz. Rev. Stat. Ann. Sec. 25–101 (West 1991) (over 65 or one is unable to reproduce); 750 Ill. Comp. Stat. Ann. 5/212 (West 1997 Supp.) (over 50 or either party permanently and irreversibly sterile); Ind. Code Ann. 31-7-1-3 (West 1996 Supp.) (over 65); Utah Code Ann. § 30-1-1 (1995) (over 65 or both over 55 and one cannot reproduce); Wis. Stat. Ann. (West 1993) § 765.03 (female 55 or either submits affadavit permanently sterile).

104. *In re Marriage of Adams* (*Adams v. Adams*), 604 P.2d 332 (Mont. 1979) (marriage between first cousins who were joined when he was 72 and she 67 was held void).

105. Polygamous marriages involve one man's having more than one wife at the same time or one woman's having more than one husband at the same time. See Peggy Cooper Davis, *Neglected Stories: The Constitution and Family Values*, 49 n.* (New York: Hill and Wang, 1997) (describing the two forms of polygamy—polyandry [the taking of multiple husbands] and polygyny [the taking of more than one wife]). The term when used in this country has tended to refer to a man's having more than one wife, so examples used here will reflect that.

106. See *Reynolds v. United States*, 98 U.S. 145, 164 (1878) ("Polygamy has always been odious among the northern and western nations of Europe, and, until the establishment of the Mormon Church, was almost exclusively a feature of the life of Asiatic and of African people"). Cf. David L. Chambers, "Polygamy and Same-Sex Marriage," 26 *Hofstra L. Rev.* 53, 61 (1997) ("Well more than half of nonindustrialized societies permit polygyny still today").

107. See Davis, *Neglected Stories*, 60 (inappropriate in a multicultural polity to rely upon the argument that polygamy is a feature of Asiatic and African people).

108. The claim that European practices should not be the sole reason offered is not merely being suggested to foreclose the same argument's being used against same-sex marriages, since several Scandinavian countries already recognize same-sex relationships. See *In re Custody of H.S.H.-K.* 533 N.W.2d 419, 439 (Wis. 1995) (Day, J., concurring and dissenting) (Sweden, Denmark, and Norway have all recognized same-sex relationships).

109. See *Reynolds*, 98 U.S. at 168.

110. See *Late Corporation of the Church of Jesus Christ of Latter-Day Saints v. United States*, 136 U.S. 1, 49 (1890).

111. *Davis v. Beason*, 133 U.S. 333, 341 (1890).

112. See generally *State v. Musser*, 175 P.2d 724 (Utah 1946), vacated and remanded by 333 U.S. 95 (1948) (discussing polygamous marriage contracted against first wife's wishes and eventually leading to divorce). See also Chambers, "Polygamy and Same-Sex Marriage," 26 *Hofstra L. Rev.* at 66 (suggesting that the divorce rate was higher in polygamous marriages in Utah in the late 1800s than in the general population).

113. See Maura I. Strassberg, "Distinctions of Form or Substance: Monogamy, Polygamy and Same-Sex Marriage," 75 *N.C. L. Rev.* 1501, 1521 (1997) ("The monogamous family . . . is less internally competitive for physical resources and emotional attention. This lack of competition would appear to promote more affectionate and sympathetic relations between family members").

114. Carlos A. Ball, "Moral Foundations for a Discourse on Same-Sex Marriage:

Looking Beyond Political Liberalism," 85 *Geo. L.J.* 1871, 1900 (1997) ("Normative arguments against polygamy include . . . the greater instability resulting from the increased jealousies and resentments in relationships with multiple sexual partners").

115. See id. See also Carrie Hillyard, Note, "The History of Suffrage and Equal Rights Provisions in State Constitutions," 10 *BYU J. Pub. L.* 117, 123 (1996) ("many outside Utah and outside the Mormon Church were concerned for the welfare of the women involved in plural marriage").

116. Keith Jaasma, Note, "The Religious Freedom Restoration Act: Responding to *Smith*; Reconsidering *Reynolds*," 16 *Whittier L. Rev.* 211, 250 (1995) (discussing the Court's view that polygamy is "patriarchal"). But see Donald L. Beschle, "Defining the Scope of the Constitutional Right to Marry: More than Tradition, Less than Unlimited Autonomy," 70 *Notre Dame L. Rev.* 39, 90 (1994) (suggesting that gender inequality will not suffice to justify polygamy prohibition). See also Nedrow, "Polygamy and the Right to Marry," 11 *Mem. St. U. L. Rev.* at 337 (discussing the allegedly "somewhat old-fashioned argument that plural marriage should be outlawed because it endangers the general welfare of women").

117. See Hillyard, "The History of Suffrage," 10 *BYU J. Pub. L.* at 122 ("Mormon women became midwives, teachers, seamstresses, hatmakers and shoemakers, produce merchants, and handmade product merchants").

118. See Chambers, "Polygamy and Same-Sex Marriage," 26 *Hofstra L. Rev.* at 83 ("the fear that polygamy will cause harms to persons not supported by a cultural or religious context does have a reasonable foundation").

119. See *Murphy v. Ramsey*, 114 U.S. 15, 45 (1885) (suggesting that "no legislation can be supposed more wholesome and necessary in the founding of a free, self-governing commonwealth" as that which prohibits polygamy). See also Strassberg, "Distinctions of Form or Substance," 75 *N.C. L. Rev.* at 1510 (suggesting that "polygamy was accurately perceived as a threat to fundamental American political ideals and was, therefore, a legitimate federal and state target").

120. Strassberg, "Distinctions of Form or Substance," 75 *N.C. L. Rev.* at 1576 ("the only legitimate basis for the *Reynolds* decision . . . is an understanding of monogamous marriage as having a fundamental role in the creation and maintenance of the modern liberal state, and an understanding of polygamy as a fundamentally illiberal institution which would undermine the modern liberal state").

121. *Bell*, 66 Tenn. at 11. See also *Smith v. Goldsmith*, 223 Ala. 155, 157 (1931) (comparing polygamy, incest, and miscegenation).

122. See Eskridge, *The Case for Same-Sex Marriage*, 149 (discussing reasons not to allow polygamy).

123. See *In re Interest of Black*, 283 P.2d 887, 889 (Utah, 1955) (discussing charge that polygamous parents could not adequately support their children).

124. See Bennett, "Leave Marriage Alone," in Sullivan ed., *Same-Sex Marriage: Pro and Con* at 275 (suggesting that if same-sex marriage is permissible then everything is permissible); Arkes, "The Role of Nature," in Sullivan ed., *Same-Sex Marriage: Pro and Con* at 277 (same); Charles Krauthammer, "When John and Jim Say 'I Do,' " in Sullivan ed., *Same-Sex Marriage: Pro and Con*, 282, 284 (same). Professor Finnis argues that if same- sex marriages are recognized, then people will wrongly think that adultery is wrong because it involves deception rather than because it is "per se" wrong. See John Finnis, "Law, Morality, and 'Sexual Orienta-

tion,' " in John Corvino ed., *Same Sex: Debating the Ethics, Science, and Culture of Homosexuality*, 31, 37 (Lanham, Md.: Rowman & Littlefield, 1997).

125. *Santosky v. Kramer*, 455 U.S. 745, 753 (1982).

126. See, for example, *Oliverson v. West Valley City*, 875 F. Supp. 1465 (D. Utah 1995); *Commonwealth v. Stowell*, 449 N.E.2d 357 (Mass. 1983).

127. See, for example, *City of Sherman v. Henry*, 910 S.W.2d 542 (Tex. App. 1995) (right to commit adultery constitutionally protected), rev'd by 928 S.W.2d 464 (Tex. 1996).

128. See, for example, *Oliverson*, 875 F.Supp. at 1477 (the act of adultery "has for centuries been viewed as totally antithetical to the family").

129. See *City of Sherman*, 928 S.W.2d at 470. See also *Oliverson*, 875 F.Supp. at 1477 (the act of adultery "has for centuries been viewed as totally antithetical to the family"); *Stowell*, 449 N.E.2d at 360 ("the act of adultery frequently has a destructive impact on the marital relationship and is a factor in many divorces"); *Chlystek v. Kane*, 412 F. Supp. 20, 23 n.7 (W.D. Pa. 1976) ("the Pennsylvania legislation [punishing adultery] assailed in the case at bar does not conflict with such a right [i.e., to marry], but indeed affords it additional protection. The statute is simply a means for protecting the sanctity of marriage, and of deterring disregard for the fundamental obligations of that 'basic' civil status").

130. See *Bowers v. Hardwick*, 478 U.S. 186, 191 (1986).

131. See *Stowell*, 449 N.E.2d at 360 ("Given this broad concern with the institution of marriage, the State has a legitimate interest in prohibiting conduct which may threaten that institution").

132. Cf. *Evans v. Romer*, 882 P.2d 1335, 1347 (Colo. 1994) (en banc) (rejecting that laws prohibiting orientation discrimination will somehow "undermine marriages and heterosexual families").

133. For a discussion of some of the parallels between same-sex and interracial unions, see generally Mark Strasser, "Family, Definitions, and the Constitution: On the Antimiscegenation Analogy," 25 *Suffolk U. L. Rev.* 981 (1991).

134. See *Bowers*, 478 U.S. at 191.

135. See Chambers, "What If?" 95 *Mich. L. Rev.* at 460 (suggesting that voluntary adult sexual conduct should not be criminalized).

136. See *Bowers v. Hardwick*, 478 U.S. 186 (1986).

137. See Andrew H. Friedman, "Same-Sex Marriage and the Right of Privacy: Abandoning Scriptural, Canonical, and Natural Law Based Definitions of Marriage," 35 *How. L.J.* 173, 214 (1992) (*Bowers* "deals a serious, if not fatal, blow to any arguments that state prohibitions against same-sex marriages are unconstitutional"); Mary F. Gardner, Note, "*Braschi v. Stahl Assocs. Co.*: Much Ado About Nothing?" 35 *Vill. L. Rev.* 361, 363 (1990) (arguing that recognition of right to same-sex marriage would conflict with state sodomy statutes). Cf. *Bowers*, 478 U.S. at 195–96 ("it would be difficult, except by fiat, to limit the claimed right to homosexual conduct while leaving exposed to prosecution adultery . . ."); *Poe v. Ullman*, 367 U.S. 497, 553 (1961) (Harlan, J., dissenting) (suggesting that the state may forbid homosexuality and adultery altogether).

138. See *State v. Schmit*, 139 N.W.2d 800, 809 (Minn. 1966) ("it is conceivable that a husband and wife could be convicted of sodomy even though the proof established consent"); *State v. Nelson*, 271 N.W. 114, 118 (Minn. 1937) ("Thus hus-

band and wife, if violating this [sodomy] statute, could undoubtedly be punished, whereas the normal sexual act would not only be legal but perhaps entirely proper").

139. See Strasser, *Legally Wed*, 42 (the majority of states do not have sodomy statutes).

140. See *Bowers*, 478 U.S. at 218 (Stevens, J., dissenting) ("our prior cases thus establish that a State may not prohibit sodomy within 'the sacred precincts of marital bedrooms' "); *Cotner v. Henry*, 394 F.2d 873, 875 (7th Cir. 1968) ("Indiana courts could not interpret the statute constitutionally as making private consensual physical relations between married persons a crime absent a clear showing that the state had an interest in preventing such relations, which outweighed the constitutional right to marital privacy."); *Lovisi v. Slayton*, 539 F.2d 349, 351 (4th Cir. 1976) ("We may thus assume that the marital intimacies shared by the Lovisis when alone and in their own bedroom are within their protected right of privacy."); *State v. Lair*, 301 A.2d 748, 753 (N.J. 1973) (sodomy statute has marital exception).

141. *Williams v. State*, 494 So.2d 819, 828–29 (Ala. App. 1986).

142. *State v. Dubish*, 675 P.2d 877, 886 (Kan. 1984) ("Since we have determined that the defendant and the victim were married, his conviction for aggravated sodomy was erroneous").

143. See id. at 882.

144. See id. at 886. But see *Williams*, 494 So.2d at 830 ("None of the rationales for the 'marital exemption' that we have discussed provide a rational basis for distinguishing between married and unmarried persons in the forcible sodomy statute").

145. *Gryczan v. State*, 942 P.2d 112, 123 (Mont. 1997).

146. Id. at 125 (Turnage, C.J., concurring and dissenting)

147. 478 U.S. 186 (1986).

148. 517 U.S. 620 (1996). For the suggestion that not much is left of *Bowers* after *Romer*, see Richards, *Women, Gays, and the Constitution*, 408–9; Thomas C. Grey, "*Bowers v. Hardwick* Diminished," 68 *U. Colo. L. Rev.* 373, 374 (1997).

149. See id. at 196 n.8.

150. See *United States v. Fagg*, 34 M.J. 179 (1992) (nonmarital sodomy not protected by right to privacy); *State v. Santos*, 413 A.2d 58 (R.I. 1980) (same).

151. *Bowers*, 478 U.S. at 191.

152. Id. at 195–196.

153. Id. at 209 n.4 (1986) (Blackmun, J., dissenting) ("a court could find simple, analytically sound distinctions between certain private, consensual sexual conduct, on the one hand, and adultery . . . on the other. . . . [A] State might conclude that adultery is likely to injure third persons, in particular, spouses and children of persons who engage in extramarital affairs").

154. *Rochin*, 342 U.S. at 173.

155. Id. at 172.

2

Equal Protection

In *Baehr v. Lewin*, a plurality of the Hawaii Supreme Court held that Hawaii's ban on same-sex marriage implicates equal protection guarantees.[1] Because sex is a suspect classification under the state constitution,[2] the case was remanded to give the state an opportunity to establish that its same-sex marriage prohibition was narrowly tailored to promote compelling state interests.[3] On remand, the circuit court held that the state had failed to meet its burden,[4] but stayed that ruling to give the supreme court an opportunity to review it.[5] Before the state supreme court had issued an opinion, the state constitution was amended to permit the state legislature to reserve marriage for opposite-sex couples. Assuming that the amendment to the Hawaii Constitution violates no federal constitutional guarantees, the state supreme court will not need to address the issues raised under the *former* constitution. Nonetheless, the court will still have to examine whether a same-sex marriage ban violates federal equal protection guarantees.

EQUAL PROTECTION ANALYSIS

To understand which issues the state supreme court will probably have to address, it will be necessary to understand some basic features of equal protection analysis. When a court examines a statute that allegedly violates the Equal Protection Clause, the court will use one of three standards of review: strict scrutiny, heightened scrutiny, or the rational basis test. In order for a contested statute to be found constitutional under the most exacting standard, strict scrutiny, the statute at issue must be narrowly tailored to promote a compelling state interest; under the intermediate standard, heightened scrutiny, the statute must be substantially related to an important state interest; under the least restrictive standard, the rational basis test, the statute must be rationally related to a legitimate state interest.

The determination of the correct standard of review will be based upon the characteristics of the class against whom the statute has been directed. If the statute is designed to adversely affect a class that has a history of having been subjected to purposeful, unjustified discrimination and also has a history of (relative) political powerlessness, the statute will be subjected to strict scrutiny.[6] The United States Constitution requires that statutes discriminating on the basis of race, religion, ethnicity, and national origin be examined with strict scrutiny. Classes that fall within this category are called "suspect classes."

Some politically powerless classes that have been subjected to purposeful, unjustified discrimination may have suffered to a lesser extent than have the suspect classes. Such classes may be afforded *some* extra protection, although less than the suspect classes are afforded. A statute designed to adversely affect one of these classes will be subjected to heightened scrutiny. The United States Constitution requires that statutes discriminating on the basis of illegitimacy or sex be examined with heightened scrutiny. Classes that fall within this category are called "quasi-suspect classes."

Suppose that a class is neither suspect nor quasi-suspect. As far as the Equal Protection Clause of the United States Constitution is concerned, statutes adversely affecting that class should merely be examined in light of the rational basis test and will be upheld as long as they are rationally related to legitimate state goals.

The likelihood that a particular statute will be held unconstitutional is strongly correlated with the level of scrutiny that will be employed—if strict scrutiny is applied, the statute at issue will usually be found unconstitutional; if heightened scrutiny is applied, the statute will often be found unconstitutional; and if the rational basis test is used, the statute will usually be found constitutional.[7] A statute that could survive rational basis review might well not survive heightened or strict scrutiny, and thus the determination of the level of scrutiny to be employed is not a matter to be taken lightly.

STATE PROTECTIONS

In *Baehr v. Lewin*, a plurality of the Hawaii Supreme Court examined the state's same-sex marriage ban with strict scrutiny because it held that: (1) sex was a suspect classification under the state constitution and thus all statutes discriminating on that basis had to be examined with strict scrutiny,[8] and (2) the same-sex marriage ban discriminated on the basis of sex, both facially and as applied.[9] Each of these aspects of the decision may have import for the future success of challenges to same-sex marriage bans.

The decision that sex was a suspect classification under the Hawaii Constitution is important because it means that any Hawaiian statute which discriminates on the basis of sex will be examined with strict rather than heightened scrutiny. While it is likely that a statute examined with heightened scrutiny will be found unconstitutional, it is even more likely that a statute examined with strict scrutiny will not pass the relevant test. Thus, the state of Hawaii would have been forced to bear a heavy burden of persuasion were its justification for its same-sex marital prohibition to have been examined with strict scrutiny.

When the *Baehr* plurality held that strict scrutiny had to be employed, the plurality was interpreting its own state constitution's equal protection guarantees. Merely because Hawaii treats gender like race and requires that the highest level of scrutiny be employed when a statute discriminates on either of those grounds does not mean that other states must do the same. Thus, statutes employing sex-based classifications may receive closer scrutiny in Hawaii than in other states. For example, when suggesting that Alaska's same-sex marriage ban discriminated on the basis of sex, the trial court in *Brause v. Bureau of Vital Statistics* stated that the statute would have to be examined with heightened scrutiny insofar as it was being challenged on those grounds.[10] Thus, although the Hawaii and Alaska courts agreed that same-sex marriage bans discriminate on the basis of sex and thus implicate equal protection guarantees, they disagreed about the level of scrutiny that would be appropriately imposed for sex discrimination because of differences in their respective state constitutions.

It should not be thought that each state can simply apply whatever level of scrutiny it deems appropriate when examining statutes discriminating on the basis of sex. Because the United States Constitution requires that any statute discriminating on the basis of sex must be examined with heightened scrutiny and because states are precluded from imposing a lower level of scrutiny than the United States Constitution demands, state courts must employ at least heightened scrutiny when examining statutes that distinguish on the basis of sex.

The Hawaii electorate decided in November, 1998, to amend the state constitution to permit the legislature to reserve marriage for opposite-sex couples. Assuming that the legislature acts in light of that grant of authority, the courts may still have to address whether reserving marriage for opposite-sex couples violates federal guarantees. By the same token, even though the Alaska electorate voted to amend the state constitution to prohibit same-sex marriages, the Alaska courts may still have to decide whether such a ban is permitted by the United States Constitution. Presumably, that issue will initially be addressed by the Hawaii and Alaska courts but might ultimately be addressed by the United States Supreme Court.

The above point has received inadequate attention because many commentators have concentrated on only one of the two important aspects of the holding that Hawaii's same-sex marriage ban implicates equal protection guarantees. The aspect that has received much attention and discussion is that because sex is a suspect classification according to the Hawaii Constitution, Hawaii's same-sex marriage ban was to have been examined with strict scrutiny. It would have been no surprise if the Hawaii Supreme Court had affirmed *Baehr v. Miike*, the lower court ruling striking down the state's same-sex marriage ban, because classifications subjected to strict scrutiny are almost invariably struck down. Indeed, it is difficult to see how the court could have upheld a same-sex marriage ban, given that the ban involved a sex-based classification and that the state constitution required that such classifications be examined with strict scrutiny.

A similar analysis would be appropriate in any states whose constitutions treat sex as a suspect classification. If the supreme courts of those states were also to hold that same-sex marriage bans implicate equal protection guarantees on the basis of sex (and there are ample reasons that the courts should so hold), then they too would likely have difficulty upholding such statutes when employing strict scrutiny.

The second important aspect of the *Baehr* decision (which was echoed by the *Brause* decision)—namely, that the same-sex marriage ban discriminates on the basis of sex—has received relatively less attention, even though that aspect of the holding may have more significant implications than did the Hawaii Supreme Court's decision to employ strict rather than heightened scrutiny when examining the constitutionality of that state's same-sex marriage prohibition. This lack of attention may be due to a misunderstanding of the basis of the court's decision.

DO SAME-SEX MARRIAGE BANS DISCRIMINATE ON THE BASIS OF SEX?

When the *Baehr* plurality held that the statute at issue implicated equal protection guarantees and thus had to be examined with strict scrutiny, the plurality might have been saying (a) there is something special about the Hawaii Constitution that makes its equal protection guaranteees cover a broader range of individuals than would the equal protection guarantees offered by other state constitutions or the United States Constitution,[11] or (b) there is something special about the Hawaii Constitution that requires strict scrutiny for sex-based classifications, whereas the United States Constitution and many other states' constitutions merely require heightened scrutiny for such classifications. The plurality was clearly saying (b),[12] and the relevant question is whether it was also saying (a).

Part of the difficulty in discerning whether *Baehr* should be read to stand for (b) or, instead, (a) and (b) is that the plurality and the concurrence in the decision were addressing different issues when trying to decide whether equal protection guarantees were implicated by the same-sex marriage ban.[13] The plurality looked at the statute and concluded that, on its face and as applied, the statute distinguished on the basis of sex.[14] The concurring judge, Judge James Burns, addressed a different issue, namely, whether sexual orientation discrimination was a subcategory that should be included within the category of sex discrimination. Judge Burns suggested that orientation discrimination should be treated as sex discrimination if it could be established that sexual orientation was "biologically fated."[15] Regrettably, it was not made sufficiently clear in the opinion that different issues were in fact being addressed by the plurality and the concurrence,[16] although the plurality did indicate that it believed Judge Burns's analysis irrelevant to the issue before the court.[17]

If orientation discrimination were to be treated as sex discrimination as a matter of law,[18] then *all* laws which explicitly imposed extra burdens or disabilities on lesbians or gays would be subjected to at least heightened scrutiny. The *Baehr* plurality did *not* address the appropriate standard of review for statutes which facially discriminate against gays, lesbians, and bisexuals, but merely made a decision about how to analyze the statute before it, which explicitly classified on the basis of *sex*.

The difference between these approaches can be illustrated by considering two different scenarios. Suppose, for example, that two *heterosexual* women, Terry and Pat, wish to marry each other, perhaps because they want to receive certain benefits that they could not receive unless they were married.[19] Suppose further that this couple wishes to marry in a state that has the current Hawaii marriage statute, which reads in relevant part, "In order to make valid the marriage contract, which shall be *only* between a man and a woman, ..."[20] The current statute *on its face* would preclude this marriage, even if the statute had only been "intended" to discriminate against gays, lesbians, and bisexuals.[21] Because the statute explicitly states that a marriage contract will not be valid unless it is between a man and a woman, these two women could not contract a valid marriage in the state, regardless of their sexual orientation. Indeed, in his *Baehr* dissent, Judge Walter Heen seemed to believe that a virtue of the statute under examination was that it prohibited "same sex marriages on the part of professed or non-professed heterosexuals, homosexuals, bisexuals, or asexuals."[22] Thus, the statute under examination involved a sex-based classification because it precluded same-sex couples from marrying regardless of their sexual orientation.

It is conceivable that a court would ignore the clear language of a statute specifying that only a marriage between a man and a woman would be valid and would only enforce the prohibition when gays, lesbians, or bisexuals wished to marry (ignoring the potential difficulties that might be posed in trying to establish the orientations of the would-be marital partners). Such a method of enforcement would itself raise equal protection difficulties, both because applying a facially neutral statute to only a subset of those to whom the statute would apply would hardly be fair[23] and because it is not clear that the statute so construed would be serving a legitimate purpose, even were it arguable that the statute as written served such a purpose. For example, even were there a legitimate purpose in restricting marriage to those who were able and willing to produce children through their union,[24] this purpose would hardly be served by allowing *same-sex heterosexual* couples to marry but not allowing gay or lesbian couples to marry. Were marriage permissibly restricted to those who had children to raise, then it would make no sense to preclude a same-sex couple from marrying *who had children to raise*, whether the couple was composed of individuals with a same-sex orientation, an opposite-sex orientation or, perhaps, one individual with a same-sex orientation and one with an opposite-sex orientation.

Perhaps it would seem that enforcing such a statute against only individuals with a same-sex orientation would promote the "legitimate" purpose of punishing bisexuals, gays, and lesbians or of expressing official state disapproval of that group. Yet, there are at least two reasons that such a tack is unpersuasive. First, if that in fact had been the legislative intent, the legislature might have passed a statute that read, in relevant part, "In order to make valid the marriage contract, which shall be only between heterosexuals . . . ." Second, the United States Supreme Court has already made clear that the state is prohibited from enacting legislation just to punish a group that it dislikes.[25]

Suppose that a state passed a statute prohibiting lesbians, gays, or bisexuals from marrying a same-sex partner. A same-sex, heterosexual couple such as Terry and Pat would be allowed to marry, although a same-sex lesbian couple would not be permitted to marry. Such a statute would be challenged as a violation of state or federal equal protection guarantees. Now, the question posed by Judge Burns would be quite relevant. If discrimination on the basis of sexual orientation is to be treated in the same way as is discrimination on the basis of sex, then this statute would be subjected to (at least) heightened scrutiny on equal protection grounds. If discrimination against gays, lesbians, and bisexuals does not trigger heightened or strict scrutiny, then the statute at issue would be examined in light of the rational basis test, at least as far as the equal protection issues were concerned.[26]

When the *Brause* court explained why it thought the Alaska same-sex marriage ban implicated the "Constitution's prohibition of classifications based on sex or gender,"[27] it offered the following hypothetical: "[I]f twins, one male and one female, both wished to marry a woman and otherwise met all of the Code's requirements, only gender prevents the twin sister from marrying under the present law."[28] The court concluded, "Sex-based classification can hardly be more obvious."[29]

There are at least two points that should be noted about the Alaska court's hypothetical: (1) it illustrates that the statute is based on sex rather than, for example, orientation, and (2) it and the accompanying implicit analysis do not involve some feature of equal protection jurisprudence that is peculiar to Alaska constitutional doctrine—the same hypothetical might have equal force in a discussion of federal constitutional guarantees. Thus, the

Alaska court's analysis would seem to have implications for the constitutionality of all states' same-sex marriage bans.

CONSTITUTIONAL PROTECTIONS

It is much too easy to conflate some of the different issues that are raised by the Hawaii Supreme Court's interpretation of the former state constitution and by the subsequent amendment to that constitution. The former constitution afforded special safeguards that prevented the legislature from passing a same-sex marriage ban unless the state had compelling interests at stake justifying that ban. Now that the amendment has passed, the Hawaii Constitution can no longer be construed as affording this *extra* protection.

The change pointed to here can be easily illustrated. Suppose that the Hawaii Supreme Court would have affirmed the lower court opinion because *strict* rather than even *heightened* scrutiny had to be employed and that the same-sex marriage ban would have been upheld in Hawaii had this "extra" protection not been afforded. This result would be important, not for Hawaii (because the amendment's passage entails that the state constitution explicitly permits the legislature to pass the relevant legislation), but for any other state in which such bans are examined with at most heightened scrutiny. However, as will be explained below, there is good reason to think that the above does not capture the Hawaii Supreme Court's position.

Before that explanation can be offered, however, it is important to understand what the approved amendment to the Hawaii Constitution does and does not do. The amendment does *not* concern itself with whether strict rather than heightened scrutiny should be employed when sex classifications are implicated. Rather, it addresses a specific issue, namely, whether the state constitution will permit the legislature to reserve marriage for opposite-sex couples. The amendment does not merely require that the Hawaii Supreme Court examine the prohibition with a less demanding level of scrutiny (e.g., heightened rather than strict) but entirely precludes the court from invalidating the same-sex marriage ban on *state* constitutional grounds. The amendment does *not* preclude the court from striking the same-sex marriage prohibition on *federal* constitutional grounds. So, too, the Alaska constitutional amendment precludes Alaska courts from invalidating the state's same-sex marriage ban on state constitutional grounds, but does not (and indeed cannot) affect federal constitutional guarantees.

Suppose that a state had a provision within its constitution that read: "Of several persons claiming and equally entitled under applicable law to administer an estate, males must be preferred to females."[30] It is clear that such a provision could not be struck down on state constitutional grounds, since the provision would have been part of the state constitution itself. However, merely because the provision was incorporated within the state constitution would not somehow make the provision immune from federal challenge.

When the Supreme Court held that interracial marriage bans were unconstitutional, the Court thereby invalidated several state constitutional provisions that had improperly restricted marriage.[31] Thus, when the case was decided, the Alabama Constitution read, "The legislature shall never pass any law to authorize or legalize any marriage between any white person and a negro, or descendant of a negro." [32] Other state constitutions also prohibited such unions.[33] Nonetheless, notwithstanding these state constitutional provisions, the United States Supreme Court held that these limitations on the right to marry violated federal constitutional guarantees.

Consider the provision discussed above which reads: "Of several persons claiming and equally entitled under applicable law to administer an estate, males must be preferred to females." The state would be unable to deny that the provision involved a classification based on sex, since the provision would have clearly and explicitly distinguished on that basis. However, a separate question would be whether the admittedly sex-based classification was invidious or, instead, closely tailored to promote important state objectives.[34]

A similar analysis is appropriate when examining the current situations in Hawaii and Alaska. The passage of the Hawaii constitutional amendment does not somehow make a statute reserving marriage for opposite-sex couples non-sex-based. Rather, it incorporates within the state constitution a grant of power to the legislature enabling it to create a sex-based classification that will escape state constitutional scrutiny. Thus, were the legislature to pass a same-sex marriage ban as authorized by the constitution and were that ban challenged in the courts, the Hawaii Supreme Court might still find that the same-sex marriage ban involves a sex-based classification because it allows a man to marry a woman but not a man and it allows a woman to marry a man but not a woman.[35] However, the court could not find that the admittedly sex-based classification violated the Hawaii Constitution, although it could and presumably would find the classification invidious in light of federal constitutional guarantees. So, too, the Alaska Supreme Court could find that the state same-sex marriage ban implicated constitutional guarantees prohibiting discrimination based on sex. While it could not find that the admittedly sex-based classification violated the state constitution, it could find that the United States Constitution precluded such discrimination.

EQUAL PROTECTION

Merely because a statute makes a sex-based distinction does not establish the constitutional infirmity of that classification.[36] It might seem that Hawaii, Alaska, or any other state could admit that its marital statute involves a sex-based classification but could simply deny that the distinction is invidious. After all, as the *Baehr* dissent points out, men and women are being treated in the same way—neither can marry a partner of the same sex.[37]

Yet, the seemingly straightforward argument offered by the *Baehr* dissent has a rather tainted history. An analogous argument was offered to justify imposing extra burdens on interracial couples, namely, that statutes prohibiting interracial marriage did not invidiously discriminate as long as each member of the interracial couple was subjected to the same penalty. Thus, it was argued that because *no one* was allowed to marry a partner of a different race, interracial marriage bans should not be held invidiously discriminatory. Various courts accepted this reasoning and held that the Fourteenth Amendment does not preclude states from enforcing antimiscegenation laws.[38] It was not until 1967 that the Supreme Court rejected this analysis of the constitutionality of interracial marriage bans.

In the late 1800s, the United States Supreme Court held that the Constitution permitted Alabama's punishing interracial fornication more severely than intraracial fornication. That Court reasoned that because both whites and blacks would be subjected to the same penalty for violating the antimiscegenation statute, there was no constitutional violation.[39] However, in 1964, the Supreme Court again examined a statute that imposed a more severe penalty for interracial than intraracial fornication.[40] The Court understood that blacks and whites who engaged in the same conduct were subject to the same penalty.[41] However, the Court explained that mere equal application was not enough.[42] A further question had to be answered, namely, whether the statutory classifications were reasonable in light of the statute's purpose.[43] The Court concluded that the statute was invidiously discriminatory,[44] thereby repudiating both the view and the reasoning that had been accepted in the late 1800s.[45]

SEX-BASED CLASSIFICATIONS

Even if bans on interracial coupling and marriage are invidiously discriminatory, that does not establish that intrasexual coupling or marriage bans are also invidiously discriminatory. The former are examined with strict scrutiny, whereas the latter are usually examined with at most "mere" heightened scrutiny. Yet, it should not be thought that heightened scrutiny imposes a relatively light burden—the Supreme Court has made clear that statutes will not survive heightened scrutiny unless an "exceedingly persuasive justification"[46] is offered to justify the employment of a sex-based classification. The Court will closely examine such classifications to make sure that they are not invidious and are not based upon "overbroad generalizations" about the proper roles of men and women.[47]

In *Mississippi University for Women v. Hogan*, the United States Supreme Court had to decide whether the school was invidiously discriminating on the basis of sex when it refused to admit men to its School of Nursing.[48] The Court made clear that the fact that the policy discriminated against males rather than females did not exempt it from intermediate scrutiny. Thus, the Court could have struck down the policy because of its adverse effect on *males*.[49] Nonetheless, notwithstanding that statute's facial discrimination against men, much of the opinion involved why the *apparently* benign classification in fact invidiously discriminated against *women*. For example, the Court suggested that the admissions policy tended to perpetuate the stereotype that nursing was exclusively a woman's profession[50] and that the policy might in fact have been penalizing the very class the State was attempting to benefit.[51] Thus, the Court made clear that facial classifications on the basis of sex, although apparently benign, might well be invidious and offensive to constitutional guarantees. Indeed, the Court has described as "axiomatic" the proposition that "intentional gender discrimination by the state violates the Equal Protection Clause, particularly where . . . the discrimination serves to ratify and perpetuate invidious, archaic, and overbroad stereotypes about the relative abilities of men and women."[52] Given that same-sex marriage prohibitions facially classify on the basis of sex, the relevant question is whether such bans implicitly if not explicitly perpetuate myths about the relative abilities of men and women. Yet, the answer to that seems clear, since men allegedly cannot fulfill the marital roles that women are supposed to fulfill and women allegedly cannot fulfill the marital roles that men are supposed to fulfill. This kind of sex-stereotyping is exactly what the Fourteenth Amendment is supposed to prevent.

The Constitution does *not* require that all differences between the sexes must be ignored. On the contrary, the inherent differences between men and women are "cause for celebration."[53] However, these differences are "not for denigration of the members of either sex or for artificial constraints on an individual's opportunity,"[54] and preventing two individuals from marrying because one of them cannot fulfill his or her "proper" role involves an obviously artificial constraint.

The Supreme Court has said that the test for determining the validity of a gender-based classification must be applied "free of fixed notions concerning the roles and abilities of males and females."[55] Further, statutory objectives themselves must not reflect "archaic and stereotypic notions."[56] Yet, precisely what is at issue are the fixed notions concerning the roles and abilities of men and women. There is no reason to think that for all women only a man can provide sexual, emotional, and spiritual fulfillment, just as there is no reason to think that for all men only a woman can provide sexual, emotional, and spiritual fulfillment.

By passing a same-sex marriage ban, the state seems to be saying that if one cannot find marital fulfillment with someone of the opposite sex then one simply will not be allowed to have marital fulfillment. The state does not seem to be making the empirically implausible claim that the individual would find fulfillment with someone of the opposite sex once he or she meets the "right" woman or man, but that the individual will simply be denied the opportunity for fulfillment with the only kind of person who might be able to provide it. Just as states acted wrongly when they said that if one could not find marital fulfillment with someone of the same race then one would simply have to forego such fulfillment, states act wrongly when they impose the analogous requirement based on the partner's sex.

APPLYING HEIGHTENED SCRUTINY TO SAME-SEX MARRIAGE BANS

In order to determine whether a state's same-sex marriage ban is based on false stereotypes or is designed to promote archaic notions about the sexes, the state's reasons for the statute must be examined. At the trial court level, the state of Hawaii argued that same-sex marriages should be precluded because lesbians and gays would not be sufficiently good parents. However, that claim has been empirically disproven and thus was rightly rejected by the trial court in *Baehr v. Miike*.[57]

Certainly, there are differences between same-sex and opposite-sex couples. For example, none of the former can have a child through their union, whereas many of the latter can. However, since there is no general requirement that couples who wish to marry must be planning on having children, much less children through their union,[58] it seems clear that this would not be the real reason that the state would be precluding same-sex couples from marrying. The state cannot plausibly maintain that it is an important state interest for those who plan to marry to be able to have children through their union if they are same-sex but not if they are opposite-sex partners.[59] Further, the state of Hawaii has already made clear that it does *not* believe that an important interest is served by restricting marriage to those able to have a child through their union, since the legislature took action to *remove* that requirement from its laws.[60]

The state of Alaska does not believe that an important interest is served by restricting marriage to those able to have a child through their union, since there is no fertility requirement for those who wish to marry.[61] Indeed, Alaska does not even make the capacity or willingness to have sexual relations a requirement of marriage, since the state makes nonconsummated marriages voidable rather than void and will recognize such marriages as long as the parties themselves do not object.[62] Further, no one but the parties themselves can have a marriage voided on the ground of nonconsummation.[63] Thus, the state of Alaska can hardly argue that the ability to have children is an essential requirement for those who wish to marrry, given its current laws.

When the United States Supreme Court evaluates the constitutionality of a statute with a sex-based classification, the Court insists that the classification at issue must have been drawn to promote important government objectives and, further, that the means employed be substantially related to the achievement of those objectives.[64] The Court also insists that the reasons for the statute be "genuine, not merely hypothesized or invented."[65] Thus, the Court will not hold a sex-based classification constitutional merely because some rationalization is invented after the fact to "sanitize" the invidious discrimination. For example, were Hawaii to try to justify its same-sex marriage ban now by arguing that marriage should be reserved for those able and willing to procreate, the claim would be unacceptable, at least in part, because of its post hoc nature, given the earlier removal of such a requirement by the legislature. By the same token, the Alaska Legislature does not currently impose such a requirement, so such an attempted justification simply would not be plausible.

It should not be thought that only Hawaii and Alaska will have difficulty in claiming to have an important interest in reserving marriage for those able and willing to have children through their union. Several states have indicated their willingness to allow first cousins to marry provided either that they are over 65 or can establish that they *cannot* have children through their union.[66] These states will also have some difficulty in plausibly claiming that the purposes of marriage require that the individuals who wish to marry be able to have a child through their union, since these states will allow certain couples to marry only if they cannot do so.

Nor should those states not making this particular first-cousin exception feel confident that they can easily maintain the importance of would-be marital couples being able to produce children through their union. If indeed this is an important or compelling state interest, then states will have to explain why they are willing to ignore that interest when opposite-sex couples desire to marry.

The Supreme Court has warned that discriminations of an unusual character require careful consideration to determine whether they are obnoxious to constitutional guarantees.[67] If the legislature is allowed to pass burdensome legislation that will only affect a small, select group of individuals, it will be able to escape the political fallout that might occur if larger numbers were affected.[68] When one considers that this requirement of procreation through the union of the to-be married individuals is (1) unusual and (2) applied to only a few who (3) themselves are relatively powerless[69] so that it will not be difficult for lawmakers to escape political retribution by the selective imposition of that requirement, the classification cries out for close examination.

The claim here is not that the state lacks a legitimate interest in the production and raising of the next generation. On the contrary, that is a legitimate interest, and lesbian and gay couples should be allowed to marry precisely because of that interest.[70] Yet, even were it true that lesbians and gays did not have children to raise, preventing their marrying would *not* promote the legitimate state objective of providing a setting for the nurturing of the young. Same-sex couples being allowed to marry would neither induce others not to have children nor would it somehow induce others to raise their children in less healthy settings. In short, preventing lesbians and gays from marrying does *not* promote the state's legitimate interest in providing a setting in which the next generation can flourish and thus is not sufficiently closely tailored to withstand constitutional scrutiny.

It is sometimes suggested that allowing same-sex couples to marry will somehow undermine opposite-sex marriage.[71] Yet, such an assertion flies in the face of the empirical evidence[72] and, in any event, other steps would be much more effective if the state really was interested in protecting the family unit.[73] It is doubtful that many would choose opposite-sex marriage because they did not have the option to marry a same-sex partner and also doubtful that such marriages (if they did occur) would be happy, healthy, and long-lasting.

If certain individuals must establish that they can produce a child through their union before they can marry but no one else has to meet that test, there is at the very least a question whether that requirement is reasonable in light of the purposes of marriage. If in addition this requirement is only imposed on a discrete, disfavored group, it is hard to see how the Court could find that this was not an arbitrary and invidious classification. By the same token, if certain people are to be barred from marrying because they cannot be good parents when (1) there is ample evidence that they are good parents,[74] and (2) other couples do not have the requirement imposed when they wish to marry, it is difficult to see how the Court could uphold the requirement as noninvidious.

In the long run, it seems likely that the more important aspect of the *Baehr v. Lewin* decision is that same-sex marriage bans involve sex discrimination, not that sex is a suspect class under the Hawaii Constitution. Just as the *Brause* court found that the Alaska statute implicated equal protection guarantees, other courts may well find that their own state prohibitions do so as well. The United States Constitution requires that sex-based classifications receive careful scrutiny and it is unlikely that an exceedingly persuasive justification could be offered to justify same-sex marriage bans. If other courts accept the *Baehr* and *Brause* conclusions that same-sex marriage bans involve a sex-based classification, it is doubtful that those prohibitions will be upheld.

ORIENTATION DISCRIMINATION

Suppose that it were rejected that the same-sex marriage ban was sex-based, *Baehr* and *Brause* conclusions to that effect notwithstanding. It still would not be clear that the statute would pass constitutional muster, notwithstanding that when using the rational basis test the Court must sustain a legislative classification if it is rationally related to a legitimate governmental interest.[75]

One governmental interest that might be suggested would be that the state wanted to make clear that it disapproved of lesbians, gays, and bisexuals. Yet, the United States Supreme Court has already made clear that statutes designed to make lesbians and gays second-class citizens "unequal to everyone else"[76] are unconstitutional. As a California appellate court pointed out, the Equal Protection Clause applies to all citizens[77]—lesbians, bisexuals, and gays are also entitled to the equal protection of the laws.[78] Indeed, the "United States Constitution forbids any effort to discriminate against a discrete group."[79] As the Supreme Court made clear years ago, equal protection has no meaning if a legislature's desire to harm a politically unpopular group constitutes a *legitimate* governmental interest.[80]

Whether or not same-sex marriage bans are held unconstitutional, some individuals will continue to hate other individuals because of their sexual orientation. By the same token, even though discrimination on the basis of race is unconstitutional, some individuals continue to hate other individuals because of their race. Yet, the persistence of prejudice does not justify incorporating those attitudes into law. As the United States Supreme Court made clear, the Constitution can neither "tolerate" such attitudes[81] nor can it give them effect, directly or indirectly.[82]

MORALITY

Perhaps it will be argued that the state's prohibiting lesbians and gays from marrying is not prompted by bias but, instead, by the state's legitimate interest in promoting morality. Yet, same-sex relationships are not immoral, just as interracial relationships are not immoral, views to the contrary notwithstanding.

Presumably, one who believes same-sex relationships immoral will not be convinced of the error of that view merely because someone else disagrees. Nor might such a person have a change of heart when it is pointed out that such relationships do not hurt anyone or that such relationships involve the love, companionship, emotional support, etc., that opposite-sex relationships involve. Indeed, it is not clear what could convince someone of the error of that view. Yet, the test for whether long-term same-sex relationships should be recognized by the state simply *cannot* be that all members of the state must find such relationships morally acceptable. Were that the test, interracial and interreligious relationships also would not be recognized.

When the states of Florida and Alabama wanted to punish nonmarital interrracial sexual relationships more severely than intraracial ones, they were presumably reflecting the moral views of their respective populaces. When the state of Virginia wanted to preclude interracial couples from marrying, it was presumably reflecting the moral views of the Virginia citizenry. Yet, the United States Supreme Court made clear that such a rationale justified neither a state's punishing interracial relationships more severely than intraracial ones nor a state's refusing to recognize interracial marriages. By the same token, the presumed moral view of the populace would not justify a refusal to recognize same-sex marriages.

The state has a legitimate interest in the promotion of morality where secular effects are at issue. It is of course true that the state can criminalize rape, murder, etc., but that is not merely because they are "immoral" but because of the actual harms that they cause. However, same-sex marriages would not be harmful; on the contrary, they would promote the same sorts of benefits that opposite-sex marriages promote, which is one of the reasons that same-sex unions should be legally recognized rather than prohibited.

THE DEFINITION OF MARRIAGE

It might seem that this entire discussion involves a misunderstanding—the state's refusing to recognize a same-sex marriage does not discriminate on the basis of sex or orientation but merely reflects the definition of marriage, which limits marriage to opposite-sex couples.[83] However, there are clear difficulties with this kind of analysis. For example, as a general matter, if equal protection scrutiny can be avoided by adopting definitions, then it would seem that states could go back to prohibiting interracial marriages by simply *defining* marriage as a union involving individuals of the same race.[84] This is something that the Constitution simply would not permit.

It might be suggested that the argument that same-sex couples are precluded by definition from marrying is not undermined by the analogy to interracial marriage because the comparison is inapt.[85] Arguably, interracial marriages should be understood to fall within the category of "traditional" marriages,[86] whereas same-sex marriages should not be so understood.[87] Yet, it is clear that many did not view interracial marriages as falling within the traditional limitations of marriage.[88] Indeed, it was only about thirty years ago that the *Loving* Court struck down antimiscegenation laws[89] and, further, the United States Supreme Court *refused* to strike down Virginia's antimiscegenation law about forty years ago.[90]

Historically, the issue for courts confronting whether the Constitution prohibited antimiscegenation laws was whether marriage itself was protected by the United States Constitution. Many courts did not think so, because the Constitution does not even mention, much less explicitly protect, the freedom to marry.[91] If Justice Scalia is willing to suggest that *Loving* was rightly decided,[92] despite the Fourteenth Amendment text's *not* being explicitly limited to race[93] and despite the absence of an explicit constitutional provision protecting the right to marry,[94] then his comments would suggest that the right to marry a same-sex partner might also be protected. Of course, judging from his comments in *Romer*,[95] it is clear that he would not find such a right, implications of his own position notwithstanding.[96]

Even if Justice Scalia's claims were more accurate historically (e.g., even if the Framers of the Civil Rights Amendmens had intended that interracial marriages should be protected by the Constitution),[97] that would not limit what could be recognized now. The Supreme Court has already indicated that it is not confined to historic notions of equality when determining which classifications are unconstitutionally discriminatory.[98]

Bracketing general claims about the appropriate definition of marriage, the precluded-by-definition argument is utterly implausible in the context discussed here. Given that the Hawaii Supreme Court would likely have affirmed *Baehr v. Miike* had the constitutional amendment not been adopted, the state would likely have had to recognize same-sex marriages had the referendum failed. Thus, not only are same-sex unions *not* definitionally precluded, they would probably have been *legally recognized* if the amendment had not passed—and probably will be if the constitutionality of the amendment is not upheld. The very *possibility* that such marriages will be recognized should lay to rest the definitional preclusion argument.[99] A separate issue is whether the same-sex marriage prohibition is sufficiently closely tailored to sufficiently important interests to withstand constitutional analysis. However, that involves an examination and weighing of the individual and state interests at issue and can only be broached once the definitional preclusion argument has been rejected.

The United States Supreme Court has made clear that discrimination against lesbians, bisexuals, and gays is not constitutionally permissible, absent a legitimate basis for the classification.[100] The Equal Protection Clause precludes states from placing individuals into different classes and then treating those classes differently if the differentiating criteria are wholly unrelated to the objective of that statute.[101] If indeed marriage is only for those who can reproduce through their union or only for those who can parent well, then the state must enforce the relevant requirements generally and in an equal-handed manner. Were the state to impose the latter requirement generally, it would allow some same-sex partners to marry but prohibit some (otherwise qualified) opposite-sex couples from marrying. The requirement that would-be marital partners be able or willing to have or raise children should not be imposed on anyone, much less on a select group as a pretext to prevent their being able to marry.

Now that the Hawaii and Alaska electorates have decided to amend their state constitutions, their same-sex marriage bans may have to be examined in light of federal constitutional guarantees. It is difficult to see how such statutes could pass the relevant constitutional test. However, another issue has now been posed, namely, whether the amendments, themselves, offend constitutional guarantees. That issue will be discussed in the next chapter.

NOTES

1. *Baehr v. Lewin*, 852 P.2d 44 (Haw.), reconsideration granted in part, 875 P.2d 225 (Haw. 1993).

2. Id. at 67.

3. Id. at 68.

4. See *Baehr v. Miike*, CIV. No. 91–1394, 1996 WL 694235 (Haw. Cir. Ct. Dec. 3, 1996).

5. See Joel R. Brandes & Carole L. Weidman, "Same-Sex Marriage," 217 *N.Y.L.J.* 3 (1/28/97) (Judge Chang stayed his own ruling pending state supreme court review).

6. As Justice Marshall pointed out, however, not all classes meeting these criteria will have statutes adversely affecting them examined with strict scrutiny. See *Massachusetts Board of Retirement v. Murgia*, 427 U.S. 307, 320 (1976) (Marshall, J., dissenting).

7. For further discussion of the standards of review, see Mark Strasser, *Legally Wed: Same-Sex Marriage and the Constitution*, Chap. 2 (Ithaca, N.Y.: Cornell University Press, 1997).

8. See *Baehr*, 852 P.2d at 67.

9. Id. at 60.

10. See 1998 WL 88743, at *6 (Alaska Super.).

11. See Vincent C. Green, Note, "Same-Sex Adoption: An Alternative Approach to Gay Marriage in New York," 62 *Brook. L. Rev.* 399, 400 (1996) (suggesting that "because the *Baehr* court's classification is based upon the Equal Protection Clause of the Hawaii Constitution," its precedential value is lessened).

12. See *Baehr*, 852 P.2d at 67 (strict scrutiny to be employed when analyzing equal protection classifications).

13. When the case was reconsidered, the *Baehr* court ordered "further proceedings consistent with the plurality opinion." See id. at 74.

14. See id. at 60.

15. See id. at 69 (Burns, J., concurring in the result).

16. Some have not appreciated this and have simply concluded that Judge Burns's position and reasoning are somewhat obscure See Andrew Koppelman, "Why Discrimination Against Lesbians and Gay Men Is Sex Discrimination," 69 *N.Y.U. L. Rev.* 197, 207 (1994).

17. See *Baehr*, 852 P.2d at 53 n.14.

18. See generally Koppelman, "Why Discrimination Against Lesbians and Gay Men Is Sex Discrimination," 69 *N.Y.U. L. Rev.* 197.

19. See Sondrea Joy King, Note, "Ya'll Cain't Do That Here: Will Texas Recognize Same-Sex Marriages Validly Contracted in Other States?" 2 *Tex. Wesleyan L. Rev.* 515, 551 (1996) (posing hypothetical of two heterosexual women who wish to marry for economic benefits).

20. See Haw. Rev. Stat. § 572–1 (1996) (italics added).

21. Cf. Craig M. Bradley, "The Right Not to Endorse Gay Rights: A Reply to Sunstein," 70 *Ind. L.J.* 29, 34 (1994) ("A ban on same-sex marriages is not perfectly tailored to further the governmental interest in not giving homosexual relationships

legal recognition since it forbids people of the same sex from entering into a legally recognized 'marriage' regardless of their sexual proclivities [or lack of same]").

22. See *Baehr*, 852 P.2d at 71 (Heen, J., dissenting).

23. Cf. *Yick Wo v. Hopkins*, 118 U.S. 356, 373–74 (1886) ("Though the law itself be fair on its face, and impartial in appearance, yet, if it is applied and administered by public authority with an evil eye and an unequal hand, so as practically to make unjust and illegal discriminations between persons in similar circumstances, material to their rights, the denial of equal justice is still within the prohibition of the constitution").

24. For reasons to doubt that this is legitimate, see Strasser, *Legally Wed*, Chap. 3.

25. See *Romer v. Evans*, 517 U.S. 620, 632 (1996) ("the amendment seems inexplicable by anything but animus toward the class that it affects; it lacks a rational relationship to legitimate state interests").

26. Arguably, a statute prohibiting same-sex marriage abridges a fundamental right and thus should be subjected to strict scrutiny. See Strasser, *Legally Wed*, Chap. 3.

27. *Brause*, 1998 WL 88743, at *6.

28. Id.

29. Id.

30. Cf. *Reed v. Reed*, 404 U.S. 71, 73 (1971).

31. See *Loving v. Virginia*, 388 U.S. 1, 6 n.5 (1967)(listing different state constitutions that barred interracial marriage).

32. Ala. Const. Art. 4, § 102.

33. See Fla. Const. Art. 16, § 24 ("All marriages between a white person and a negro, or between a white person and a person of negro descent to the fourth generation, inclusive, are hereby forever prohibited"); Miss. Const. Art. 14, § 263 ("The marriage of a white person with a negro or mulatto, or person who shall have one-eighth or more of negro blood, shall be unlawful and void"); N.C. Const. Art. XIV, § 8 ("All marriages between a white person and a negro, or between a white person and a person of negro descent to the third generation, inclusive, are hereby forever prohibited"); S.C. Const. Art. III, § 33 ("The marriage of a white person with a negro or mulatto, or person who shall have one-eighth or more of negro blood, shall be unlawful and void"); Tenn. Const. Art. XI, § 15 ("The intermarriage of white persons with negroes, mulattoes, or persons of mixed blood, descended from a negro to the third generation inclusive or their living together as man and wife in this State is prohibited").

34. Cf. *Loving*, 388 U.S. at 8 ("the State contends that, because its miscegenation statutes punish equally both the white and the Negro participants in an interracial marriage, these statutes, despite their reliance on racial classifications do not constitute an invidious discrimination based upon race").

35. See *Baehr*, 852 P.2d at 60.

36. See *Michael M. v. Superior Court*, 450 U.S. 464, 469 (1981) ("this Court has consistently upheld statutes where the gender classification is not invidious, but rather realistically reflects the fact that the sexes are not similarly situated in certain circumstances").

37. *Baehr*, 852 P.2d at 71 (Heen, J., dissenting).

38. See *Naim v. Naim*, 87 S.E.2d 749 (Va. 1955) (upholding antimiscegenation

law); *Ex parte Kinney*, 14 Fed. Cas. 602, 603 (Case No. 7,825) (E.D. Va. 1879) ("there is nothing in the national constitution expressly forbidding a state from abridging the right of marrying").

39. *Pace v. Alabama*, 106 U.S. 583, 585 (1883).

40. *McLaughlin v. Florida*, 379 U.S. 184, 188 (1964).

41. Id.

42. Id. at 191.

43. Id.

44. Id. at 195.

45. Id. at 188.

46. See *United States v. Virginia*, 518 U.S. 515, 534 (1996).

47. Id. at 533.

48. *Mississippi University for Women v. Hogan*, 458 U.S. 718, 719 (1982) ("This case presents the narrow issue of whether a statute that excludes males from enrolling in a state-supported professional nursing school violates the Equal Protection Clause of the Fourteenth Amendment").

49. See id. at 723 (citing *Caban v. Mohammed*, 441 U.S. 380, 394 [1979]).

50. Id. at 729.

51. Id. at 729 n.15.

52. *J.E.B. v. Alabama ex rel. T.B.*, 511 U.S. 127, 130–131 (1994).

53. *Virginia*, 518 U.S. at 533.

54. Id.

55. *Mississippi University for Women*, 458 U.S. at 724–25.

56. Id. at 725.

57. See *Baehr v. Miike*, 1996 WL 694235 (Hawai'i Cir. Ct. 1996) (rejecting state's claim that lesbians and gays are not sufficiently good parents).

58. See Mark Strasser, "Domestic Relations Jurisprudence and the Great, Slumbering *Baehr*: On Definitional Preclusion, Equal Protection, and Fundamental Interests," 64 *Fordham L. Rev.* 921, 955–62 (1995).

59. See id. at 955.

60. See *Baehr*, 852 P.2d at 48 n.1. See also Richard D. Mohr, "The Case for Gay Marriage," 9 *Notre Dame J. L., Ethics & Pub. Pol'y* 215, 223 (1995) (noting that Hawaii had amended its marriage statute to delete the requirement that neither of the parties was impotent); Nancy Klingeman & Kenneth May, Recent Development, "For Better or Worse, in Sickness and in Health, until Death Do Us Part: A Look at Same-Sex Marriage in Hawaii," 16 *U. Haw. L. Rev.* 447, 473 n.185 (1994) (same); Erik J. Toulon, "Call the Caterer: Hawaii to Host First Same-Sex Marriage," 3 *S. Cal. Rev. L. & Women's Stud.* 109, 127 (1993) (same).

61. See Alaska Stat. § 25.05.011 (Michie 1998) (fertility not listed under requirements for marriage).

62. See Alaska Stat. § 25.05.031 (1998).

63. Id.

64. See *Virginia*, 518 U.S. at 533.

65. See id.

66. See Ariz. Rev. Stat. Ann. § 25–101 (West 1991) (over 65 or one is unable to reproduce); Ind. Code Ann. 31–11–1-2 (over 65) (West 1997); Utah Code Ann. § 30–1-1(2) (Supp. 1997) (over 65 or both over 55 and one cannot reproduce);

Wis. Stat. Ann. 765.03 (West 1993) (female 55 or either submits affadavit permanently sterile).

67. *Louisville Gas and Electric Co. v. Coleman*, 277 U.S. 32, 37 (1928).

68. *Eisenstadt v. Baird*, 405 U.S. 438, 454 (1972).

69. For a discussion of the relative powerlessness of lesbians, gays, and bisexuals compared to other groups that have been held to be suspect or quasi-suspect, see Mark Strasser, "Unconstitutional? Don't Ask; If It Is, Don't Tell: On Deference, Rationality, and the Constitution," 66 *U. Colo. L. Rev.* 375, 407–11 (1995).

70. See Strasser, *Legally Wed*, Chap. 4.

71. Cf. *Evans v. Romer*, 882 P.2d 1335, 1347 (Colo. 1994) (en banc) (defendants suggest that prohibiting discrimination against lesbians and gays will undermine marriage).

72. See id.

73. See *Equality Foundation of Greater Cincinnati, Inc. v. City of Cincinnati*, 860 F. Supp. 417, 442 (S.D. Ohio 1994) (heterosexual males are far more responsible than gays for the breakdown of the family unit), rev'd, 54 F.3d 261 (6th Cir. 1995), cert. granted, judgment vacated by 116 S. Ct. 2519 (1996), rev'd, judgment vacated by 128 F.3d 289 (6th Cir. 1997).

74. See *Baehr v. Miike*, 1996 WL 694235 (Hawai'i Cir. Ct. 1996) (rejecting state's claim that lesbians and gays are not sufficiently good parents).

75. *United States Dept. of Agriculture v. Moreno*, 413 U.S. 528, 533 (1973).

76. *Romer*, 517 U.S. at 635.

77. *Citizens for Responsible Behavior v. Superior Court*, 2 Cal. Rptr.2d 648, 654 (Ct. App. 1991).

78. Id. See also *Evans v. Romer*, 854 P.2d 1270, 1275 (Colo. 1993) (en banc) ("the Equal Protection Clause of the United States Constitution applies to all citizens, and not simply those who are members of traditionally 'suspect' classes such as racial or ethnic minorities") (citing *Yick Wo*, 118 U.S. 356).

79. *Citizens for Responsible Behavior*, 2 Cal. Rptr.2d at 654.

80. *United States Dept. of Agriculture*, 413 U.S. at 534.

81. *Palmore v. Sidoti*, 466 U.S. 429, 433 (1984).

82. Id.

83. Several courts have made this suggestion. See *Adams v. Howerton*, 486 F. Supp. 1119, 1124 (C.D. Cal. 1980) (concept of marriage requires individuals of different sexes); *Baker v. Nelson*, 191 N.W.2d 185, 185–86 n.1 (Minn. 1971) (marriage can only be between individuals of different sexes); *Singer v. Hara*, 522 P.2d 1187, 1191–92 (Wash. Ct. App. 1974) (same); *Jones v. Hallahan*, 501 S.W.2d 588, 590 (Ky. 1973) (same).

84. See Mark Strasser, "Family, Definitions, and the Constitution: On the Antimiscegenation Analogy," 25 *Suffolk U. L. Rev.* 981, 982–89 (1991) (discussing definitional preclusion argument). See also Strasser, *Legally Wed*, Chap. 1.

85. See *Baehr*, 852 P.2d at 588 (Heen J., dissenting).

86. Donald L. Beschle, "Defining the Scope of the Constitutional Right to Marry: More than Tradition, Less than Unlimited Autonomy," 70 *Notre Dame L. Rev.* 39, 64 (1994) (suggesting that the Court's recognizing the right to marry an interracial partner should be understood as the Court's recognizing a "right to be free of obstacles to entering a traditional marriage").

87. But see William N. Eskridge, Jr., *The Case for Same-Sex Marriage: From*

Sexual Liberty to Civilized Commitment, Chap. 2 (New York: Free Press, 1996) (discussing the history of same-sex marriages).

88. For example, the *Loving* Court discussed the trial court's view that interracial marriages violated God's plan. See *Loving*, 388 U.S. at 3. Some courts believed that the state's power to prevent interracial marriage was of great importance. See *State v. Gibson*, 36 Ind. 389, 403 (1871) ("The right, in the states, to regulate and control, to guard, protect, and preserve this God-given, civilizing, and Christianizing institution is of inestimable importance, and cannot be surrendered, nor can the states suffer or permit any interference therewith").

89. The case was decided in 1967.

90. In *Naim v. Naim*, the Court refused to strike down Virginia's antimiscegenation law, instead remanding for a fuller record. See 350 U.S. 891 (1955). In *Naim v. Naim*, 350 U.S. 985 (1956), the Court refused to rehear the case because it was allegedly "devoid of a properly presented federal question." See id. at 985. The Court even refused to strike down antimiscegenation laws in 1964. See *McLaughlin*, 379 U.S. at 195 (refusing to reach "the question of the validity of the State's prohibition against interracial marriage . . . For even if we posit the constitutionality of the ban against the marriage of a Negro and a white, it does not follow that the cohabitation law is not to be subjected to independent examination under the Fourteenth Amendment").

91. See *Zablocki v. Redhail*, 434 U.S. 374, 392 (1978) (Stewart, J., concurring in the judgment).

92. See *Planned Parenthood of Southeastern Pennsylvania v. Casey*, 505 U.S. 833, 980 n.1 (1992) (Scalia, J., concurring and dissenting).

93. U.S. Const. Amend XIV.

94. But see *Planned Parenthood*, 505 U.S. at 980 (Scalia, J., concurring and dissenting) (there is no fundamental right if "(1) the Constitution says absolutely nothing about it, and (2) the longstanding traditions of American society have permitted it to be legally proscribed").

95. See *Romer*, 517 U.S. at 644 (Scalia, J., dissenting) (suggesting that animus towards gays and lesbians is acceptable).

96. See Michael J. Gerhardt, "The Pressure of Precedent: A Critique of the Conservative Approaches to Stare Decisis in Abortion Cases," 10 *Const. Comment.* 67, 79–80 (1993) (suggesting that Justice Scalia's position is neither credible nor consistent).

97. For reasons to believe that the Framers had not intended this, see generally Alfred Avins, "Anti-Miscegenation Laws and the Fourteenth Amendment: The Original Intent," 52 *Va. L. Rev.* 1224 (1966).

98. See *Harper v. Virginia State Bd. of Elections*, 383 U.S. 663, 669 (1966).

99. See Strasser, "Domestic Relations Jurisprudence," 64 *Fordham L. Rev.* at 928 (*Baehr v. Lewin* establishes the inapplicability of the definitional preclusion argument to this issue).

100. *Shahar v. Bowers*, 114 F.3d 1097, 1126 (11th Cir. 1997) (Birch, Circuit J., dissenting) ("The import of *Romer* . . . is to elucidate what the Supreme Court considers not to be a rational basis for discrimination against homosexuals").

101. *Reed*, 404 U.S. at 75–76.

3

The Referenda

In November, 1998, the Hawaii and Alaska electorates voted to amend their state constitutions to prevent the legal recognition of same-sex marriages. Both *Baehr* and *Brause* might now seem irrelevant, since they were based on interpretations of the former state constitutions. Yet, the reasoning offered in these cases remains quite relevant, even if the decisions have been legislatively overruled. Contrary expectations notwithstanding,[1] the passage of the referenda will only bring about more litigation rather than provide an end to it.

Further, it is not at all clear that the referenda themselves will survive constitutional scrutiny. Recently, an attempt in Colorado to amend that state's constitution to disadvantage lesbians, bisexuals, and gays was struck down,[2] and these attempts to amend the Hawaii and Alaska Constitutions may suffer the same fate. Indeed, there are a number of reasons to believe that the amendments in Hawaii and Alaska more clearly violate federal constitutional guarantees than did the amendment at issue in Colorado.

THE CONSTITUTIONALITY OF REFERENDA

The United States Supreme Court has had numerous opportunities to consider the constitutionality of referenda that were at least arguably aimed at minorities. The Court has upheld amendments that were facially neutral, even if disproportionately impacting a minority, as long as the Court was confident that the amendment was not intended to disadvantage that minority. The Court's willingness to uphold such referenda should be of little comfort to those supporting the amendments in Hawaii and Alaska, however, since they were not facially neutral and were clearly aimed at disadvantaging a particular minority.

Whenever the constitutionality of a statute or state constitutional amendment is at issue, that statute or amendment must be authoritatively construed. The Hawaii Supreme Court has already construed the same-sex marriage ban as discriminating on the basis of sex, both facially and as applied, and in Alaska a trial court has offered reasons that the Alaska Supreme Court should do the same with respect to that state's ban. As suggested in the last chapter, the amendments in Hawaii and Alaska did not somehow make the statutory classification at issue non-sex-based, but instead made these sex-based classifications immune from state constitutional scrutiny. Both of the amendments should be struck down because they violate federal constitutional guarantees.

MINORITIES AND THE STATE AMENDMENT PROCESS

An analysis of the amendments in Hawaii and Alaska requires an examination of various other decisions involving proposed amendments to charters or state constitutions that, at least arguably, were directed at disfavored minorities. In several decisions, the United States Supreme Court invalidated popularly mandated amendments that were not facially neutral or that intentionally picked out disfavored groups for adverse treatment.

In various states and localities, voters have attempted to disadvantage minorities by making it more difficult for those groups to get housing, to pass antidiscrimination ordinances, or even to have their votes count as much as others' votes counted. Sometimes, the proposed amendments would seek to accomplish more than one goal—for example, both to dilute votes and to make it more difficult to acquire protection from invidious discrimination. For example, the Colorado amendment would have made it more difficult to use the political process to pass antidiscrimination laws.

The proposed amendment to the Colorado Constitution (Amendment 2) would have withdrawn "from homosexuals, but no others, specific legal protection from the injuries caused by discrimination," and would have forbidden "reinstatement of these laws and policies."[3] The Amendment read:

> Neither the State of Colorado, through any of its branches or departments, nor any of its agencies, political subdivisions, municipalities or school districts, shall enact, adopt or enforce any statute, regulation, ordinance or policy whereby homosexual, lesbian or bisexual orientation, conduct, practices or relationships shall constitute or otherwise be the basis of or entitle any person or class of persons to have or claim any minority status, quota preferences, protected status, or claim of discrimination.[4]

Amendment 2 might have been analyzed in terms of its effect on voting (voters' attempts to pass certain kinds of legislation would have been thwarted by the amendment) or in terms of its effect on the ability of a particular group to compete on an equal playing field with others (the amendment would have precluded antidiscrimination protection). The former tack has proven to be quite powerful in a whole series of cases and was adopted by the Supreme Court of Colorado when it originally heard the case.[5]

Every citizen has a fundamental right to vote and the Court will vigilantly protect that right.[6] That right cannot be modifed on the basis of such irrelevant factors as race, sex, economic status, or place of residence within the State.[7] That some of these factors receive heightened scrutiny (race, sex) while others do not (economic status, place of residency)[8] *perhaps* suggests that the consideration motivating the Court to employ close scrutiny in these kinds of cases is the nature of the right at issue (the right to vote) and not the nature of the group whose rights are being diluted. After all, the right to vote is a "fundamental matter" in a democracy.[9] Especially when one considers that voting helps to preserve other basic civil and political rights, any attempts to limit or circumvent the citizen's right to vote must be "carefully and meticulously scrutinized."[10] Thus, one explanation of the holdings in these cases is that the right to vote is so important that any attempts to infringe upon that right must be closely examined.

Voting rights might be impaired in a variety of ways. For example, a state might provide that the votes of citizens in one part of the state should be given two, five, or ten times the weight of votes of citizens in another part of the state,[11] thereby effectively diluting the votes of those in the latter part of the state.[12] Yet, it is not necessary for a state to diminish a vote's effectiveness by 50 percent or more for the Court to find a constitutional violation. The Court has pointed out that a more subtle system that nonetheless places special burdens on the ability of minority groups to achieve beneficial legislation may also be constitutionally infirm.[13]

Not every voting system will be subjected to close and careful examination, however. For example, the state of West Virginia had a law that on bond referenda three-fifths of the voters had to give their approval before the issuance of the bonds would be authorized.[14] The West Virginia Supreme Court concluded that such a requirement could not pass constitutional muster because the votes of those favoring the issuance of the bonds had a proportionately smaller impact on the outcome of the election than did the votes of those opposing issuance of the bonds.[15] The United States Supreme Court reversed because the Court could discern no independently identifiable group that was being harmed by the requirement [16] Election provisions do not violate the Equal Protection Clause as long as they do not discriminate against, or authorize discrimination against, any identifiable class.[17] Thus, while the Court will be vigilant to protect the voting rights of identifiable groups and, for example, might strike down a poll tax precisely because it was aimed at those with little wealth,[18] the Court will tend to uphold the suggested classification if the voting system is rationally based and does not pick out a particular group for adverse treatment.

TARGETING MINORITIES

A central concern in the West Virginia case was whether the voting rules under examination targeted an identifiable class. When the United States Supreme Court considered the Colorado amendment, the Court was struck by the amendment's breadth, which seemed inexplicable by anything but animus toward the class that it affected.[19] The Court pointed out that states should rarely if ever single out a particular class of citizens for disfavored legal status or general hardships.[20]

To assure that classifications are not drawn for the purpose of disadvantaging a particular group, the Court requires that the classification bear a rational relationship to an *independent* and legitimate legislative end.[21] When there is such an end, the statute at issue may be constitutional, even if an unpopular group is adversely affected by that statute. It is a truism that whenever classifications are made, some but not other groups will be subject to some restrictions or receive certain advantages,[22] and the Constitution does not require that statutes affect every individual equally, since the Fourteenth Amendment guarantees equal laws, not equal results.[23]

Notwithstanding the Court's acceptance of the principle that equal results are not guaranteed, however, the Court realizes that some statutorily imposed inequalities are constitutionally impermissible. For example, a statute which facially discriminates against racial minorities can be upheld only upon an extraordinary justification.[24] Indeed, even if the statute is ostensibly neutral,[25] it will be held unconstitutional if it is an obvious pretext for racial discrimination.[26]

When a facially neutral statute is attacked on equal protection grounds, the Court must discern intent.[27] If such a statute is invidiously motivated, it will be struck down as violating the protections of the Fourteenth Amendment. However, it may be quite difficult to discern the intent of or motivation behind a particular statute.[28] An individual advocating the adoption of a particular measure for invidious reasons will be unlikely to admit his purpose. Rather, he will articulate neutral-sounding reasons to support his position and will likely not be so imprudent as to admit his animosity towards the group to be adversely affected.[29] Further, individuals may have a variety of intentions and motivations when supporting a proposition that they know will adversely affect a group whom they hate. As Justice Thurgood Marshall suggested, "That a legislature seeks to advantage one group does not, as a matter of logic or of common sense, exclude the possibility that it also intends to disadvantage another. Individuals in general and lawmakers in particular frequently act for a variety of reasons."[30] Thus, merely because an individual has a noninvidious reason to support a particular proposal does not establish the absence of a stronger, invidious reason to support that same proposal.

When there are numerous reasons articulated to support a particular proposal, it will be difficult to discern which are the "real" reasons. One way to distinguish between real and specious reasons is to see whether the asserted reasons prompt the state to adopt practices that adversely affect groups that do not have a history of having been subjected to discriminatory practices. If it turns out that allegedly compelling reasons justifying policies adversely affecting disfavored groups are noncompelling or, perhaps, nonexistent when the interests of other groups are at issue, then there may be reason to doubt that the asserted reasons are reasons at all.

Once the "real" reasons are discerned, the Court will still have to decide whether the predominant motivating factor is invidious. The Supreme Court has suggested that where a legislature passes a law because of, rather than in spite of, its adverse effects upon an identifiable group, the Court will find that a discriminatory purpose exists.[31]

When the state of Colorado tried to offer noninvidious justifications for Amendment 2, it cited respect for other citizens' freedom of association and the state's interest in conserving resources to fight discrimination against other groups.[32] However, the United States Supreme Court found it impossible to credit those as the real reasons.[33] Indeed, the Court could not believe that the amendment had any identifiable legitimate purpose or discrete objective,[34] concluding that because Amendment 2 was designed to make bisexuals, gays, and lesbians unequal to everyone else,[35] the amendment violated the Equal Protection Clause and was unconstitutional.[36]

When disfavored groups are disadvantaged by statutes, whether facially or as applied, those statutes will be examined to make sure that they are employing rational means to achieve legitimate ends. The Court will attempt to uncover illicit motivation and will attempt to discern which classifications constitute invidious discrimination, claims of innocuous or benign classification notwithstanding.

DETERMINING THE RELEVANT BASELINE

Even bracketing the issue of whether a particular classification will in fact be to the advantage or detriment of a particular class, the United States Supreme Court has expressed another concern when seeking to determine the constitutionality of a voter-initiated modification, namely, determining the baseline from which to judge whether the change at issue is in fact disadvantageous. Would the recission of a statute benefiting a group involve disadvantaging that group or simply putting it back in the position in which it would have been found before the statute had been passed? As a public policy matter, it would be counterproductive to say that whenever a recission measure puts a traditionally disfavored group in a worse position than it would have been without that measure, that group has been disadvantaged in a constitutionally significant way.[37] Were the Court to adopt such an approach, cities and states might be encouraged *not* to provide any protections above those required by federal law for fear that such protections once enacted would have to become part of the permanent legal landscape.[38] The United States Supreme Court has rejected the contention that once a state chooses to do more than the Fourteenth Amendment requires, it may never go back to merely doing what is required.[39]

In Colorado, one of the questions at hand was whether the amendment at issue merely repealed or rescinded the antidiscrimination laws that had already been adopted in Boulder, Denver, and Aspen.[40] The United States Supreme Court rejected the claim that the amendment was a mere recission, pointing out that Amendment 2 not only rescinded existing provisions, but prohibited all legislative, executive, or judicial action at the local or state level which was designed to protect gays and lesbians.[41] This analysis may have import for the constitutionality of the Hawaii and Alaska amendments, since the citizens of those states were not "simply" trying to rescind a statute or local ordinance barring discrimination. Rather, those constitutions were amended to limit their protections.

The amendments in Hawaii and Alaska suffer from one of the defects found in the Colorado amendment, although the manifestations are somewhat different. In all of these cases, the *kind* of legislation subject to popular vote has been altered, and that alteration is intended to disadvantage a disfavored group. In Colorado, the amendment would have deprived voters of the right to enact protective legislation. In Hawaii, the amendment gives voters the right to determine through their legislators whether particular individuals will be allowed to marry, whereas before that amendment's passage the right of same-sex couples to marry was (probably) protected by the state constitution and thus not subject to popular referendum. In Alaska, the amendment prohibits the legislature from passing legislation recognizing same-sex marriages,[42] whereas before that amendment's passage the right to marry a same-sex partner was arguably protected by the state constitution and certainly could have been granted by the legislature.

In addition, as a separate matter, some rights simply should not be subject to popular referendum. As a federal district court in Ohio pointed out, "one of the most important roles of the federal courts [is] to ensure that the constitutional rights of the few or the powerless are not infringed."[43] In both Alaska and Hawaii, the referenda are obvious attempts to infringe upon the rights of a minority.

PREVIOUS AMENDMENT ATTEMPTS

Historically, there have been several attempts to modify state constitutions, city charters, etc., in ways that would have adversely impacted minorities. The Court has developed a jurisprudence that explains why some but not all of these attempts were constitutionally infirm and which suggests that the amendments in Hawaii and Alaska do not pass constitutional muster.

The voters in the city of Akron approved an amendment to the city charter which provided that any "ordinance enacted by the Council of The City of Akron which regulates the use, sale, advertisement, transfer, listing assignment, lease, sublease or financing of real property of any kind or of an interest therein on the basis of race, color, religion, national origin or ancestry must first be approved by a majority of the electors voting on the question at a regular or general election before said ordinance shall be effective."[44] The United States Supreme Court held the amendment unconstitutional, holding that the state could no more disadvantage any particular group by making it more difficult to enact legislation in its behalf than it could dilute someone's vote.[45] Further, the Court was not persuaded that this amendment had to be upheld because it was adopted in a referendum, suggesting that the fact that this change came about through a popular referendum did not immunize it,[46] since the sovereignty of the people is itself subject to constitutional limitations.[47]

The Akron amendment is helpfully contrasted with a California amendment to the state constitution providing that "no low-rent housing project should be developed, constructed, or acquired in any manner by a state public body until the project was approved by a majority of those voting at a community election."[48] The United States Supreme Court not only described this amendment as facially neutral but also held that it was not aimed at a racial minority,[49] thereby distinguishing it from the Akron provision, which rested on race-based distinctions.[50]

The Akron ordinance distinguished between two groups: (1) those who sought protection against racial, religious, or ancestral discrimination in the sale and rental of property, and (2) those who sought regulations regarding property transactions for other reasons.[51] In the Akron case, the Court understood that the ordinance's aim was to disadvantage minorities seeking protection,[52] whereas in the California case the Court offered no suggestion that racial minorities in particular had an extra burden as a result of the amendment.[53]

Certainly, it might be suggested that the referendum at issue in California was not aimed at a particular racial class but instead was aimed at a particular economic class, singling them out for special disadvantageous treatment,[54] since the referendum concerned the conditions under which low-rent housing projects might be constructed.[55] However, the Court rejected this analysis, suggesting that persons advocating low-income housing had not been singled out for mandatory referenda,[56] and pointing out that referenda were required in a variety of contexts having nothing to do with the relative wealth of the groups or individuals that might be affected.[57]

The United States Supreme Court has also had to consider other kinds of amendments (e.g., those involving measures limiting or prohibiting busing). For example, a Washington statewide initiative provided that no school board could require any student to attend a school that was not geographically very close to the student's place of residence.[58] However, there were several broad exceptions to this requirement.[59] Basically, this initiative was designed to stop the use of mandatory busing for racial integration purposes,[60] although the initiative did not mention race or integration anywhere.[61] The Court held that the initiative was effectively drawn for racial purposes,[62] noting the initiative's proponents' claim that 99 percent of the school districts in the state—those lacking mandatory integration progams—would not be affected by the initiative.[63] Because the initiative was designed to promote invidious racial purposes, the Court held that it violated constitutional guarantees.

At the same time that the Court was considering the Washington busing initiative, it was considering a proposed amendment to the California constitution also involving busing.[64] The California amendment provided that state courts could not order mandatory pupil assignment or transportation unless a federal court would do so to remedy a Fourteenth Amendment Equal Protection violation.[65] The Supreme Court denied that the proposition embodied a racial classification, since it neither said nor implied that persons were to be treated differently on account of their race.[66] (Had the Proposition employed a racial classification, it would have been unconstitutional unless necessary to further a compelling state interest.[67])

The Court's failing to find a facial racial classification in the California amendment did not end the matter. As the Court indicated when discussing the Washington initiative, a facially neutral statute will not pass constitutional muster if it has a discriminatory purpose.[68] In the California case, the Court rejected that the voters of the state had so voted because of a discriminatory purpose[69] and, further, refused to characterize the proposition as anything more than a mere repeal of existing legislation.[70] In the Washington case, the Court had found a discriminatory purpose[71] and had found that the initiative had been more than a mere repeal.[72]

The point here is not to question the particular findings of fact in each of the cases—for example, whether it was true that no invidious purpose had been involved in the adoption of the California proposition—but to see what conclusions of law might be inferred from the two cases. The Court's position seems to be that an initiative or proposition that (1) is neutral on its face,[73] (2) is a mere repeal or recission,[74] and (3) is not invidiously motivated[75] passes constitutional muster as long as no federal guarantees are violated.[76]

When the constitutionality of a facially neutral statute is at issue, the measure may be at risk unless proponents convince the Court that no particular group has been selected for adverse treatment. The Court suggested that one of the fatal weaknesses of the Washington amendment was that race-related busing was subjected to requirements to which other kinds of busing would not be subjected.[77]

In yet another California case, the Court considered a ballot initiative that would have given absolute discretion to any private person to refuse to sell, lease, or rent property to any other person.[78] This amendment would have protected the right of a would-be seller/lessor to refuse to contract with someone of the "wrong" race or religion. The United States Supreme Court upheld the California Supreme Court's invalidation of the amendment, agreeing with the state court's determination that the amendment at issue would have a wider impact than a mere repeal of existing statutes.[79] Because the California court had concluded that the state could be prohibited not only from commanding but also from even encouraging discrimination[80] and because the court had concluded that this amendment would encourage discrimination, the court held the amendment unconstitutional.

Just as the California Supreme Court and the United States Supreme Court had worried that the amendment "protecting" would-be sellors/lessors would encourage discrimination, the amendment in Hawaii might do the same. To include within the state constitution an explicit provision that the legislature would be allowed to impose a limitation on same-sex couples that is not imposed on other couples might induce individuals to believe that other kinds of discrimination against same-sex couples would also be permissible. If the state constitution allows the legislature to deprive individuals of something as fundamental as the right to marry,[81] then it might be argued that the legislature is obviously empowered to restrict other non-fundamental rights.[82] Further, arguably, this will encourage private individuals to engage in discriminatory activities, just as the California Supreme Court found would occur were the ballot issue upheld. So, too, by making a same-sex marriage ban part of the Alaska Constitution, the populace has been invited to discriminate against a class of individuals allegedly so different from everyone else that they must be constitutionally barred from marrying the only individuals whom they would want to marry.

A California appellate court examined the constitutionality of a proposed ordinance that would have repealed existing ordinances offering protection on the basis of sexual orientation and HIV status.[83] The proposed ordinance further required that any future ordinances prohibiting such discrimination would have to be submitted to the voters for approval.[84] The court explained that "under the proposed ordinance, persons seeking protective legislation against discrimination based on sexual orientation or AIDS must attempt to persuade a majority of the voters that such an ordinance is desirable,"[85] and noted that this arrangement was strikingly similar to the Akron ordinance that the United States Supreme Court had found unconstitutional.[86]

The proposed local ordinance was a response to the city council's having already passed antidiscrimination resolutions.[87] The court refused to characterize the proposed ordinance as a mere repeal, instead suggesting that the ordinance would implicitly affirm the right of all persons to discriminate against the affected classes.[88] Indeed, the court held that the ordinance was plainly designed to encourage discrimination.[89] Because the ordinance was not a mere repeal but would in addition encourage discrimination, the appellate court held it unconstitutional.

Not only has the United States Supreme Court suggested that proposed ordinances or propositions that are intended to promote discrimination are unconstitutional, but the Court has also indicated its misgivings about the constitutionality of propositions that will prevent various state actors from rectifying discrimination against minorities. The Court worried that when California citizens wanted to allow sellers absolute discretion with respect to refusing to sell, let, or rent to anyone, the state was including the right to discriminate within the State constitution[90] and, further, was making the right to discriminate immune from regulation.[91] When examining the Colorado amendment, the United States Supreme Court worried that all state legislative, executive, or judicial action designed to protect gays and lesbians would now be prohibited.[92] Presumably, the Court will also worry that all state legislative, executive, or judicial action designed to gain same-sex marriage rights for same-sex couples have been prohibited in Alaska.

The amendment to the Hawaii Constitution authorizes the legislature to discriminate against an identifiable group. This itself is presumably enough to establish its constitutional impermissibility, although the amendment seems to have even more serious flaws, depending upon how it is construed.

JUDICIAL CONSTRUCTION

To determine the kinds of effects that a particular amendment will have, one must know how it will be construed by the courts. As suggested above, it may matter, for example, whether an amendment will be construed to permit or encourage discrimination rather than merely to repeal a statute. An additional element for consideration is that it will matter which court is construing the amendment. Because the issues under discussion here involve state constitutional amendments, the Hawaii and Alaska Supreme Courts' constructions will be considered definitive or, at the very least, will be given great deference.

DEFERENCE TO STATE COURTS

The United States Supreme Court has consistently held that only state courts may authoritatively construe state statutes.[93] Thus, when the Court must decide whether a particular state statute violates federal constitutional guarantees, the Court will defer to the state supreme court's construction of that statute rather than impose its own interpretation.

Suppose that there are several possible interpretations of a state amendment or statute. Even if the United States Supreme Court would have offered a different interpretation than was offered by the state supreme court, it is not the United States Supreme Court's function to construe a state statute contrary to the construction given it by the state's highest court.[94] This is true even if, as construed, the statute or amendment violates Fourteenth Amendment guarantees and thus must be held unconstitutional.[95]

That the United States Supreme Court should defer to state supreme court constructions of their own state statutes was established long ago. By the middle of the nineteenth century, the Court had made clear that it would adopt and follow the decisions of the state high courts in the construction of their own laws[96] and constitutional provisions.[97] Further, the statutory construction offered by the state supreme court is to be viewed as if that meaning had been specifically expressed within the statute itself[98] and is to be considered just as binding as the text itself.[99] The only exception to this rule concerning the deference owed by the United States Supreme Court to the highest state court's statutory construction is when no settled construction has been offered and the proper interpretation of the statute or amendment is still an open question.[100]

The determining factor for when deference is owed is *not* whether the United States Supreme Court agrees with the correctness of the state high court's interpretation.[101] For example, suppose that the United States Supreme Court would have offered an interpretation of a particular state statute that would have made it constitutional but the state supreme court offered an interpretation of that statute which entailed that the legislature had exceeded its power. As a general rule, if a statute might be interpreted in two different ways and one of the ways would make that statute constitutional while the other would not, courts will adopt the former because it is presumed that the legislature would not have passed an unconstitutional statute.[102] Here, however, the general rule would be trumped by the requirement that the United States Supreme Court defer, and the state supreme court's interpretation would be accepted.

The point here is not that citizens have no recourse once their supreme court offers an interpretation of the state constitution that they do not like. On the contrary, the citizens can change their constitution,[103] as long as the appropriate procedures are followed and federal guarantees are not violated.

FEDERAL PROTECTIONS

By adopting this deferential attitude toward the highest state court with respect to the construction of the state statutes and constitution, the Court is not thereby ceding all authority. On the contrary, the Court is deferring to the state supreme courts on some matters and reserving for itself the right to decide others. For example, although the Court is bound by the state court's construction and application of the law, the Court will decide for itself whether the statute so construed or applied violates federally protected rights.[104] The Court is thus striking a balance, deferring to the state courts in their area of expertise but reserving the right to make its own decisions about the federal Constitution's protections.[105]

The Court's reserving this power cuts both ways. The Supreme Court will not defer to a state supreme court's judgment that a statute is permitted or, for that matter, prohibited by the United States Constitution. If a state supreme court strikes a state statute on federal constitutional grounds, the United States Supreme Court can make its own judgment about whether that statute is constitutional, even if, for example, the state high court might instead have struck down the statute on state constitutional grounds.[106]

Insofar as the amendment to the Hawaii Constitution is at issue, the Hawaii Supreme Court will not even be considering whether it is in accord with the state constitution, since that is the document that has been amended. Rather, the Hawaii Supreme Court will offer its construction of the purpose, scope, and operative effect of a provision of the state constitution,[107] and then judge the constitutionality of that amendment in light of federal constitutional guarantees. So, too, the Alaska Supreme Court will have to decide whether the state constitution now incorporates a sex-based provision, and then whether that provision passes federal constitutional muster.

One of the issues posed by the Colorado initiative was how to construct Amendment 2. The state of Colorado had characterized it as simply denying a particular group special rights.[108] The Court found this position implausible, especially given the authoritative construction offered by Colorado's Supreme Court,[109] and then upheld the Colorado Supreme Court's determination that the Amendment violated the United States Constitution. Assuming that the amendments to the Hawaii and Alaska Constitutions are challenged in the state courts, the Hawaii and Alaska Supreme Courts will construe those amendments, and then make judgments about whether they pass federal constitutional muster. If those decisions are appealed, the United States Supreme Court should defer to the state supreme courts' interpretations of the meaning and application of the amendments but make its own determination concerning whether those amendments violate the United States Constitution.

ONE POSSIBLE SCENARIO

The amendments to the Hawaii and Alaska Constitutions are clearly designed to deprive a discrete, disfavored group of a right that was (probably) guaranteed under the former state constitution. Further, the amendments involve facial gender classifications. Not only has there been no showing that such classifications are closely tailored to promote important state interests, the interests themselves have thus far not been articulated in a way that can be credited.[110]

The United States Supreme Court has already held that states are not allowed to create classifications just to establish the inequality of gays and lesbians.[111] Yet, that is exactly what the Hawaii and Alaska amendments do. For example, Hawaii has decided to afford many of the financial benefits of marriage to same-sex couples in the hope that the emotional, religious, and symbolic aspects of marriage do not also need to be extended.[112] Many of the purportedly compelling interests justifying the same-sex marriage bans are clearly pretextual.[113] The amendments are simply a way to deprive a particular group of a very important right that most take for granted and that this group would probably enjoy but for the amendments.

A plurality of the Hawaii Supreme Court has already held that the same-sex marriage ban discriminates on the basis of gender, both facially and as applied. Presumably, it will so hold again should the issue be presented. If the United States Supreme Court must decide the constitutionality of Hawaii's same-sex marriage ban, it should defer to the Hawaii Supreme Court's construction of the statute or amendment but decide for itself whether the challenged classification passes intermediate scrutiny.

It would strain credulity were the Court to employ heightened scrutiny and uphold such a classification. The amendments in Hawaii and Alaska should not be upheld using a rational basis test, much less a higher level of scrutiny,[114] since they involve exactly the kind of stigmatization and unequal treatment that the Equal Protection Clause is designed to prevent. If the Hawaii and Alaska amendments do not provide examples of amending a state constitution to impose a badge of inequality and second-class citizenship on a discrete group, then it is not clear what would qualify.

The analysis offered here will be relevant whenever the citizens of any state try to amend their constitutions to deprive gays and lesbians of the right to marry when that right would have been guaranteed by the state constitution absent that amendment. Thus, should the constitution in a different state protect the right to marry a same-sex partner, any attempt to amend the state constitution to abridge that right would be constitutionally suspect for the reasons outlined here.

Suppose that a different state supreme court were to hold that same-sex marriages are protected by the state constitution. Suppose further that some same-sex couples living there were to marry and then a referendum were to pass that modified the state constitution to prohibit those marriages. Bracketing the constitutionality of the amendment, a separate issue would involve the validity of those same-sex marriages that had already been celebrated. The next chapter discusses whether a legislature could retroactively nullify those same-sex marriages that had already been celebrated before the modification to the state constitution had been approved.

NOTES

1. See Cal Thomas, "Marriage from God, Not Courts," in Robert M. Baird & Stuart E. Rosenbaum eds., *Same-Sex Marriage: The Moral and Legal Debate*, 42, 42 (New York: Prometheus Books, 1997) (the "main event" involves the constitutional amendment).

2. See *Romer v. Evans*, 517 U.S. 620 (1996).

3. Id. at 627.

4. Id. at 624.

5. See *Evans v. Romer*, 854 P.2d 1270, 1276 (Colo. 1993) (en banc) ("the Equal Protection Clause guarantees the fundamental right to participate equally in the political process and . . . any attempt to infringe on an independently identifiable group's ability to exercise that right is subject to strict scrutiny") (citing *Dunn v. Blumstein*, 405 U.S. 330, 336 [1972]).

6. *Harper v. Virginia State Bd. of Elections*, 383 U.S. 663, 670 (1966) ("where fundamental rights and liberties [like the right to vote] are asserted under the Equal Protection Clause, classification which might invade or restrain them must be closely scrutinized and carefully confined").

7. *Reynolds v. Sims*, 377 U.S. 533, 560–61 (1964).

8. Race is suspect (see *Loving v. Virginia*, 388 U.S. 1 [1967]), gender is quasi-suspect (see *Craig v. Boren*, 429 U.S. 190 [1976], employing intermediate scrutiny), while economic status and location within the state are non-suspect. See *San Antonio School Dist. v. Rodriguez*, 411 U.S. 1 (1973) (poverty not suspect). See also *Gray v. Sanders*, 372 U.S. 368, 380 (1963) (suggesting that neither occupation nor homesite is a legitimate basis for distinguishing between qualified voters, but also not suggesting that special scrutiny is required or even appropriate for that determination).

9. *Reynolds*, 377 U.S. at 561–62.

10. Id.

11. Id. at 562.

12. Id. at 562–63.

13. *Washington v. Seattle School District No. 1*, 458 U.S. 457, 467 (1982).

14. *Gordon v. Lance*, 403 U.S. 1, 8 (1971).

15. Id. at 4.

16. Id. at 5.

17. Id. at 7.

18. *Harper*, 383 U.S. at 666 ("a State violates the Equal Protection Clause of the Fourteenth Amendment whenever it makes the affluence of the voter or payment of any fee an electoral standard").

19. *Romer*, 517 U.S. at 632.

20. Id. at 633.

21. Id.

22. *Kotch v. Bd. of River Port Pilot Com'rs*, 330 U.S. 552, 556 (1947).

23. *Personnel Administrator of Massachusetts v. Feeney*, 442 U.S. 256, 273 (1979).

24. Id. at 272 (citing *Brown v. Board of Education*, 347 U.S. 483 [1954]; *McLaughlin v. Florida*, 379 U.S. 184 [1964]).

25. Id.

26. Id.

27. *Washington*, 458 U.S. at 484–85 ("when facially neutral legislation is subjected to equal protection attack, an inquiry into intent is necessary to determine whether the legislation in some sense was designed to accord disparate treatment . . .").

28. For a discussion of the difference between intention and motivation, see Mark Strasser, "The Invidiousness of Invidiousness: On the Supreme Court's Affirmative Action Jurisprudence," 21 *Hastings Const. L.Q.* 323, 341–43 (1994).

29. But see *Romer*, 517 U.S. at 636 (Scalia, J., dissenting) (chastising the Court for placing "the prestige of this institution behind the proposition that opposition to homosexuality is as reprehensible as racial or religious bias"). Justice Scalia implies that the imposition of disadvantages was appropriate because what was involved was a "Kulturkampf" rather than "a fit of spite." See id. Justice Scalia seems not to appreciate that individuals who promote policies involving racial or religious bias may also view what they are doing as a culture war rather than a fit of spite. Were that all that was needed to make policies constitutionally permissible, much of the Fourteenth Amendment equal protection jurisprudence would be rendered worthless.

30. *Personnel Administrator*, 442 U.S. at 282 (Marshall, J., dissenting).

31. Id. at 279.

32. *Romer*, 517 U.S. at 635. See also Richard F. Duncan, "Wigstock and the Kulturkampf: Supreme Court Storytelling, the Culture War, and *Romer v. Evans*," 72 *Notre Dame L. Rev.* 345, 350 (1997) (offering purportedly rational reasons justifying the discrimination). Professor Duncan seems not to appreciate that these same reasons might be offered to legitimate discrimination against a variety of racial and religious groups.

33. *Romer*, 517 U.S. at 635.

34. Id.

35. Id. at 1629.

36. Id.

37. See *James v. Valtierra*, 402 U.S. 137, 142 (1971) ("But of course a lawmaking procedure that 'disadvantages' a particular group does not always deny equal protection").

38. See *Crawford v. Board of Education*, 458 U.S. 527, 539 (1982).

39. Id. at 535.

40. Each of these cities had "enacted ordinances which banned discrimination in many transactions and activities, including housing, employment, education, public accommodations, and health and welfare services." See *Romer*, 517 U.S. at 623–24.

41. Id. at 1623. See also *Washington*, 458 U.S. at 483 ("Initiative 350, however, works something more than the 'mere repeal' of a desegregation law by the political entity that created it. It burdens all future attempts to integrate Washington schools in districts throughout the State, by lodging decisionmaking authority over the question at a new and remote level of government").

42. The Alaska Legislature had not manifested any inclination to pass such legislation. See Alaska Stat. § 25.05.013 (Michie 1998) (prohibiting same-sex marriages and treating same-sex marriages celebrated in other states as void).

43. *Equality Foundation of Greater Cincinnati, Inc. v. City of Cincinnati*, 838 F.Supp. 1235, 1236 (S.D. Ohio 1993).

44. *Hunter v. Erickson*, 393 U.S. 385, 387 (1969).

45. Id. at 393. See also *Evans*, 854 P.2d at 1285 ("In short, gay men, lesbians, and bisexuals are left out of the political process through the denial of having an 'effective voice in the governmental affairs which substantially affect their lives' ") (citing *Kramer v. Union Free School District*, 395 U.S. 621, 627 [1969]).

46. *Hunter*, 393 U.S. at 392 (citing *Lucas v. Forty-Fourth General Assembly of State of Colorado*, 377 U.S. 713, 736–37 [1964]).

47. Id.

48. *James*, 402 U.S. at 139.

49. See id. at 141.

50. See id.

51. Id.

52. Id. at 391.

53. See *James*, 402 U.S. at 141 ("The Article requires referendum approval for any low-rent public housing project, not only for projects which will be occupied by a racial minority").

54. See id. at 144 (Marshall, J., dissenting) ("The article explicitly singles out low-income persons to bear its burden").

55. See id. at 139.

56. See id. at 142.

57. See id.

58. *Washington*, 458 U.S. at 462.

59. Id.

60. Id.

61. See id. at 471.

62. Id.

63. Id.

64. Both *Washington v. Seattle School District*, 458 U.S. 457 (1982) and *Crawford v. Board of Education*, 458 U.S. 527 (1982) were argued on March 22, 1982 and announced on June 30, 1982.

65. *Crawford*, 458 U.S. at 529.

66. Id. at 537.

67. Id. at 536

68. Id. at 537–38 (citing *Washington v. Davis*, 426 U.S. 229, 238–48 [1976]).

69. See id. at 545.

70. See id. at 539–40.

71. See *Washington*, 458 U.S. at 471.

72. See id. at 483.

73. Compare *Crawford*, 458 U.S. at 537 (neutral) with *Washington*, 458 U.S. at 471 (neutral).

74. Compare *Crawford*, 458 U.S. at 539–40 (implying that proposition is mere repeal) with *Washington*, 458 U.S. at 483 (more than mere repeal).

75. Compare *Crawford*, 458 U.S. at 545 (not invidiously motivated) with *Washington*, 458 U.S. at 485–86 (invidiously motivated).

76. Compare *Crawford*, 458 U.S. at 535 (meets and indeed adopts Fourteenth Amendment guarantees) with *Washington*, 458 U.S. at 487 (Fourteenth Amendment violated).

77. *Washington*, 458 U.S. at 487.

78. *Reitman v. Mulkey*, 387 U.S. 369, 371 (1967).

79. Id. at 376.

80. Id. at 375. See also Teresa M. Bruce, Note, "Neither Liberty Nor Justice: Anti-Gay Initiatives, Political Participation, and the Rule of Law," 5 *Cornell J.L. & Pub. Pol'y* 431, 455–56 (1996) ("States cannot, without running afoul of the Constitution, authorize conduct that would violate the Fourteenth Amendment if engaged in directly by government").

81. *Zablocki v. Redhail*, 434 U.S. 374 (1978) (right to marry is fundamental).

82. But see *Romer*, 517 U.S. at 633 ("By requiring that the classification bear a rational relationship to an independent and legitimate legislative end, we ensure that classifications are not drawn for the purpose of disadvantaging the group burdened by the law").

83. *Citizens for Responsible Behavior v. Superior Court*, 2 Cal. Rptr.2d 648, 655 (Ct. App. 1991).

84. Id.

85. Id.

86. Id.

87. Id. at 657.

88. Id.

89. Id.

90. Id. But see *Reynolds*, 377 U.S. at 584 ("With respect to the operation of the Equal Protection Clause, it makes no difference whether a State's apportionment scheme is embodied in its constitution or in statutory provisions").

91. *Reitman*, 387 U.S. at 377.

92. See *Romer*, 517 U.S. at 624.

93. *BMW of North America, Inc. v. Gore*, 517 U.S. 559, 577 (1996).

94. *O'Brien v. Skinner*, 414 U.S. 524, 531 (1974). See also *Gooding v. Wilson*, 405 U.S. 518, 520 (1972) ("Only the Georgia courts can supply the requisite construction, since of course 'we lack jurisdiction authoritatively to construe state legislation' ") (citing *United States v. Thirty-seven (37) Photographs*, 402 U.S. 363, 369 [1971]); *Groppi v. Wisconsin*, 400 U.S. 505, 507 (1971) ("we must, of course, accept the construction that the Supreme Court of Wisconsin has put upon the state statute") (citing *Kingsley International Pictures Corp. v. Regents of the University of the State of New York*, 360 U.S. 684, 688 [1959]).

95. *O'Brien*, 414 U.S. at 531.

96. *Nesmith v. Sheldon*, 48 U.S. 812, 818 (1849).

97. *Webster v. Cooper*, 55 U.S. 488, 504 (1852) ("there is no sound distinction between the construction of a law enacted by the legislature of a State, and the construction of the organic law, ordained by the people themselves. The exposition of both belongs to the judicial department of the government of the State, and its decision is final").

98. *Supreme Lodge, K. P. v. Meyer*, 265 U.S. 30, 32 (1924).

99. *Leffingwell v. Warren*, 67 U.S. 599, 603 (1862).

100. *Groves v. Slaughter*, 40 U.S. 449, 497 (1841).

101. *Elmendorf v. Taylor*, 23 U.S. 152, 165 (1825).

102. *St. Louis Southwestern Railway Co. v. Arkansas ex rel. Norwood*, 235 U.S. 350, 369 (1914).

103. *Webster*, 55 U.S. at 504.

104. *Storaasli v. Minnesota*, 283 U.S. 57, 62 (1931).

105. *Chapman v. California*, 386 U.S. 18, 21 (1967) (The Court cannot "leave to the States the formulation of the authoritative laws, rules, and remedies designed to protect people from infractions by the States of federally guaranteed rights").

106. See *Indiana ex rel. Anderson v. Brand*, 303 U.S. 95, 98 (1938).

107. Cf. *Reitman*, 387 U.S. at 374.

108. *Romer*, 517 U.S. at 631.

109. Id.

110. Cf. id. at 1629.

111. See id.

112. See Bettina Boxall, "A New Era Set to Begin in Benefits for Gay Couples Domestic Partners: Hawaii Law, Which Takes Effect Tuesday, Will Allow Unmarried People to Qualify for Many Things Typically Reserved for Wedded Couples," *L.A. Times*, July 7, 1997, at A3 (describing domestic partnership benefits).

113. See *Baehr*, 1996 WL 694235, *3 (Hawaii Cir. Ct.) (rejecting state claim that the public fisc would be significantly adversely affected if same-sex marriages were recognized). The state's claim seems even less plausible in light of the legislature's willingness to award these partnership benefits.

114. For a discussion of the different levels of constitutional scrutiny, see generally Mark Strasser, "Suspect Classes and Suspect Classifications: On Discriminating, Unwittingly or Otherwise," 64 *Temple L. Rev.* 937 (1991).

4

Retroactive Legislation

Suppose that the supreme court of a state holds that the state constitution protects same-sex marriage. Suppose further that some same-sex couples domiciled in that state marry in accord with the relevant statutes and regulations and that the electorate *then* amends the state constitution to prohibit same-sex marriages. Same-sex couples who had married before the state constitution had been modified would still have a legally valid marriage unless, for example, the legislature *retroactively nullified* those same-sex unions that had already been celebrated.

Retroactive legislation is sometimes constitutionally permissible. For example, the Court often upholds retroactive tax legislation. However, a retroactive nullification of marriages is paradigmatic of what legislatures are constitutionally precluded from doing. Even were state same-sex marriage bans held to pass constitutional muster, a retroactive nullification of marriage contrary to the wishes of the individual parties would itself violate constitutional guarantees.

RETROACTIVE MARRIAGE NULLIFICATION

A retroactive nullification of a marriage by a *legislature* might seem to pose no constitutional difficulties because retroactive nullifications of marriages by *courts* already take place. Courts sometimes declare marriages void, either because the union was void ab initio[1] without possibility of becoming legally recognized or because it was voidable and the defects in the marriage were never corrected. A different example of a court's retroactively modifying marital status would seem to be offered by nunc pro tunc decrees,[2] since the decree is treated as if it had been officially recorded earlier than it in fact was. Upon close analysis, however, it will be clear that these court practices do not support the permissibility of a legislature's retroactively nullifying a marriage.

VOID MARRIAGES

Marriages are sometimes declared void ab initio and treated as if they had never existed,[3] even if years have passed between the ceremony and the court declaration. For example, a marriage between individuals too closely related by blood might be declared void, even if the parties had lived together for years as man and wife and even if one of the parties had already died.[4]

An incestuous marriage that was subsequently declared void by a court would have been retroactively invalidated in at least one sense, namely, that the marriage would not have been officially declared void until years after its celebration. Yet, in a more important sense, there would have been no retroactive nullification, since in the eyes of the law the marriage would never have existed.[5] As a New York court made clear, "Where a marriage is void, it is void from its inception without any decree of the court and for all purposes despite any acts or intentions of the parties."[6] Thus, it would be inaccurate to say that a void marriage was one that had been legally recognized and then was retroactively nullified by a court; rather, the union simply never existed in the eyes of the law, even if it took awhile for a court to officially declare that lack of legal validity.

The paradigmatic example of a void marriage involves two individuals who attempt to marry, notwithstanding the *prior* existence of a law in their domicile making such a marriage void. The individuals who suspect or know that their marriage would be void in their domicile might do something so that the person officiating would not know that any difficulties were posed[7] or they might go to another state to evade their domicile's law.[8] For example, consider the couple whose marriage was at issue in *Loving v. Virginia*.[9] Richard Loving and Mildred Jeter went to Washington D.C. to marry because Virginia, their domicile, had an antimiscegenation law that precluded their marrying.[10] After legally marrying in the District of Columbia, the Lovings went back to Virginia to live.

Loving was not a case in which a couple had married in accord with the laws of their domicile and then had later moved elsewhere hoping that their new domicile would recognize the union.[11] Rather, Virginia had always been their domicile and the question for the state was whether it would recognize its domiciliaries' marriage, which was void at home although legally celebrated elsewhere.

Virginia treated the Lovings' marriage as void ab initio,[12] notwithstanding the District of Columbia's having permitted the celebration of their marriage.[13] When the United States Supreme Court held that the Lovings' marriage had to be recognized, it did so because Virginia's law had created an invidious racial distinction[14] that had denied the fundamental right to marry.[15] The Court did not suggest that any difficulty was posed by the state's having treated a marriage of its own domiciliaries as void ab initio.

While states are constitutionally permitted to treat their domiciliaries' marriages as void ab initio under certain conditions, states disfavor such an extreme measure, especially because (1) no court decree is required for that marital union to be treated as if it had never existed, and (2) the consequences of treating a marriage as void can be quite harsh.[16] As the Minnesota Supreme Court points out, precisely because there are so many important ramifications of treating a marriage as void ab initio even absent a court decree, this should occur only if the marriage has been *expressly* declared void by statute.[17]

Not only should the statute expressly declare that the marriage is void rather than, say, voidable, but the statute should predate the attempted marriage.[18] As a New Jersey appellate court explained, "A judgment of nullity can be issued only for an impediment which existed at the time of the contract."[19] For a marriage to be declared void, the "defect" in the marriage should have existed at the time that the marriage was celebrated.[20]

VOIDABLE MARRIAGES

It would be a mistake to claim that void marriages involve retroactively nullified marriages, since a void marriage was never legally recognized. However, voidable marriages would seem to be retroactively nullified marriages, at least potentially, since a voidable marriage is legally recognized until it is declared void by a court.[21] Thus, a voidable marriage might have been an existing marriage in the eyes of the law at a particular time, T_1, and then later be held not to have existed *at* T_1.[22]

Voidable marriages provide a sharp contrast to void marriages. A voidable marriage might be contracted in one year, valid the next year, and then be held never to have existed the following year, whereas a void marriage would have been void from the beginning and would never have existed in the eyes of the law. Thus, insofar as one wishes to find a judicial analog of a retroactively nullified marriage, the voidable marriage is a better example than is the void marriage.

The issue of concern in this chapter is whether a legislature could retroactively nullify marriages that had been valid at the time of their celebration. There is a difference between a court's and a legislature's annulling a marriage and so a court's being able to retroactively nullify a marriage would not establish that a legislature could do so, notwithstanding that legislatures were dissolving marriages at one point in United States history.[23] However, the argument here is not merely that courts being able to nullify marriages does not entail that legislatures can do so as well. Rather, it is that the annulments that might be secured in a court differ in important ways from the legislative annulment under discussion here. Further, there are additional compelling reasons to believe that a legislature could not retroactively nullify a legally celebrated marriage without running afoul of constitutional guarantees, since the reasonable and justified expectations of the parties would be undermined, vested interests would be destroyed, and manifest injustice would result.

When individuals contract a voidable marriage, at least one of them knows or should know that there is a legal impediment to the marriage at the time it is celebrated. If, unbeknown to the partner, an individual is planning on marrying but on never consummating the marriage, at least that individual would know that the marriage was voidable.[24] If both individuals know that according to state law they are too young to marry, then they both would know that there is a legal impediment to their marriage. Thus, in the paradigmatic case involving a voidable marriage, at least one of the parties knows or should know that the marriage is legally defective in some way.

Notwithstanding that at least one of the parties would or should know that the marriage had a legal defect, there might seem to be something counterintuitive about the retroactive nullification of a marriage. It might seem difficult to understand how a marriage could have been recognized as legally existing at a particular point in time and then subsequently be held not to have been legally existing at that same point in time. Indeed, it might seem easier to understand a void marriage in which the union had never legally existed, despite the observance of certain formalities, than a voidable marriage in which the union would have legally existed until it was retroactively nullified and held never to have existed at all.

The anomaly presented by the voidable marriage is more easily understood in light of the fact that voidable marriages are viewed as *less* odious to public policy than are void marriages.[25] The voidable marriage is potentially salvageable. The union will be recognized as legal and not voidable once certain conditions have been met, for example, once the underage individuals attain majority and then ratify the marriage by cohabitation[26] or once the individual who knows that he or she was fraudulently induced to marry nonetheless ratifies the marriage by cohabiting with the marital partner after the fraud has come to light.[27]

The rationale underlying a court's ability to declare a marriage void is that the parties were incapable of contracting a marriage in the first place,[28] e.g., because they were too closely related by blood,[29] or were underage,[30] or were non compos mentis.[31] If the marriage is voidable rather than void, the "defect" in the marriage is viewed as correctable.[32] Further, even if "uncorrected," a voidable marriage cannot be made void after the death of one of the parties to the marriage.[33]

When a voidable marriage is declared void by a court, it is not as if the "formerly married" individuals have been unjustly, retroactively deprived of their marital status. Basically, despite having been *precluded* from marrying by the law existing at the time of the wedding, these individuals nonetheless chose to go through a marriage ceremony. Their marriage has been subsequently declared void because either there was no opportunity or no desire on the part of each of the individuals to correct the original defect and thereby make the marriage valid.[34]

It seems more appropriate to view a voidable marriage not as one that was retroactively changed from a stable and certain legal union to one that had never existed but as an analog to a contractual agreement subject to a condition subsequent.[35] In the case of a voidable marriage, there is a condition the existence of which will operate to discharge the marital duties. Here, the condition is that one of the parties goes to court to annul the marriage before the defect has been cured by ratification or cohabitation.[36]

Admittedly, the analogy is not exact. A paradigmatic example of a case involving a condition subsequent might involve an individual's failing to make an insurance claim in a timely manner,[37] whereas here the individual must go to court before the voidable marriage can in fact be voided. Nonetheless, the point remains that a voidable marriage is one that will be contingently recognized. The certainty and stability of marriage as an institution is not endangered by a court's holding that a contingency (ratification) has not come to pass and that the failure to correct the defect entails that the voidable marriage should be held void and of no legal effect, just as the institution of contract is not undermined when a court refuses to enforce certain obligations if one of the parties has failed to assert his claim in a timely manner.

NUNC PRO TUNC DECREES

A nunc pro tunc decree would seem to involve a retroactive application of law, since such an entry gives retroactive effect to something that is in fact recorded at a later date. Normally, such entries are made to correct a past irregularity.[38] Thus, suppose that a judgment of divorce is granted but the judgment is not recorded.[39] The failure to record that judgment might make a subsequent marriage bigamous.[40] By recording the date of the divorce as of when it was issued rather than as of when it was finally recorded, the record would reflect what should have happened in the first place. Various interests might thereby be protected.[41]

Courts tend not to allow nunc pro tunc decrees when they are being made to create new rights[42] rather than to correct clerical errors,[43] although it is of course true that someone's rights or responsibilities will be changed depending upon whether a nunc pro tunc entry is made. For example, if an individual's marriage is declared bigamous and void, she may not be entitled to claim compensation as a result of her putative husband's death on the job[44] and someone else may instead be entitled to make that claim.[45] Thus, one individual will have a right to the compensation if the nunc pro tunc order is made and a different individual will have such a right if the order is not made.

Yet, merely because a third party would benefit were the nunc pro tunc decree not granted would not establish the inappropriateness of granting such a decree.[46] A court might in addition look to see whether the third party had reasonably relied on the legal state of affairs that had existed immediately prior to the possible granting of the nunc pro tunc decree.[47] As long as there was no reasonable reliance by an innocent third party and as long as the nunc pro tunc decree "did not change, modify, or correct a judgment but merely made the record speak the truth by recording the judicial action previously and actually taken,"[48] such a decree might be made.

As the Colorado Supreme Court made clear, while the "general rule is that judgments will be entered nunc pro tunc only when they have actually been rendered and the entry omitted,"[49] there may be certain extremely rare cases in which such a decree may be "both rendered and entered."[50] For example, one Colorado case involved an individual who was entitled to a divorce.[51] However, she failed to apply for it at the appropriate time and the decree was never entered.[52] Nonetheless, both she and her "ex"-husband remarried, and he had a child with his second wife.[53] The court entered the decree nunc pro tunc, explaining that "the harm which follows a failure to grant the relief demanded is that two couples have for years maintained bigamous relations and a child is bastardized."[54] Thus, the Colorado court may have been considering the innocent third parties who would have been hurt by the failure to grant the nunc pro tunc decree.

A different interpretation of that opinion is that the court was implicitly estopping[55] the second husband from pressing the claim that his own marriage had been bigamous[56] or that he should not be ordered to pay support of "the woman whom, for fifteen years, he has held out to the world as his lawful wife."[57] Or, it may be that the combination of the protection of innocent third parties and the very unsympathetic position of the second husband convinced the court that the usual rules concerning nunc pro tunc orders might be relaxed. Certainly, in other cases, the courts have considered those kinds of factors when they had to decide whether to issue such an order. As the Supreme Court of Washington explained, when a court is deciding whether to issue a nunc pro tunc order, the interests of innocent third parties or the complicity of an individual seeking such an entry would justify a court's refusing to grant a nunc pro tunc decree, notwithstanding that the decree would otherwise have likely been granted.[58]

Neither the existence of void marriages nor of merely voidable ones warrants the inference that legislatures are constitutionally empowered to enact statutes that retroactively nullify marriages. Void and voidable marriages were so classified at the time that they were "contracted." A court's holding that a void marriage is in fact void merely involves the court's making clear that a particular marriage had never been legally recognized; a court's holding a voidable marriage void merely involves the court's making clear that the defects that had existed at the time the marriage was "contracted" had never been corrected. Indeed, the state's willingness to treat a voidable marriage as valid until declared void by a court only serves to underscore that "the law favors marriage and its continuance and frowns upon dissolution of the status by annulment or divorce."[59]

Nunc pro tunc decrees are almost always entered to correct mere clerical errors. They will not be entered unless doing so promotes justice and does not adversely affect the interests of innocent third parties. The existence of such orders or decrees also does not support the permissibility of a legislature's retroactively nullifying a marriage that was legally valid at the time it was celebrated.

THE CONTRACTS CLAUSE

The state might seem to be precluded by Article 1, Section 10, of the United States Constitution from retroactively nullifying marriages. Section 10 reads, "No State shall . . . pass any Bill of Attainder, ex post facto Law, or Law impairing the Obligation of Contracts." Insofar as a statute retroactively nullifying a marriage is impairing a contractual obligation, the Contracts Clause would seem to preclude state legislatures from passing such legislation.

On one reading, the Contracts Clause would prevent states from impairing contractual obligations of or setting limitations on *any* contracts.[60] However, it is clear that states may regulate certain kinds of contracts. Indeed, even in a case in which the Court was overly protective of the freedom of contract,[61] the Court recognized that the state "has power to prevent the individual from making certain kinds of contracts, and in regard to them the Federal Constitution offers no protection."[62]

The Contracts Clause has been interpreted to limit the state's ability to affect existing contracts rather than those which have not yet been made.[63] Thus, the state power to regulate contracts that might be made in the future are limited by the Fourteenth Amendment but not the Contracts Clause,[64] although those Fourteenth Amendment protections are relatively weak, since they only imply "freedom from arbitrary restraint, not immunity from reasonable regulations and prohibitions."[65]

While the limitations imposed by the Contracts Clause are more robust than those offered by the Fourteenth Amendment, states are still constitutionally permitted to impair contractual obligations under certain conditions. The Supreme Court has rejected that the Contracts Clause can be taken literally[66] or as an absolute bar to the state's power to modify contracts,[67] recognizing that the Contracts Clause does not "operate to obliterate the police power of the States."[68] Nonetheless, as the Court has explained, if that clause is to retain any meaning at all, it must be understood to impose some limits upon the "power of a State to abridge existing contractual relationships, even in the exercise of its otherwise legitimate police power."[69]

THE CONTRACTS CLAUSE TEST

The Court has explained that its Contracts Clause analysis involves an inquiry with three components: "whether there is a contractual relationship, whether a change in law impairs that contractual relationship, and whether the impairment is substantial."[70] However, even if the Court is convinced that state legislation substantially impairs certain contractual obligations, there may be no violation of the Contracts Clause if the state can establish that the regulation supports a significant, legitimate public purpose.[71] Thus, the fourth component, which the Court sometimes fails to make explicit, is that a substantial contract impairment may be justified if the state's need is sufficiently compelling and the means chosen sufficiently closely tailored.

The Constitution prevents states from destroying vested rights without good reason. Thus, while there will be some cases in which the legislature will be permitted to destroy vested rights,[72] there will be other cases in which the legislature will be unable to meet the relevant burden and thus will not be able to destroy such rights without offending constitutional guarantees.[73] The Court has reserved for itself the right to override both legislative and state judicial judgments about the nature and extent of particular contractual impairments and the need therefor,[74] that is, the Court will decide for itself whether a particular contractual impairment violates the Contracts Clause.[75]

THE CONTRACTS CLAUSE'S PURPOSES

The Contracts Clause has a variety of purposes. For example, it is designed to prevent the states from obstructing interstate commerce.[76] In one case, the Court refused to allow Mississippi to alter the terms of a contract that had been lawfully made in Tennessee.[77] The Court held that Mississippi could not "extend the effect of its laws beyond its borders so as to destroy or impair the right of citizens of other states to make a contract not operative within its jurisdiction and lawful where made."[78] However, protecting interstate commerce is not the only purpose served by the Clause. Even were a particular contract viewed as solely impacting individuals within a state, the Contracts Clause would still prevent that state from reneging on a contract merely because it wanted to spend the owed money in a way which it thought would better promote the public good.[79]

When deciding whether the state's impairment[80] of a contract is precluded by the Contracts Clause, the Court considers whether individuals relied on representations made by the state.[81] The Court also considers the exigencies that prompted the state to want to alter the contract. If there is an emergency, a state may be permitted to impair a contract that it would not normally be allowed to impair.[82] For example, if the honoring of a contract would somehow jeopardize the government, then there would be sufficient reason to justify a modification of that contract. The Court has explained that contracts will not be enforced if doing so would destroy the goverment's ability to secure the peace and good order of society.[83] The Contracts Clause should not be interpreted to prevent an enforcement of a contract if made necessary by a "great public calamity such as fire, flood, or earthquake."[84] Of course, if the states would be justified in impairing contracts in those kinds of circumstances, other kinds of circumstances in which an urgent need is created would likewise justify temporary relief.[85] Nonetheless, a kind of balancing is required. The Contracts Clause clearly limits the kinds of retroactive contractual modifications that states are permitted to make.[86] Absent sufficiently significant state interests or absent justification establishing that the admittedly significant interests can only be protected by impairing the contractual obligations at issue, the Contracts Clause will prevent the state from impairing existing contracts.

THE MARITAL CONTRACT

Some state supreme courts have held that the Contracts Clause does not apply to the marital contract.[87] Other courts have suggested that whether the Clause is relevant depends upon whether the state views marriage as a contract or as a status.[88] The United States Supreme Court has spoken to this issue, although no one interpretation of the Court's view on this matter has been universally accepted.[89]

The Contracts Clause has never been understood to limit the right of legislatures to legislate on the subject of divorce.[90] Laws specifying the conditions under which courts might grant divorces were not viewed as the state's impairing the marriage contract but as the state's providing a means by which to liberate one of the parties when the other party had already violated the marital agreement.[91] However, the Court has explicitly *refused* to establish that all issues involving the marital contract are beyond the reach of the Contracts Clause.[92]

Historically, marriage has always been subject to the control of the legislature.[93] For example, the legislature "prescribes the age at which parties may contract to marry, the procedure or form essential to constitute marriage, the duties and obligations it creates, its effects upon the property rights of both, present and prospective, and the acts which may constitute grounds for its dissolution."[94] However, the issue under examination in this chapter is not, for example, whether adultery, abuse, etc., should be grounds for dissolution or even whether states should limit divorce no-fault options, but whether the state may retroactively nullify a marriage when neither of the married individuals wishes to have that marital union dissolved.

At one time, legislatures granted divorces. Further, the Court has upheld the constitutionality of legislatures doing so, even while conceding that the determination of the appropriateness of dissolving a marriage might more properly be performed by courts.[95] However, it is important to understand why the Court believed that legislative divorces were constitutional. The Court explained that when the courts do not have jurisdiction to grant a divorce, legislatures should be permitted to put an end to marriages in the interests of society and of the individual parties themselves.[96]

Currently, there is no reason to worry that if legislatures are unable to grant divorces, then individuals will be forced to remain married to each other when the continuation of that union would be contrary to the interests of the individuals themselves and of society as a whole.[97] Given the advent of no-fault divorce and the possibility of securing a divorce through the courts, that concern is no longer relevant and can no longer be used to justify permitting legislatures to dissolve marital unions.[98] It certainly could not be so used when the dissolution would be contrary to the interests of all concerned parties.

In addition and more important for purposes here, the Supreme Court has cautioned that a legislature's attempt to interfere with the vested rights of the individuals involved in a marriage might have constitutional implications.[99] Clearly, a *retroactive* nullification of a marriage legally valid at the time of its celebration might affect vested property rights. Thus, there is reason to think that a legislature's retroactive nullification of a same-sex marriage might well violate constitutional guarantees.

The Supreme Court has warned that legislative acts affecting marital status must not adversely affect the children of a marriage (e.g., by delegitimating them).[100] Yet, the refusal to recognize same-sex marriages and, especially, a retroactive nullification of such marriages might greatly harm any children of the marriage. Because the partners in a same-sex couple would probably not each be genetically related to any child that they were raising, a legally recognized tie between the spouses might be necessary for each of the adults to be recognized as a legal parent of the child.[101] Without that legal tie, an individual who in fact had been raising a child for that child's entire life might be viewed by the law as a legal stranger to that child. Should something happen to that caregiver's partner and should the legal tie between the caregiver and the child not be recognized, that adult and child might be separated by the law to the detriment of each of the parties and of society as a whole.[102]

Some commentators argue that the marriage contract is not subject to Contract Clause limitations.[103] However, the Court has suggested that the marital contract might indeed fall within the protections of that clause under certain conditions and that those conditions might include those in which a legislature tried to retroactively nullify a marriage contrary to the wishes of each of the individual parties.

RETROACTIVE LEGISLATION

Suppose that marital contracts are not covered by the Contracts Clause and that the only limitations on the retroactive nullification of marriages would be those which apply to any legislation. Even were that the sole limiting factor, a legislature's retroactively nullifying marriages would not be constitutionally permissible.

Traditionally, statutes have been viewed as forward-looking[104] and judicial decisions have been viewed as backward-looking.[105] This is true whether the legislation at issue was civil or criminal, although there are additional protections against retroactive criminal laws, since the Ex Post Facto Clause specifically prohibits such laws.[106] The different treatment of statutes and judicial decisions with respect to their presumed retrospectivity is in part a result of a tradition in which judges are viewed as discovering law and legislatures are viewed as creating law,[107] although there are other rationales that also support that legislation as a general matter should not be retrospective. As the United States Supreme Court explained, "Retroactive legislation presents problems of unfairness that are more serious than those posed by prospective legislation, because it can deprive citizens of legitimate expectations and upset settled transactions."[108] Retroactive legislation undermines the ability of individuals to act in ways they know will benefit them and to avoid acting in ways they know will harm them.[109]

Where manifest injustice would result from the law being retrospectively applied, there is a presumption that the legislation should be applied prospectively only.[110] Because retroactively destroying rights that had come into existence as a result of same-sex marriages would qualify both as manifestly unjust and as a deprivation of vested rights, a statute declaring marriages reserved for opposite-sex couples would be presumed to be prospective. However, that presumption is rebuttable. The Court has indicated that where legislative intent is clear, the legislation should be applied as intended.[111] Suppose, then, that a legislature had made clear that the new law banning same-sex marriages was to be applied retroactively. The issue then would be whether the retroactive application of the legislation would be consitutional.[112]

The Supreme Court has held that not all retroactive legislation violates constitutional guarantees.[113] The Court is relatively deferential with respect to the permissibility of retroactivity in economic matters[114] and, at least arguably, especially deferential with respect to the constitutional permissibility of tax legislation being retroactive.[115] For example, the Court's very lax standard to determine the constitutionality of the latter[116] entails that even a good faith detrimental reliance claim will not suffice to prevent the retrospective application of a tax statute.[117]

Nonetheless, the Court has made clear that the mere fact that a statute would be constitutionally permissible if prospectively applied would not establish that its being retroactively applied would also be constitutionally permissible.[118] Further, the Court has indicated its reluctance to "infringe upon or deprive a person of a right that had matured or become unconditional,"[119] although the Court has also indicated that it will sometimes allow a retroactive application where no rights are implicated.[120] This suggests that the willingness of the Court to permit tax statutes to be applied retroactively (where no vested rights are at issue) does not establish that it would also permit the retroactive destruction of marital rights (where vested rights may well be at issue).

At least one further point is important to remember in the context of the present discussion. The Court may be less deferential with respect to retroactive *social* legislation than it is with respect to retrospective *economic* legislation. Indeed, the Supreme Court has articulated a concern that seems especially applicable in the context of deciding the constitutionality of a legislature's retroactively nullifying legally recognized same-sex marriages—namely, that the legislature's "responsivity to political pressures poses a risk that it may be tempted to use retroactive legislation as a means of retribution against unpopular groups or individuals."[121] Thus, the Court might well view a retroactive nullification of same-sex marriages as an impermissible attempt by the Legislature to disadvantage a disfavored group in an attempt to gain political advantage.

DOMESTIC RELATIONS CONTEXT

One reason that the analysis of whether a Legislature would be constitutionally permitted to retroactively nullify marriages is somewhat complicated is that such an action would be historically unprecedented. One might expect that this would have occurred earlier, for example, when states adopted antimiscegenation laws or when they modified antimiscegenation laws already on the books prohibiting marriages between people previously allowed to marry. Or, one might have expected that this would have occurred when states did away with common law marriages. Yet, all of these statutes were made prospective only.

A different legislative practice that is less closely analogous to a retroactive marriage nullification but nonetheless merits examination involves the ways that legislatures would adopt or modify divorce laws. Yet another practice instructive to examine involves whether changes made to rules regarding the disposition of property after divorce may themselves be implemented retroactively. A close examination of each of these practices reveals that a legislative, retroactive nullification of marriages legally valid at the time of celebration would pose insurmountable constitutional difficulties.

ANTIMISCEGENATION LAWS

A close analogy to a retrospectively applied same-sex marriage ban might involve newly adopted antimiscegenation laws that declared marriages invalid and void even if those unions had previously been legally recognized. However, laws preventing interracial unions were made prospective *only*. Sometimes, a legislature would explicitly state the date upon which these laws would be effective. At other times, the courts had to construe the effective date because the legislature had failed to include one. The courts would construe these laws as applying as of the date of ratification, and thus refused to apply them retroactively.

For example, despite the alleged importance of preventing interracial marriage,[122] North Carolina's antimiscegenation law was held not to be retroactive.[123] The state legislature had not included within the relevant statute the date that the antimiscegenation law would go into effect,[124] and the North Carolina Supreme Court held that it was effective as of the day of its ratification.[125]

In Louisiana, the antimiscegenation prohibition was written into the state Constitution. That prohibition modified the state's antimiscegenation law. Once it took effect, it would preclude a white person's marrying "a person who shall have one eighth, or more, of negro blood,"[126] whereas before it had taken effect the "then existing statute fixing the permissible limit of negro blood at one-fourth could be invoked."[127] When the Supreme Court of Louisiana decided a case in which it would have been important to decide whether the one-fourth or the one-eighth rule was applicable, the Court did not say that it could apply the more restrictive policy, (e.g., because of the importance of the social policy at issue) but instead was careful to note that the marriage had not been celebrated until *after* the Louisiana Constitution's prohibition had taken effect.[128]

Often, legislatures would specify when the antimiscegenation law would take effect. For example, the Montana antimiscegenation statute, which explicitly prohibited "Marriage between a Japanese and a white person,"[129] only applied to those marriages "hereafter contracted or solemnized."[130] Not surprisingly, in these cases as well, the statutes were applied prospectively only.

It has been suggested that the refusal to attempt to apply antimiscegenation laws retroactively may have been due to the "understanding that once a marriage was solemnized, it could not be undone by mere statute."[131] That may be so, although there may be other reasons as well. Consider, for example, the statutes specifying that common law marriages would not be recognized. Statutes would indicate that such marriages would no longer be recognized if "contracted" after a certain date.[132] Such unions would not be retroactively nullified, despite the strong public policy in having such marriages celebrated in accord with state requirements.[133] Further, there would have been no worry about desolemnizing common law marriages, since such marriages had not been solemnized in the first place.[134] Nonetheless, perhaps out of a desire to be fair and perhaps out of a fear of the implications of retroactively invalidating such marriages, the denial of the recognition to common law marriages was prospective only.

Whether one examines the statutes prohibiting interracial marriages or those declaring common law marriages invalid, one sees that they operated prospectively only. The antimiscegenation statutes provide a closer analogy to the issue under discussion here, both because they entirely prevented the couples from marrying and because they had invidious overtones.[135] The common law marriage statutes, which did not prevent the individuals from marrying but merely required that those individuals go through a ceremony, nonetheless also did not try to "undo" existing marriages.

DIVORCE LAWS

Divorce statutes were alleged to be unconstitutional, either because they violated the Contracts Clause or because they involved retroactive legislations that detroyed vested rights. Both claims were ultimately rejected, although it will be helpful to understand why those arguments failed.

Legislation can be retroactive in the sense that it is said to be effective as of some date prior to its enactment[136] or in the sense that it affects rights and obligations that had been established under prior law.[137] The divorce laws were alleged to be retroactive in the latter sense, since they would affect rights and obligations established under previous law.

Allegedly, new divorce laws changed the marriage contract[138] or deprived one of the parties of a vested interest in the marital status.[139] However, the claim that the state's divorce laws involve an impermissible interference with contract has been rejected by the United States Supreme Court as well as by various state courts,[140] as has the claim alleging a deprivation of marital status.[141] Certainly, it would hardly be inequitable for the state to grant a divorce if, for example, an individual had made the life of his or her innocent spouse intolerable, the spouse had desperately wanted to get out of the marriage, but the legislature had only realized after the marriage had been contracted that these kinds of circumstances should allow the innocent spouse to be set free. Such a situation is hardly comparable to one in which two individuals were legally married, both wanted to stay in the marriage, but the legislature nonetheless wanted to retroactively nullify that marital union.

That courts have upheld the constitutionality of applying new divorce laws to existing marriages does not establish that a retroactive nullification of a marriage would be permissible. An act modifying the conditions under which a divorce could be granted would not retroactively nullify the existence of a marriage that had been valid (and not even voidable) under then-existing law, as would occur were a state to retroactively nullify those same-sex marriages already celebrated. Rather, the new divorce law would simply modify the conditions under which the individuals might be relieved of their (continuing) marital obligations when at least one of the parties wished to be relieved of those obligations.

PROPERTY

Perhaps ironically,[142] while the interest in marital status has not been held sufficiently important to justify preventing the retroactive application of divorce laws to marriages "contracted" under the previously existing laws, interests in property have been held sufficiently important to prevent retroactive application of laws in the domestic relations context. However, before property interests can have that effect, it must first be established that the individual has property interests at stake that must be respected by the state.

For example, the Supreme Court of Indiana examined the permissibility of the legislature's changing the laws regarding dower.[143] The court suggested that the right to dower was not vested until after the death of the husband and thus was subject to legislative modification.[144] Thus, because the rights had not yet vested, the legislature was free to modify those rights without offending constitutional guarantees.

When the property right has become vested or unconditional, however, retroactive modifications by a legislature will not simply be upheld as a matter of course. As the California Supreme Court explained, "While the Legislature generally is free to apply changes in rules of evidence or procedure retroactively when no vested rights are involved, it is not so unrestrained when these changes directly affect such rights."[145]

To say that a legislature is restrained is not to say that the legislature is absolutely prohibited from impairing vested rights.[146] For example, a retroactive statute impairing vested rights might be justified if it were correcting a situation that was manifestly unfair or would correct an obvious injustice.[147] The California Supreme Court explained that rank, patent injustice "might justify retroactive impairment of a vested property right."[148] However, legislatures cannot impair vested rights without a very important justification, such as the prevention of manifest unfairness or the correction of an obvious injustice.

The California Supreme Court has outlined some of the considerations to be taken into account when determining whether a retroactive application that would abrogate vested rights may nonetheless be justified. The court included the significance of the state interest served by the law and the importance of retroactively applying that law to promote that interest, and the extent and legitimacy of the reliance upon the former law.[149] Thus, if innocent parties might otherwise be left unprotected, the state's interest in retroactively modifying the notion of marital property to achieve a fair and equitable result might meet the relevant test.[150]

The kinds of considerations that are taken into account when judging whether a retroactive application of a law abrogating vested rights is appropriate are similar to those taken into account when judging whether the state has violated the Contracts Clause when impairing contractual obligations.[151] Insofar as rights to community or marital property are acquired through being married,[152] a state's retroactively nullifying those marriages thereby destroying any accrued, vested property rights would be subject to the same kind of analysis as would be appropriate were the state impairing contractual obligations. Unless the state has legitimate, significant interests supporting its retroactive nullification, such a nullification will be constitutionally impermissible.

Suppose that a state had recognized same-sex marriages until the legislature had reserved marriage for opposite-sex couples. If the legislature had either made clear that the statute only applied prospectively (e.g., by including an effective date) or remained silent with respect to the effective date, then the statute would only be appropriately applied prospectively. If the legislature had stated that the statute was to be applied retrospectively, then the statute would be subject to constitutional scrutiny, either because of the Contracts Clause or because such an unprecedented retroactive nullification of marriages and the rights accompanying them would involve a denial of due process. The question here is not whether a same-sex marriage ban can be justified prospectively, which itself seems unlikely, but whether in addition a retrospective application would be constitutionally permitted. Because such a retroactive nullification would not correct rank injustice but, on the contrary, would itself be rank injustice, it could never withstand constitutional scrutiny.

MASS DISSOLUTION

Suppose that a legislature had not retroactively nullified existing same-sex marriages but instead had passed legislation specifying that all such unions would be dissolved as of a certain date. This would have to be distinguished from saying that no *more* same-sex couples would be allowed to marry as of a certain date, which was the tack taken with interracial couples, common law marriages, etc. Although the mass dissolution scenario would have *fewer* constitutional difficulties than the retroactive nullification scenario, it would also be constitutionally impermissible.

Whenever a legislature passes legislation, that legislation must be rationally related to the promotion of legitimate goals. The legislature would have to address which legitimate goals would be promoted by such a dissolution statute, which might be a daunting task given that the promotion of marriage and family is a legitimate state interest and that this legislation would be undermining that interest. Further, by dissolving all of its domiciliaries' same-sex marriages that had been celebrated there, the state would be enacting very unusual legislation designed to impose a substantial burden on a distinct minority. It is difficult to see how this legislation could survive an equal protection challenge. Further, when the Supreme Court upheld the power of legislatures to grant divorces, it explained that this was permissible to promote the interests of society *and* the individuals themselves.[153] It would require great ingenuity, indeed, to show how such divorces could be in the interests of the individuals themselves, their own wishes notwithstanding. Thus, although a legislative dissolution of all of the domiciliaries' same-sex marriages that had been celebrated there might avoid some of the difficulties posed by retroactively nullifying vested rights, it nonetheless seems quite unlikely that such a law could withstand constitutional scrutiny.

Neither Hawaii nor Alaska will be forced to decide how to treat those same-sex marriages that had been celebrated prior to the referenda because no same-sex marriages had been legally performed prior to the passage of the constitutional amendments. However, at least two points should be noted. First, this issue might well be raised in a different state in which the state supreme court struck down a same-sex marriage ban on state constitutional grounds and the electorate later passed a state constitutional amendment in response to that decision. Second, some of the reasons that a state could not retroactively nullify a marriage also help establish why states will sometimes be precluded from refusing to recognize marriages validly celebrated in other domiciles.

As a separate matter, if a state had once recognized same-sex marriages, its no longer doing so would not affect whether other states would have to recognize those marriages that had already been validly celebrated. Suppose, then, that Hawaii or Alaska had recognized same-sex marriages or that the state constitutional amendments are invalidated on federal constitutional grounds. Other states may have to decide whether to recognize those same-sex marriages validly celebrated in Hawaii or Alaska. The next chapter discusses the Full Faith and Credit Clause and its implications for the recognition of marriages celebrated in other states.

NOTES

1. See *Black's Law Dictionary*, 6 (6th ed. 1990) (ab initio— "From the beginning; from the first act; from its inception").

2. See id. at 1069 (Nunc pro tunc—"Now for then. A phrase applied to acts allowed to be done after the time when they should be done, with a retroactive effect, i.e., with the same effect as if regularly done").

3. See *Succession of Gabisso*, 44 So. 438, 441 (La. 1907) ("The marriage here relied on, being an absolute nullity in contravention of public policy and good morals, was not susceptible of ratification, acquired no validity by the lapse of time, remains open to attack, and cannot serve as the basis of an action; in short, in legal contemplation, it has never existed").

4. See, for example, *Ex parte Bowen*, 247 S.W.2d 379 (Ky. 1952) (marriage between first cousins treated as void ab initio).

5. Sometimes, states treat certain incestuous marriages as voidable rather than void. See 23 Pa. Cons. Stat. Ann. §1703 (West 1991) ("All marriages within the prohibited degrees of consanguinity as set forth in this part are voidable, but, when any of these marriages have not been dissolved during the lifetime of the parties, the unlawfulness of the marriage shall not be inquired into after the death of either of the parties to the marriage").

6. *Kay v. Kay*, 252 N.Y.S. 518, 523 (1931).

7. See *Karin T. v. Michael T.*, 484 N.Y.S.2d 780, 781 (Fam. Ct. 1985) (woman dressed as man went through official marriage ceremony with female partner).

8. See *Kinney v. Commonwealth*, 71 Va. 858, 865 (1878) (discussing individuals who attempt to evade the domicile's antimiscegenation law by going to a different state).

9. 388 U.S. 1 (1967).

10. See id. at 2.

11. For a discussion of whether subsequent domiciles could refuse to recognize marriage valid in the domicile at the time of the marriage, see generally Mark Strasser, "For Whom *Bell* Tolls: On Subsequent Domiciles' Refusing to Recognize Same-Sex Marriages," 66 *U. Cin. L. Rev.* 339 (1998).

12. See *Loving*, 388 U.S. at 4 & n.3.

13. For a discussion of choice of law and full faith and credit in the domestic relations context, see generally Mark Strasser, "Judicial Good Faith and the *Baehr* Essentials: On Giving Credit Where It's Due," 28 *Rutgers L.J.* 313 (1997).

14. See *Loving*, 388 U.S. at 11.

15. See id. at 12.

16. See Homer H. Clark, *The Law of Domestic Relations in the United States*, 2nd ed., § 2.9 (St. Paul, Minn.: West Publishing Co., 1988).

17. See *Seeley v. Erringer*, 57 N.W.2d 628, 633 (Minn. 1953) ("the far-reaching ramifications of treating a marriage as a nullity forbid that it should be held invalid without a decree of dissolution unless it is expressly declared void by statute").

18. *Wilson v. Cook*, 100 N.E. 222, 223 (Ill. 1912) ("where a state has enacted a statute lawfully imposing upon its citizens an incapacity to contract marriage . . . , a marriage contracted in disregard of the prohibition of the statute, wherever celebrated, will be void").

19. *Wilkins v. Zelichowski*, 129 A.2d 459, 464 (N.J. Super. Ct. App. Div. 1957), rev'd 140 A.2d 65 (N.J. 1958) (reversed on other grounds). See also *Bernstein v. Bernstein*, 201 A.2d 660, 661 (Conn. Super. 1964) ("a divorce is based on a valid marriage and a cause which arises subsequently for terminating it, while an annulment is decreed on the theory that the marriage is void ab initio").

20. But see *Lang v. Reetz-Lang*, 488 N.E.2d 929, 931 (Ohio App. 1985) ("the preexistence of a condition preventing consummation is not a requisite for annulment for nonconsummation").

21. *Kinney v. Commonwealth*, 71 Va. 858, 860 (1878) (voidable marriages are "declared to be void only from the time they shall be so declared by decree of divorce or nullity"). See also *In re Interest of S.I.*, 173 A.2d 457, 469 (N.J. Super. Ct. 1961) ("Until so annulled, however, this court is required to recognize the marriage as valid").

22. For an example of a court that both nullified a marriage and held that the marriage once existed, see *Taylor v. Taylor*, 31 So.2d 579, 580 (Ala. 1947) ("The father has the right of annulment, but the annulment is effective only from this date").

23. See *Maynard v. Hill*, 125 U.S. 190, 206 (1888) ("until a recent period, legislative divorces have been granted, with few exceptions, in all the states"); Laura Bradford, Note, "The Counterrevolution: A Critique of Recent Proposals to Reform No-Fault Divorce Laws," 49 *Stan. L. Rev.* 607, 609 (1997) ("Many of the divorces granted prior to the middle of the nineteenth century were granted on an ad hoc basis through special legislative acts of annulment in the state legislature.")

24. See, for example, *Bernstein*, 201 A.2d at 661–62 ("Since the defendant had the intention which existed at the time of the marriage ceremony of not cohabiting or consummating the marriage with the plaintiff, and the plaintiff was unaware of that intention at the time of the ceremony and would not have entered into the marriage if he had known of that intention, and the defendant continuously and wrongfully refused to carry out the purposes of the marriage, there is such legal cause as justifies the annulment of the marriage").

25. See *Wilkins*, 129 A.2d at 462.

26. See, for example, *Mangrum v. Mangrum*, 220 S.W.2d 406, 408 (Ky. 1949) ("a marriage under age may be ratified by later cohabitation"); *Abelt v. Zeman*, 179 N.E.2d 176, 178 (Ohio Ct. Common Pleas 1962) ("even though a wife is less than 16 years of age when she enters into the marriage, the same becomes irrevocable by cohabitation . . . after she becomes of age").

27. See *Gassman v. Gassman*, 296 N.W.2d 518 (S.D. 1980). The wife falsely denied having had an abortion before the marriage. Id. at 520. The court was unwilling to hold that such a lie would make the marriage voidable, but did suggest that the husband cohabited with the wife after learning of her abortion and thus would not have been able to void the marriage on that account anyway. See id.

28. *Payne v. Payne*, 214 P.2d 495, 497 (Colo. 1950) (en banc) ("We appreciate the difference between actions for divorce and annulment, the former being based on a valid marriage and a cause of divorce arising post-nuptially, while the latter presupposes and is based entirely upon the assumption that by reason of some legal impediment the parties were incapable of contracting a valid marriage. In other words, in the latter case, because of the legal impediment, the attempted marriage is void ab initio").

29. See *In re Marriage of Adams* (*Adams v. Adams*), 604 P.2d 332 (Mont. 1979) (marriage between first cousins held void ab initio).

30. See *Demoss v. Demoss*, 195 N.E.2d 496 (Ind. App., 1964) (in banc) (marriage between underage individuals voided).

31. See *Mahan v. Mahan*, 88 So.2d 545 (Fla. 1956) (marriage annulled because

plaintiff was so intoxicated during the ceremony that she did not know what she was doing and because she never ratified the marriage).

32. See *Kleinfield v. Veruki*, 372 S.E.2d 407, 410 (Va. App. 1988) ("if the parties can subsequently ratify the marriage and give it legal effect, the marriage could not have been void from commencement").

33. See *Rickard v. Trousdale*, 508 So.2d 260 (Ala. 1987); *Dibble v. Meyer*, 278 P.2d 901 (Or. 1955) (in banc); *Davidson v. Davidson*, 151 N.W.2d 53 (Wis. 1967); *Arnelle v. Fisher*, 647 So.2d 1047 (Fla. App. 1994); *Coulter v. Melody*, 489 S.W.2d 156 (Tex. App. 1972).

34. For example, the marriage may be declared void while one of the individuals is still a minor and thus there would not yet have been an opportunity to ratify the marriage. See *Warner v. Warner*, 256 S.W.2d 734 (Ark. 1953) (marriage voided while the teenager was still a minor); *In re Marriage of Fetters*, 584 P.2d 104 (Colo. App. 1978) (same).

35. See John D. Calamari & Joseph M. Perillo, *The Law of Contracts*, 3rd ed., § 11–7 (St. Paul, Minn: West Publishing Co., 1987) ("A condition subsequent is any event the existence of which, by agreement of the parties, operates to discharge a duty of performance that has arisen"). The *Restatement (Second) of Contracts* no longer uses this terminology. See American Law Institute, *Restatement (Second) of Contracts*, Chap. 9, § 224(e) (St. Paul, Minn: American Law Institute Publishers, 1981). See also E. Allan Farnsworth, *Farnsworth on Contracts*, vol. 2, § 8.2 (Boston: Little, Brown, and Co., 1990) ("The *Restatement Second* has abandoned the term *condition subsequent*").

36. See *In re Marriage of Rabie* (*Rabie v. Rabie*), 115 Cal. Rptr. 594 (Ct. App 1974) (marriage not ratified once wife learned that her husband had married her to facilitate his getting a "green" card, so annulment could be granted).

37. See Calamari & Perillo, *The Law of Contracts*, § 11–7; Farnsworth, *Farnsworth on Contracts*, § 8.2.

38. See *Bockemehl v. Bockemehl*, 604 S.W.2d 466, 467 (Tex. Civ. App. 1980) ("the circumstances in this record are sufficient to show that the error was clerical rather than judicial, and, therefore, was properly corrected nunc pro tunc"); *Dauderman v. Dauderman*, 263 N.E.2d 708, 710 (Ill. App. 1970) ("The function of a nunc pro tunc order is merely to correct the record of the judgment and not to alter the judgment actually rendered").

39. See, for example, *In re Stewart*, 721 P.2d 405, 406 (N.M. 1986) (discussing an attorney who "neglected to file a decree of divorce and, five years later, his client was forced to retain other counsel and request a decree to be entered nunc pro tunc to the date the divorce had been granted in order to legitimize her child from a subsequent marriage").

40. See *McCown v. Quillin*, 344 S.W.2d 576 (Tenn. App. 1960) (nunc pro tunc decree entered to correct failure to enter final divorce decree when granted, which had caused subsequent marriage to be bigamous). See also *Malott v. Malott*, 703 P.2d 531 (Ariz. App. 1985) (decree merely requiring preparation and signature given nunc pro tunc effect so that second marriage would not be bigamous and child would be legitimate).

41. See *Ladd v. Ladd*, 640 A.2d 29, 31 (Vt. 1994) (purpose of nunc pro tunc order is to set effective date of a present order at a particular, appropriate time in the past because the correct entry was not entered when it should have been).

42. See *Merrick v. Merrick*, 194 N.E. 55, 56 (N.Y. 1934) ("New rights, arising out of a matrimonial relationship, cannot be created by a judicial declaration in 1933 concerning an assumed fact which concededly did not exist in 1925 and the existence of which was an essential element of a lawful marriage.") See also *Harvey v. Harvey*, 298 S.E.2d 467, 473–74 (W.V. 1982) (court refuses to issue nunc pro tunc decree annulling marriage, even though husband convicted of bigamy, because wife had not initiated proceedings to have marriage annulled and no mistake or judicial delay had prevented the annulment from being ordered or decreed).

43. See *George v. Sullivan*, 909 F.2d 857, 861 (6th Cir. 1990) (nunc pro tunc decree to correct record rather than to change an order previously made). See also *Merrick*, 194 N.E. at 56 ("When a ruling has in fact been made but is improperly evidenced by a defective mandate, or by no mandate at all, an appropriate and suitable order or judgment which manifests the existence of a determination may subsequently be granted to take effect as of the date of such determination"); *Bruce v. Bruce*, 296 P.2d 310, 311 (Wash. 1956) ("The office of such order or decree [nunc pro tunc] is to record judicial action taken, and not to remedy inaction").

44. Cf. *Toler v. Oakwood Smokeless Coal Corp.*, 173 Va. 425 (1939) (woman denied compensation for putative husband's death because the marriage was held to be bigamous and void).

45. See *Hobson v. Dempsey Const. Co.*, 7 N.W.2d 896, 900 (Iowa 1943) (mother claims her deceased son's marriage was void and thus that she rather than his putative wife should receive compensation).

46. See id. ("Appellant contends she is an innocent third person who acquired vested interests before said nunc pro tunc entry was made").

47. See id. ("It is not contended that appellant took any action or parted with any rights in the belief that appellee was not divorced").

48. Id. at 899.

49. *Perdew v. Perdew*, 64 P.2d 602, 604 (Colo. 1936). See also *Cornell v. Cornell*, 164 N.E.2d 395, 397 (N.Y. 1959) ("an order nunc pro tunc may not serve to record a fact, such as a divorce, as of a prior date when the fact did not then exist").

50. *Perdew*, 64 P.2d at 604.

51. *Perdew v. Perdew*, 64 P.2d 602 (Colo. 1936).

52. Id. at 603.

53. Id.

54. Id.

55. See *Black's Law Dictionary*, 551 (Estoppel—"A principle that provides that an individual is barred from denying or alleging a certain fact or state facts because of that individual's previous conduct, allegation, or denial").

56. *Perdew*, 64 P.2d at 604 ("the entry is in fact to his advantage, because it will relieve him from the stigma of bigamy").

57. See id. at 603. See also id. at 604 (Fifer "cannot complain because he was primarily at fault in the contracting of this marriage before the entry of final decree. The record discloses that Fifer himself filed the verified application for the marriage license issued to himself and Alfreada, and therein swore that her divorce decree had been entered August 9, 1921").

58. See *State ex rel. Tufton v. Superior Court*, 90 P. 258, 259 (Wash. 1907) ("If it appears that the party seeking the entry has himself been guilty of conduct that would make the entry improper, or that third persons have acquired interests or rights

which will be injuriously affected by the entry, the application will be denied, and the party left to his ordinary remedies").

59. *Wilkins*, 129 A.2d at 461.

60. It is unlikely that the Court would countenance such a position. See Robert M. Phillips, Comment, "Good Faith and Fair Dealing under the Revised Uniform Partnership Act," 64 *U. Colo. L. Rev.* 1179, 1219 (1993) (The "extreme 'freedom to contract' position is not likely to be adopted given that courts have always assumed some role as protectors of the community's interest in promoting decent, fair and reasonable conduct.")

61. *Lochner v. New York*, 198 U.S. 45 (1905). In *Lochner*, the Supreme Court struck New York's law limiting the daily and weekly work hours of bakers on 14th Amendment grounds. *Lochner* has been roundly criticized, although commentators disagree about why that decision was wrong.

62. Id. at 54.

63. See *Ogden v. Saunders*, 25 U.S. 213. 303 (1827) (Thompson, J., concurring) ("The law must have a present effect upon some contract in existence, to bring it within the plain meaning of the language employed").

64. See *Lochner*, 198 U.S. at 53 (discussing protection offered by Fourteenth Amendment).

65. *Hardware Dealers' Mut. Fire Ins. Co. v. Glidden Co.*, 284 U.S. 151, 157 (1931) (citing *Chicago, Burlington, & Quincy R. R. Co. v. McGuire*, 219 U.S. 549 [1911]). See also *Barbier v. Connolly*, 113 U.S. 27, 31 (1884).

66. *Allied Structural Steel Co. v. Spannaus*, 438 U.S. 234, 240 (1978) ("The language of the Contract Clause appears unambiguously absolute: "No State shall . . . pass any . . . Law impairing the Obligation of Contracts." U.S. Const. Art. 1, § 10. The Clause is not, however, the Draconian provision that its words might seem to imply").

67. See *United States Trust Co. v. New Jersey*, 431 U.S. 1, 25 (1976) ("The Contract Clause is not an absolute bar to subsequent modification of a State's own financial obligations. As with laws impairing the obligations of private contracts, an impairment may be constitutional if it is reasonable and necessary to serve an important public purpose"). See also *W. B. Worthen Co. v. Thomas*, 292 U.S. 426, 432-33 (1934) ("the constitutional prohibition against the impairment of the obligation of contracts [does] not make it impossible for the State, in the exercise of its essential reserved power, to protect the vital interests of its people"); *Energy Reserves Group, Inc. v. Kansas Power & Light Co.*, 459 U.S. 400, 410 (1983) ("Although the language of the Contract Clause is facially absolute, its prohibition must be accommodated to the inherent police power of the State 'to safeguard the vital interests of its people' ".) (quoting *Home Bldg. & Loan Ass'n v. Blaisdell*, 290 U.S. 398, 434 [1934]).

68. *Allied Structural Steel Co.*, 438 U.S. at 241.

69. Id. at 242.

70. *General Motors Corp. v. Romein*, 503 U.S. 181, 186 (1992).

71. See *Energy Reserves Group*, 459 U.S. at 411.

72. *Treigle v. Acme Homestead Ass'n*, 297 U.S. 189, 197 (1936).

73. Id. ("The statute impairs the obligation of the appellant's contract and destroys his vested rights in contravention of article 1, s 10, and Amendment 14, s 1, of the Constitution").

74. Thus, the Court will defer to a state supreme court's "construction of [its] own constitution and laws." See *Rowan v. Runnels*, 46 U.S. 134, 139 (1847). However, the Court will not defer to a state supreme court's decision about whether contracts may be retroactively invalidated. See id. Nor will the Court defer to legislative judments about whether the Contracts Clause has been violated. See *United States Trust Co.*, 431 U.S. at 22.

75. *El Paso v. Simmons*, 379 U.S. 497, 506–7 (1964) (some do not violate) and id. at 509 (some do).

76. See Michael W. McConnell, "Contract Rights and Property Rights: A Case Study in the Relationship between Individual Liberties and Constitutional Structure," 76 *Calif. L. Rev.* 267, 285 (1988) (suggesting that the contracts clause and other constitutional provisions "prevent the states from obstructing interstate commerce, and thus foster the development of the United States into an integrated commercial republic").

77. *Hartford Accident & Indemnity Co. v. Delta & Pine Land Co.*, 292 U.S. 143, 149–50 (1934).

78. Id. at 149.

79. See *United States Trust Co.*, 431 U.S. at 29 ("Thus a State cannot refuse to meet its legitimate financial obligations simply because it would prefer to spend the money to promote the public good rather than the private welfare of its creditors").

80. The Court defined "impairment" in *Home Building and Loan Ass'n*. See *Home Building and Loan Ass'n*, 290 U.S. at 431 ("The obligations of a contract are impaired by a law which renders them invalid, or releases or extinguishes them and impairment, as above noted, has been predicated of laws which without destroying contracts derogate from substantial contractual rights") (citing *Sturges v. Crowninshield*, 17 U.S. [4 Wheat.] 197, 198 [1819]).

81. See *El Paso*, 379 U.S. at 514 ("We note at the outset that the promise of reinstatement . . . was not the central undertaking of the seller nor the primary consideration for the buyer's undertaking").

82. See *Home Building and Loan Ass'n*, 290 U.S. at 426 ("While emergency does not create power, emergency may furnish the occasion for the exercise of power").

83. Id. at 435.

84. Id. at 439 (citing *American Land Co. v. Zeiss*, 219 U.S. 47 [1911]).

85. Id. at 439–40 ("if state power exists to give temporary relief from the enforcement of contracts in the presence of disasters due to physical causes such as fire, flood, or earthquake, that power cannot be said to be nonexistent when the urgent public need demanding such relief is produced by other and economic causes").

86. *United States Trust Co.*, 431 U.S. at 17 ("It long has been established that the Contract Clause limits the power of the States to modify their own contracts as well as to regulate those between private parties"). (citing *Fletcher v. Peck*, 10 U.S. [6 Cranch] 87, 137–39 [1810]; *Dartmouth College v. Woodward*, 17 U.S. [4 Wheat.] 518 [1819]).

87. See *Needham v. Needham*, 33 S.E.2d 288, 290 (Va. 1945) ("Rules applicable to ordinary contracts are not applied to marriage contracts because of the nature of the marriage relation and for reasons of sound public policy"); *In re Marriage of Franks*, 542 P.2d 845, 850 (Colo. 1975) (en banc) ("a marriage is not a 'contract' within the meaning of the contract clause of the constitution"); *In re Marriage of*

Semmler, 481 N.E.2d 716, 718 (Ill. 1985) ("any argument based upon the State or Federal constitutions' impairment-of-contract clauses [U.S. Const. art. 1, sec. 10; Ill. Const.1970, art. I, sec. 16] is inapplicable. This court has specifically held that marriage contracts are not protected by the contract clause").

88. *McGinley v. McGinley*, 295 S.W.2d 913, 915 (Tex. Civ. App. 1956) ("In certain jurisdictions where marriage is regarded as a contract rather than a status, constitutional provisions against retrospective and retroactive laws . . . have been held to restrain retrospective operation of amending statutes such as the one in question") (citing *Clark v. Clark*, 10 N.H. 380 [1839]). See also *Clark*, 10 N.H. at 387 ("A statute which attempts to confer authority upon the court to grant a divorce, for matters already past, and which, at the time when they occurred, furnished no ground for a dissolution of the marriage, or for other legal proceedings, is, in our view, clearly a retrospective law, and well entitled to the epithets applied to such laws in the constitution"). Cf. *Hamlet v. Hamlet*, 242 Ala. 70, 71 (1941) ("It is established in this jurisdiction that marriage is in law a civil contract between the parties").

89. In *In re Hobbs*, 12 Fed. Cas. 262, 263 (N.D. Ga. 1871), the court suggested that "it is plain that the institution of marriage is not technically a contract." The court cited *Dartmouth College v. Woodward*, 17 U.S. (4 Wheat.) 518 (1819) in support. See id. See also Steven A. Bank, "Anti-Miscegenation Laws and the Dilemma of Symmetry: The Understanding of Equality in the Civil Rights Act of 1875," 2 *U. Chi. L. Sch. Roundtable* 303, 338 (1995) (suggesting that the *Dartmouth College* Court clearly laid to rest the notion that the Contracts Clause might apply to marriage). Others disagree. See Michael Joseph Woodruff, "Lawyers and Sacred Gold," 27 *Tex. Tech L. Rev.* 1411, 1423 n.29 (1996) (suggesting that in *Dartmouth College*, "marriage was treated as a contract within the Contracts Clause"); David P. Currie, "The Constitution in the Supreme Court: State and Congressional Powers, 1801–1835," 49 *U. Chi. L. Rev.* 887, 906 n.132 (1982) (suggesting that *Dartmouth College* was about whether and under what conditions unilateral divorce would be unconstitutional).

90. *Dartmouth College*, 17 U.S. at 629.

91. Id.

92. See id. ("When any state legislature shall pass an act annulling all marriage contracts, or allowing either party to annul it, without the consent of the other, it will be time enough to inquire, whether such an act be constitutional").

93. *Maynard*, 125 U.S. at 205.

94. Id.

95. Id.

96. Id. at 205–6.

97. Cf. id.

98. Cf. Bingham v. Miller, 17 Ohio 445, 448–49 (1848) ("the exercise of granting divorces on the part of the legislature is unwarranted and unconstitutional—an encroachment upon the duties of the judiciary, and a striking down of the dearest rights of individuals, without authority of law").

99. Id. at 206.

100. Id. at 208.

101. Some states allow unmarried individuals to each be legally related to the same child. See *Adoption of Tammy*, 619 N.E.2d 315 (Mass. 1993); *In re Jacob*, 660 N.E.2d 397 (N.Y. 1995); *Adoptions of B.L.V.B. & E.L.V.B.*, 628 A.2d 1271 (Vt.

1993). However, others do not. See, for example, *Georgina G. v. Terry M. (In re Angel Lace M.)*, 516 N.W.2d 678 (Wis. 1994). For further discussion of this issue, see generally Mark Strasser, "Legislative Presumptions and Judicial Assumptions: On Parenting, Adoption, and the Best Interests of the Child," 45 *U. Kan. L. Rev.* 49, 90–110 (1996).

102. See generally Mark Strasser, *Legally Wed: Same-Sex Marriage and the Constitution*, Chap. 4 (Ithaca, N.Y.: Cornell University Press, 1997).

103. See Bank, "Anti-Miscegenation Laws and the Dilemma of Symmetry," 2 *U. Chi. L. Sch. Roundtable* at 338 (suggesting that the *Dartmouth College* Court clearly laid to rest the notion that the Contracts Clause might apply to marriage); Woodruff, "Lawyers and Sacred Gold," 27 *Tex. Tech L. Rev.* at 1423 n.29 (suggesting that in *Maynard*, "marriage was treated as an exception outside the Contracts Clause").

104. See *Winfree v. Northern Pacific Railway Co.*, 227 U.S. 296, 301 (1913) (discussing "the almost universal rule that statutes are addressed to the future, not to the past").

105. See *Great Northern Ry. Co. v. Sunburst Oil & Refining Co.*, 287 U.S. 358, 365 (1932) (discussing "the ancient dogma that the law declared by its courts had a Platonic or ideal existence before the act of declaration, in which event the discredited declaration will be viewed as if it had never been, and the reconsidered declaration as law from the beginning"). See also William N. Eskridge, "Reneging on History? Playing the Court/Congress/President Civil Rights Game," 79 *Calif. L. Rev.* 613, 666 (1991) ("The traditional, but not iron-clad, rule has been that legislation only applies prospectively, whereas judicial interpretation of legislation applies retroactively").

106. *Landgraf v. USI Film Products*, 511 U.S. 244, 266 (1994) ("The Ex Post Facto Clause flatly prohibits retroactive application of penal legislation"). See also Nelson Lund, "Retroactivity, Institutional Incentives, and the Politics of Civil Rights," 1995 *Pub. Int. L. Rev.* 87, 87 (The Ex Post Facto Clause has been applied only to penal legislation).

107. See Eskridge, "Reneging on History?" 79 *Calif. L. Rev.* at 666–67 (discussing "the traditional view of the different roles of Court and Congress. Since the Court 'declares' the preexisting law, its decisions apply not only to the case or controversy at hand, but also to all others pending. Since Congress 'creates' new law through the political process, it would be unfair to apply its 'new' rules to preexisting transactions"); Lund, "Retroactivity, Institutional Incentives," 1995 *Pub. Int. L. Rev.* at 87 ("Legislatures declare in general terms what the law shall henceforth be, while courts resolve disputes by declaring the specific effects of preexisting general laws"); Michele A. Estrin, Note, "Retroactive Application of the Civil Rights Act of 1991 to Pending Cases," 90 *Mich. L. Rev.* 2035, 2047 (1992) ("The American legal system evolved from the assumption that courts find the law made by the legislature. This strict dichotomy, in which courts discover the past and legislatures regulate the future, disfavors retroactive laws").

108. *General Motors Corp. v. Romein*, 503 U.S. 181, 191 (1992). See also Elmer E. Smead, "The Rule against Retroactive Legislation: A Basic Principle of Jurisprudence," 20 *Minn. L. Rev.* 775, 780 (1936) ("Retroactive laws were held to be oppressive and unjust, and it was maintained that the essence of a law was that it be a rule for the future"); Brian Neff, Comment, "Retroactivity and the Civil Rights Act of 1991: An Opportunity for Reform," 1993 *Utah L. Rev.* 475, 476 ("Retro-

active legislation has long been recognized as carrying special potential for unfairness").

109. See Laura Ricciardi & Michael B.W. Sinclair, "Retroactive Civil Legislation," 27 *U. Tol. L. Rev.* 301, 329–30 (1996) ("If law is to guide and delimit behavior, . . . then legislation has to be available to those whose behavior is subject to that limitation, ordering, and control. If a law has yet to be enacted, limiting or adjusting one's behavior according to the law is a temporal impossibility"); Laura Ricciardi, Comment, "The Aftermath of *United States v. Carlton*: Taxpayers Will Have to Pay for Congress's Mistakes," 40 *N.Y.L. Sch. L. Rev.* 599, 638 (1996) ("retroactive legislation fails to provide individuals, before they act, with notice of the laws with which they must comply"). See also Charles B. Hochman, "The Supreme Court and the Constitutionality of Retroactive Legislation," 73 *Harv. L. Rev.* 692, 692 (1960) ("a person should be able to plan his conduct with reasonable certainty of the legal consequences"); Andrew C. Weiler, Note, "Has Due Process Struck Out? The Judicial Rubberstamping of Retroactive Economic Laws," 42 *Duke L.J.* 1069, 1069 (1993) ("Retroactive application of the law . . . denies individuals the ability both to conform their conduct to what society expects and to forecast the benefits or punishments associated with what they do").

110. See *Bowen v. Georgetown University Hospital*, 488 U.S. 204, 208 (1988) and *Bradley v. School Board of City of Richmond*, 416 U.S. 696, 720 (1974).

111. See *Kaiser Aluminum & Chemical Corp v. Bonjourno, 494 U.S. 827, 837 (1990).*

112. See *Fuqua v. Fuqua*, 268 Ala. 127, 129 (1958) ("Where the language of the statute clearly requires retroactive construction it must be so construed even through it may be held to be unconstitutional"); *Semmler*, 481 N.E.2d at 719 ("when the legislature clearly intends a law to be applied retrospectively, it is the duty of the courts to so apply it, subject only to due process limitations") (citing *United States Steel Credit Union v. Knight*, 204 N.E.2d 4 [Ill. 1965]).

113. See *Chase Securities Corp. v. Donaldson*, 325 U.S. 304, 315–16 (1945). See also *Cohen v. Beneficial Indust. Loan Corp.*, 337 U.S. 541, 554 (1949) ("The mere fact that a statute applies to a civil action retrospectively does not render it unconstitutional") (citing *Blount v. Windley*, 95 U.S. 173, 180 [1877]); Hochman, "The Supreme Court," 73 *Harv. L. Rev.* at 694–95 ("The Court has consistently held that not all retrospective statutes are unconstitutional, but only those which, upon a balancing of the considerations on both sides, are felt to be unreasonable").

114. See *Usery v. Turner Elkhorn Mining Co.*, 428 U.S. 1, 15 (1976) ("It is by now well established that legislative Acts adjusting the burdens and benefits of economic life come to the Court with a presumption of constitutionality").

115. See Weiler, "Has Due Process Struck Out?", 42 *Duke L.J.* at 1069–70 ("Alongside this mild scrutiny of retroactive economic legislation generally [the 'general deference' doctrine], the Court has enunciated for tax legislation specifically an alternative due process standard that, in practice, elevates such legislation to an even higher level of presumptive validity").

116. *United States v. Carlton*, 512 U.S. 26, 30 (1994) ("The due process standard to be applied to tax statutes with retroactive effect, therefore, is the same as that generally applicable to retroactive economic legislation").

117. Id. at 33 ("Although Carlton's reliance is uncontested—and the reading of

the original statute on which he relied appears to have been correct—his reliance alone is insufficient to establish a constitutional violation").

118. *Usery*, 428 U.S. at 16–17 ("The retrospective aspects of legislation, as well as the prospective aspects, must meet the test of due process, and the justifications for the latter may not suffice for the former").

119. *Bradley*, 416 U.S.at 720.

120. See *Crane v. Hahlo*, 258 U.S. 142, 147 (1922) ("No one has a vested right in any given mode of procedure") (citing *Railroad Co. v. Grant*, 98 U.S. 398, 401 [1878]); *Irving Trust Co. v. Day*, 314 U.S. 556, 562 (1942) ("Expectations or hopes of succession, whether testate or intestate, to the property of a living person, do not vest until the death of that person").

121. *Landgraf*, 511 U.S. at 266. See also Bryant Smith, "Retroactive Laws and Vested Rights," 6 *Tex. L. Rev.* 409, 417 (1928) (suggesting that because the lawgiver is exposed "to greater temptation to partiality and corruption," the lawgiver must "leave the past alone"); Estrin, "Retroactive Application," 90 *Mich. L. Rev.* at 2076 ("One objection to retroactive laws is that lawmakers can use them to burden certain groups unfairly").

122. See *State v. Ross*, 76 N.C. 242, 245 (1877) (discussing claim that "a marriage between persons of different races is as unnatural and as revolting as an incestuous one"); id. at 246 (describing interracial marriage as "revolting"). See also *Kinney*, 71 Va. at 865 (discussing antimiscegenation policy "upon which social order, public morality, and the best interests of both races depend"). Cf. *Scott v. State*, 39 Ga. 321, 323 (1869) ("The amalgamation of the races is not only unnatural, but is always productive of deplorable results").

123. See Session Laws, Chapter XXIV (1938–39) ("any marriage, hereafter solemnized or contracted beween any free negro or free person of color and a white person, shall be null and void. [Ratified 8th January, 1839]").

124. See Session Laws, Chapter XXIV (1938–39).

125. See *State v. Hairston*, 63 N.C. 439, 440 (1869) (holding that the interracial ban applied to all marriages contracted after the date of ratification).

126. See *Succession of Gabisso*, 44 So. 438, 441 (La. 1907).

127. See id.

128. See id. ("It is undisputed that the Constitution had been adopted and was in force, so far as it was self-acting") and id. ("article 274, which has been offered in evidence, provides that, with certain exceptions, the laws repugnant to the Constitution should continue in force only until April 1, 1892, and plaintiff's marriage was not celebrated until May 15, 1892").

129. See *In re Takahashi's Estate*, 129 P.2d 217, 219 (Mont. 1942).

130. Id.

131. See Paul Finkelman, "The Crime of Color," 67 *Tul. L. Rev.* 2063, 2086 (1993).

132. See, for example, Alaska Stat. § 25.05.311 (Michie 1996) (listing Jan. 1, 1964 as relevant date); Fla. Stat. Ann. § 741.211 (West 1997) (listing Jan. 1, 1968 as relevant date); Ga. Code Ann. 19-3-1.1 (Supp. 1997) (listing Jan. 1, 1997 as relevant date); 750 Ill. Comp. Stat. Ann. 5/214 (West 1993) (listing June 30, 1905 as relevant date); Mich. Comp. Laws Ann. § 551.2 (West 1988) (listing Jan. 1, 1957 as relevant date); Minn. Stat. Ann. § 517.01 (West 1990) (listing April 26, 1941 as relevant date); Miss. Code Ann. § 93-1-15 (1994) (listing April 5, 1956 as relevant

date); S.D. Codified Laws § 25–1-29 (Michie 1992) (listing July 1, 1959 as relevant date).

133. See *Laikola v. Engineered Concrete*, 277 N.W.2d 653, 656 (Minn. 1979) (discussing the strong public policy against common law marriages).

134. See *Black's Law Dictionary*, 277 (Common-law marriage—"One not solemnized in the ordinary way [i.e., nonceremonial] but created by an agreement to marry, followed by cohabitation").

135. Cf. *Romer v. Evans*, 517 U.S. 620, 632 (1996) (discussing Colorado's Amendment 2, which disadvantaged bisexuals, gays, and lesbians and was described by the Court as seeming "inexplicable by anything but animus toward the class that it affects").

136. See Ricciardi & Sinclair, "Retroactive Civil Legislation," 27 *U. Tol. L. Rev.* at 332 ("A newly enacted statute . . . can by its terms come into effect at a date earlier than its enactment").

137. See id. ("A newly enacted statute can be retroactive in [that] . . . it can have effects on legal rights and relations established under prior law").

138. *Ryan v. Ryan*, 277 So.2d 266, 273 (Fla. 1973) ("It is urged as unconstitutional to apply the new law to existing contracts of marriage entered into under the prior law which, it is claimed, was a part of that marriage contract"); *In re Marriage of Walton (Walton v. Walton)*, 104 Cal. Rptr. 472, 475–76 (Ct. App. 1972) (discussing wife's "contention that dissolution of her marriage on the ground of irreconcilable differences as prescribed in The Family Law Act constitutes an unconstitutional impairment of her contract rights").

139. *Walton*, 104 Cal. Rptr. at 476 (discussing wife's "contention that the dissolution of her marriage on the ground of irreconcilable differences under The Family Law Act unconstitutionally deprives her of a vested interest in her married status").

140. *Noel v. Ewing*, 9 Ind. 37, 49 (1857) ("marriage is not technically a contract within the protection of the constitution of the United States"); *Fuqua*, 268 Ala. at 129 (Marriage "is not a contract whose obligation the Constitution protects"); *Raia v. Raia*, 214 Ala. 391, 392 (1926) ("Marriage . . . is not within the provisions of the impairment of the obligation of contracts").

141. *Semmler*, 481 N.E.2d at 720 (rejecting deprivation of marital status claim); *Walton*, 104 Cal. Rptr. at 476–77 (same).

142. *Barrington v. Barrington*, 200 Ala. 315, 323 (1917) (Somerville, J., concurring) (describing matrimonial rights as "legal and moral rights in the highest sense of the word; perhaps, indeed, the most sacred and important of any that are recognized by law and by society").

143. See *Black's Law Dictionary*, 492 (Dower—"The provision which the law makes for a widow out of the lands or tenements or her husband, for her support and the nurture of her children"). See also *Noel*, 9 Ind. at 40 (The object of dower "was the maintenance of the widow, and the nurture and education of the children").

144. *Noel*, 9 Ind. at 42. See also *Ryan*, 277 So.2d at 269 ("Dower is not a vested right"). Various courts have discussed the implications of no rights having vested. See *Fuqua*, 268 Ala. at 129 ("It was within legislative competency to enact retroactive legislation affecting the marital status, just so no vested rights were affected"); *Barrington*, 200 Ala. at 316 ("Remedial statutes—those which do not create, enlarge, diminish, or destroy vested rights—are favored by the courts, and their retrospective operation is not obnoxious to the spirit and policy of the law"). But see

Semmler, 481 N.E.2d at 720 ("In assessing the validity of retrospective legislation from a due process standpoint the question should not be whether the 'rights' allegedly impaired are 'vested' or 'non-vested' ").

145. *In re Marriage of Buol*, 705 P.2d 354, 358 (Cal. 1985) (in bank).

146. See *In re Marriage of Fabian (Fabian v. Fabian)*, 715 P.2d 253, 257 (Cal. 1986) (in bank) ("Impairment of a vested property interest, alone, does not invalidate retroactive application of a statutory measure. Retroactivity is barred only when such impairment violates due process of law"). See also *In re Marriage of Giroux*, 704 P.2d 160, 162 (Wash. App. 1985) ("to determine the constitutionality of retroactive legislation, the proper inquiry is not whether vested rights have been interfered with, but whether 'settled expectations honestly arrived at with respect to substantial interests' will be defeated").

147. *In re Marriage of Slivka (Slivka v. Slivka)*, 228 Cal. Rptr. 76, 81 (Ct. App. 1986) ("retroactive application of section 4800.3 cures an injustice in the former law and advances the state interest in equitable division of community property in the dissolution of the marital partnership"). See also *In re Marriage of Bouquet (Bouquet v. Bouquet)*, 546 P.2d 1371, 1377 (Cal. 1976) (in bank) ("the legislation sprang . . . from an appreciation of the rank injustice of the former law"); *In re Marriage of Powers (Powers III v. Powers)*, 267 Cal. Rptr. 350, 355–56 (Ct. App. 1990) ("the state's paramount interest in the equitable dissolution of the marital partnership justifies legislative action abrogating rights in marital property where those rights derive from manifestly unfair laws").

148. *In re Marriage of Heikes*, 899 P.2d 1349, 1356 (Cal. 1995).

149. *Bouquet*, 546 P.2d at 1376.

150. *Addison v. Addison*, 399 P.2d 897, 903 (Cal. 1965) (in bank).

151. *In re Marriage of Barnes (Barnes v. Barnes)*, 743 P.2d 915, 918 (Cal. 1987) (suggesting that the tests are similar).

152. See *Smith v. Smith*, 486 S.E.2d 516, 519 (S.C. Ct. App. 1997) (defining marital property as all real and personal property acquired by the parties during the marriage); *Findlen v. Findlen*, 695 A.2d 1216, 1218 (Me. 1997) (defining marital property as all property acquired during the marriage except that: which is acquired by gift, devise, descent; which is acquired by a spouse after a decree of legal separation; which is excluded by valid agreement; or which involves an increase in value to property acquired prior to the marriage). See also *Gessner v. Gessner*, 614 So.2d 307, 308 (La. App. 1993) (defining community property as property acquired during the marriage through the effort, skill, or industry of either spouse); *Leland v. Leland*, 847 P.2d 518 (Wash. Ct. App. 1993) (suggesting that community property is all property acquired during the marriage that is not defined as separate property by statute, assuming no valid contract between the parties declaring otherwise).

153. See *Maynard*, 125 U.S. at 205–6.

5

Full Faith and Credit

Suppose that the Hawaii Legislature chooses not to reserve marriage for opposite-sex couples or that the referendum is invalidated and the Hawaii Supreme Court then holds that same-sex marriages are protected by the Hawaii Constitution. Even if states have the right not to allow same-sex marriages to be celebrated within their own jurisdiction, states would have to decide whether to recognize those same-sex marriages validly celebrated in Hawaii.

The Full Faith and Credit Clause might seem to require that such marriages be recognized.[1] However, that view has certain difficulties. First, the Full Faith and Credit Clause has traditionally been viewed as incorporating an exception so that, for example, a state would not have to recognize a judgment if doing so would be strongly offensive to its public policy, although the Court has recently suggested that the Clause incorporates no such exception. Second, although the Full Faith and Credit Clause refers to the acts and records and judicial proceedings of the states, the Clause has been interpreted not to require that the acts or records of a sister state be given as much or the same kind of credit as are the judgments of a sister state. Because decisions about whether a state should recognize a marriage validly celebrated in another state have traditionally been viewed as a choice of law question, there has never been a question whether a state could refuse to recognize a marriage of its own domiciliaries validly celebrated elsewhere if certain *narrow* conditions had been met. However, a different and more difficult question involves determining the conditions, if any, under which nondomiciliary states will be permitted to refuse to recognize those unions valid in the domicile at the time of their celebration.

FULL FAITH AND CREDIT

The Full Faith and Credit Clause reads: "Full Faith and Credit shall be given in each State to the public Acts, Records, and judicial Proceedings of every other State."[2] There is some controversy whether this means that (a) *full* faith and credit must be given to acts and records and judgments but, because these are different kinds of entities, giving full faith and credit to an act, for example, would be quite different from giving full faith and credit to a judgment,[3] or (b) *less* credit is due to an act or record than a judgment.[4] The latter seems to be a more accurate interpretation, although in many instances it would not matter which was chosen as long as the former was properly understood.

JUDGMENTS

Courts and commentators agree that judgments are entitled to full faith and credit, although they disagree about what giving a judgment full faith and credit entails. As a general matter, the full faith and credit guarantee has been interpreted to require that each state must treat the judgment of a sister state as it would be treated in the state in which the judgment was rendered.[5] If the judgment is not subject to modification in the state rendering it, then the judgment is not subject to modification in other states either.

There is some controversy whether one state may *ever* refuse to give full faith and credit to a judgment rendered in another state. Justice Felix Frankfurter suggested that "*exceptional* circumstances may relieve a State from giving full faith and credit to the judgment of a sister State because 'obnoxious' to an overriding policy of its own."[6] However, this obnoxiousness exception was to be read quite narrowly. Even on his view, states were not permitted to ignore foreign judgments merely because they disagreed with the policies underlying those judgments. States might have to submit "even to hostile policies reflected in the judgment of another state."[7] Thus, a mere policy conflict would not establish that a judment of one state would be obnoxious to the public policy of another.[8]

In 1998, the Supreme Court made clear that the Full Faith and Credit Clause imposes an "exacting" obligation upon states to enforce the judgments of sister states.[9] A final judgment issued in one State must be recognized throughout the United States as long as the court issuing the judgment had jurisdiction over the subject matter and the parties before it.[10] The Supreme Court denies that there is a "roving 'public policy exception' to the full faith and credit due judgments."[11]

It is not clear that the difference between the view articulated by Justice Frankfurter and the view recently articulated by the Supreme Court has any practical ramifications. Basically, the question will be just how obnoxious a judgment must be in order for the exception included within Justice Frankfurter's account to be triggered. If, for example, the exception referred to by Justice Frankfurter was so narrow that it would be practically impossible to trigger, then the difference in theory might not have any practical significance.[12] If, however, there might be a variety of judgments that would be viewed as sufficiently obnoxious to trigger this exception, then it would matter that the Court has rejected Justice Frankfurter's view and has made clear that, at least for judgments, no obnoxiousness exception to the Full Faith and Credit Clause will be recognized.

LAWS

As currently interpreted, the Full Faith and Credit Clause requires that judgments issued in one state be given full faith and credit in all of the other states. However, the same is not true where Acts are concerned. The term 'Acts' in the Full Faith and Credit Clause refers to statutes,[13] and there is general agreement that a state is not required by the Full Faith and Credit Clause to substitute the laws of another state for its own,[14] although there is some disagreement about *why* statutes and judgments should be accorded different treatment.

Commentators have offered a few different explanations of why the Full Faith and Credit Clause may not be violated when a state refuses to subordinate its own laws to those of another state.[15] One explanation implies that statutes and judgments are not really being treated differently and that Acts are appropriately analogized to *modifiable* judgments. This explanation cannot be understood without a little background concerning the faith and credit due other states' modifiable judgments.

If a judgment is modifiable in the issuing state, the Full Faith and Credit Clause would permit it to be modified in other states as well,[16] because the Clause only requires that parity be maintained and that sister states treat a judgment as it would be treated in the originating state. For example, if a divorcing parent is awarded custody of a child but that decree can be modified in the future to give custody to the other parent should conditions warrant such a change, then the Full Faith and Credit Clause would permit other states to modify that decree, too.[17]

The Clause's merely requiring parity of treatment might seem to have important implications for how much faith and credit the statutes of sister states must be given. Legislative acts are modifiable, since legislatures can repeal or amend those statutes that have already been enacted.[18] Arguably, if legislative acts can be made and remade at will by the legislature of the state whose law is at issue, then it is not clear why any other state should be bound by such laws.[19] Thus, it might seem that sister states treat laws as they would treat modifiable judgments issued elsewhere.

Although initially appealing, this analysis is somewhat misleading. Suppose, for example, that State A's law is incorporated within the state constitution and thus cannot be changed at the whim of the legislature. Suppose further that a court in State B must decide whether to subordinate State B's law to State A's in a particular case. When making this decision, the State B court will not consider whether or how easily State A's constitution can be changed but, instead, whether State A's law violates an important public policy of State B.[20] Thus, the decision whether to give a sister state's law full faith and credit will not be based upon how readily the sister state's law can be changed but on whether that law is obnoxious to the forum's public policy.

The difference between the obligations imposed by the Full Faith and Credit Clause with respect to other states' judgments and with respect to other states' statutes can be illustrated by considering how some states treat gambling debts. Suppose that an individual borrows money to pay for chips at a gambling casino.[21] Suppose further that the casino sues the individual in *its* home state, the court has jurisdiction over the parties and the subject matter,[22] and that judgment is entered in favor of the casino. The casino then goes to court in the individual's home state to have the judgment enforced. The Full Faith and Credit Clause would require that the latter state enforce the judgment, even if enforcement of gambling debts *violated* that state's important public policy.[23]

Suppose that the example is a little different. The casino tries to enforce the gambling debt by suing the individual in *his* home state. However, the individual's home state has already made clear that the enforcement of gambling debts is obnoxious to an important public policy.[24] Notwithstanding that the debt would be valid in the state in which it was incurred, the court might nonetheless refuse to enforce the debt as a matter of public policy.[25] Thus, the gambling debt would be enforceable in Florida, for example, if a judgment had been entered in a different jurisdiction and the individual who was owed the money then went to court in Florida and argued that the Full Faith and Credit Clause required that the judgment be enforced. Public policy could not be used to preclude enforcement of that valid judgment. However, if the case was originally heard in Florida, public policy might preclude enforcement of that gambling debt.

Merely because the law of a foreign state differs from the law of the forum state would not be sufficient to justify the forum's invocation of the public policy exception. The Supreme Court has noted that the Full Faith and Credit Clause requires states to submit to "hostile policies" of other states "because the practical operation of the federal system, which the Constitution designed, demand[s] it."[26] Indeed, it is "when a clash of policies between two states emerges that the need of the Clause is the greatest."[27] Thus, the mere fact that two state statutes differ does not mean that the statute of the former would be obnoxious to the latter's public policy. For example, although Florida might refuse to enforce gambling debts validly incurred in other jurisdictions, a different state might enforce such debts, even if they could not have been validly incurred in that state.[28] Thus, the public policy exception does not allow the forum state to refuse to enforce other states' laws merely because their laws conflict, although it does allow the forum state to refuse to enforce a law that is contrary to one of its important public policies.

RECORDS

Determining the full faith and credit obligations of the states with respect to other state's records is complicated for several reasons. First, it is important to distinguish between records of *judgments* issued by other states' courts and other kinds of records. The United States Supreme Court has explained that the Full Faith and Credit Clause requires that "the judgments of each State [have] the same conclusive effect, *as records*, in all the States, as they had at home,"[29] although such records must be duly authenticated if they are to have this conclusive effect.[30] Even if authenticated, however, records will be given full faith and credit for certain purposes but not for others. For example, a record would not be given full faith and credit insofar as the sister state court's jurisdiction was itself at issue.[31] Because a court's having rendered a judgment in one state would not establish that the court in fact had jurisdiction to do so and because "a want of jurisdiction over either the person or the subject matter is of course open to inquiry,"[32] it would not make sense to allow the record to establish that the court had jurisdiction to issue the judgment. Otherwise, "a court's record would establish its power and the power would be proved by the record."[33] Thus, records of judgments in sister states must be given full faith and credit only if they are duly authenticated and the jurisdiction of that court over the subject matter and the parties is not itself at issue.

Suppose that the record is of something other than a judgment. It, too, might be used for a variety of purposes. For example, one party might wish to have a birth certificate from another jurisdiction entered into evidence. Just as would be true were this a record of a judgment, the certificate would have to be duly authenticated.[34] Even if authenticated, it might be admissible for certain purposes but not for others. Thus, a court might accept it to establish the date of birth of a particular individual,[35] but not to establish the identity of that person's father,[36] especially if establishing paternity might have significant legal implications, such as establishing support obligations, affecting custody awards, or who might inherit.

Records themselves are subject to modification in the originating state. For example, an individual might petition to have his marriage license changed to reflect a different racial identity, perhaps because he might thereby be entitled to certain benefits to which he would not otherwise be entitled (e.g., benefits reserved in a minority set-aside program).[37]

Suppose that the individual seeking the change in racial identity designation had been born in one state but had moved to another where he had married and continued to live. He might petition in his current home state to have his marriage license amended to reflect his true racial identity. However, he might in addition want to have his birth certificate amended and might try to get a court in his current home state to order his birth state to make that change. Because the courts in his current home state would lack jurisdiction to order an official in charge of vital statistics in a different state to change the records,[38] the request to have the birth certificate changed would be denied. The individual would have to go back to his birth state to petition to have that change made.

If the individual did not go back to his birth state to petition to have the changes made, the marriage certificate in one state might have information that contradicted the information that was included on the *same* individual's birth certificate in another state. However, the Full Faith and Credit Clause does not require that the information on the records of different states be consistent. For example, the Clause's guarantees would not be violated by a state court's authorizing a name change, even if the state in which the person had been born did not recognize the new name.[39]

The information that might be kept on official records might have great legal significance. For example, historically, the racial identity of the parties was very important if they wished to marry in certain states. Further, whether criminal penalties would be imposed might have depended upon that racial classification. Thus, not only were racial intermarriages viewed as null and void, but individuals might have been prosecuted for attempting to marry someone of a different race.[40]

To make matters even more complicated, although various states prohibited racial intermarriage, the states were not in agreement with respect to how the races were to be defined. The Florida Constitution read, "All marriages between a white person and a negro or between a white person and a person of negro descent to the *fourth* generation, inclusive, are hereby forever prohibited."[41] The Tennessee Constitution read, "The intermarriage of white persons with negroes, mulattoes, or persons of mixed blood, descended from a negro to the *third* generation inclusive of their living together as man and wife in this State is prohibited."[42] Other states might employ a "one drop rule," so that individuals with one drop of nonwhite blood would be so classified.[43]

Marriage licenses might only specify "black" or "white" without specifying lineage.[44] A state that tried to make use of records from a different state to determine racial classification and thus, perhaps, whether a "crime" had been committed would have difficulty, both because an individual might be considered white in one state and black in another and because there would be no lineage specification. The Full Faith and Credit Clause would not require that the same "effect" be given to the record in the sister state as it was given in the originating state, at least in part, because of the allegedly important public policy decisions that were based on specifications of who should be counted as belonging to one race and who to another.

THE FULL FAITH AND CREDIT CLAUSE'S PURPOSES

When deciding whether a state is constitutionally required to give full faith and credit to a sister state's judgment, act, or record, it is helpful to consider the purposes of the Full Faith and Credit Clause. That clause is a "nationally unifying force"[45] that is designed to make the several states "integral parts of a single nation."[46] However, states cannot be integral parts of a single nation without surrendering some of their autonomy. Thus, as the Supreme Court has recognized, the Full Faith and Credit Clause requires that states sometimes sacrifice local policies as a price of being a member of a federal system.[47]

The Supreme Court has suggested that the function of the Full Faith and Credit Clause is to "resolve controversies where state policies differ."[48] Because the purpose of the Full Faith and Credit Clause is to transform an "aggregation of independent, sovereign States into a nation,"[49] and because one cannot "weld the independent states into a nation"[50] without requiring particular local policies to "give way,"[51] the Full Faith and Credit Clause restricts state power to enforce local policy. While there is "room for some play of conflicting policies,"[52] the space that has been "left for the play of conflicting policies is a narrow one."[53]

The Full Faith and Credit Clause is designed to promote interstate harmony.[54] However, it is important to distinguish between the kind of harmony sought between *states* and the kind of harmony sought between different sovereign *nations*. The deference that may be appropriate to accord to a sovereign nation may be quite different from the deference owed to one state by another when each is part of the same country. As Justice Robert Jackson suggested, the Constitution "created a political union among otherwise independent and sovereign states."[55] One goal was to integrate the economic life of the country.[56] Another goal was to "guard the new political and economic union against the disintegrating influence of provincialism in jurisprudence, but without aggrandizement of federal power at the expense of the states."[57] Thus, the Full Faith and Credit Clause was designed to force states to surrender some of their provincial policies while not at the same time increasing the power of the United State Congress.

COMITY

A court in one state might enforce a judgment rendered in another jurisdiction because the court was required to do so or because there were clear public policy reasons to do so, notwithstanding the *lack* of an obligation to enforce that judgment. A state court that enforces a judgment from a different state court does so as a matter of constitutional obligation, since the Full Faith and Credit Clause requires that enforcement. The same cannot be said of the enforcement of a judgment from a foreign country, since neither the Full Faith and Credit Clause in particular nor the United States Constitution more generally requires United States courts to recognize the judgments of other countries. [58]A state court that enforces a judgment from the court of another country may well be doing so out of comity[59] rather than obligation.[60]

Courts respecting foreign judgments out of comity are acting out of deference and respect as well as good will.[61] Nonetheless, deference is more easily overcome than a constitutionally imposed obligation, a point especially important to consider in those cases in which the state's declared public policy would militate against enforcing the judgment. Thus, were it simply a matter of comity, a state court might hold that a foreign judgment that was obnoxious to local public policy did not have to be enforced; however, were it a matter of constitutional obligation, the court would have no such choice, obnoxiousness to local public policy notwithstanding. The Full Faith and Credit Clause places sister state judgments in the latter category. As the Supreme Court explained, the Clause "substituted a command for the earlier principles of comity and thus basically altered the status of the States as independent sovereigns."[62]

It is a serious mistake to treat domestic and international choice of law cases as interchangeable.[63] The way that the United States courts treat the laws of other countries is a matter of comity and diplomacy.[64] The way that states treat the laws of their sister states is subject to considerations that simply have no bearing on the way that other countries' laws should be treated.[65] It is thus at best misleading to suggest that just as Hawaii and Alaska cannot impose their own marital laws on the world, so, too, they cannot impose their own marital laws on any other states.[66] Hawaii and Alaska stand in a different relation to their sister states than they do to foreign countries and thus might be able to impose obligations on the former which they could not impose on the latter. If, indeed, Hawaii and Alaska come to recognize same-sex marriages (e.g., because the referenda themselves are held to violate federal constitutional guarantees), some states should be forced to recognize those marriages while other states should not. To understand which states should be bound and which not requires an examination and analysis of choice of law practices.

CHOICE OF LAW

Above, it is suggested that the Full Faith and Credit Clause requires states to enforce the judgments of sister states' courts, as long as those courts had the requisite jurisdiction. States are permitted not to enforce obligations validly incurred in other states if those obligations have not been reduced to judgment and if enforcement of those obligations would be obnoxious to an important public policy. Records will be given full faith and credit depending upon the purpose for which they were offered and whether they were properly authenticated.

Sometimes, when commentators are discussing what the Full Faith and Credit Clause requires, they are discussing the limitations it imposes on which state's laws may be applied to a particular occurrence or transaction. This issue must be differentiated from whether the Full Faith and Credit Clause requires, for example, that a forum enforce a debt validly incurred elsewhere. The latter is determined by looking to see whether that enforcement would violate an important public policy of the forum. The former is determined by looking to see whether particular states have enough of a connection to the parties and the transaction or occurrence at issue to justify application of those states' laws.

Suppose that a resident of Minnesota buys an insurance policy from an insurance company in Wisconsin. One evening, the Minnesota resident is driving in Wisconsin when a Wisconsin resident who has had several drinks crosses the double yellow line in the center of the road, has a head-on collision with the Minnesota driver, and kills him.

The Minnesota driver's widow tries to collect the insurance proceeds due her. However, it turns out that she will be entitled to more generous insurance proceeds if Minnesota rather than Wisconsin law is applied.[67] The widow goes to court in Minnesota where she lives and sues the insurance company, claiming that she is entitled to the more generous benefits provided by Minnesota law rather than the less generous benefits provided by Wisconsin law. The Minnesota court applies local law and the widow is awarded the more generous benefits.

Both Minnesota and Wisconsin had significant contacts to the occurrence. The accident occurred in Wisconsin, involved a Wisconsin driver, and the insurance company was based in Wisconsin. The innocent party was a Minnesota resident, the insurance policy was bought while the individual was a resident of Minnesota, and the individual's widow still lives in Minnesota. The issue here is *not* whether one state's law is obnoxious to an important public policy of another, but merely whether the different states (Minnesota and Wisconsin) each have sufficient contacts with the event at issue to have its own law applied. Here, each state would have more than sufficient contacts with the parties and the event to justify application of local law.

Courts and commentators agree that the recognition of marriages validly celebrated in other states involves a choice of law question because the law of more than one state is potentially applicable when the ceremony takes place.[68] Various states have a significant interest in whether a particular marriage will be recognized: the state or states where the parties are domiciled, the state where the marriage ceremony is performed, and the state where the couple plans to live immediately after they are married. The laws of any of these states *might* be applied to determine the validity of a marriage. However, precisely because such important interests are at stake when the validity of a marriage is at issue, there are clear rules for determining whose law will apply to determine the validity of a particular marriage.

CHOICE OF LAW RULES

As a general matter, choice of law is a difficult and confusing area.[69] To make it even more complicated, a number of different questions might be asked when examining a case involving choice of law, and the failure to carefully identify the relevant question might yield confusing or inaccurate answers. For example, it is important to distinguish between two different questions: (1) what is the best rule for deciding which law should be applied,[70] and (2) which choice of law rules are required by the United States Constitution.[71] Merely because some choice of law rules are thought non-optimal or unwise does not render them unconstitutional.[72] Further, it would be a mistake to think that there is only one "wise" choice of law rule. There is no universal agreement about which choice of law system would be best and different scholars offer different approaches that they claim should be adopted.[73] Sometimes, theorists claim that certain other approaches are not only inferior but unconstitutional,[74] although the Supreme Court has been unwilling to declare that any of those allegedly unconstitutional approaches actually violates constitutional guarantees.

The Court has explained that there are some minimal constitutional limits on which states' laws are applicable to a particular occurrence or transaction. For example, "if a state has only an insignificant contact with the parties and the occurrence or transaction, application of its law is unconstitutional."[75] However, the Court has failed to make sufficiently clear how minimal those contacts must be,[76] having recognized that "it is frequently the case under the Full Faith and Credit Clause that a court can lawfully apply either the law of one State or the contrary law of another."[77] Some commentators have concluded that as a general matter the forum state can apply its own law without much fear of being overturned on constitutional grounds.[78]

Nonetheless, it would be implausible to claim that a state can always apply its own law, since that would undermine the Constitution's having constrained state powers to create a federal system.[79] The Court has recognized that "the statute of a state may sometimes override the conflicting statute of another, *both at home and abroad*."[80] Thus, in some cases states must apply a sister state's law. Regrettably, the Court has refused to offer explicit guidelines to help establish when a state is permitted to apply its own law, believing it "unavoidable" that in particular cases the Court will be forced to "determine for itself the extent to which the statute of one state may qualify or deny rights asserted under the statute of another."[81]

CHOICE OF LAW IN THE DOMESTIC RELATIONS CONTEXT

In the context of marriage and divorce, decisions about which state's law is applicable are relatively clear, in part because of the importance of the implicated interests. For example, an individual who secures a divorce and then remarries may be charged with bigamy if the first divorce is not given full faith and credit in the state in which the charge has been brought.[82] An individual whose marriage is held invalid may lose a variety of rights including the right to inherit, the right to have custody of a child, the right to bring certain actions in tort, etc.

DIVORCE

In order for a court to grant a divorce, it must have jurisdiction over at least one of the parties and jurisdiction over the subject matter. The court will have personal jurisdiction over the party before the court who is voluntarily seeking a divorce and thus the more difficult question will be whether the court has subject matter jurisdiction. The court will have subject matter jurisdiction over the marriage if one of the parties is domiciled in that state.[83] Thus, assuming that the party before the court has met the state's residency requirement and is domiciled in that state,[84] the court's having issued a decree of divorce will constitute the court's having issued a judgment that itself will be subject to full faith and credit requirements in all of the states.

As is the case with judgments generally, however, a court's having had jurisdiction to issue a divorce decree is itself subject to challenge in sister states, assuming that the jurisdictional issue was not litigated in the initial divorce proceeding. Thus, a spouse might challenge the divorce decree issued in a sister state by claiming that the court had not had jurisdiction because, for example, the divorce-seeker had never intended to become domiciled in the decree-granting state. The United States Supreme Court has made clear that a court in a sister state can decide for itself whether any of the parties to the marriage had in fact been domiciled in the state issuing the decree, and thus whether the decree-granting court had subject matter jurisdiction.[85]

The Supreme Court realizes that one state court's being allowed to decide for itself whether another state court's determination of domicile is correct will itself cause uncertainty about marital status. However, the Court believes this an inevitable result "in a federal system in which regulation of domestic relations has been left with the States and not given to the national authority."[86] Yet, the Court is not claiming that marital status will simply be indeterminate when one spouse gets a divorce in a relatively new domicile. On the contrary, there are certain protections in place. As long as each spouse participates in the divorce proceeding and thus has an opportunity to contest the jurisdictional issues, the Full Faith and Credit Clause will prevent either from later attacking the decree elsewhere.[87]

Suppose that Mr. Smith is seeking a divorce from Mrs. Smith. He moves from State A to State B, meets State B's residency requirement for divorce, gives his wife notice that he will be getting a divorce in State B, and then is granted that divorce by a State B court. Suppose further that as soon as the divorce decree is granted, Mr. Smith immediately returns to his previous home state where Mrs. Smith continues to live. If Mrs. Smith did not contest jurisdiction in the original divorce proceeding, she might now go to court challenging the divorce, claiming that Mr. Smith had never changed domiciles.[88] If the State A court agrees that Mr. Smith had never become domiciled in State B, the court could refuse to recognize the divorce decree issued in State B, because State B would not have had jurisdiction to issue it. As far as State A is concerned, the Smiths might still be married.

While the State A court can decide for itself whether Mr. Smith was in fact domiciled in State B when he secured the decree and thus might refuse to recognize the divorce on jurisdictional grounds, that court cannot decide whether State B's criteria for divorce are, for example, too liberal. The only matter before the court would be whether the court in State B had personal and subject matter jurisdiction when it granted the divorce decree. If indeed the State B court had the requisite jurisdiction, the State A court could not refuse to recognize the divorce—indeed, all other states would have to give full faith and credit to that decree.

MARRIAGE

Traditionally, choice of law rules are relatively clear in the context of the interstate recognition of marriages. For example, if a marriage is celebrated in the domicile, only that state's marriage law may be applied to determine the validity of the marriage. Thus, suppose that John Jones is the uncle of Bernice Brown. Because Bernice is the daughter of John's half-sister, Carol, John is Bernice's half-uncle. Suppose further that John and Bernice live in California, which allows half-uncles and half-nieces to marry.[89] It would not matter that, for example, Oregon does not permit half-uncles and half-nieces to marry.[90] John and Bernice will have a valid marriage when they marry and live in California.

Suppose that two individuals are domiciled in one state, California. Suppose further that they go to another state, Massachusetts, to marry, all the while intending to live in California. The two states whose laws are potentially applicable to determine the validity of the marriage are California and

Massachusetts. If the marriage is valid in both of those states, then the marriage is valid. It would not matter that some third state, Montana, precludes such marriages. For example, suppose that David and Ellen are first cousins. The laws of Massacusetts[91] and California[92] both allow first cousins to marry, although the law of Montana does not.[93] The validity of the marriage will be determined by looking at the law of the state of celebration (Massachusetts) and the law of the domicile (California), but not at the law of some third state that has nothing to do with the marriage.

Above, there is no difficulty in determining the validity of the marriages discussed because the law of the domicile and the law of the state of celebration agree. However, suppose that those laws conflict. If the law of the state of celebration is applied the marriage will be valid, but if the law of the domicile is applied the marriage will be invalid.

In cases in which the laws of the states of celebration and domicile conflict, there is a generally accepted decision rule for determining which law to apply. The law of the place of celebration will apply unless the marriage violates an important public policy of the domicile, in which case the domicile's law will apply and the marriage will be invalid.

The *First Restatement of the Conflict of Laws* suggests that "a marriage is valid everywhere if the requirements of the marriage law of the state where the contract of marriage takes place are complied with."[94] However, the *Restatement* lists some exceptions. Section 132 reads:

Marriage Declared Void by Law of Domicil

> A marriage which is against the law of the state of domicil of either party, though the requirements of the law of the state of celebration have been complied with, will be invalid everywhere in the following cases:
> (a) polygamous marriage,
> (b) incestuous marriage between persons so closely related that their marriage is contrary to a strong public policy of the domicil,
> (c) marriage between persons of different races where such marriages are at the domicil regarded as odious,
> (d) marriage of a domiciliary which a statute at the domicil makes void even though celebrated in another state.

Comment c is no longer applicable because the Supreme Court has held that *no* state may prohibit interracial marriage.[95] However, the remaining exceptions entail that a marriage will be valid unless it is polygamous, incestuous, or declared *void* by the domicile.

The *Second Restatement of the Conflict of Laws* suggests a similar policy, since a "marriage which satisfies the requirements of the state where the marriage was contracted will everywhere be recognized as valid unless it violates the strong public policy of another state which had the most significant relationship to the spouses and the marriage at the time of the marriage."[96] Both *Restatements* suggest that a marriage valid where celebrated will be valid everywhere unless the marriage would be treated as *void* in the domicile,[97] although the *Second Restatement* formulation may include one exception.

Suppose that Wanda Williams and Trent Thomas are domiciled in one state, celebrate their marriage in another state, and then immediately move to a third state where they expect to spend the rest of their lives. Arguably, the third state has the most significant relationship to the spouses and marriage at the time of the marriage because that is where the marital couple will permanently reside. The *Second Restatement* suggests that if the union is void according to the law of the state that will be the couple's domicile *immediately after* the marriage, then the marriage may not be valid.

According to the *First* and *Second Restatements*, the only states whose law might be applicable to determine the validity of a marriage are the states where the parties are domiciled before the marriage, the state where the marriage is celebrated, and the state where the couple will live after they have married. Because the states whose laws might be applicable are limited in this way, the parties will know whether their marriage will be valid. They can make plans and have justified expectations based on their knowledge that because their marriage was valid according to the laws of the relevant states, their marriage will be recognized throughout the United States.

One further point must also be considered. A state may prohibit a marriage by declaring it void or voidable or, perhaps, merely prohibited. The general rule for the validity of marriages is that only marriages *void* in the domicile will be invalid when validly celebrated in another state. As the Supreme Court explained, "Marriages not polygamous or incestuous or otherwise declared void by statute [in the *domicile*] will, if valid by the law of the state where entered into, be recognized as valid in every other jurisdiction."[98]

The point in this chapter is not to oversimplify when marriages will be recognized. For example, some marriages treated as void in the domicile might nonetheless be recognized for certain purposes if validly celebrated elsewhere.[99] Some marriages that were merely prohibited and not declared void in the domicile would not be recognized even if validly celebrated elsewhere if the domicile had passed an Evasion Statute.[100] These exceptions notwithstanding, however, the general rule is that marriages void in the domicile will be void everywhere and that marriages not void in the domicile and valid where celebrated will be valid throughout the country.

A point that bears emphasis is that both the *First* and the *Second Restatements* determine the validity of a marriage by looking at the domicile at the time of the marriage or, perhaps, immediately following the marriage. This way, marital status can be established early and with certainty. Important rights involving family or property will not suddenly be destroyed years after the wedding has taken place without the parties having had any notice at the time of the marriage that the validity of their marriage might be in doubt. Individuals can make plans and have reasonable and justified expectations about their marriage and about how they might go about living their lives.

DECLARATORY JUDGMENTS

Suppose that states adopt choice of law rules that do not follow the *First* or *Second Restatements* but instead allow those states to refuse to recognize same-sex marriages.[101] Assuming that such laws would pass constitutional muster, there might nonetheless be a way to prevent states from refusing to recognize *some* marriages. One suggestion that has been made in the secondary literature is that same-sex couples could get declaratory judgments affirming the validity of their marriages.[102]

Declaratory judgments may be issued when an actual controversy exists that requires a judgment to determine legal rights and relations.[103] Where marital status is in doubt and there is some dispute whether two individuals are (or were) married to one another,[104] an individual might want a legal declaration of marital status in order to determine whether he or she is still free to marry.[105]

A declaratory judgment can have the force and effect of a final judgment,[106] although there is some controversy whether a declaratory judgment would be subject to full faith and credit. The United States Supreme Court has given an indication of how that issue would be decided were it before the Court, suggesting that such decrees are not "outside the full faith and credit domain."[107]

Two different kinds of scenarios should be distinguished. In the first scenario, a couple from a state declaring same-sex marriages void travels to a state recognizing such marriages, marries, and then seeks a declaratory judgment from a court in the celebratory state that their marriage is valid.[108] Assuming that the celebratory state follows the *First* or the *Second Restatement of the Conflict of Laws*, the court should consult the *domicile's* law to determine whether the marriage was treated by the domicile as void or whether the domicile had an evasion statute. If, for example, the domicile would treat the marriage as void and of no legal effect, the forum court should rule that the marriage is *invalid*, notwithstanding its validity in the celebratory state.[109] Otherwise, individuals could always evade the domicile's marital laws by simply going to a celebratory state that recognized the marriage and then getting a declaratory judgment that the marriage was valid.

The above scenario should be distinguished from one in which a same-sex marriage is valid according to the laws of the states of celebration and domicile at the time of the marriage. A same-sex couple might still seek a declaratory judgment, either because they were planning on moving to a state that refused to recognize such marriages or because the couple would be travelling through such a state.[110] Arguably, notwithstanding both members of the couple claiming to have a valid marriage, an actual controversy would still be posed because the new state would have a statute on the books precluding recognition of such marriages.[111] Assuming that the forum state followed either the *First* or the *Second Restatement of the Conflict of Laws*, the court would declare the marriage *valid*, because the states of celebration and domicile at the time of the marriage had recognized the union. It would not matter that there were other states (having no relation to the parties or the marriage at the time of the marriage) that would not recognize the union.

A court might be precluded from issuing a declaratory judgment in a scenario in which both parties wanted their marriage declared valid because there would be an absence of a controversy *between the parties.*[112] That would depend upon the law of the state where the proceeding was to take place.[113]

Consider Vermont's Declaratory Judgments Act, the purpose of which "is to settle and to afford relief from uncertainty and insecurity with respect to rights, status and other legal relations and . . . is to be liberally construed and administered."[114] Perhaps a court would liberally construe the conditions under which it could issue a judgment so as to afford the parties relief from uncertainty and insecurity with respect to their marital status and rights, although a court might decide instead that it could not issue a declaratory judgment in the circumstances hypothesized here.[115] In any event, a case in which there were adversarial parties (e.g., one claiming that the parties were married and the other claiming that they were not) would presumably give the court jurisdiction to issue such a judgment,[116] assuming that there was no fraud involved.[117] Were the same parties to relitigate the issue in a sister state, that state might have to give full faith and credit to the declaratory judgment issued in the first state, even if that meant recognizing the marriage.

The analysis offered here might seem to be inaccurate for the following reason. If one looks at some of the older cases in which the validity of marriages was at issue, one might see that courts offered the following formulation as the test for determining the validity of a marriage. A marriage that is "valid where it is celebrated is valid everywhere, but there are two well-recognized exceptions, viz., marriages which are contrary to the *law of nature*, as generally recognized by Christian nations, and those which are declared by positive law to have no validity [i.e., are void]."[118] The law of nature criterion might *seem* to indicate that same-sex marriages need not be recognized. However, that view is incorrect because, as will be explained in the next chapter, the law of nature exception has a special, narrow meaning within the domestic relations context.

NOTES

1. Robert Cordell II, "Same-Sex Marriage: The Fundamental Right of Marriage and an Examination of Conflict of Laws and the Full Faith and Credit Clause," 26 *Colum. Hum. Rts. L. Rev.* 247, 265 (1994) ("Facially, the Full Faith and Credit Clause would [seem to] mandate that marriages performed in one state be honored in another").

2. U.S. Const. Art. 4, § 1.

3. See, for example, *Chicago & A. R. Co. v. Wiggens Ferry Co.*, 119 U.S. 615, 622 (1887) ("Without doubt the constitutional requirement [article 4, § 1] that 'full faith and credit shall be given in each state to the public acts, records, and judicial proceedings of every other state,' implies that the public acts of every state shall be given the same effect by the courts of another state that they have by law and usage at home"); Douglas Laycock, "Equal Citizens of Equal and Territorial States: The Constitutional Foundations of Choice of Law," 92 *Colum. L. Rev.* 249, 296 (1992) ("the Clause is most plausibly read as requiring each state to give the law of every other state the same faith and credit it gives its own law—to treat the law of sister states as equal in authority to its own").

4. *Baker v. General Motors Corp.*, 118 S. Ct. 657, 663 (1998) ("Our precedent differentiates the credit owed to laws [legislative measures and common law] and to judgments"); Lea Brilmayer, "Credit Due Judgments and Credit Due Laws: The Respective Roles of Due Process and Full Faith and Credit in the Interstate Context," 70 *Iowa L. Rev.* 95, 97 (1984) ("The credit due judgments is, unmistakably, greater than the credit due laws").

5. See *Morris v. Jones*, 329 U.S. 545, 547 (1947).

6. *Vanderbilt v. Vanderbilt*, 354 U.S. 416, 426 (1957) (Frankfurter, J., dissenting) (italics added). See also *Magnolia Petroleum Co. v. Hunt*, 320 U.S. 430, 439 (1943) ("there are some limitations upon the extent to which a state will be required by the full faith and credit clause to enforce even the judgment of another state, in contravention of its own statutes or policy"); *Pacific Employers Ins. Co. v. Industrial Accident Comm'n*, 306 U.S. 493, 502 (1939); American Law Institute, *Restatement (Second) of the Conflict of Laws* §103 (St. Paul, Minn.: American Law Institute Publishers, 1971) ("A judgment rendered in one State of the United States need not be recognized or enforced in a sister State if such recognition or enforcement is not required by the national policy of full faith and credit because it would involve an improper interference with important interests of the sister State"). But see William L. Reynolds, "The Iron Law of Full Faith and Credit," 53 *Md. L. Rev.* 412, 438 (1994) ("it is quite doubtful that Section 103 provides an accurate statement of the law"). Professor Reynolds' view has been confirmed by the *Baker* Court.

Some commentators seem unaware that there has been an ongoing debate about this issue. See Andrew Koppelman, "Dumb and DOMA: Why the Defense of Marriage Act Is Unconstitutional," 83 *Iowa L. Rev.* 1, 15 (1997) ("It has been settled for nearly a century that no state may invoke its public policy in order to withhold enforcement of a final judgment issued by the courts of another state").

7. *Estin v. Estin*, 334 U.S. 541, 546 (1948).

8. *Bradford Electric Light Co. Inc. v. Clapper*, 286 U.S. 145, 162 (1932).

9. *Baker*, 118 S. Ct. at 663.

10. Id. at 663–64.

11. Id. at 664.

12. See *FMS Management Systems Inc. v. Thomas*, 309 S.E.2d 697, 699 (N.C. App. 1984) (area of state public policy that provides relief from mandates of Full Faith and Credit Clause with respect to judgments narrows almost to the vanishing point).

13. Laycock, "Equal Citizens," 92 *Colum. L. Rev.* at 290 ("The Full Faith and Credit Clause extends to all sources of state law. It is clear that 'public Acts' means statutes").

14. Brilmayer, "Credit Due Judgments," 70 *Iowa L. Rev.* at 104 ("full faith and credit is not offended when the domestic rule of the other state is chosen").

15. *Pink v. A.A.A. Highway Express, Inc.*, 314 U.S. 201, 210 (1941).

16. See Jean A. Mortland, "Interstate Federalism: Effect of Full Faith and Credit to Judgments," 16 *U. Dayton L. Rev.* 47, 66 (1990) ("The courts generally have found that judgments subject to modification in the state of rendition are not entitled to full faith and credit").

17. Congress passed the Parental Kidnapping Prevention Act (PKPA) to limit the rights of states to modify the custody decrees of sister states.

18. See Brilmayer, "Credit Due Judgments," 70 *Iowa L. Rev.* at 98.

19. Id.

20. See *Black's Law Dictionary*, 655 (6th ed. 1990) (Forum—"A court of justice, or judicial tribunal; a place of jurisdiction; a place of litigation; an administrative body. Particular place where judicial or administrative remedy is pursued").

21. See *M & R Investments, Co., Inc. v. Hacker*, 511 So.2d 1099 (Fla. App. 1987).

22. See id. at 1099.

23. See id. at 1100–1101. See also *Coghill v. Boardwalk Regency Corp.*, 396 S.E.2d 838 (Va. 1990) (The Full Faith and Credit Clause requires that New Jersey judgment involving payment of gambling debt be enforced, notwithstanding Virginia's strong public policy prohibiting the enforcement of such debts).

24. See *Barquin v. Flores*, 459 So.2d 436 (Fla. App. 1984).

25. See id. at 436–37. See also *The Casanova Club v. Bisharat*, 458 A.2d 1 (Conn. 1983) (refusal to enforce gambling debt valid where incurred).

26. See *Estin*, 334 U.S. at 546.

27. *Union National Bank v. Lamb*, 337 U.S. 38, 42 (1949).

28. See *Intercontinental Hotels Corporation v. Golden*, 254 N.Y.S.2d 527 (N.Y. 1964) (gambling debts enforceable under Puerto Rican law are enforceable in New York). See also *Caribe Hilton Hotel v. Toland*, 307 A.2d 85 (N.J. 1973) (same).

29. *Thompson v. Whitman*, 85 U.S. (18 Wall.) 457, 462 (1873) (italics added).

30. *Mills v. Duryee*, 11 U.S. (7 Cranch) 481, 484 (1813) ("The act declares that the record duly authenticated shall have such faith and credit as it has in the state Court from whence it is taken").

31. *Thompson*, 85 U.S. at 468 ("But if it is once conceded that the validity of a judgment may be attacked collaterally by evidence showing that the court had no jurisdiction, it is not perceived how any allegation contained in the record itself, however strongly made, can affect the right so to question it. The very object of the evidence is to invalidate the paper as a record").

32. *Milliken v. Meyer*, 311 U.S. 457, 462 (1940) (citing *Grover & Baker Sewing Machine Co. v. Radcliffe*, 137 U.S. 287 [1890]).

33. *Williams v. North Carolina*, 325 U.S. 226, 234 (1945) ("*Williams II*").

34. See *Hinson v. Hinson*, 356 So.2d 372 (Fla. App. 1978) (New Jersey birth certificate inadmissible because not duly authenticated).

35. See *Steele v. Campbell*, 82 N.E.2d 273, 275 (Ind. App. 1948).

36. See id. at 275 (refusing to accept birth certificate to establish paternity without additional evidence to that effect). See also *Johnson v. Branson*, 319 S.E.2d 735 (Va. 1984). The court refused to accept that a West Virginia birth certificate established paternity, see id. at 737, even though West Virginia law specified that the name of the putative father would not be entered without his consent. See id. at 736. But see *Hinson*, 356 So.2d at 374 (duly authenticated birth certificate is prima facie evidence of paternity).

37. See *Phillips v. Consolidated Supply Co.*, 895 P.2d 574 (Idaho 1995) (individual seeks to have race designation on marriage certificate changed from "white" to "American Indian").

38. See *Arnold v. Department of Health of City of New York*, 571 N.Y.S.2d 14, 14–15 (App. Div. 1991) (Maryland court lacked jurisdiction to order New York City Department of Health to issue new birth certificates); *Phillips*, 895 P.2d at 577 (court lacked jurisdiction to order Missouri to change individual's birth certificate).

39. See *Don v. Don*, 114 A.2d 203, 205 (Conn. 1955) (full faith and credit does not prevent Connecticut from permitting name change, notwithstanding record in New York that lists individual's old rather than new name).

40. See *Jones v. Commonwealth*, 79 Va. 213, 217 (1884).

41. See *Ellis v. State*, 42 Ala. 525, 526 (1868) (penalty for intermarriage 2–7 years hard labor); *Frasher v. State*, 30 Am. Rep. 131, 131 (Tex. Ct. App. 1877) (penalty for intermarriage 2–5 years in penitentiary).

42. See Fla. Const. Art. 16, §25 (italics added).

43. See Tenn. Const. Art. XI, §15 (italics added).

44. See Julie C. Lythcott-Maims, Note, "Where Do Mixed Babies Belong? Racial Classification in America and Its Implications for Transracial Adoption," 29 *Harv. C.R.-C.L. L. Rev.* 531, 532 (1994) (discussing one drop rule).

45. *Magnolia Petroleum Co.*, 320 U.S. at 439.

46. *Milwaukee County v. M. E. White Co.*, 296 U.S. 268, 277 (1935).

47. *Sherrer v. Sherrer*, 334 U.S. 343, 355 (1948).

48. *Morris*, 329 U.S. at 553.

49. *Sherrer*, 334 U.S. at 355.

50. See *Johnson v. Muelberger*, 340 U.S. 581, 584 (1951).

51. *Sherrer*, 334 U.S. at 355.

52. *Bradford*, 286 U.S. at 160.

53. *Williams v. North Carolina*, 317 U.S. 287, 294 (1942) ("*Williams I*") (quoting *Broderick v. Rosner*, 294 U.S. 629, 642 [1935]).

54. See David P. Currie, "Full Faith and Credit to Marriages," 1 *Green Bag* 7, 12 (1997) ("The full faith and credit clause is designed to promote interstate harmony").

55. Robert H. Jackson, "Full Faith and Credit—The Lawyer's Clause of the Constitution," 45 *Colum. L. Rev.* 1, 17 (1945).

56. Id. See also Charles B. Nutting, "Suggested Limitations on the Public Policy Doctrine," 19 *Minn. L. Rev.* 196, 208 (1935).

57. Jackson, "Full Faith and Credit," 45 *Colum. L. Rev.* at 17.

58. *Bradford*, 286 U.S. at 154. See also *Golden v. Golden*, 68 P.2d 928, 832 (N.M. 1937) ("the 'full faith and credit' clause of the Constitution of the United States (art. 4, Sec. 1) . . . is not applicable to the judgments of foreign countries").

59. See *Black's Law Dictionary*, 267 (Comity—"Courtesy, complaisance; respect; a willingness to grant a privilege, not as a matter of right, but one of deference and good will").

60. *Hilton v. Guyot*, 159 U.S. 113, 163–64 (1895) (" 'Comity', in the legal sense, is neither a matter of absolute obligation, on the one hand, nor of mere courtesy and good will, upon the other").

61. *Bobala v. Bobala*, 33 N.E.2d 845, 849 (Ohio App. 1940).

62. *Estin*, 334 U.S. at 546 (citing *Williams I*, 317 U.S. at 301, 302).

63. See Laycock, "Equal Citizens," 92 *Colum. L. Rev.* at 259 ("It is a serious mistake to discuss domestic and international choice-of-law cases interchangeably, even though that practice is nearly universal in the conflicts literature").

64. See id. at 259 ("How U.S. courts treat foreign law is a matter of comity and diplomacy").

65. See id. ("How Texas courts treat the law of a sister state is a matter of law, not comity, and the choice is . . . [not] voluntary").

66. See, for example, David P. Currie, "Full Faith and Credit," 1 *Green Bag* at 12 (italics added) ("The answer to the old question whether the island of Tobago can make laws for the *whole world* is still No; and neither can the islands of Hawaii, unless other *states* are willing to let them").

67. This case is based on *Allstate Insurance Co. v. Hague*, 449 U.S. 302 (1981), although the facts have been changed to make even clearer that either state's law might be applied.

68. C.W. Taintor, II, "What Law Governs the Ceremony, Incidents and Status of Marriage," 19 *B.U. L. Rev.* 353, 367 (1939) ("Since the question of the creation of the marriage status must be referred to the law of some state or to the laws of two states acting together, the problem is one of choice of law "); Cordell, "Same-Sex Marriage," 26 *Colum. Hum. Rts. L. Rev.* at 265 ("the decision to honor a marriage from another state, especially a marriage which conflicts with the laws in the state deciding, involves a choice of laws question").

69. See Stewart Sterk, "The Marginal Relevance of Choice of Law Theory," 142 *U. Pa. L. Rev.* 949, 1030 (1994) (discussing choice of law "chaos").

70. Jackson, "Full Faith and Credit," 45 *Colum. L. Rev.* at 24 ("Where there is a choice under the full faith and credit clause, the one should be made, I should say, which best will meet the needs of an expanding national society for a modern system of administering, inexpensively and expeditiously, a more certain justice").

71. Id. at 16 ("I think it difficult to point to any field in which the Court has more completely demonstrated or more candidly confessed the lack of guiding standards of a legal character than in trying to determine what choice of law is required by the Constitution").

72. *Sun Oil Co. v. Wortman*, 486 U.S. 717, 728–29 (1988).

73. See, for example, Robert A. Leflar, "Conflicts Law: More on Choice-Influencing Considerations," 54 *Cal. L. Rev.* 1584, 1587–88 (1966) (discussing the

better rule of law criterion); Laycock, "Equal Citizens," 92 *Colum. L. Rev.* 249 (offering a sophisticated territorialist approach); David E. Seidelson, "Resolving Choice of Law Problems through Interest Analysis in Personal Injury Actions: A Suggested Order of Priority among Competing State Interests and among Available Techniques for Weighing Those Interests," 30 *Duq. L. Rev.* 869 (1992) (offering interest anaysis approach).

74. See John Hart Ely, "Choice of Law and the State's Interest in Protecting Its Own," 23 *Wm. & Mary L. Rev.* 173, 187 (1981) (suggesting that interest analysis is constitutionally suspect), Laycock, "Equal Citizens," 92 *Colum. L. Rev.* at 312 (suggesting that better rule of law theory is constitutionally suspect).

75. *Allstate Insurance Co.*, 449 U.S. at 310–11.

76. See id. at 334–38 (Powell, J., dissenting) (describing the insignificant contacts that the Court nonethless held were sufficient).

77. *Sun Oil Co.*, 486 U.S. at 727.

78. See, for example, Louise Weinberg, "Choosing Law: The Limitations Debates," 1991 *U. Ill. L. Rev.* 683, 719.

79. Jackson, "Full Faith and Credit," 45 *Colum. L. Rev.* at 26 (Such a policy would "be at odds with the implication of our federal system that the mutual limits of the states' powers are defined by the Constitution").

80. *Alaska Packers Ass'n v. Industrial Accident Commission of California*, 294 U.S. 532, 548 (1935) (italics aded).

81. Id. at 547.

82. *Williams I*, 317 U.S. at 289 ("Petitioners were tried and convicted of bigamous cohabitation under s 4342 of the North Carolina Code, 1939, and each was sentenced for a term of years to a state prison").

83. See *Black's Law Dictionary*, 484 (Domicile—"A person's legal home. That place where a man has his true, fixed, and permanent home and principal establishment, and to which whenever he is absent he has the intention of returning").

84. State residency requirements for divorce vary. See, for example, Ala. Code § 30–2-5 (1989) (6 months if defendant not resident); Ariz. Rev. Stat. Ann. § 25-312 (West 1991) (90 days); Cal. Fam. Code § 2320 (West 1994) (6 months); Del. Code Ann. tit. 13 § 1504 (1993) (6 months); Fla. Stat. Ann. § 61.021 (West 1997) (6 months); Ga. Code Ann. § 19–5-2 (1991) (6 months); Idaho Code § 32–701 (1996) (6 weeks); 750 Ill. Comp. Stat. Ann. § 5/401 (West Supp. 1997) (90 days); Iowa Code Ann. § 598.6 (West 1996) (1 year); Kan. Stat. Ann. § 60–1603 (1994) (60 days); Ky. Rev. Stat. Ann. § 403.140 (Banks-Baldwin 1994) (180 days); Md. Code Ann., Family Law, § 7–101 (1991) (1 year, if grounds for divorce occurred outside of state); Mich. Comp. Laws Ann. § 552.9 (West Supp. 1997) (180 days); Minn. Stat. Ann. § 518.07 (West 1990) (180 days); Mo. Ann. Stat. § 452.305 (West Supp. 1998) (90 days); Mont. Code Ann. § 40–4-104 (1997) (90 days); Nev. Rev. Stat. § 125.020 (1993) (6 weeks unless other exceptions met); N.J. Stat. Ann. § 2A:34–10 (West 1987) (1 year, unless it is an action for adultery); N.M. Stat. Ann. § 40–4-5 (Michie 1997) (6 months); N.Y. Dom. Rel. § 230 (McKinney 1986) (1 year unless both parties are residents); N.D. Cent. Code §14–05–17(1997) (6 months); Ohio Rev. Code Ann. § 3105.03 (Banks-Baldwin 1994) (6 months); R.I. Gen. Laws § 15–5-12 (1996) (one year); S.C. Code Ann. § 20–3-30 (Law Co-op. Supp. 1997) (1 year unless both residents, in which case only 3 months required); Vt. Stat. Ann. tit. 15 § 592 (1989) (6 months to bring action but 1 year before divorce may be

decreed); Va. Code Ann. § 20–97 (Michie 1995) (6 months); Wyo. Stat. Ann. § 20-2–107 (Michie 1997) (60 days unless marriage solemnized there and plaintiff had resided there since).

85. *Williams II*, 325 U.S. at 230.

86. Id. at 237.

87. *Sherrer*, 334 U.S. at 351.

88. See N.D. Cent. Code § 14–05–08.1 (1997) ("If a person obtains a decree of divorce or of annulment of marriage from a court of another jurisdiction and was domiciled in this state within less than twelve months prior to obtaining the decree and resumes residence in this state within six months after obtaining the decree, it is prima facie evidence that such person did not abandon his or her domicile in this state prior to obtaining the decree").

89. See Cal. Fam. Code § 2200 (West 1994) (prohibiting marriages between uncles and nieces of the whole blood but not of the half blood). See also *People v. Baker*, 442 P.2d 675, 676 (Cal. 1968) (in bank) (construing incest statute to exclude half-uncle and half-niece from the prohibition).

90. See Or. Rev. Stat. § 106.020 (1997) (half-uncles and half-nieces are included within the incest prohibition).

91. See Mass. Gen. Laws. Ann. ch. 207, § 1 (West 1987).

92. See Cal. Fam. Code § 2200 (West 1994).

93. See Mont. Code Ann. § 40–1-401 (1997).

94. § 121.

95. See *Loving v. Virginia*, 388 U.S. 1 (1967).

96. § 283.

97. For a discussion of why "violates the strong public policy" is equivalent to "void," see Strasser, *Legally Wed*, 111, 193 n.47.

98. *Loughran v. Loughran*, 292 U.S. 216, 223 (1934).

99. See Strasser, *Legally Wed*, 111–14 (discussing marriages void in the domicile that might nonetheless be recognized for certain purposes).

100. See id. at 122–24 (discussing Evasion Statutes).

101. Some states passed laws indictating that they would not recognize same-sex marriages validly celebrated elsewhere even before DOMA was passed. See, for example, N.C. Gen. Stat. § 51–1.2 (Supp. 1997) (passed in 1995).

102. See Deborah M. Henson, "Will Same-Sex Marriages Be Recognized in Sister States?: Full Faith and Credit and Due Process Limitations on States' Choice of Law Regarding the Status and Incidents of Homosexual Marriages Following Hawaii's *Baehr v. Lewin*," 32 *U. Louisville J. Fam. L.* 551, 588 (1994); Julie L. B. Johnson, Comment, "The Meaning of 'General Laws': The Extent of Congress's Power under the Full Faith and Credit Clause and the Constitutionality of the Defense of Marriage Act," 145 *U. Pa. L. Rev.* 1611, 1628 (1997); Jon-Peter Kelly, Note, "Act of Infidelity: Why the Defense of Marriage Act Is Unfaithful to the Constitution," 7 *Cornell J.L. & Pub. Pol'y* 203, 217 (1997); Rebecca S. Paige, Comment, "Wagging the Dog—If the State of Hawaii Accepts Same-Sex Marriage Will Other States Have To?: An Examination of Conflict of Laws and Escape Devices," 47 *Am. U. L. Rev.* 165, 173 (1997).

103. *Demorest v. DiPentima*, 324 N.W.2d 634, 636 (Mich. App. 1982).

104. See id. at 635.

105. Sometimes, a dispute about marital status (e.g., whether a valid common law

marriage had in fact been contracted) will determine who will be entitled to inherit. See *In re Danza*, 591 N.Y.S.2d 197 (App. Div. 1992) (woman not entitled to elect against will because she was held not to have entered into common law marriage with the person now deceased); *Smith v. Winder (In re Winder's Estate)*, 219 P.2d 18 (Cal. Ct. App. 1950) (woman held not to have had common law marriage and thus not to have been precluded from marrying the person now deceased).

106. See *Wall v. Wall*, 534 A.2d 465, 467 (Penn. 1987) ("a declaration as to the validity of a marriage, pursuant to section 206 of the Code, would be final").

107. *Baker*, 118 S. Ct. at 664.

108. See Henson, "Will Same-Sex Marriages Be Recognized?" 32 *U. Louisville J. Fam. L.* at 588 (suggesting this scenario).

109. A separate question would be raised if the court in the celebratory state in good faith misconstrued the domicile's law and declared the marriage valid. In that event, the judgment would seem subject to full faith and credit guarantees. Cf. *Fauntleroy v. Lum*, 210 U.S. 230, 237 (1908) ("[A]s the jurisdiction of the Missouri court is not open to dispute the judgment cannot be impeached in Mississippi even if it went upon a misapprehension of the Mississippi law").

110. See Kelly, "Act of Infidelity," 7 *Cornell J.L. & Pub. Pol'y* at 218.

111. See id. But see Currie, "Full Faith and Credit," 1 *Green Bag* at 11 (suggesting that insulating a ruling "from judicial reexamination in the absence of a meaningful opportunity—even in theory—to contest the order in the original proceeding would be difficult to reconcile with the rule of law").

112. *See Fergusson v. Fergusson*, 149 N.Y.S.2d 836 (1956) (declaratory judgment could not be issued because plaintiff and defendant agreed that there was no marriage); Maurice J. Holland, "The Modest Usefulness of DOMA Section 2," 32 *Creighton L. Rev.* 395, 399–400 (1998) (parties must be adversaries). But see *Zizzo v. Zizzo*, 247 N.Y.S.2d 38 (1964) (declaratory judgment on existence of marriage issued despite parties not being adversaries).

113. See Holland, "The Modest Usefulness of DOMA," 32 *Creighton L. Rev.* at 399–400.

114. See Vt. Stat. Ann. tit. 12 § 4722 (1973).

115. See Vt. Stat. Ann. tit. 12 § 4725 (1973) ("This chapter shall be so interpreted and construed as to effectuate its general purpose to make uniform the law of those states which enact it, and as far as possible to harmonize with federal laws and regulations on the subject of declaratory judgments and decrees").

116. See *Demorest*, 324 N.W.2d at 635 (declaratory judgment could be issued because defendant had earlier filed a complaint for divorce alleging that she and plaintiff were lawfully married).

117. Cf. *Henley v. Foster*, 125 So. 662 (Ala. 1930) (fradulent decree that marriage was null was successfully challenged by child to establish her legitimacy).

118. *Wilson v. Cook*, 100 N.E. 222, 222 (Ill. 1912) (italics added); see also *Lanham v. Lanham*, 117 N.W. 787, 788 (Wis. 1908).

6

Subsequent Domiciles and Full Faith and Credit

Domiciles that wish to prevent their domiciliaries from marrying a same-sex partner can manifest that intention quite clearly by making such marriages void. That way, their domiciliaries will know that marrying a same-sex partner in a state in which such marriages are valid will not guarantee that their domicile will recognize the validity of their marriage.

A separate question that has not received adequate attention is whether states will have to recognize same-sex marriages that were recognized by both the states of celebration and domicile at the time of the marriage. Thus, suppose that Hawaii and Alaska come to recognize same-sex marriages and that a same-sex couple domiciled in either state marries and then, a few years later, moves to another state because of some employment opportunity. Even if a state could have precluded its own domiciliaries from going to Hawaii or Alaska, marrying, and then insisting that the marriage be recognized, much more argument would be needed to establish that the state was entitled to refuse to recognize the marriage of the Hawaiian or Alaskan same-sex couple, since such a refusal would implicate both constitutional and policy issues that simply are not involved when a state denies recognition to a marriage of its own domiciliaries.[1]

Historically, states had to confront whether subsequent domiciles could refuse to recognize a marriage valid in a previous domicile when a couple was married in one state and then, after some time had passed, moved to a new state that did not recognize such marriages. The marriage might have violated the latter state's law because, for example, the individuals were too closely related by blood (e.g., first cousins) or because the individuals were of different races. Many courts confronting this issue understood that such marriages had to be recognized, local law notwithstanding.[2] A minority of courts reached the opposite conclusion, although their opinions were sometimes noteworthy for their lack of clarity and reasoning.[3] For example, the Tennessee Supreme Court upheld a conviction of an interracial couple for cohabiting in that state, notwithstanding the couple's having legally married while being domiciled in Mississippi.[4] A close examination of that opinion reveals not only a lack of argumentation but, paradoxically, a holding which is consistent with the view that the validity of such marriages must be recognized.

THE RESTATEMENTS

Both the *First Restatement* and the *Second Restatement of the Conflict of Laws* suggest that a marriage recognized as valid by the states of celebration and domicile at the time of the marriage must be recognized by every state. While neither Restatement explicitly and concisely states this proposition, each Restatement is not only consistent with that view but also cannot plausibly be interpreted as incorporating anything but that view. This is important for two reasons: (1) if a state has adopted either Restatement's position with respect to which marriages will be considered valid, then the state will be bound as a matter of its own law to recognize those marriages valid in the states of celebration and domicile at the time of the marriage, and (2) even if the state has not adopted either Restatement's position as its own law, the Restatement views might be very persuasive with respect to the position the state should take.

THE *FIRST RESTATEMENT*

The *First Restatement of the Conflict of Laws* states, "Except as stated in §§ 131 and 132, a marriage is valid everywhere if the requirements of the marriage law of the state where the contract of marriage takes place are complied with."[5] Section 131 applies to individuals who have been barred from remarrying. Section 132 discusses the conditions under which a marriage that violates a law of the "domicil" will be "invalid everywhere."

Regrettably, § 132 is ambiguous, since it does not specify whether "domicil" refers to the domicile at the time of the marriage ($domicile_m$) or to some future domicile ($domicile_f$). Suppose that two individuals legally marry in their current domicile, D. Suppose further that someone contests whether these individuals are in fact married. As far as the marriage's validity is concerned, it is irrelevant that a different state, N, does not recognize such marriages. As long as State D recognizes such marriages, the *First Restatement* suggests that the marriage is valid in *all* states.[6]

Suppose that after a few years the couple who had married in State D moves to State N, perhaps because of some unanticipated opportunity. Suppose further that someone now contests whether these individuals are in fact married. It may be important to establish whether the rule determining the validity of the marriage refers to the law of the domicile$_m$ or the domicile$_f$. If the former is the relevant law, then the marriage is clearly valid and, further, will be valid no matter where the couple moves within the United States. If the latter is the relevant law, then the marriage's validity cannot be determined without examining the current domicile's law.[7] Further, the union will always be at least potentially invalid because some state might declare such marriages void ab initio.[8]

Suppose that subsequent domiciles were empowered to declare marriages null and void despite their having been valid in the states of celebration and domicile at the time of the marriage. An individual who had been married to the same person for the preceding twenty years might try to avoid her marital obligations by (1) moving to a state that had declared marriages like hers void, and then (2) getting a court to declare her own marriage null and void.

Section 132 does not include language that expressly resolves this difficulty. Fortunately, § 134 casts considerable light on the appropriate resolution of this problem. Section 134 reads, "If any effect of a marriage created by the law of one state is deemed by the courts of another state sufficiently offensive to the policy of the latter state, the latter state will refuse to give that effect to the marriage."[9]

On first reading, this section might seem to imply that each state is permitted to refuse to recognize the validity of a marriage if that marriage was "sufficiently offensive" to that state's public policy. However, *comment a* to § 134 makes clear that the "action of the state in refusing to give effect to a marriage on the ground stated in this Section does *not* deny the validity of the marriage, but precludes the enjoyment within the state of some particular right or other interest incident to the marriage."[10] Thus, § 134 does not permit a subsequent domicile to refuse to recognize the validity of a marriage offensive to its public policy, but merely to refuse to afford some of the rights incident to marriage, assuming that such a refusal does not offend constitutional guarantees. The example offered to illustrate the point is that an individual who had entered into a polygamous marriage that was recognized by the domiciliary state might nonetheless be prevented from cohabiting with both of his wives in a state in which polygamy was very offensive to local public policy.[11]

Consider a different scenario. Two individuals are precluded by their current domicile from marrying, so they go to a neighboring state, marry, and then return to their domicile claiming to be legally married. In this case, the domicile might not only refuse to give effect to the marriage—that is, might preclude the enjoyment of some particular right or interest incident to the union—but might also refuse to recognize the validity of the marriage.[12] *Comment a* to § 134 specifically discusses how such a marriage should be treated, suggesting, "Wherever a particularly strong policy of the state at the time of the marriage is concerned, the validity of the marriage may be involved under the rule stated in §§ 131 and 132."[13] However, the comment points out, "If the question is that of giving effect to a marriage in a state where neither party was domiciled at the time of the marriage, the case does not fall under §131 or 132 but is within the rule stated in this Section."[14] Thus, § 134 of the *First Restatement* makes clear that the validity of a marriage may be at issue if it offends the public policy of the domiciliary state at the time of the marriage, but not if it offends the public policy of some future domiciliary state.

THE *SECOND RESTATEMENT*

Just as there has been unnecessary confusion about how to interpret the *First Restatement* with respect to whether subsequent domiciles can refuse to recognize marriages valid in the domicile at the time of the marriage, there has been similar unnecessary confusion with respect to the position articulated in the *Second Restatement of the Conflict of Laws.* Section 283(1) reads, "The validity of a marriage will be determined by the local law of the state which, with respect to the particular issue, has the most significant relationship to the spouses and the marriage under the principles stated in § 6."[15]

Section 6 reads,

> (1) A court, subject to constitutional restrictions, will follow a statutory directive of its own state on choice of law.
> (2) When there is no such directive, the factors relevant to the choice of the applicable rule of law include
> (a) the needs of the interstate and international systems,
> (b) the relevant policies of the forum,
> (c) the relevant policies of other interested states and the relative interests of those states in the determination of the particular issue,
> (d) the protection of justified expectations,
> (e) the basic policies underlying the particular field of law,
> (f) certainty, predictability and uniformity of result, and
> (g) ease in the determination and application of the law to be applied.[16]

Arguably, § 6(2) directs that the law of the domicile at the time of the marriage rather than the law of some future domicile be applied. Certainly, the needs of the interstate and international systems would support recognizing marriages valid in the domicile$_m$.[17] States, interested third parties, and the parties themselves could make plans based on the legal validity of their marriage if the law of the domicile at the time of the marriage determined that union's validity. If instead the law of the future domicile were the relevant standard, marriages could be retroactively nullified if one of the "married" parties were to subsequently move to a state that did not recognize such marriages and then were to challenge the validity of the marriage there.[18] Insofar as the interstate or international system would benefit from having a clear rule that promotes the continuity and certainty of marriage, it would be important to establish a system that would not make the validity of a marriage contracted years ago dependent upon where a couple decides to retire or where an individual seeking to avoid his or her marital obligations is willing to be domiciled.

Consider a marriage that is celebrated in the state where both parties are domiciled and that they intend to make their home. This would be the paradigmatic example of a valid marriage, assuming that the marriage is valid according to the law of that state.[19] Yet, if the law of some future domicile might apply, even the validity of this marriage would be at risk. A system that allowed this result would be a public policy nightmare.[20]

The forum would have an interest in recognizing marriages valid in the domicile$_m$, at least in part, because it would have an interest in assuring that the valid marriages of its own current domiciliaries will be recognized elsewhere, even if those domiciliaries decide sometime in the future to move and make another state their home. If State A reserves the right to decide whether to recognize marriages celebrated in State B by State B's domiciliaries, State B might reserve for itself the same right with respect to State A's domiciliaries. If each state reserves for itself the right to decide whether to recognize marriages that were valid in the domicile at the time of the marriage, domiciliaries will never be certain that their current marriages will continue to be recognized should they decide to move elsewhere.

Having State A reserve the right to decide whether to recognize the marriages of State B's former domiciliaries and vice versa might not have such terrible consequences if our society were an extremely immobile one in which married couples rarely if ever changed their domiciles.[21] In a very mobile society like ours, however, such a system would be disastrous, since all of the rights and obligations attendant on marriage[22] would depend upon the eventual choice of domicile of either or both parties to the marriage. Such a system might induce individuals not to marry, since a couple who did not plan on making a state their permanent home might defer marriage because their union would have to be "revalidated" in their future home state anyway. Further, even a couple who had decided that one state would be their permanent home might not feel secure. Given the relatively low success rate of marriage,[23] each member of the couple might wonder whether their marriage might fall apart like so many others and, if so, whether the other member of the couple might move to a jurisdiction which would hold that the marriage was void and thus had never existed.

The state has an interest in promoting marriage[24] and will undermine rather than promote that interest by acting in ways that induce other states to refuse recognition of marriages that do not meet their local requirements.[25] State A's reserving judgment about the validity of State B's domiciliaries' marriages, State B's recognition notwithstanding, may induce State B to do the same with respect to State A's domiciliaries' marriages. By the same token, State A's recognizing those marriages of State B's domiciliaries that State B recognizes may induce State B to do the same with respect to State A's domiciliaries' marriages.[26] Thus, a state's willingness to recognize marriages valid in a different state which was the domicile at the time of the marriage will promote the stability and certainty of marriage, and a state's unwillingness to do so may promote the opposite result.

The reciprocity concern[27] discussed above is implicated whether two different states[28] or two different countries[29] are concerned, although there may be many more instances in which the domiciliaries of one state (for example, Ohio) marry and then subsequently move to another state (for example, Illinois) than in which domiciliaries of one country (for example, France) marry and then move to a particular state (for example, Ohio).[30] While the state interest in recognizing marriages valid in other countries should not be underestimated, there are even greater interests at stake in recognizing marriages that were valid in other states.

The rule of comity is based upon notions of reciprocity.[31] States will be more willing to give effect to sister states' laws and policies if confident that their sister states will respond in kind. Thus, in situations in which application of either law would be constitutionally permissible, a state might lean more heavily towards the application of its own law if the other state was viewed as applying its own law whenever possible. Indeed, there could be spillover effects into other areas of law if a state believed that its own law was not being given its due by another state. Thus, if State A refuses to recognize marriages celebrated by State B's domiciliaries in State B, State B might decide not only to do the same with respect to State A's domiciliaries' marriages but also might refuse to enforce other kinds of contracts having their inception in State A.[32]

Certainty, predictability, and uniformity of result are obviously promoted by using the domicile$_{m}$'s law, since it would be clear whether the marriage was valid by referring to the domicile$_{m}$'s law at the time of the marriage. Otherwise, one would never be certain about the validity of the marriage as long as one state refused to recognize such unions, since there would always be the possibility that one of the "married" partners would move to that state and then contest the validity of the marriage.[33]

The protection of justified expectations would militate in favor of recognizing using the domicile$_{m}$'s law.[34] Otherwise, it would seem that there could be no "justified" expectations as long as one state refused to recognize such marriages, since one of the parties to the marriage could always move to that state to contest the validity of the union there.[35] Indeed, precisely because a state's currently recognizing a marriage would not guarantee that the state would continue to recognize that marriage, the mere fact that no state currently refused to recognize particular unions would not preclude some state in the future from refusing to recognize such marriages. Thus, one's expectations about the validity of the marriage might not be "justified," even if all states currently recognized a particular marriage.

Most if not all of the factors in § 6 militate in favor of using the domicile$_m$'s law to determine the validity of a marriage. Yet, the point is not merely that the § 6 factors would support looking to the domicile$_m$'s rather than the domicile$_f$'s law; rather, it is that the *Second Restatement*, properly understood, requires that the domicile$_m$'s law rather than the domicile$_f$'s law be used to determine the validity of the marriage.

When § 283(1) suggests that a marriage's validity is "determined by the local law of the state which, with respect to the particular issue, has the most significant relationship to the spouses of the marriage," the section does not specify which states should be considered as candidates for "the state with most significant contacts." It is unclear whether this only refers to interested states at the time of the marriage[36] or, instead, can include any states with contacts during the lifetime of that union.[37] *Comment c* to subsection (1) explains that there are two states whose laws might potentially apply to determine the validity of a marriage: the "state where the spouses were domiciled before the marriage and where they make their home immediately thereafter" and the "state where the marriage was celebrated." The factors discussed in § 6 will help determine which of these two states' laws should apply. There simply is no provision discussing when a domicile acquired years in the future may invalidate a marriage.

The domicile at the time of the marriage "has an obvious interest in the application of a rule forbidding the marriage of persons with certain degrees of relationship" but "may have little interest in the application to an out-of-state marriage of a rule regulating the form in which a marriage should be celebrated."[38] The state of celebration will have different priorities, since the "state where the marriage was celebrated may have a real interest in the application to non-residents of a rule regulating the form that a marriage ceremony should take and little interest in the application of a rule directed to incestuous marriages."[39] Section 283(1) is not designed to allow some future domicile to determine the validity of a marriage[40] but, rather, to help establish whether the law of the domicile or the state of celebration should be controlling.[41]

The position of the *Second Restatement* is even clearer when one considers § 283(2), which states that a "marriage which satisfies the requirements of the state where the marriage was contracted will everywhere be recognized as valid unless it violates the strong public policy of another state which had the most significant relationship to the spouses and the marriage at the time of the marriage."[42] It would make no sense for § 283(1) to suggest that the law of the state with the most significant contacts at any time during the marriage would determine the union's validity and also that a marriage will be valid unless it violates the strong public policy of the state with the most significant relationship to the marriage and the parties at the time of the marriage. Rather, the only plausible interpretation is that the "most significant relationship" test will pick out one of the following potential candidates: (a) the domicile of either party at the time of the marriage, (b) the state of celebration, and (c) the state where the couple plans to live immediately after the marriage.[43] It simply is not reasonable to interpret the *Second Restatement* as allowing subsequent domiciliary states to undermine the validity of a marriage that the states of celebration and domicile at the time of the marriage had recognized.

Both *Restatements* suggest that a subsequent domiciliary state must recognize a marriage valid in both the states of celebration and domicile at the time of the marriage. It will be easier to understand that claim once it is understood why a subsequent domicile can refuse to recognize a marriage validly celebrated in a former domicile that is a foreign country rather than a sister state.

DOMICILE AT THE TIME OF THE MARRIAGE

Traditionally, states were viewed as having virtually unlimited discretion with respect to their local marriage laws because domestic relations were not viewed as a matter of constitutional concern.[44] Late in the nineteenth century, the United States Supreme Court made clear that marriage was subject to the control of the legislature.[45] For example, the legislature prescribes the "age at which parties may contract to marry, the procedure or form essential to constitute marriage, the duties and obligations it creates, its effects upon the property rights of both, present and prospective, and the acts which may constitute grounds for its dissolution."[46] Further, the Court made clear that the state rather than the federal legislature has the responsibility of setting up the marriage laws—"the whole subject of the domestic relations of husband and wife, parent and child, belongs to the law of the state, and not to the laws of the United States."[47] Numerous courts ruled that domestic relations were not appropriately regulated by Congress.[48] Indeed, some courts suggested that the power of a state to set up its own marriage laws was no more constrained than was the power of a foreign country to set up its own marriage laws.[49]

Current domestic relations jurisprudence suggests that the traditional view accorded too much power to the states. First, traditional claims to the contrary notwithstanding, Congress can legislate in the area of domestic relations if clear and substantial federal interests are at stake,[50] for example, Congress passed the Parental Kidnapping Prevention Act.[51] Second, states are limited with respect to the kinds of burdens they can place on the fundamental right to marry,[52] for example, they cannot enact a blanket prohibition barring all prisoners from marrying.[53]

Although the state's power over domestic relations is not as robust as courts in the previous century suggested, states are still given great deference with respect to their marital laws. Yet, the point here is not to establish which of the domicile's marital prohibitions are constitutional, but to see which if any of a *subsequent* domicile's prohibitions may be applied to a couple who had been previously married elsewhere. The practices of legislatures and courts of the nineteenth and twentieth centuries are important to examine because they will help identify those prohibitions that may permissibly be imposed by the domicile at the time of the marriage but that nonetheless may *not* be imposed by a subsequent domicile. Thus, cases involving interracial marriage must be examined, not because states would or could now enact such a prohibition,[54] but because the ways that such marriages were treated by the courts may nonetheless be instructive with respect to the issues raised here. So, too, irrespective of current laws on the subject, it will be instructive to examine how courts treated the marriages of individuals barred by their then-current domiciles from marrying their marital partners,[55] precisely because that may help explain some of the distinctions at issue here.

AVOIDING THE DOMICILE'S MARITAL PROHIBITION

Individuals who had been precluded from marrying another individual by a state might have decided to accept that fate[56] or might have decided to move to a different state that did not preclude their marrying.[57] The latter option would have clear costs, however, such as the loss of one's job and the distance from one's friends and family. A less costly alternative might be to go to a different state to marry but return to the domicile hoping that the home state would recognize the marriage which had been validly celebrated elsewhere.

When a couple goes to another state to marry and then returns to the domicile asking that the marriage be recognized, two separate issues should not be conflated: (1) whose law applies, and (2) what does the relevant law say about the contested marriage. As suggested in the previous chapter, the interplay of (1) and (2) is not as straightforward as might be supposed. If one were simply to determine which state had the most significant contacts with the parties or the marriage and then apply that state's laws, then one might expect that a marriage violating the laws of the state with the most significant contacts would not be recognized whether that union was prohibited or declared void, since in either case the marriage would not be permitted in the state.[58] As a general matter, however, when a domicile merely prohibits a marriage rather than declares it void, the domicile will recognize the prohibited union if it is validly celebrated elsewhere; if the domicile declares the marriage void, however, the union's validity will not be recognized.[59]

Often, a state that found a particular marital union strongly offensive to its public policy would declare that marriage void and would not recognize such a marriage of its domiciliaries even if they had married in a state recognizing such unions. Several courts made clear their unwillingness to recognize the marriages of domiciliaries who had gone elsewhere to evade the laws of the domicile.[60] For example, the marriage of individuals who were too closely related by blood might not be recognized, even if their marriage was in fact permissible in the state of celebration.[61]

Many southern states viewed interracial marriages as strongly offensive to their public policy and would not recognize them even if validly celebrated elsewhere.[62] Northern states seemed to view such marriages as less offensive to public policy and were more likely to recognize them if they were celebrated in a state where such unions were legally recognized.[63] Thus, if an interracial couple tried to evade a southern domicile's refusal to allow them to marry by marrying in a state that permitted such unions and then returned to the domicile claiming to have a valid marriage, the southern domicile would likely not recognize the marriage whereas a northern domicile in similar circumstances might recognize the marriage, notwithstanding the state's own prohibition.[64]

A separate question would be whether the union was in fact an interracial marriage as defined by the statute. An antimiscegenation statute might be held not to have been violated if, for example, the mixed-race individual did not have the requisite amount of "negro blood."[65] Even a statute prohibiting whites and mulattoes from marrying might be held not to have been violated by a white's marrying a child of a mulatto man and a white woman.[66] Nonetheless, in most southern states with antimiscegenation laws, marriages that fell within the statutorily defined prohibition were held to be void and of no legal effect.[67]

SUBSEQUENT DOMICILES

Bracketing constitutional constraints, the domicile at the time of the marriage can refuse to recognize a marriage validly celebrated elsewhere if that union violates local law and the state has made clear that such marriages will not be recognized. That does not imply, however, that a subsequent domicile has the same power. Different issues are raised if (a) a couple domiciled in State A goes to State B, marries, and then returns to State A to live, despite State A's having made that marriage void, and (b) a couple domiciled and married in State B subsequently moves to State A to live, despite State A's having made that marriage void.[68] The relevant question is whether the two scenarios are sufficiently dissimilar to require different outcomes with respect to the validity of the marriages.[69]

The Supreme Court of North Carolina had to decide whether the state should recognize an interracial marriage validly celebrated in South Carolina.[70] The court found that there had been no intention to evade the law of North Carolina, since there had been no intent to return to the state after the marriage,[71] and further found that an interracial marriage valid in the domicile and the state of celebration at the time of the marriage had to be recognized by the subsequent domicile.[72] The state supreme court made clear that its ruling would not protect an interracial couple who had purposely tried to evade the laws of North Carolina with the intent of living in the state after having married elsewhere.[73] Indeed, the same court held void an interracial marriage which had been celebrated by North Carolina domiciliaries in a state where such marriages were legal.[74]

The North Carolina decision was predicated on the couple's having been domiciled in South Carolina rather than in North Carolina at the time of the marriage.[75] The defendant had been domiciled in North Carolina, but had left the state and married in South Carolina.[76] The issue that had to be determined by the trier-of-fact was whether the defendant had abandoned North Carolina with the intention of making South Carolina her domicile or instead had remained a North Carolina domiciliary.[77] The validity of her marriage depended upon her having done the former.

Identification of a couple's current domicile can sometimes be rather difficult.[78] Further, there is no requirement that states agree about which state is in fact the domicile of a particular individual.[79] Thus, it could have been (but in fact was not) that South Carolina had determined that the couple had become domiciled in South Carolina but that, later, North Carolina had determined that at least one of the parties had always been domiciled in North Carolina.[80]

Once the North Carolina Supreme Court found that the defendant had been domiciled in South Carolina, the court had to address whether North Carolina could refuse to recognize a marriage recognized by the states of celebration and domicile at the time of the marriage. The North Carolina Attorney General argued that just as incestuous and polygamous marriages, although valid where celebrated, need not be recognized as valid in a subsequent domicile, so, too, interracial marriages need not be recognized in a subsequent domicile even if valid in the states of celebration and domicile at the time of the marriage.[81] However, the court rejected that argument and reasoned that the costs of recognizing the marriage would be less dear than the costs of refusing to do so.[82]

It is instructive to examine the reasoning of the court. First, it is important to understand why the attorney general analogized interracial marriages to polygamous or incestuous unions. Such marriages are considered to be contrary to the law of civilized nations ("the law of nature") and thus need not be recognized in a subsequent domicile even if they are celebrated in a country which recognizes such unions.[83] Since it might seem that no court would recognize a polygamous or incestuous marriage,[84] the attorney general's argument would seem to have much persuasive force if, indeed, interracial marriages are appropriately analogized to polygamous or incestuous unions.

The rhetorical force of the attorney general's analogy diminishes significantly upon closer examination. The attorney general likened an interracial marriage to an incestuous one, but not only did not mention the obvious disanalogies between the two kinds of marriages but also neglected to mention that not all incestuous marriages are thought to violate the law of nature and thus to be subject to nonrecognition by subsequent domiciles.[85] Only marriages between those "in the direct lineal line of consanguinity . . . [or] those contracted between brothers and sisters"[86] are thought to violate natural law[87] and thus need not be recognized even if validly celebrated in another domicile.[88] For example, in *Sutton v. Warren*, the Supreme Judicial Court of Massachusetts recognized a marriage between aunt and nephew that had been validly celebrated in a different domicile, notwithstanding the impermissibility of such a union in Massachusetts,[89] precisely because the marriage had not violated natural law.[90]

The distinction between different kinds of incestuous relationships is important, although not because it provides a universal standard defining incest. (There is no such universal standard since, for example, some states define first-cousin marriages as incestuous while others do not.) Rather, the distinction is important because it undermines the persuasiveness of the analogy offered by the North Carolina Attorney General.

Basically, the issue as framed by the attorney general was whether a marriage that a subsequent domicile viewed as no less offensive than a polygamous or incestuous union could be treated as void by that state, despite its having been valid in the states of domicile and celebration at the time of the marriage. The implications of such a position would be important and far-reaching, because a subsequent domicile could claim that *any* prohibited marriage was as offensive to public policy as an incestuous union and thus would not need to be recognized.[91] Were the court to have accepted the attorney general's argument, it would have provided a way for any state to refuse to recognize any marriage of which it did not approve, regardless of whether or how long it had been valid elsewhere.

It is clear, however, that the attorney general's argument was flawed. There is no closer "analogy" to incest than another example of incest. Yet, as the Supreme Judicial Court of Massachusetts had made clear in *Sutton*, even another example of incest is not included within the rule of comity, which permits subsequent domiciles to refuse to extend recognition to a marriage by individuals domiciled elsewhere. The law of nature exception does not provide a loophole whereby subsequent domiciles can refuse to recognize a marriage whenever it is too offensive to local taste. Rather, that exception is narrowly drawn and provides a bright line rule about which kinds of marriages are subject to this kind of treatment.[92]

The claim here is not that a state is precluded from defining what constitutes incest but rather that a couple domiciled and married in a different state may not be subjected to the local laws regarding their incapacity to marry if they later move to that state, assuming that the law of nature exception is not applicable.[93] Of course, a separate question is whether the latter state could criminalize the couple's having sexual relations, marriage notwithstanding.[94] Thus, a state might criminalize sexual relations between married individuals too closely related by blood.[95] Or, the state might allow marriage between such individuals to be an affirmative defense to a charge of incest.[96]

Natural law is used in different senses, sometimes referring to the law of civilized nations ("law of nature") and sometimes referring to what God allegedly forbids. For example, the North Carolina Supreme Court called the interracial marriage "unnatural,"[97] but was not thereby implying that the marriage violated the law of nature or that the marriage did not have to be recognized.[98]

Natural law, where that refers to the law of civilized nations as used in the domestic relations context, is very narrowly defined. The case law makes clear that it refers only to polygamous and certain incestuous relationships. It does not refer to a particular level of disapproval of particular marriages; else, as long as North Carolinians had disapproved of interracial marriages with at least as much intensity as they had disapproved of incestuous unions, the North Carolina Supreme Court could have refused to recognize the South Carolina marriage, regardless of the domicile of the marital couple at the time of their marriage. By the same token, if the North Carolina Attorney General's argument had accurately reflected the law, then the Supreme Judicial Court of Massachusetts might have said in *Sutton* that marriages between uncle and niece were void in Massachusetts, regardless of the law of the domicile at the time the parties had married, as long as the citizens of Massachusetts had disapproved of incestous marriages between uncle and niece with the same intensity as they had disapproved of incestuous marriages between father and daughter. However, neither the Massachusetts nor the North Carolina court tried to assess the degree of disapproval accorded to the prohibited marriages, for example, by seeing whether interracial or uncle-niece marriages, like father-daughter marriages, were void in the domicile, or by seeing whether a sexual relationship between uncle and niece or between interracial partners would be subject to the same criminal penalties as would a relationship between father and daughter. The courts instead recognized the narrow confines of the "law of nature" exception and thus refused to apply it.

A different sense of natural law refers to what God allegedly forbids. For example, in 1955, the Virginia Supreme Court cited with approval an opinion by the Indiana Supreme Court in which the latter court claimed that natural law fordbids intermarriage.[99] However, as the United States Supreme Court made clear, states cannot preclude their own domiciliaries from entering into an interracial marriage, purported natural or divine law notwithstanding.[100] Thus, the law of nature exception cannot be understood to apply merely because some group claims that a particular marriage violates their own view of natural law. Rather, this particular exception refers only to polygamous and certain incestuous marriages.

The view offered here regarding when marriages must be recognized might seem to be contradicted by a case in which the Tennessee Supreme Court considered whether an interracial couple domiciled and legally married in Mississippi at the time of their union had violated Tennessee law by living together in the state of Tennessee.[101] That opinion is noteworthy for its terseness since, for example, it did not include the wording of the relevant statute, but merely referred to "the act of the General Assembly of the 27th of June, 1870."[102] The statute that the couple had allegedly violated read: "That the intermarriage of white persons with negroes, mulattoes, or persons of mixed blood, descended from a negro to the third generation inclusive, or their living together as man and wife in this State, is hereby prohibited."[103]

The opinion also did not specify whether the accused interracial couple had been domiciliaries of Tennessee and had attempted to evade local law by going elsewhere to marry or, instead, had been domiciliaries of a different state, had married there, and had then attempted to cohabit in the state of Tennessee.[104] Although other courts had found this distinction crucial, the Tennessee court did not seem to believe this factual matter relevant, since the court framed the relevant question as whether "a marriage in Mississippi protect[s] persons who live together in this State in violation of [law]."[105] To make matters even more complicated, on one reading of the opinion, it would not have mattered whether the couple's marriage was valid,[106] since Tennessee law prohibited interracial couples from "living together as man and wife in this State."[107] The court could have been suggesting that, even if validly married, the couple was not entitled to live together in Tennessee.[108] Thus, the court might have held that cohabitation was a right or incident of marriage the enjoyment of which the state was unwilling to allow in that particular case at that time. Just as the state would not allow an individual to cohabit "with his numerous wives" merely because he had lawfully married them elsewhere,[109] the state would not allow this individual to live with his wife in Tennessee.

Although the above would have provided an explanation of the court's position, there is reason to believe that the court was in fact refusing to recognize the Mississippi marriage. The court implied that the "capacity of the parties to contract the marriage"[110] was at issue in this case and that these parties could not contract a marriage with each other, law of the state of celebration and domicile at the time of marriage notwithstanding. Further, when later offering an explanation of its own opinion, the Tennessee

Supreme Court suggested that the marriage had been held to have been void and of no legal effect.[111]

When explaining the rationale for its holding, the Tennessee court suggested that a state "cannot be subjected to the recognition of a fact or act contravening its public policy and against good morals, as lawful, because it was made or existed in a State having no prohibition against it or even permitting it."[112] Basically, the court argued that merely because a marriage was validly celebrated in a different domiciliary state would not establish that the marriage was not contrary to local public policy and thus would not establish that Tenneesee should recognize the union.

Unless suitably modified, however, such a position would simply do away with comity. Presumably, whenever a marriage is prohibited in a state, that union is thought to violate public policy; else, it would not have been prohibited. Thus, the position articulated by the Tennessee court would imply that any marriage not in accord with local policy could therefore simply not be recognized, even if validly celebrated in the neighboring domiciliary state twenty years earlier.[113]

The Tennessee Supreme Court understood that a state's reserving for itself the right to refuse to recognize any marriage validly celebrated elsewhere merely because that union was not in accord with local requirements would have unpalatable results. In a different case, the court explained that it "will not do to say that every provision of a statute prohibiting marriage, under certain circumstances, or between certain parties, is indicative of a state policy in the sense in which it is used in this connection. To so hold would be to overturn this most solemn relation, involving legitimacy of offspring, homestead dower, and the rights of property."[114] Nonetheless, the court basically suggested that the decision about whether to recognize a marriage validly celebrated in another domiciliary state must be left up to each state. "Each state or nation has ultimately to determine for itself what statutory inhibitions are by it intended to be imperative, as indicative of the decided policy of the state concerning the morals and good order of society, to that degree which will render it proper to disregard the *jus gentium* of 'valid where solemnized, valid everywhere.' "[115]

The Tennessee Supreme Court refused to distinguish between: (1) individuals who had been domiciliaries attempting to evade the laws of the state, and (2) individuals who had married in good faith in their own domicile. The court held that the legislature has the "power to enact what marriages shall be void in its own state, notwithstanding their validity in the state where celebrated, whether contracted between parties who were in good faith domiciled in the state where the ceremony was performed, or between parties who left the state of domicile for the purpose of avoiding its statutes."[116]

Yet, this analysis is faulty both because it undermines the domicile's power to determine the conditions under which its own domiciliaries may be wed and because it ignores the traditional exceptions of polygamy and certain incestuous relations which other courts have found so important. Rather than respect the power traditionally given to the domiciliary state at the time of the marriage and rather than respect the traditional international exceptions to comity involving incestuous or polygamous marriages, the Tennessee Supreme Court was willing to allow each state to decide for itself which marriages would be recognized, notwithstanding the justified expectations of couples who may have marrried years earlier and notwithstanding the legitimacy of children and the property rights that are allegedly such important considerations.

The court reasoned that if the Mississippi marriage were recognized, "we might have in Tennessee the father living with his daughter, the son with the mother, the brother with the sister, in lawful wedlock, because they had formed such relations in a State or country where they were not prohibited. The Turk or Mohammedan, with his numerous wives, may establish his harem at the doors of the capitol, and we are without remedy."[117] Yet, the court's reasoning was disingenuous for two reasons. First, it gave as examples precisely those marriages that violated the "law of nature" and thus did not have to be recognized. Second, as suggested above, even if a marriage's validity is recognized, this does not establish that all of the incidents of the marriage must be recognized—for example, allowing the individual to live with both of his wives.[118] Thus, if the fears articulated were the genuine concerns of the court, the court could have recognized the interracial marriage and still not have been forced to recognize the polygamous or incestuous marriages, both because they were included within the law of nature exception discussed by the supreme courts of Massachusetts and North Carolina among others, and because the individuals would not have been allowed to cohabit anyway, since the incidents of marriage are treated differently than is the validity of the marriage itself.

Perhaps the most ironic aspect of the Tennessee Supreme Court opinion was that the court ignored its own precedents to reach the desired result. In a previous case, the court had upheld the validity of a polygamous marriage contracted "according to the usages of the Cherokee tribe of Indians."[119] The court wrote, "Our courts of justice recognize as valid all marriages of a foreign country, if made in pursuance of the forms and usages of that country; and there is no reason why a marriage made and consummated in an Indian Nation should be subject to a different rule of action."[120] Yet, if a polygamous marriage should have been recognized, the same would be true of an interracial union, given that both were treated as void by the state of Tennessee.

The court recognized the apparent inconsistency of the holdings in the two cases and tried to distinguish the former by arguing that it concerned the "manner and form of marriage, and not the capacity of the parties to contract the marriage."[121] Yet, if a polygamous marriage did not involve the power of the parties to contract, given that the marriage was in accord with local law, then the same analysis would be appropriate for an interracial marriage. Ironically, the Tennessee court implied that it had to recognize a polygamous marriage valid in a foreign country but did not have to recognize an interracial marriage valid in a sister state. Yet, this is backwards, both because a sister state's marital law should be given at least as much deference as a foreign country's and because the existing domestic relations jurisprudence required the opposite conclusion.

COMITY

When criticizing the Tennessee opinion, one might argue that it reflected a bad policy choice or, instead, a failure to recognize the state's obligation to recognize those marriages valid in the states of celebration and domicile at the time of the marriage. The former would simply be questioning the wisdom of a decision while the latter would be making a much more damning criticism. The determination of which kind of criticism is appropriate in this kind of case depends on whether states should recognize the marriages performed in other state domiciles as a matter of comity or, instead, as a matter of constitutional obligation.[122]

The Supreme Court has described comity as "the recognition which one nation allows within its territory to the legislative, executive, or judicial acts of another nation, having due regard both to international duty and convenience, and to the rights of its own citizens, or of other persons who are under the protection of its laws."[123] Although there is no obligation to recognize a marriage celebrated in another country out of comity,[124] the impetus to do so is stronger than it would be were the question simply one of good will.

If the United States is to be more than a loose federation of independent sovereignties,[125] however, states do not and cannot stand in the same relation to each other as they do to foreign countries.[126] The comity that the acts of foreign nations are due is simply too weak a standard when the acts of a sister state are at issue. Further, precisely because the states are all part of one nation, there is less of a need to resort to the flexibility offered by comity, since there is no need to "be flexible enough to deal with totalitarian states, revolutionary states, legally unsophisticated states, or states with legal and cultural traditions fundamentally different from our own."[127]

The Supreme Court has suggested that comity may be "too fluid [and] ill-defined" a concept for domestic relations purposes insofar as the marital status conferred by another state is at issue.[128] The Court has expressed concern that "if decrees of a state altering the marital status of its domiciliaries are not valid throughout the Union even though the requirements of procedural due process are wholly met, a rule would be fostered which could not help but bring 'considerable disaster to innocent persons' and 'bastardize children hitherto supposed to be the offspring of lawful marriage.' "[129] The difficulties envisioned by the Court would certainly occur were the rule suggested by the Tennessee court adopted.

Justice Robert Jackson suggested that if "there is one thing that the people are entitled to expect from their lawmakers, it is rules of law that will enable individuals to tell whether they are married and, if so, to whom."[130] If a marriage can be retroactively invalidated by having one or both members of a couple move across state lines, individuals will not be secure in their knowledge concerning their marital status. Indeed, precisely because there is so much travel among the states,[131] it is important as a matter of public policy to establish that a marriage is valid anywhere in the United States if valid in the states of celebration and domicile at the time of the marriage.

A close examination of the *First* and *Second Restatements of the Conflict of Laws* reveals the important difference between the invalidation of a marriage by the domicile at the time of the marriage and such an invalidation by a domicile acquired years after the marriage had been celebrated. Even when states viewed themselves as independent sovereignties rather than as parts of a single nation, they realized the difficulties posed by refusing to recognize marriages valid in the states of domicile and celebration at the time of the marriage. Those refusing to recognize such marriages offered reasoning that obliterated the existing jurisprudence and significantly weakened the force of comity, as well as undermined the respect owed by states to sister states of the same federal union. Indeed, given the paucity of analysis and the specious reasoning, one infers that the Tennessee Supreme Court knew that it could not justify the result that it had nonetheless decided to reach.

Much has happened in this country since the North Carolina and Tennessee Supreme Courts were deciding whether to recognize interracial marriages validly celebrated in another domiciliary state. The United States Supreme Court has made clear that states do not have the power to prohibit such marriages, much less to refuse to recognize them when validly celebrated elsewhere. Further, to a much greater extent now than was true then, the states are integral parts of a single nation rather than a loose collection of independent sovereignties. Arguably, the Tennessee court was wrong both because its ruling deprived individuals of their fundamental right to marry and because it did not give the respect due to a marriage validly celebrated in a sister state that was the parties' domicile at the time of the marriage.

The claim that same-sex marriages trigger the law of nature exception is false, because that exception is very narrowly defined within the domestic relations context. Yet, the claims that same-sex marriage violate natural law in a broader sense and that such a violation justifies the state's refusal to recognize such marriages are also false, as will be explained in the next chapter.

NOTES

1. Harvey M. Applebaum, "Miscegenation Statutes: A Constitutional and Social Problem," 53 *Geo. L.J.* 49, 55 (1964) (suggesting that the "issue is more complex when parties domiciled and married elsewhere later move to a state which condemns the marriage").

2. P. H. V., Annotation, "Marriage Valid Where Celebrated, 127 *A.L.R.* 437, 444 (1940) ("by the greater weight of authority, a marriage celebrated in a state where it is valid, between parties resident at the time in that state, will be recognized at the forum as valid, although such a marriage, if celebrated in the latter state, would be invalid, regardless of the residence of the parties").

3. For example, in *Ex parte Kinney*, 14 F. Cas. 602, 606 (Case No. 7,825) (E.D. Va. 1879), the court argued that the Supreme Court had decided that states need not recognize marriages validly celebrated in other domiciliary states, citing *Paul v. Virginia*, 75 U.S. (8 Wall.) 168 (1868), a case in which the Court had discussed the power of a legislature to regulate insurance companies carrying on business within the state. The court ignored the important differences between natural and artificial persons (e.g., that only the former are protected by the Privileges and Immunities Clause of the Fourteenth Amendment—see *Paul*, 75 U.S. at 178–182; *Hague v. Committee for Industrial Organization*, 307 U.S. 496, 514 [1939]) and ignored the choice of law considerations. See *Kinney*, 14 F. Cas. at 606. *Paul* was later overruled on other grounds in *United States v. South-Eastern Underwriters Ass'n*, 322 U.S. 533 (1944), in which the Court held that the business of insurance was within the regulatory power of Congress under the Commerce Clause. See id. at 553.

In *Calma v. Calma*, the lower court held that because miscegenous marriages were not recognized in Virginia, an interracial marriage valid in New Jersey between individuals not domiciled in Virginia was nonetheless void in the state, choice of law issues notwithstanding. See 128 S.E.2d 440, 442 (Va. 1962) (describing lower court opinion). That opinion was not appealed. See id. In the subsequent case between the same parties, the Supreme Court of Virginia ruled that the "plaintiff's marriage was adjudicated in the first suit and cannot be relitigated." See id. at 444. It was unclear whether this meant that the Virginia Supreme Court believed that the state could ignore valid marriages contracted in other states by their own domiciliaries if those marriages violated Virginia public policy. See Walter Wadlington, "The *Loving* Case: Virginia's Anti-Miscegenation Statute in Historical Perspective," 52 *Va. L. Rev.* 1189, 1206–7 (1966) ("Although some might urge that the second *Calma* case indicates that the Supreme Court of Appeals would be reluctant to recognize a foreign miscegenous marriage valid at the domicile and not designed to evade Virginia's marriage law, this is not really inferable from the opinion").

4. See *State v. Bell*, 66 Tenn. (7 Baxt.) 9 (1872).

5. American Law Institute *Restatement of the Law of the Conflict of Laws*, § 121 (St. Paul, MN: American Law Institute Publishers, 1934) (*Restatement [First] of the Conflict of Laws*).

6. See id.

7. Even though these marriages are not permitted in N, it is not clear whether they are merely prohibited or made void, which in turn would influence whether N would recognize those marriages.

8. See, for example, *In re Estate of Stiles*, 391 N.E.2d 1026, 1027 (Ohio 1979) ("We hold that the marriage of an uncle to his niece is incestuous and void ab initio. To hold otherwise would be a mockery of the statute and emasculate the purpose of marriage laws"). For a discussion of some of the effects of declaring a marriage void ab initio, see *Garcia v. Garcia*, 127 N.W. 586, 589 (S.D. 1910) ("The consequences of declaring a marriage void ab initio and annulling the same are very serious. Its effect is to bastardize innocent children, deprive them of their inheritance, and to make the parties whose marriage was legal and valid in the state where contracted [potentially] criminally liable").

9. See *First Restatement*, § 134.

10. Id. (emphasis added).

11. See § 134, cmt. c, illustration.

12. See id., cmt. a. ("Wherever a particularly strong policy of the state at the time of the marriage is concerned, the validity of the marriage may be involved under the rule stated in §§ 131 and 132. If the question is that of giving effect to a marriage in a state where neither party was domiciled at the time of the marriage, the case does not fall under §131 or 132 but is within the rule stated in this Section.") See also Anthony Dominic D'Amato, Note, "Conflict of Laws Rules and the Interstate Recognition of Same-Sex Marriages," 1995 *U. Ill. L. Rev.* 911, 922 ("states are free, within constitutional limitations, to delineate the circumstances under which they will recognize a marriage involving their domiciliaries").

13. See *First Restatement*, § 134, cmt a.

14. See id., cmt a.

15. American Law Institute, *Restatement (Second) of the Conflict of Laws*, § 283(1) (St. Paul, Minn.: American Law Institute Publishers, 1971).

16. Id. § 6.

17. See *Vandever v. Industrial Commission of Arizona*, 714 P.2d 866, 869 (Ariz. App. 1985) ("Justifications for the rule include predictability and the interstate order arising from society's interest in marriage."); Candace L. Sage, Note, "Sister-State Recognition of Valid Same-Sex Marriages; *Baehr v. Lewin*—How Will It Play in Peoria," 28 *Ind. L. Rev.* 115, 116–17 (1994) ("Interstate recognition of marriages exists not merely as a matter of comity, but also because public policy favors predictability, certainty, and uniformity of result in protecting the justified expectation of the parties").

18. See *Medway v. Needham*, 16 Mass. 157, 159 (Mass. 1819) ("it would produce greater inconveniences than those attempted to be guarded against, if a contract of this solemn nature [marriage] valid in a neighboring state, could be dissolved at the will of either of the parties, by stepping over the line of a state, which might prohibit such marriages").

19. C. W. Taintor II, "What Law Governs the Ceremony, Incidents and Status of Marriage," 19 *B.U. L. Rev.* 353, 367 (1939) ("If the parties are both domiciled at the place of ceremony and intend to make their home there, no other state is interested; and if the law of that state will create the status, the marriage is valid; otherwise it is void"). But see Monrad G. Paulsen & Michael I. Covern, " 'Public

Policy' in the Conflict of Laws," 56 *Colum. L. Rev.* 969, 994–95 (1956) ("A marriage valid when made both at the place of celebration and at the domicil of the parties may possibly be disregarded on public policy grounds if the parties move to a new domiciliary state").

20. See Mark Strasser, "*Loving* the *Romer* Out for *Baehr*: On Acts in Defense of Marriage and the Constitution," 58 *U. Pitt. L. Rev.* 279, 311 (1997) ("Allowing states to invalidate previously valid marriages would be a public policy disaster—the justified and settled expectations of the parties would be disappointed, the status of the children would be unclear, title to property would be clouded, and third party creditors would be in a tenuous position"). See also Maurice J. Holland, "The Modest Usefulness of DOMA Section 2," 32 *Creighton L. Rev.* 395, 404 (1998) ("it would be an intolerable situation in the United States if couples who were lawfully married in the state where they lived at the time of the marriage regularly faced the prospect of their marriages not being recognized should they subsequently move to a new domiciliary state under whose laws they would not have been issued a marriage license").

21. Even when societies were much less mobile, however, countries would tend to recognize those marriages validly celebrated elsewhere. See, for example, *Sutton v. Warren*, 51 Mass. 451, 452 (Mass. 1845) ("It is a well settled principle in our law, that marriages celebrated in other States or countries, if valid by the law of the country where they are celebrated, are of binding obligation within this Commonwealth, although the same might, by force of our laws, be held invalid, if contracted here").

22. *Williams v. North Carolina*, 317 U.S. 287, 298 (1942) ("*Williams I*") ("The marriage relation creates problems of large social importance. Protection of offspring, property interests, and the enforcement of marital responsibilities are but a few of commanding problems in the field of domestic relations with which the state must deal.")

23. See Ellyn Ferguson, "Marriage Activists Seek Help in Cutting U.S. Divorce Rates," *Courier-Journal* (Louisville, Ky.) May 25, 1996 at 3A ("About 40 percent of first marriages in the United States end in divorce.")

24. Beth A. Allen, Comment, "Same-Sex Marriage: A Conflict-of-Laws Analysis for Oregon," 32 *Willamette L. Rev.* 619, 626 (1996) ("Generally, states encourage marriage because it creates stability, limits the social costs of disorganized breakdown of relationships, encourages continuation of the population, and provides an environment for education of the young").

25. See Brainerd Currie & Herma Hill Schreter, "Unconstitutional Discrimination in the Conflict of Laws: Privileges and Immunities," 69 *Yale L.J.* 1323, 1361 (1960) ("In general, withholding the benefits of local laws from citizens of other states will invite retaliation, to the detriment of local citizens"); Gary J. Simson, "State Autonomy in Choice of Law: A Suggested Approach," 52 *S. Cal. L. Rev.* 61, 80 (1978) ("If, however, a particular foreign jurisdiction's courts repeatedly ignore American interests in influencing outcome that rival or outweigh any other jurisdiction's, then the court at least arguably should opt for an approach that, without sacrificing uniformity, denies the specific jurisdiction's interests their due").

26. Indeed, it may be that only after provincial attitudes yield retaliatory measures by other states will states become more cooperative. See Currie & Schreter, "Unconstitutional Discrimination in the Conflict of Laws," 69 *Yale L.J.* at 1361 ("In

general, withholding the benefits of local laws from citizens of other states will invite retaliation, to the detriment of local citizens; retaliation will lead to reciprocity—a cumbersome device for ameliorating the effects of provincialism.")

27. See *Black's Law Dictionary*, 1270 (6th ed. 1990) (Reciprocity—"The term is used to denote the relation existing between two states when each of them gives the subjects of the other certain privileges, on condition that its own subjects shall enjoy similar privileges at the hands of the latter state.")

28. See *Forgan v. Bainbridge*, 274 P. 155, 158 (Ariz. 1928) ("when a sister state does not recognize and will not enforce in her courts our rule of law in regard to a certain class of contracts having their inception in this state, we are not required under the doctrine of comity to enforce similar contracts according to her rule, when such rule is directly opposed to our public policy").

29. *Hilton v. Guyot*, 159 U.S. 113, 227 (1895) ("judgments rendered in France, or in any other foreign country, by the laws of which our own judgments are reviewable upon the merits, are not entitled to full credit and conclusive effect when sued upon in this country").

30. To some extent, this would depend upon the state and countries at issue. For example, California would seem to attract more foreigners than other states. See David Wessel, "Nevada's Population Growth Outpaced Any Other State's in the Latest Year," *The Wall Street J.*, Dec. 31, 1996, at 2 (more foreigners moved to California than to any other state).

31. *Forgan*, 274 P. at 158 ("The rule of comity is essentially based upon the principle of reciprocity"); *Union Securities Co. v. Adams*, 236 P. 513, 517 (Wyo. 1925) ("the principle of comity is throughout the civilized world based upon mutuality and reciprocity, and, where it appears that no such reciprocity is extended, none is generally granted in return").

32. See Larry Kramer, "Return of the Renvoi," 66 *N.Y.U. L. Rev.* 979, 1026 (1991) (discussing "diffuse reciprocity").

33. *Stevenson v. Gray*, 56 Ky. 154, 169 (17 B. Mon. 193, 212–13) (Ky. 1856) ("The confusion and uncertainty with regard to the legitimacy of offspring, and the rights of property and succession, are not the only evils which would follow if the validity of a marriage were subject to be tried by the various laws to which the parties might at different times be personally subject"). See also *Medway*, 16 Mass. at 159 ("If the marriage takes place in a state whose laws allow it, the marriage is certainly good there; and it would produce greater inconveniences than those attempted to be guarded against, if a contract of this solemn nature valid in a neighboring state, could be dissolved at the will of either of the parties, by stepping over the line of a state, which might prohibit such marriages").

34. Willis L. M. Reese, "Marriage in American Conflicts of Laws," 26 *Int'l & Comp. L.Q.* 952, 955 (1977) ("parties enter marriage with forethought and in the expectation that their relationship will be a valid one. It is desirable that these expectations should not be disappointed"). Cf. *Garrett v. Chapman*, 449 P.2d 856, 860 (Or. 1969) ("The tenor of the *Restatement (Second)* is a recognition of the policy of upholding the validity of marriages entered into in good faith").

35. This would undermine an important feature of the current system. See Reese, "Marriage in American Conflicts of Laws," 26 *Int'l & Comp. L.Q.* at 955 ("parties enter marriage with forethought and in the expectation that their relationship will be a valid one. It is desirable that these expectations should not be disappointed. It

is also desirable that, to the extent possible, the choice-of-law rules applicable to marriage should be clear and precise so that the parties may be able to foretell with fair confidence what law will be applied to govern their relationship").

36. This might include the state that the couple was planning to make their domicile. See *Succession of Hernandez*, 46 La. Ann. 962, 990 (1894) ("The principle is well settled that the matrimonial rights of the wife, who marries with the intention of removing into another State, must be governed by the laws of her intended domicile.") See also D'Amato, "Conflict of Laws Rules," 1995 *U. Ill. L. Rev.* at 943 ("if Hawaii residents of the same sex marry in that state and if at the time of the marriage they intend to move to Illinois, Illinois would have a basis for arguing that it has the most significant relationship to the marriage").

37. Sondrea Joy King, Note, "Ya'll Cain't Do That Here: Will Texas Recognize Same-Sex Marriages Validly Contracted in Other States?" 2 *Tex. Wesleyan L. Rev.* 515, 537 (1996) ("section six does not address when the most significant relationship should be applied in a choice of law issue").

38. See *Second Restatement*, § 283, cmt. c.

39. Id.

40. See J. Phillip Johnson, "The Validity of a Marriage under the Conflict of Laws," 38 *N.D. L. Rev.* 442, 452 (1962) ("a subsequent state where the parties are domiciled may also rule on validity and should base its decision on the law of the domicil of the parties at the time of the marriage").

41. *In re Estate of Lenherr*, 314 A.2d 255, 258 (Pa. 1974) (applying *Second Restatement* to conclude that because "Leo and Sarah were residents of Pennsylvania before and after their West Virginia marriage, we have no trouble concluding that Pennsylvania has the most significant relationship to the spouses and the marriage"); *In re Takahashi's Estate*, 129 P.2d 217, 221–22 (Mont. 1942) ("it is the residence immediately prior to and at the time of the marriage that is of importance here").

42. King, "Ya'll Cain't Do That Here," 2 *Tex. Wesleyan L. Rev.* at 531 ("Subsection two applies the most significant relationship test at the time of the marriage. Although subsection one does not state the most significant relationship test should be applied at the time of marriage, the language in subsection two may be read in conjunction with subsection one to create this presumption.")

43. See Taintor, "What Law Governs," 19 *B.U. L. Rev.* at 367 ("The intrinsic validity of this status may be referred to the law of the place of ceremony, to the law of the domicil of both parties if they live in the same state, to the law of the domicils of either or both of the parties if they live in different states, or to the law of the state in which the parties intend to live as husband and wife.").

44. *Kinney*, 14 F. Cas. at 603 ("there is nothing in the national constitution expressly forbidding a state from abridging the right of marrying").

45. *Maynard v. Hill*, 125 U.S. 190, 204 (1888).

46. Id.

47. *Ex parte Burrus*, 136 U.S. 586, 593–94 (1890).

48. *Kinney*, 14 F. Cas. at 605 ("The fourteenth amendment gives no power to congress to interfere with the right of a state to regulate the domestic relations of its own citizens, and if a state enact such laws as those which have been quoted, the federal courts must respect them as they stand, without inquiring into the reasons of them"); *State v. Gibson*, 36 Ind. 389, 403 (1871) ("The right, in the states, to regulate and control, to guard, protect, and preserve this God-given, civilizing, and

Christianizing institution is of inestimable importance, and cannot be surrendered, nor can the states suffer or permit any interference therewith").

49. *Kinney*, 14 F. Cas. at 605 ("If Virginia were in the midocean or on the antipodal continent, her control over the rights and privileges of her citizens as members of society, including marriage, would be, no more certainly than now, unrestrained by any provision of the national constitution").

50. For a discussion of the "major damage to clear and substantial federal interests" doctrine, see Mark Strasser, *Legally Wed: Same-Sex Marriage and the Constitution*, 150–52 (Ithaca, N.Y.: Cornell University Press, 1997).

51. Pub. L. No. 96–611, 94 Stat. 3568 (codified as amended at 28 U.S.C. § 1738A [1994]).

52. See *Zablocki v. Redhail*, 434 U.S. 374 (1978) (individual could not be precluded from marrying because of his failure to support his child). For a discussion of these and other cases, see Strasser, *Legally Wed*, 59–65.

53. See *Turner v. Safley*, 482 U.S. 78 (1987) (prisoner could not be precluded from marrying).

54. In *Loving v. Virginia*, 388 U.S. 1 (1967), the Supreme Court struck down Virginia's antimiscegenation statute.

55. See *Dickson v. Dickson*, 9 Tenn. (I Yerg.) 110, 113 (1826) (discussing individual who had divorced in Kentucky and had been prohibited from remarrying); *Putnam v. Putnam*, 25 Mass. (8 Pick.) 433, 434 (1829) (discussing individual who had committed adultery and had been prohibited from remarrying after his divorce); *Van Storch v. Griffin*, 71 Pa. 240, 242 (1872) (discussing individual who had been forbidden from remarrying while her husband was still alive even though he was free to remarry after their divorce); *West Cambridge v. Lexington*, 18 Mass. (1 Pick.) 506, 507–8 (1823) (discussing individual precluded from remarrying after his divorce because he had committed adultery). See also *State v. Shattuck*, 69 Vt. 403, 406 (1897) ("our statute provides that it shall not be lawful for a divorced libelee to marry a person other than the libellant for three years from the time the divorce is granted, unless the libellant dies, and imposes a penalty on a person who violates that provision, or lives in this State under a marriage relation forbidden by it; and we have recently held that a marriage celebration in this State in violation thereof, between parties domiciled here, was void here").

56. The individuals might be charged with fornication if they had sexual relations outside of marriage. See *Jones v. Commonwealth*, 80 Va. 18, 20 (1885) ("There may be illicit intercourse and even lewd and lascivious intercourse between man and woman, which would be *fornication* or *adultery*, as the case might be, and which are punishable by the law as offences against sound morals and good government"); *State v. Hairston*, 63 N.C. 439, 441 (1869) ("Among other things, our marriage law declares that the white and colored races shall not intermarry. The pretended marriage in this case was therefore invalid and the parties guilty of fornication and adultery"); *Hood v. State*, 56 Ind. 263, 271 (1877) ("Fornication is sexual intercourse between a man, married or single, and an unmarried woman").

57. See *Dickson*, 9 Tenn. at 113 (discussing individual who had been precluded from remarrying in Kentucky but could remarry in Tennessee); *Kinney v. Commonwealth*, 71 Va. (30 Gratt.) 858, 870 (1878) ("If the parties desire to maintain the relations of man and wife, they must change their domicile and go to some state or country where the laws recognize the validity of such marriages").

58. Some commentators seem not to appreciate this. See King, Note, "Ya'll Cain't Do That Here," 2 *Tex. Wesleyan L. Rev.* at 537 (suggesting that if subsequent domicile prohibits union then marriage need not be recognized).

59. *Loughran v. Loughran*, 292 U.S. 216, 223 (1934) ("Marriages not polygamous or incestuous, or otherwise declared void by statute, will, if valid by the law of the state where entered into, be recognized as valid in every other jurisdiction.")

60. *Estate of Stull*, 183 Pa. 625, 630 (1898) ("But where a man and woman, citizens of the same state, and subject to an absolute statutory prohibition against entering into a marriage contract which is against good morals and contrary to public policy, leave their domicil and enter another for the express purpose of violating the law of their domicil in this respect, the case is highly exceptional, and the great weight of authority is against the validity of such a marriage in the place of their domicil"); *Dupre v. Executor*, 10 La. Ann. 411, 412 (1855) ("Whatever validity might be attached in France to the singular marriage contract, and subsequent unnatural alliance there celebrated between the plaintiff and the deceased testatrix, it is plain that, under the facts in evidence, the Courts of Louisiana cannot give effect to these acts, without sanctioning an evasion of the laws, and setting at naught the deliberate policy of the State"); *Eggers v. Olson*, 231 P. 483, 485 (Okla. 1924) ("the marriage of William Yates with Emily Lewis was prohibited by the laws of this state, and they could not, while citizens of this state, evade the law of marriage by going out of the state and marrying under the laws of another state and then return to this state to live and maintain the marriage assumed in that state, which was prohibited in this state, and expect the marriage to be recognized and protected in this state"); *Kinney*, 71 Va. at 866 ("The laws enacted to further and uphold this declared policy would be futile and a dead letter if in fraud of these salutary enactments, both races might, by stepping across an imaginary line, bid defiance to the law, by immediately returning and insisting that the marriage celebrated in another state or country, should be recognized as lawful, though denounced by the public law of the domicile as unlawful and absolutely void"). See also Ernest G. Lorenzen, "Territoriality, Public Policy and the Conflict of Laws," 33 *Yale L.J.* 736, 749 (1924) ("Suppose, for example, that two citizens of the forum to go into another state for the purpose of contracting a marriage which they could not enter into under the local law of the forum. In such a case the courts might reach the conclusion that the local interests of the state demand that its law should not be allowed to be evaded by its own citizens and that its local rule should therefore prevail").

61. See *Osoinach v. Watkins*, 180 So. 577, 578 (Ala. 1938) ("Dr. Watkins and Mrs. Viola Watkins, then Viola Chapman, well knowing the relationship existing between them, and that the laws of Alabama inhibited, under severe penalty, their intermarriage, for the purpose of evading such law, did go from their domicile in Alabama to the city of Atlanta, in the state of Georgia, and did there intermarry").

62. *Kinney*, 71 Va. at 865 ("Whenever the question has arisen in the southern states, it has been held that a marriage between a white person and a negro, although the marriage be celebrated in a state where such marriages are not prohibited, is void in the state of the domicile").

63. See *Medway v. Needham*, 16 Mass. 157 (1819) (recognizing interracial marriage validly celebrated elsewhere).

64. See Joseph H. Beale, "Marriage and the Domicil," 44 *Harv. L. Rev.* 501, 512–13 (1931) ("If parties domiciled in a southern state leave the state and go to

another state which permits such a union, and are there married, the marriage is nevertheless void by reason of this overwhelming policy of the domicil. If, on the other hand, parties to such a marriage are domiciled in a northern state the marriage will be held good in spite of a prohibition at the domicil").

65. See *McPherson v. Commonwealth*, 69 Va. (28 Gratt.) 939, 940 (1877) ("It thus appears that less than one-fourth of her blood is negro blood. If it be but one drop less, she is not a negro"). See also *Keith v. Commonwealth*, 181 S.E. 283, 284 (Va. 1935) ("These circumstances, as a matter of law, fail to demonstrate beyond a reasonable doubt that the accused Bascomb Keith has negro blood, and therefore we conclude that his marriage with Reda Baker did not violate Code, §4546, as amended by Acts 1932, c. 78"); *Jones*, 80 Va. at 544–45:

> From the certificate of facts in this case we find, that the accused was not a full-blooded negro, but had white blood in his veins, but there was no evidence to show the quantity of negro blood in his veins, and no evidence of his parentage except that his mother was a yellow woman. If his mother was a yellow woman with more than half of her blood derived from the white race, and his father a white man, he is not a negro. If he is a man of mixed blood he is not a negro, unless he has one-fourth at least of negro blood in his veins, and this must be proved by the commonwealth as an essential part of the crime, without which it cannot exist. The commonwealth, as we have seen in this case, has produced no evidence of this fact, and if every accused person is to be presumed to be innocent until his guilt is proved, this person must be presumed not to be a negro until he is proved to be as such.

But see *Weaver v. State*, 116 So. 893, 894–95 (Ala. Ct. App. 1928) ("Whatever may be the holdings in other jurisdictions [and they seem to be different in North Carolina and Virginia], a negro, within the meaning of section 5001 of the Criminal Code of 1923, is a descendant of the whole blood from the black woolly-headed race of South Africa and his and her descendants, to and including the third generation, where one parent of each generation is a white person").

66. See *Thurman v. State*, 18 Ala. 276, 278 (1850) ("A marriage took place there between a white man, and a woman, who was the child of a mulatto man by a white woman, and the court held that the child of such parents was not a mulatto. It was their unanimous opinion that a mulatto is a person begotten between a white and a black, and that this agreed with the popular use of the term").

67. See *Succession of Minvielle (Domec v. Barjac)*, 15 La. Ann. 342, 342–43 (1860):

> The prohibition contained in this article is one eminently affecting the public order. Hence the nullity declared by the same is absolute, and cannot be cured by ratification. The law is of that rigorous nature that it will not permit a marriage to exist between persons of the two different races for a moment. No suit is needed to declare the nullity of such an union. Either party may disregard it, and neither can pretend to derive from it any of the consequences of a lawful marriage.

Greenhow v. James' Ex'or, 80 Va. (6 Hansbrough) 636 (1885) (marriage held void though validly celebrated elsewhere).

68. *Kinney*, 14 F. Cas. at 606:

If this petitioner had been born a citizen of the District of Columbia, and had there married a white woman in conformity to the laws of that jurisdiction, and had afterward migrated with his lawful wife to Virginia, and had been, after becoming thus domiciled here, prosecuted under that provision of the law of Virginia which has been quoted, and convicted and imprisoned, and had filed his petition here, praying for an inquiry into the cause of his detention in prison, the cause presented would have been essentially different from that actually under consideration.

69. See id. at 607 (denying that the difference mandated a different result).

70. *State v. Ross*, 76 N.C. 242 (1877).

71. Id. at 243 ("It is difficult to see how, in going to South Carolina to marry a negro, without an intent to return with him to this State, she could evade or intend to evade the laws of this State").

72. Id. at 244–45 ("the decided weight of English and American authority requires us to hold that the relation thus lawful in its inception continues to be lawful here"). See also *Succession of Caballero v. Executor*, 24 La. Ann. 573, 574 (1872) (interracial marriage upheld because domicile changed); Johnson, "The Validity of a Marriage," 38 *N.D. L. Rev.* at 446 ("Though the forum may prohibit miscegenous marriages, a valid marriage contracted in another state when the parties were not residents of the forum will be recognized as valid"); Sage, "Sister-State Recognition of Valid Same-Sex Marriages," 28 *Ind. L. Rev.* at 123 (discussing *Ross* decision in which interracial marriage recognized).

73. *Ross*, 76 N.C. at 243 ("Such a case differs essentially from one in which both persons, being domiciled in North Carolina, leave the State for the purpose of contracting a marriage forbidden by its law, and with an intent to return to and reside in North Carolina after such marriage").

74. *State v. Kennedy*, 76 N.C. 251, 252 (1877) ("when the law of North Carolina declares that all marriages between negroes and white persons shall be void, this is a personal incapacity which follows the parties wherever they go so long as they remain domiciled in North Carolina"). See also *Hairston*, 63 N.C. at 441 ("Among other things, our marriage law declares that the white and colored races shall not intermarry. The pretended marriage in this case was therefore invalid and the parties guilty of fornication and adultery").

75. See *Ross*, 76 N.C. at 243. Everyone is presumed to be domiciled somewhere. See *In re Estate of Banks*, 629 N.E.2d 1223, 1225 (Ill. App. 1994) ("A person must have a domicile at all times, but there can be only one domicile at a time, and once a domicile is established, it continues until a new one is acquired").

76. See *Ross*, 76 N.C. at 243.

77. See *Banks*, 629 N.E.2d at 1225 ("A change of domicile is effected by an actual abandonment of the first domicile, an intent not to return to it, and physical presence in another place with the intention of making the last-acquired residence the permanent home"). See also *Texas v. Florida*, 306 U.S. 398, 427 (1939) ("Proof is wanting also that the domicile established in Massachusetts was abandoned in favor of the Florida house which he built there in 1927").

78. See *Texas v. Florida*, 306 U.S. 398 (1939) (Texas, Florida, Massachusetts, and New York each claimed that a particular individual had been domiciled in that state and thus that the state was owed estate taxes).

79. *Worcester County Trust Co. v. Riley*, 302 U.S. 292, 299 (1937) ("Neither the Fourteenth Amendment nor the full faith and credit clause (art. 4, sec. 1) requires uniformity in the decisions of the courts of different states as to the place of domicil").

80. See *Ross*, 76 N.C. at 244 (lower court had determined an intent to evade North Carolina law, although the North Carolina Supreme Court ruled that such a conclusion was "unsupported by or repugnant to the facts").

81. Id. at 245:

> It is contended, however, by the attorney-general that there is an exception to this rule as well established as the rule itself, viz.: that incestuous and polygamous marriages, although lawful in the country in which they are contracted, will not be recognized in other States in which such marriages are deemed immoral and are prohibited. And it is further argued that a marriage between persons of different races is as unnatural and as revolting as an incestuous one, and is declared void by the law of North Carolina.

82. Id. at 247 ("The inconveniences which may arise from this view of the law are less than those which result from a different one. The children of such a marriage, if born in South Carolina, could migrate here and would be considered legitimate. The only evil which could be avoided by a contrary conclusion is that the people of this State might be spared the bad example of an unnatural and immoral but lawful cohabitation").

83. *Stevenson*, 56 Ky. at 165:

> It is, however, understood to be the settled general rule of law in England, and in most, or all, of the United States, and especially in Kentucky that a marriage valid by the law of the country where it is celebrated, is to be held valid in other countries in which the parties may be resident or domiciled, though it would have been invalid by the law of the subsequent domicile if it had been originally celebrated there. Cases of polygamous or inestuous marriages are, in Christian countries, established exceptions to this rule.

People v. Ezeonu, 588 N.Y.S.2d 117 (1992) ("a polygamous marriage legally consummated in a foreign country will be held invalid in New York").

84. But see Strasser, *Legally Wed*, 112–14.

85. *Ross*, 76 N.C. at 246 ("all Christian countries agree that marriages in the direct line and between the nearest collaterals are incestuous. . . . But beyond these few cases in which all States agree, there is a difference as to what marriages are incestuous, and in such cases the admitted international law leaves it to each State to say what is incestuous in respect to its own subjects").

86. *Sutton*, 51 Mass. at 452.

87. See *Van Voorhis v. Brintnall*, 86 N.Y. 18, 26 (1881) (discussing the exception of "incest or polygamy coming within the prohibitions of natural law").

88. See P. H. V., "Marriage Valid Where Celebrated," 127 *A.L.R.* at 439 ("where the fundamental policy of the forum condemning the marriage is based on a universal principle recognized throughout Christendom, there is no doubt that the foreign marriage will not be recognized, though valid where performed").

89. *Sutton*, 51 Mass. at 453–54 ("In the present case, the marriage of these

parties was not void by the laws of England, though voidable in the spiritual court. It never was avoided, and though absolutely prohibited by our laws, yet not being within the exception, as against natural law, we do not feel warranted in saying the parties are not husband and wife"). See also *Fensterwald v. Burk*, 129 Md. 131, 138 (1916) ("The provision contained in the statute of this State, Act of 1777, Chapter 12, prohibiting the marriage of uncles and nieces, does not, we think, fall within any of the enumerated exceptions to the general rule. It is not incestuous 'according to the generally accepted opinion of Christendom.' "); *Campione v. Campione*, 107 N.Y.S.2d 170 (1951) (upholding marriage between uncle and niece); *State ex. rel. Miesner v. Geile*, 747 S.W.2d 757, 758 (Mo. App. 1988) (upholding marriage between "uncle and niece by reason of adoption"); *In re May's Estate*, 114 N.E.2d 4, 6 (N.Y. 1953) (upholding marriage between uncle and niece). But see *Catalano v. Catalano*, 170 A.2d 726 (Conn. 1961) (marriage between uncle and niece void); *Stiles*, 391 N.E.2d at 1027 ("We hold that the marriage of an uncle to his niece is incestuous and void ab initio").

90. *Sutton*, 51 Mass. at 453–54 ("In the present case, the marriage of these parties was not void by the laws of England, though voidable in the spiritual court. It never was avoided, and though absolutely prohibited by our laws, yet not being within the exception, as against natural law, we do not feel warranted in saying the parties are not husband and wife"); *Fensterwald*, 129 Md. at 137 (discussing "marriages which are deemed contrary to the law of nature as generally recognized in Christian countries" and making clear that those involve "polygamy and incest; and in the sense in which the term incest is used, are embraced only such marriages as are incestuous according to the generally accepted opinion of Christendom, which relates only to persons in direct line of consanguinity, and brothers and sisters"); *Commonwealth v. Lane*, 113 Mass. 458, 463 (1873) (discussing marriages "which are deemed contrary to the law of nature as generally recognized in Christian countries, namely, "those void for polygamy or for incest"); *In re Miller's Estate*, 214 N.W. 428, 429 (Mich. 1927) (discussing marriages "which are deemed contrary to the law of nature as generally recognized in Christian countries, namely "only those void for polygamy or for incest") (quoting *Commonwealth v. Lane*, 113 Mass. 458 [1873]).

91. See *Brinson v. Brinson*, 96 So.2d 653, 659 (La. 1957) (Louisiana claims right not to recognize common law marriage valid in Mississippi of Mississippi domiciliaries because that marriage was in "bad faith" and thus violated Louisiana public policy); see also id. at 660 (on rehearing).

92. *Ross*, 76 N.C. at 247:

> It is impossible to identify this case with that of an incestuous or polygamous marriage admitted to be such *jure gentium*. The law of nations is a part of the law of North Carolina. We are under obligations of comity to our sister States. We are compelled to say that this marriage being valid in the State where the parties were *bona fide* domiciled at the time of the contract must be regarded as subsisting after their immigration here.

93. But see *Osoinach*, 180 So. at 581 ("The Legislature is fully competent to declare what marriages shall be void in its own state, notwithstanding their validity in the state where celebrated, whether contracted between parties who were in good

faith domiciled in the state where the ceremony was performed, or between parties who left the state of domicile for the purpose of avoiding its statute, when they come or return to the state").

94. Id. at 580 ("The statute not only prohibits the intermarriage of persons standing in relationship of the parties to the marriage under consideration in this case, but it also prohibits any act of sexual intercourse between them"); *State v. Brown*, 23 N.E. 747, 750 (Ohio 1890):

> The act is little, if any, less repulsive to a correct sense of decency, and no less a violation of sound public policy, because it is perpetrated by persons living together publicly under the form of marriage, than if done by them clandestinely and occasionally only. We hold, therefore, that by section 7019, Rev. St., sexual commerce, as between persons nearer of kin than cousins, is prohibited, whether they have gone through the form in intermarriage or not; nor is it material that the marriage was celebrated in a country where it was valid, for we are not bound, upon principles of comity, to permit persons to violate our criminal laws, adopted in the interest of decency and good morals, and based on principles of sound public policy, because they have assumed, in another state or country where it was lawful, the relation which led to the acts prohibited by our laws.

95. See Mass. Gen. Laws Ann. ch. 272 § 17 (West 1987) ("Persons within the degrees of consanguinity within which marriages are prohibited or declared by law to be incestuous and void, who intermarry or have sexual intercourse with each other, shall be punished by imprisonment in the state prison for not more than twenty years or in jail for not more than two and one half years").

96. *State v. Nakashima*, 114 P. 894, 896 (Wash. 1911) ("If there in fact existed between the defendants a marriage relation contracted in a foreign jurisdiction, which would have to be regarded as legal here and which would relieve them from the crime charged, such marriage relation should be pleaded and proven by them as a defense, and need not be negatived by the information").

97. *Ross*, 76 N.C. at 247.

98. Id. at 246 ("However revolting to us and to all persons who, by reason of living in States where the two races are nearly equal in numbers, have an experience of the consequences of matrimonial connections between them, such a marriage may appear, such cannot be said to be the common sentiment of the civilized and Christian world").

99. *Naim v. Naim*, 87 S.E.2d 749, 752 (Va. 1955), vacated on alternative grounds, 550 U.S. 891 (1955) (citing *State v. Gibson*, 36 Ind. 389 [1871]).

100. See *Loving*, 388 U.S. at 3 (discussing trial court's view that God prohibited interracial marriages).

101. *State v. Bell*, 66 Tenn. (7 Baxt.) 9 (1872).

102. Id. at 9. However, in the summary, the act is referred to as the act of 1870 (second sessions), ch. 39. See id.

103. Ch. 39 (1870) (2nd session of the 36th Assembly). Compare *Frasher v. State*, 30 Am. Rep. 131, 131 (Tex. Ct. App. 1877)

> Art. 2016. If any white person shall, within this State, knowingly marry a negro or a person of mixed blood descended from negro ancestry to the third gen-

> eration inclusive, though, one ancestor of each generation may have been a white person, or having so married in or out of the state, shall continue within this State to cohabit with such negro or such descendant of a negro, he or she shall be punished by confinement in the penitentiary not less than two nor more than five years.

104. P. H. V., "Marriage Valid Where Celebrated," 127 *A.L.R.* at 441:

> Thus, in *State v. Bell* (1872) 7 Baxt. (Tenn.) 9, 32 Am. Rep. 549, it was held that a marriage of a white man and a negro woman in Mississippi, according to the law of which it was valid, would not be recognized as valid in Tennessee, so as to protect the parties from a criminal prosecution, under the act of the general assembly, for living together in that state. It does not expressly appear whether the parties were domiciled in Mississippi at the time of their marriage, but the ground upon which the decision is based seems to be broad enough to cover a case where the parties were residents of the state in which the marriage was celebrated.

Some commentators assume that this case involved a couple who had been domiciled in Tennessee who had attempted to evade Tennessee's law. See Steven A. Bank, Comment, "Anti-Miscegenation Laws and the Dilemma of Symmetry: The Understanding of Equality in the Civil Rights Act of 1875," 2 *U. Chi. L. Sch. Roundtable* 303, 338 and n.242 (1995). However, the summary of the case makes clear that the individuals had not been Tennessee domiciliaries before the marriage. See *Bell*, 66 Tenn. at 9 ("The defendant, a white man, was married to a woman of color, in the State of Mississippi [where such marriages are not forbidden by law], and removed to this State with his wife, and continued to live with her as his wife").

105. *Bell*, 66 Tenn. at 9.

106. In a Texas case, the individual was charged with attempting to enter into an interracial marriage while he was a domiciliary of the state of Texas. See *Frasher*, 30 Am. Rep. at 131 ("The indictment in this case charges that on March 18, A. D. 1875, in the county of Gregg and State aforesaid, one Charles Frasher, late of the said county, being then and there a white man, did then and there unlawfully, knowingly, and feloniously marry a negro, contrary to the form of the statute in such cases made and provided, and against the peace and dignity of the State"). Had he instead attempted to cohabit in Texas with his interracial spouse whom he had married while a domiciliary of a state recognizing such marriages, he might nonetheless have been charged with breaking the same law.

107. Ch. 39 (1870) (2nd session of the 36th Assembly).

108. See Sage, "Sister-State Recognition of Valid Same-Sex Marriages," 28 *Ind. L. Rev.* at 123 ("The Tennessee Supreme Court in *Bell* held that it was an indictable offense for a man to live in Tennessee with his wife, whom he validly married in Mississippi, in violation of the antimiscegenic laws of Tennessee").

109. See *Bell*, 66 Tenn. at 11.

110. See id. at 10.

111. *Pennegar v. State*, 10 S.W. 305, 307 (Tenn. 1889) ("this court held that a marriage betwen a white person and a negro, valid in Mississippi, where celebrated, was void here, in a case where the parties were domiciled in Mississippi at the time of the marriage"). Cf. *State v. Tutty*, 41 F. 753, 761 (S.D. Ga. 1890) ("To illustrate

the proposition, the court cites the case of *State v. Bell*, 7 Baxt. 9, where a marriage between a white person and a negro, valid in Mississippi, where celebrated, and where the parties were domiciled at the time of the marriage, was held void in Tennessee"). Professor Koppelman suggests that one way of thinking about *Bell* is to say that the marriage ceased to exist when the couple entered the forum and another way is to say that the couple had remained married but had not been permitted to cohabit. See Andrew Koppelman, "Same-Sex Marriage, Choice of Law, and Public Policy," 76 *Tex. L. Rev.* 921, 984–85 (1998). But these are not two different ways to think about the case. Rather, they were two possibilities open to the court. The court chose the former, which involved a rejection of the existing jurisprudence. The latter choice, which the court did not make, would have been within the existing jurisprudence.

112. *Bell*, 66 Tenn. at 10–11.

113. Herbert F. Goodrich, "Foreign Facts and Local Fancies," 25 *Va. L. Rev.* 26, 31 (1938) (criticizing the "simple rule of Conflict of Laws . . . that the rule of another state will not be applied in a given situation if it differs from that of the forum," suggesting that such a policy "would destroy practically all of our modern rules of Conflict of Laws").

114. *Pennegar v. State*, 10 S.W. 305 (Tenn. 1889).

115. Id.

116. *Bell*, 66 Tenn. at 11.

117. Id.

118. See Applebaum, "Miscegenation Statutes," 53 *Geo. L.J.* at 55 ("Suppose, again, that a Mohammedan having two wives should attempt to cohabit with both within the limits of the forum. In this case, there would be no doubt that the local rule should have precedence").

119. *Morgan v. M'Ghee*, 24 Tenn. (5 Humph.) 13, 13 (1844).

120. Id. at 14.

121. *Bell*, 66 Tenn. at 10.

122. Cf. *Nevada v. Hall*, 440 U.S. 410, 425 (1979) ("this Court has presumed that the States intended to adopt policies of broad comity toward one another. But this presumption reflected an understanding of state policy, rather than a constitutional command").

123. *Hilton*, 159 U.S. at 164.

124. *United States ex rel. Devine v. Rodgers*, 109 F. 886, 887 (E.D. Pa. 1901) ("If the relation thus entered into elsewhere, although lawful in the foreign country, is stigmatized as incestuous by law of Pennsylvania, no rule of comity requires a court sitting in this state to recognize the foreign marriage as valid").

125. Robert H. Jackson, "Full Faith and Credit—The Lawyer's Clause of the Constitution," 45 *Colum. L. Rev.* 1, 27 (1945) ("Always to be kept in mind in dealing with these problems is that the policy ultimately to be served in application of the clause is the federal policy of 'a more perfect union' of our legal systems"); Russell Weintraub, "Due Process and Full Faith and Credit Limitations on a State's Choice of Law," 44 *Iowa L. Rev.* 449, 477 (1959) ("The purpose of the full faith and credit clause was and is to help forge a federal nation out of individual sovereign states. If the United States is to be more than just a loose alliance of independent sovereignties, if it is to be a nation, then the individual states must act as parts of a nation").

126. Indeed, the *Ross* court talked about an obligation of comity to a sister state.

See *Ross*, 76 N.C. at 247 ("We are under obligations of comity to our sister States"). Cf. Douglas Laycock, "Equal Citizens of Equal and Territorial States: The Constitutional Foundations of Choice of Law," 92 *Colum. L. Rev.* 249, 259 (1992) ("international choice of law is derived from wholly different sources. How U.S. courts treat foreign law is a matter of comity and diplomacy, the voluntary choice of a sovereign power. How Texas courts treat the law of a sister state is a matter of law, not comity, and the choice is no longer voluntary").

127. Laycock, "Equal Citizens," 92 *Colum. L. Rev.* at 260.

128. *Williams v. North Carolina*, 325 U.S. 226, 228 (1945).

129. *Williams I*, 317 U.S. at 301 (citing *Haddock v. Haddock*, 201 U.S. 562, 628 [1906] [Holmes, J., dissenting]).

130. *Estin v. Estin*, 334 U.S. 541, 553 (1948) (Jackson, J., dissenting). See also Deborah M. Henson, "Will Same-Sex Marriages Be Recognized in Sister States?: Full Faith and Credit and Due Process Limitations on States' Choice of Law Regarding the Status and Incidents of Homosexual Marriages Following Hawaii's *Baehr v. Lewin*," 32 *U. Louisville J. Fam. L.* 551, 588 (1993–1994) ("Marriage is one of the most basic civil rights of women and men. It would seem that one should be at least as certain of the creation of an institution of this caliber [one which creates such a multitude of tangible and symbolic benefits], as one is of the dissolution of the same institution. The parties and their children need protection of their justified expectations for legitimate family structuring").

131. *Lenherr*, 314 A.2d at 258 ("In an age of widespread travel and ease of mobility, it would create inordinate confusion and defy the reasonable expectations of citizens whose marriage is valid in one state to hold that marriage invalid elsewhere"). See also Habib A. Balian, Note, " 'Til Death Do Us Part: Granting Full Faith and Credit to Marital Status," 68 *S. Cal. L. Rev.* 397, 413 (1995) ("this unification policy is needed even more in the area of marriage because marriage possesses a migratory relationship to the union. Because married individuals can easily move between states, the problems that call for unification are magnified").

7

Natural Law and Same-Sex Marriage

Some natural law theorists argue that same-sex marriages cannot be true marriages and thus cannot be recognized by any state. The analyses that such theorists offer are unconvincing, because they not only undermine each other and as readily establish that the state should recognize same-sex marriages as that it should not, but they also at least implicitly involve a misunderstanding of the relation between natural law as a moral system and American domestic relations jurisprudence. Even if natural law had a determinative content which specified that same-sex marriages were morally impermissible, this would not establish what states must or even should do, because the alleged dictates of natural law are ignored in other areas of domestic relations jurisprudence regarding who may marry whom and regarding the conditions under which marriages will be recognized as legally valid. Indeed, not only does current domestic relations law reject the natural law rationales, but the individual and state interests implicated in marriage that have already been recognized in the law strongly support the recognition of such unions.

NATURAL LAW AND DETERMINATIVE CONTENT

Natural law as a legal theory must be distinguished from natural law as a moral theory. In neither form will the dictates of the system be completely determinate. Thus, some natural law *moral* theories will yield dictates that directly contradict those of other natural law *moral* theories, and some natural law *legal* theories will yield dictates that directly contradict those of other natural law *legal* theories. Indeed, part of the difficulty in determining whether natural law supports, permits, or prohibits same-sex marriage is that natural law might refer to any number of legal and moral positions.

Even were one to limit one's focus to natural law as a moral theory, one would still find that the term might refer to a number of different, potentially conflicting theories. When one examines some of the particular natural law theories that ostensibly establish the impermissibility of same-sex marriage, one finds that the claimed clarity and consistency of these theories are lacking and, further, that the dictates of the systems as easily support as undermine the permissibility if not obligatoriness of the state's recognizing same-sex marriages.

THE LEGAL THEORY VERSUS THE MORAL THEORY

Natural law as a legal theory posits that there is a necessary connection between law and morality.[1] Such a position might helpfully be contrasted with legal positivism, which denies that necessary connection.[2] However, natural law legal theorists are not wedded to any particular moral theory. Thus, one such theorist might be a utilitarian, another might be a deontologist, and yet another might subscribe to her particular society's conventional morality.[3]

Natural law legal theorists do not only disagree about which moral system is correct; they also disagree about the nature of the required connection between law and morality. For example, while claiming that law must have its own inner morality,[4] some natural law legal theorists merely mean that the law must meet certain procedural requirements.[5] Others claim that the content of the law must itself be in accord with certain moral requirements, and that laws which fail to meet that standard are not in fact laws.

Natural law as a moral theory makes claims about the nature of morality (e.g., that moral principles are objectively valid and are discoverable by reason).[6] Yet, a variety of moral theorists might claim that the moral system to which they subscribe meets those conditions. For example, a utilitarian might claim that the "Greatest Happiness Principle [which] holds that actions are right in proportion as they tend to promote happiness, wrong as they tend to produce the reverse of happiness"[7] is objectively true and discoverable by reason.[8] Other theorists might make similar claims about the discoverability and objective validity of their own moral systems.

An individual might be a natural law moral and legal theorist. However, such a theorist might have any number of positions—for example, that her moral theory is true and objectively discoverable by reason and, further, that laws which require or even permit immoral practices are not in fact laws[9] or that morality is objective but also that law must merely have certain procedural protections in order to qualify as law.

THE NATURAL LAW POSITION ON SAME-SEX MARRIAGE

Various theorists claim that natural law precludes same-sex marriages.[10] Yet, the validity of such a claim cannot be established until that claim has been analyzed more fully. For example, it would be important to know whether this was a claim about natural law as a legal theory or as a moral theory. Since natural law as a legal theory addresses the necessary connection between law and morality but does not specify which moral theory must be true,[11] the claim that natural law prohibits same-sex marriages is presumably, at the very least, a claim that natural law as a moral theory condemns such marriages. There might be an additional implicit assertion at work here—namely, that because natural law as a moral theory (allegedly) condemns such marriages and because natural law as a legal theory posits a necessary connection between law and morality, the law therefore must not recognize such marriages. However, that additional assertion would require further justification even were the first claim accurate, and so can only be examined after the first claim has been discussed.

It would not be surprising if a natural law moral theorist *claimed* that same-sex marriages were morally impermissible. Natural law has been cited to establish the moral permissibility *and* impermissibility of a variety of practices.[12] For example, it has been described both as permitting and as prohibiting interracial marriages,[13] and both as permitting and as prohibiting nonprocreative marital sex. One would expect the same lack of consensus with respect to same-sex unions, especially because some of the issues dividing natural law moral theorists about the moral permissibility or impermissibility of interracial marriages or nonprocreative sex will also divide theorists on this issue.

That there are debates among natural law moral theorists about what is permitted and prohibited is itself significant, since the claimed obviousness and certainty of the moral dictates of the system are undermined if reasonable individuals can come to opposite conclusions about the morality of particular practices. Thus, if it is claimed that natural law is a preferable alternative to other systems because it offers certainty while other theories do not[14] and if natural law is itself indeterminate, then the claims about its superiority in this respect are at best unpersuasive.

The more compelling difficulty for the natural law moral theorist, however, is not merely that the claimed obviousness and certainty of the system are in fact illusory, since such a criticism might be made about a variety of systems.[15] Rather, it is that some of the justifications for the permissibility of interracial marriage and nonprocreative sex undermine the purported justifications for the impermissibility of same-sex marriage. Indeed, some commentators suggest that natural law *supports* same-sex marriage.[16]

INTERRACIAL MARRIAGE

Natural law has long been cited to explain why interracial marriages are impermissible.[17] Further, those claims were not only made in the 1700s and 1800s—in the 1950s and 1960s, courts were making clear their belief that God does not permit individuals of different races to marry.[18] Court cases involving the religious view that interracial marriage is contrary to God's Will have occurred even more recently.[19]

The difficulties posed for the natural law moral theorist by the disagreement about whether interracial marriages are morally permissible cannot be easily dismissed. Such theorists must explain how individuals could have believed and, perhaps, still believe that natural law precludes such marriages. Of course, a theorist might suggest that such individuals are correct, although such a theorist would then have to explain how others who claim that natural law permits such marriages could be wrong and, in any event, would risk the charge that natural law as currently interpreted is a mask for bigotry and thus should not be incorporated within the civil law.

A natural law moral theorist might suggest that some of the dictates of natural law are unclear and are subject to disagreement among reasonable people or, perhaps, that natural law at one time prohibited interracial marriage but no longer does. However, either of these responses would undermine the constancy and determinacy of the system's dictates[20] and would invite the response that same-sex marriage might also be one of those subjects about which reasonable natural law moral theorists might disagree or which once might have been impermissible but now is permissible.

The natural law moral theorist might instead suggest that an individual believing interracial marriage impermissible probably had his or her judgment corrupted in some way. As Francis Hutcheson explained, "When the strain of conversation and popular maxims have long represented certain actions or events as good, and others as evil; we find it difficult to break the association, even after our reason is convinced of the contrary."[21] Yet, the same might be said of the reactions of many to same-sex relationships—namely, that the associations inculcated since childhood are affecting the ability to make a correct, unbiased moral judgment.

WHAT DOES NATURAL LAW FORBID?

When two individual disagree about what natural law as a moral system requires or forbids, there must be some way to settle the disagreement. A theorist who suggests that natural law is a system of "rules and principles for the guidance of human conduct" that may be "discovered by the rational intelligence of man"[22] will not help resolve the disagreements at issue here, because each of the disagreeing parties would claim to have used reason to discover the permissibility or impermissibility of such marital unions. By the same token, an appeal to revelation will be of no help here,[23] because either or both of the disagreeing parties might claim to have had his or her understanding enhanced through revelation. Unless some non-question-begging way to resolve these disputes is offered, the credibility of the natural law claims to clarity and certainty will be severely undermined.

There are additional ways to establish the superiority of one position over another without appealing to reason or revelation. For example, if it could be established that permitting a particular practice would be disastrous, that would seem to be a compelling reason to believe the practice impermissible. However, it should be noted that the mere claim that permitting a particular practice will be disastrous will not make it so.

When courts discussed why interracial marriages were impermissible, they suggested that allowing interracial couples to marry would result in dire consequences.[24] When Isaac Jones was convicted of having married a woman of a different race, Martha Auther, he was "convicted of a crime, not only against the law of Virginia, but against the just sensibilities of her civilization."[25] That conviction was overturned, not because it was believed that there was anything wrong with punishing individuals for marrying outside of their race, but because the state could not prove that Isaac Jones and his wife were of different races.[26]

A different Virginia court had already explained the importance of preventing the races from intermarrying. "The purity of public morals, the moral and physical advancement of both races, and the highest advancement of our cherished southern civilization . . . all require that . . . [the races] should be kept distinct and separate, and that connections and alliances so unnatural that God and nature seem to forbid them, should be prohibited by positive law."[27] Not surprisingly, the claimed disastrous consequences of permitting interracial marriages have not materialized. The public morals have not become impure and the advancement of civilization has not been arrested.

Professor John Finnis suggests that the state's endorsing same-sex relationships would involve "an active threat to the stability of existing and future marriages"[28] because, for example, doing so would allegedly make nonsense of the view that adultery is per se immoral rather than because it may involve deception or the breaking of an agreement.[29] Because the stability of family life is of "fundamental importance"[30] and because the recognition of same-sex marriages would allegedly threaten that stability, he suggests that such marriages need not and should not be recognized. However, if same-sex marriage is not in fact a threat to the traditional family, as has been suggested in the courts,[31] then one must wonder how a community could rightly judge that it had a compelling interest in denying same-sex marriages, contrary view notwithstanding.[32]

Perhaps it will be argued that a difficulty in Professor Finnis's account is the arguably instrumental claim that same-sex marriages will somehow lead to the destruction of the traditional family.[33] If that contention can be shown to be false or if various other practices that are much more likely to lead to the destruction of the family are ignored whereas something much less likely to do so like same-sex marriage is prohibited,[34] then the argument against recognizing such marriages is substantially weakened if not totally undermined.

Natural law moral theorists who argue that the recognition of same-sex marriages would have deplorable consequences seem to have at least two worries: (1) their arguments seem subject to empirical disconfirmation, and (2) their arguments are strikingly analogous to arguments previously offered against permitting interracial couples to marry. Indeed, these theorists' offering implausible empirical claims to justify policies that do not seem to have a rational basis only supports the suspicion that the suggested policies are a product of prejudicial attitudes.[35]

In a related context, Justice Harry Blackmun suggested both that existing disabilities imposed on lesbians, gays, and bisexuals often do not in fact promote their purported goals and that the impositions of those disabilities have often been invidiously motivated. For example, he suggested that disagreements about which sexual acts are morally permissible will not induce people to abandon morality or to think better of murder, cruelty, or dishonesty,[36] thus rejecting the asserted claim that protecting sodomy within the right to privacy would promote rampant immorality. He further suggested that efforts to punish sodomy are the product of bias rather than legitimate social policy and that a "State can no more punish private behavior because of religious intolerance than it can punish such behavior because of racial animus."[37] Not only did he thus imply that legal prohibitions imposed on lesbians, bisexuals, and gays are comparable to those that have been imposed on the basis of race, but also that both types of prohibitions often stem from illicit intentions and motivations.

Sometimes, it is not the historical moral teachings themselves but the method of applying those precepts that suggests invidious treatment. Thus, arguments based on historical religious and moral teachings may be used selectively to burden gays, lesbians, and bisexuals but not others, even though the traditions themselves made no such distinction. For example, the Supreme Court of Kentucky asked whether a "society that no longer criminalizes adultery, fornication, or deviate sexual intercourse between heterosexuals, has a rational basis to single out homosexual acts for different treatment."[38] The court rejected that there was a "a rational basis for declaring this one type of sexual immorality so destructive of family values as to merit criminal punishment whereas other acts of sexual immorality which were likewise forbidden by the same religious and traditional heritage of Western civilization are now decriminalized,"[39] and struck down the state's sodomy law on state constitutional grounds.

When considering whether the right to commit sodomy was protected by the right to privacy, the United States Supreme Court had before it a statute that did not distinguish between same-sex and opposite-sex sodomy.[40] The majority itself chose to ignore the statutory language and to characterize the issue in terms of same-sex sodomy rather than sodomy generally.[41] The Court could have held that nonmarital sodomy was not protected by the fundamental right to privacy,[42] although equal protection issues might still have been implicated in such an analysis given the state's refusal to allow same-sex couples to marry. However, the Court took special pains to indicate that it was not addressing opposite-sex sodomy,[43] as if same-sex sodomy was so different that it required a special, wholly different analysis.[44] When courts offer selective applications of moral teachings and selective interpretations of statutes, they do not inspire confidence in the impartiality or sincerity of those offering the interpretations.

Historically, courts would attempt to justify antimiscegenation statutes by suggesting that interracial marriages posed a threat to civilization. Yet, civilization would seem to be much more at risk by allowing prejudice and bigotry to reign than by allowing same-sex or interracial couples to marry. When concurring in a judgment striking down that state's antimiscegenation statute, Justice Jesse Carter of the California Supreme Court noted, "Prejudice and intolerance are the cancers of civilization."[45] There is no reason to think that prejudice on the basis of orientation is any healthier for the body politic than is prejudice on the basis of race.

It would be false to suggest that commentators are not sensitive to the possibility that they will be charged with bias when offering arguments against same-sex marriage that, at the very least, sound strikingly familiar to those previously offered against interracial marriage.[46] Indeed, commentators sometimes try to explain why laws preventing same-sex marriage are disanalogous to laws that prevented interracial marriage. For example, Professor Wardle suggests that they are dissimilar because the former protect "the basic unit of society—the family," whereas the latter did not,[47] as if supporters of antimiscegenation laws would never have argued that those laws aimed to support the family and civilization itself. He also suggests that because it was "permissible" to criminalize sodomy, it is also permissible to prevent same-sex marriage.[48] Yet, this was exactly the kind of piggybacking argument that was used to justify laws invidiously discriminating on the basis of race.

In 1964, the state of Florida attempted to justify its law penalizing interracial fornication more heavily than intraracial fornication by suggesting that the fornication statute supported its antimiscegenation statute.[49] The Supreme Court rejected this analysis, perhaps realizing the difficulties that accepting such an analysis might pose. For example, had that argument been accepted, then as long as there were two laws, each imposing a related kind of disability against one particular group, each law might be thought a reasonable exercise of the police power because it would be viewed as helping the state to enforce the other law.[50] When either law was challenged, the state would claim that it was not attempting to act invidiously but, instead, merely to support the other existing law.

Merely because some theorists offer specious distinctions that are strikingly similar to those offered to justify antimiscegenation laws does not imply that no arguments can be offered to prohibit same-sex marriages that were not analogously used to prohibit interracial marriage. Indeed, one obvious possibility might seem to suggest itself, namely, that same-sex couples should not be allowed to marry because they cannot produce a child through their union. Because many interracial couples can and could reproduce through their union whereas no same-sex couples can, this might seem to be an argument against same-sex marriages that would not have been analogously used against interracial unions.

NONPROCREATIONAL SEX

Commentators who differentiate between former laws prohibiting interracial marriage and current laws prohibiting same-sex marriage by focusing on whether the couples can have children through their union are ignoring the historical bases used to justify the "unnaturalness" of interracial unions, since courts would sometimes point to the children of such marriages to justify the prohibition, either by claiming that children of interracial unions might themselves be unable to reproduce[51] or by claiming that children of interracial unions were "inferior."[52] Further, when one considers that St. Augustine approved even of sterile marriages because communion and companionship of the spouses was an additional goal of marriage,[53] one must wonder about the accuracy of the claim that natural law requires that individuals be able to procreate through their union if they are to be allowed to marry.

Although discussing with approval Plutarch's comment that intercourse with a sterile spouse is a desirable mark of esteem and affection,[54] Professor Finnis claims that gay and lesbian relationships "cannot express or do more than is expressed or done if two strangers engage in [sexual] . . . activity to give each other pleasure or a prostitute gives pleasure to a client in return for money."[55] This goes well beyond a claim about the possibility of procreation and instead relies on a theory of expression which very few if any theorists would be willing to embrace. Indeed, one wonders whether such a theory would even be offered in any context other than this one.

Suppose that Lynn has sexual relations with her longtime female partner, Kim. By and in having sexual relations with her partner, Lynn means to express her love for her partner and is so understood by Kim. Notwithstanding Kim's having understood the meaning that Lynn had intended to convey, Professor Finnis would deny that any such expression had occurred. All that Lynn allegedly could have expressed to Kim would be what two strangers could express to each other during anonymous sex or what a prostitute could express to a client.

Professor Finnis argues that same-sex couples cannot marry because their sexual relations cannot be marital in the appropriate sense. "Because their activation of one or even each of their reproductive organs cannot be an actualizing and experiencing of the marital good . . . [their coupling] can do no more than provide each partner with an individual gratification."[56] He suggests that sexual acts are not marital unless they have "procreative significance, not necessarily of being intended to generate or capable in the circumstances of generating but at least of being, as human conduct, acts of the reproductive kind."[57] Because same-sex sexual activity allegedly does not have procreative significance, it cannot be marital. However, because the naturally sterile couple can engage in acts of the right reproductive kind, their acts can be marital. Professor Finnis thus offers a theory that *might* explain why the naturally sterile couple may marry, although it is not at all clear that he can distinguish between intentionally and nonintentionally sterile couples.

One difficulty for this theory is in the specification of the relevant reproductive kind. He suggests that the acts of the sterile couple may be marital, because their sexual relations are as procreative as they can make them. However, were the requirement merely that the spouses make the act as reproductive as much as they "then and there [could],"[58] there would be no bar to same-sex spouses marrying and having intercourse, since they might indeed fulfill that requirement. The theory described above requires that there be a way to differentiate between those kinds of sexual relations that have the possibility of producing a child and those kinds of sexual relations that do not.

Professor Finnis suggests that individuals may perform an act of the correct kind, even if "some biological condition happens to prevent that unity resulting in generation of a child."[59] Presumably, by including those who *happen* to be unable to procreate, he means to exclude those who were intentionally sterilized. Yet, it is at best unclear why a particular act would be of the right type if performed by individuals *involuntarily* sterile but not if by individuals *voluntarily* sterile. In each case, the individuals involved would intend to have sexual relations, knowing that they could not produce a child through their lovemaking.

Suppose that Bill has a permanent and irrevocable vasectomy because he has decided that he never wants to father any children. Suppose further that he then meets and marries Caroline. Their sexual relations would not be unitive in the appropriate sense. Bill does not merely happen to be unable to father a child but, instead, has intentionally brought about that condition. It would be untenable to claim that contracepted sex is not unitive for married couples[60] but that noncontracepted sex is, if the only reason that the latter does not involve contraception is that one of the partners has intentionally and voluntarily become sterilized.[61]

Suppose, however, that Bill now sincerely regrets his decision to have had a vasectomy. He would undo the procedure if he could but he has been reliably informed by his physician that this particular procedure cannot be undone. Perhaps the relations between Bill and Carol would now be unitive in the appropriate sense because he sincerely regrets his decision, even though he is now no more able to father a child than he would have been had he never changed his mind about the desirability of obtaining a vasectomy. Regardless of whether regretful Bill can engage in the appropriate unitive relations, it would be quite difficult to offer a non-question-begging way to distinguish between the behaviors of regretful Bill, the behaviors of nonregretful Bill, and the behaviors of someone naturally sterile.

If the relevant issue is how to morally evaluate individuals who are naturally sterile versus individuals who intentionally and voluntarily bring about their own sterility, then there are a variety of approaches that might be taken. One could, following John Stuart Mill, distinguish between acts and characters and, perhaps, argue that the characters of those who intentionally became sterilized would deserve a different moral evaluation than would those of the individuals who did nothing to bring about their sterility. Yet, such an approach would not be helpful in this context, because it might not be clear what the moral evaluation of the intentionally sterilized individual would be (arguably, the person was praiseworthy for acting responsibly) and because this evaluation would be even more complicated in a case in which the individual now sincerely regrets his former decision to become sterilized. Perhaps he is no longer blameworthy (or praiseworthy) because of that sincere regret. Or, perhaps he is less (or more) blameworthy (or praiseworthy) because he should have foreseen that he might change his mind but nonetheless had a vasectomy anyway.

The important issue for Professor Finnis's theory is not moral blameworthiness or praiseworthiness per se but rather the proper way to individuate actions.[62] He must show how the acts or behaviors of the different marital couples can be distinguished so that some are of the right kind but others are not, even though the couples' current sexual behaviors are identical. The theory of act-individuation that is required in his account is much more complicated than might first be realized.

Indeed, it may be even more complicated than the above suggests. Consider two lesbians in a long-term, committed relationship who sometimes make artificial insemination an integral part of their lovemaking. Or, consider two gay men who sometimes make it a part of their lovemaking to produce sperm that is to be used in artificial insemination. The lovemaking of either of these couples might have to be included as being of the "right" kind, because it may in fact result in the production of a child. If their lovemaking is not so classified, assuming that a non-question-begging distinction could somehow be offered, then there will be the surprising result that sexual relations that cannot result in the production of children are of the correct reproductive kind[63] but that sexual relations which can produce children are not.[64]

Professor Finnis does not helpfully explain how his theory should account for the same-sex lovemaking that might result in the production of a child. He suggests that although biological union between men and women does not result in generation in most circumstances, "it is the behaviour that unites biologically because it is the behaviour which, as behaviour, is suitable for generation."[65] Yet, the behavior of sterilized individuals is not suitable for generation in that it will never result in generation. Further, the same-sex lovemaking described above is suitable in that it might result in generation. Thus, suitability is not to be defined in terms of reproductive possibility but, instead, in a different way.

Professor Finnis suggests that marital sexual acts are "of the reproductive kind" because "in willing such an act one wills sexual behavior which is (1) the very same as causes generation (intended or unintended) in every case of human *sexual* reproduction, and (2) the very same as one would will if one were intending precisely sexual reproduction as a goal of a particular marital sexual act."[66] However, unless modified, this definition is too inclusive for the theory that he wants to offer. For example, his definition would seem to include acts of the intentionally sterile couple, since they would be the same behaviors as cause generation in cases involving human sexual reproduction and would be the very same that would be willed if one were intending sexual reproduction as a goal. Further, it is simply unclear what to say about this definition insofar as it is to be applied to the same-sex acts referred to above. Would it be sexual reproduction if part of the lovemaking included artificial insemination? One infers that the answer is "No," although it is not clear why that should not be included.

Presumably, Professor Finnis would argue that same-sex relations should not count as acts of the reproductive kind because additional behaviors would have to be performed to achieve conception (e.g., use of artificial insemination) that are not included in many other cases of reproduction. Yet, such a view seems to have some surprising implications. Consider the opposite-sex couple who cannot reproduce without some sort of external assistance. Their sexual relations when they were not doing what was necessary for them to procreate might count as acts of the reproductive kind but their behaviors when they were doing what was necessary for them to be able to conceive (which would involve some sort of external assistance) would not count as acts of the reproductive kind. Further, if this couple believed that sexual relations were only appropriate for procreative purposes, they might never engage in any "marital acts" at all. For many couples, the system described above would undermine both the stability of their marriages and the possibility of their having and raising children.

Professor Finnis builds a great deal into what one is supposed to will when engaging in marital acts. For example, he suggests that intercourse with a spouse that is solely for pleasure is nonmarital,[67] although such sexual activity would seem to meet his definition of marital acts, since it is the same behavior as causes unintended generation and is the same as one would will if one were intending to reproduce. Further, he suggests that "the *complete* exclusion of non-marital sex acts from the range of human options is a precondition for the truly marital character of any spouse's intercourse."[68] Not only must married individuals refrain from these acts, but they must refrain from them for the right reasons, since "indifference to the inherent wrongness of non-marital acts is among the states of mind which render nonmarital the choosing and carrying out of even those actual sex acts which in all other respects are marital in kind."[69] Thus, for a sexual act with one's *spouse* to be marital, one must take the "appropriate" moral stance towards nonmarital acts (e.g., oral, anal, or digital stimulation).[70] If one regards one or more of these acts with one's spouse as morally acceptable, one will thereby undermine the marital character of *any* sexual acts with one's spouse.[71] Notwithstanding that his theory seems to require a somewhat complicated set of beliefs and dispositions in order for individuals to be able to engage in "marital acts," Professor Finnis claims that his position is "no more than the articulation of married people's commonsense appreciation of the offensiveness of adultery and of being treated by one's spouse as a mere object of sexual relief, sexual servicing, depersonalized sex."[72]

Professor Finnis claims that same-sex partners cannot have "a *common good* that could be actualized and experienced by . . . bodily union,"[73] presumably because the comon good involved in an expression of same-sex love does not count as the "right" kind of good or the "right" kind of love. He then argues that because this common good cannot be experienced, a kind of disintegration of self occurs.[74] Yet, this disintegration occurs, *subjective experience notwithstanding*, since the individuals themselves may feel united in a kind of oneness. Further, Professor Finnis may well be underestimating the frequency with which marital partners may feel alienated—for example, because one spouse is only having sexual relations to placate the other.[75]

Allegedly all "who accept that homosexual acts can be a humanly appropriate use of sexual capacities must, if consistent, regard sexual capacities, organs and acts as instruments for gratifying the individual 'selves' who have them."[76] As illustrated above, that claim is false if such a conclusion is not required as long as the act can be reproductive. Further, same-sex couples, like opposite-sex couples, can use their lovemaking as an expression of their love rather than "merely" as instruments for self-gratification. Bracketing whether seeking sexual gratification should have the moral taint that Professor Finnis seems to want to ascribe to it,[77] there is no reason to think that he is offering an accurate description of same-sex or opposite-sex relations between unmarrieds.

Professor Finnis takes great pains to explain why the naturally sterile person can enage in the appropriately unitive marital act. Presumably, this is because it is no fault of the individual that he or she is unable to reproduce. Suppose that orientation is either genetic or fixed early in childhood so that it, too, is not chosen. The same claims about lack of "fault" might be made here, too.

It might be thought (although Finnis does not suggest this) that the difference between the naturally sterile person and the naturally gay or lesbian person would seem to be the following. Although one's orientation would be towards individuals of the same sex, one still could have children if one were to be married to someone of the opposite sex.[78] Thus, natural inclinations notwithstanding, one might *choose* an opposite-sex partner. The individual might not be able to love his or her marital partner but nonetheless should choose him or her so that children might be produced or so that "unitive" acts might take place. Of course, the disintegration and alienation that would be felt here would be quite real. Further, as a separate matter, it is unlikely that this would be a happy or healthy home for any of the parties involved, although perhaps it might be suggested that this would be a small price to pay for the possibility of engaging in appropriately "unitive" acts.

Consider the individual who loves an opposite-sex, would-be marital partner who is sterile. Should this potentially procreating individual be pressured into choosing a different mate? While the sterile individual might not have chosen his or her condition, the nonsterile individual would be *choosing* to enter into a marriage that could not result in children. Arguably, just as the lesbian or gay person should allegedly choose another mate if there is to be a marriage, this person should as well. Further, it will not help that a way has been offered for the nonvoluntarily sterile person to be able to engage in "procreative-like" acts, because the potentially procreating person would have chosen to be with someone who could not procreate.

Professor Finnis criticizes same-sex marriage because he claims it makes no sense of the commitment that is utterly central to marriage.[79] This is because such marriages allegedly cannot account for marital fidelity that is essentially related to "the generation, nurture, and education of children who each can have only two parents and who are fittingly the primary responsibility (and object of devotion) of *those two parents*."[80] Not only must there be children, but (it seems) the children must be biologically related to each of the parents. Certainly, he is correct that same-sex couples will generally not have children biologically related to both of them.[81] Yet, he seems to be implying that marital fidelity would be problematic in blended families. Thus, where there is a remarriage after the death or divorce of a first spouse, the members of the couple would allegedly have no reason for fidelity unless they produced their own children through their union, even if each had brought children to this marriage from the previous one. If that is not correct—because one can, of course, love one's spouse's children and have as much reason to be faithful on their account as one would have were they one's own biological claim[82]—then same-sex couples might also have reason to be faithful.

Professor Finnis's analysis seems to suggest that a sterile couple would have no reason to be faithful. Perhaps sensing that his theory poses some difficulties for the fidelity of nonfertile couples, he suggests that a man and woman who engage in marital acts "but who have reason to believe that in their case those very same acts will never result in children, can still opt for this form of life as one that makes good sense."[83] Yet, he does not seem to appreciate the implications of his point. It might also make sense for same-sex couples to opt for this "form of life," although he is trying very hard to prevent the state from affording them that opportunity.

It makes no sense to preclude individuals from marrying solely because they cannot have children or because they do not want any (more) children. Further, it would rightly be viewed as insulting to question whether such individuals could be faithful. This is true regardless of the sexes of the individuals involved.

A DIFFERENT APPROACH

A different tack might be adopted to justify differing assessments of same-sex and opposite-sex relationships. Professors George and Bradley offer a different natural law critique of same-sex marriage. According to their theory, individuals who engage in the appropriate kind of sexual behavior can achieve a basic marital good, "whether or not they are capable of conceiving children in their acts of genital union."[84] These theorists reject the tradition within natural law which asserts that sexual acts are only instrumentally good insofar as they can produce children,[85] asserting that such an instrumentalist view "damages the basic good of human integrity."[86] These theorists also seem to reject, at least implicitly, that individuals who intentionally become sterilized will be engaging in an unacceptable practice when having sexual relations.

Professors George and Bradley understand that others may not appreciate the intrinsic goodness of the marital practices of which they speak. However, that is not a worry, since "[i]intrinsic value cannot, strictly speaking, be demonstrated."[87] They further warn that "whatever undermines the sound understanding and practice of marriage in a culture—including ideologies that are hostile to that understanding and practice—makes it difficult for people to grasp the intrinsic value of marriage and marital intercourse."[88]

They thus imply that those who are knowledgeable and, perhaps, whose understanding has not been corrupted will have the proper appreciation of the intrinsic value of marriage and of marital intercourse.

Professors George and Bradley do not seem to appreciate the irony of suggesting that they *can* appreciate the worth of same-sex relationships and same-sex intercourse while at the same time suggesting that the uninitiated or the corrupted will be unable to understand the intrinsic worth of marriage and family. Apparently, these commentators believe that the knowledge of the value of same-sex practices should not be "corrupted" by an actual experiencing of them (i.e., that the *initiated* will be unable to appreciate the intrinsic worth of such relationships and will not have anything relevant to say).

The point here should not be misunderstood. These theorists are correct to point out that there are difficulties in establishing or appreciating intrinsic worth and value, especially by those who due to personal or cultural circumstances have little acquaintance with the matter at issue.[89] Yet, they seem unable to appreciate the implications of such a point, since they themselves may have difficulty in grasping the intrinsic value of same-sex relationships, given the ideologies that are hostile to such an understanding.

John Stuart Mill argued that some pleasures were intrinsically superior to others. However, because others (e.g., Jeremy Bentham) claimed that no pleasures were intrinsically superior to any other,[90] Mill sought to provide a neutral method by which to determine which pleasures were intrinsically superior. He asked that it be supposed that one of two pleasures "is, by those who are competently acquainted with both, placed so far above the other that they prefer it, even though knowing it to be attended with a greater amount of discontent, and would not resign it for any quantity of the other pleasure which their nature is capable of."[91] In that case, we would be "justified in ascribing to the preferred enjoyment a superiority in quality, so far outweighing quantity as to render it, in comparison, of small account."[92]

Mill's approach is helpful to consider in this context. At issue here are claims both about which relationships are superior and about the implications of that superiority. Yet, when one is challenged about a claim that one practice is intrinsically superior to another, it is at best unconvincing to simply reassert that position. Presumably, the other individual will simply reassert the denial of the alleged intrinsic superiority of the practice at issue and no progress will have been achieved. Thus, when Professors George and Bradley claim that the marital relationship is intrinsically superior, they seem to have no helpful response to someone who challenges that claim.

Perhaps, following Mill, one should see whether those who have familiarity with both same-sex and opposite-sex relationships or practices would universally choose one type over the other. Indeed, one wonders what Professors George and Bradley would say if "knowledgeable" judges chose same-sex over opposite-sex practices and relationships, despite some of the societally imposed, extrinsic costs of doing so.[93] Would these theorists suggest that opposite-sex marriages should not be permitted?

There is no need to actually have such a test, because the point here is not to make an assertion about which practices are intrinsically superior to which or which practices have intrinsic worth, but to suggest that the intrinsic worth argument is much less compelling than might first appear and as readily supports as undermines recognizing same-sex marriages.[94] Further, the theorist's argument itself is of the sort that would never be offered in any other marital context. Basically, these theorists are suggesting that because one marriage is intrinsically superior to another, the inferior marriage simply should not exist. Yet, they would never assert such a claim if, for example, same-sex marriages were shown to be intrinsically superior. By the same token, were marriages of fertile couples intrinsically superior to marriages of nonfertile couples, these theorists would never claim that the latter couples should be prohibited from marrying. Indeed, these theorists have already suggested that a position that would preclude nonfertile couples from marrying does not account for the basic good of human integrity.

Natural law theorists who claim that the law cannot recognize same-sex marriages at best illustrate the difficulties in determining what their theory requires, permits, and prohibits.[95] The justifications involving extrinsic and intrinsic worth seem at least as well suited to establishing that such marriages must be recognized than that they should not be. Indeed, other commentators claim that natural law supports the permissibility of same-sex marriage.[96] Yet, even were the natural law critique of same-sex marriage more convincing, it is not at all clear that it would have the import that some theorists suggest.

EXISTING DOMESTIC RELATIONS LAW

One issue is whether natural law as a moral theory permits or prohibits same-sex marriage. Even were it possible to establish that natural law as a moral theory had a determinate position on the permissibility of same-sex unions, a different issue is whether the law should take account of that position and, if so, how. Numerous state and individual interests are implicated in marriage, and those must be considered either instead of or in addition to the natural law position before one can establish that the state should or should not permit same-sex couples to marry.

THE PROMOTION OF MORALITY

The state has a legitimate interest in promoting morality.[97] Yet, as suggested above, the correct moral evaluation of same-sex relationships is at the very least a contested issue. A variety of moral theories suggest that such relationships are morally permissible if not praiseworthy.[98] Thus, even were natural law as a moral theory clearly to hold that same-sex marriages were impermissible, that would not establish that such unions were immoral, since there are a variety of moral systems of which natural law is but one example.[99] The state has a legitimate interest in the promotion of morality generally rather than natural law moral theory in particular or, more to the point, a particular version of natural law moral theory. Thus, even were the natural law positions allegedly establishing the impermissibility of same-sex marriage more persuasive, this would not establish that the state's interest in morality would be promoted by incorporating any of those positions into the law.

When individuals discuss what is moral or immoral, they might not have in mind what a particular theory says but, instead, the majority view of a particular society. Yet, merely because the majority of a particular society happens to believe that a particular practice is immoral does not make it so. For example, those believing interracial marriages immoral are simply wrong, even if in fact they are the majority in a particular community.

Even were there unanimity about which practices were morally permissible or impermissible, it would not follow that the law should reflect those views. As Justice John Paul Stevens suggested in a related context, the "fact that the governing majority in a State has traditionally viewed a particular practice as immoral is not a sufficient reason for upholding a law prohibiting the practice."[100] Presumably, at least one of the points that Justice Stevens has in mind is that there are a variety of individual and state interests that must be considered before a law is enacted or declared constitutional, regardless of the prevailing view about the moral permissibility of the practice at issue.

IMPLICATED INTERESTS IN MARRIAGE

While the state has an interest in promoting morality, it has a number of other interests that must be considered when marriage laws are at issue. State interests in the recognition and promotion of marriage include the promotion of stability, the limitation of the disorganized breakdown of relations, and the provision of a home for the production and rearing of children.[101] All of these interests would be promoted by recognizing same-sex marriages. It should be noted, for example, that same-sex couples are having and raising children, even if those children are not produced through their union. Indeed, some states recognize both members of same-sex couples as the legal parents of the same child, precisely because this will promote the best interests of that child.[102] Thus, some commentators' claims notwithstanding, the state's interest in assuring that children will have a healthy, supportive environment in which to thrive militates in favor of the recognition of same-sex marriage rather than against it.[103] Indeed, a court in Hawaii has already recognized that many individuals in same-sex relationships have good parenting skills.[104]

Ironically, just as the state's interests would be promoted by recognizing same-sex marriages, various individual interests would also be promoted by affording that recognition. The United States Supreme Court has articulated some of the individual interests that are implicated in marriage. Marriages are "expressions of emotional support and public commitment."[105] They have spiritual significance and are the precondition to a variety of government benefits.[106] These interests are implicated whether one is discussing same-sex or opposite-sex couples. Indeed, although the Supreme Court of Hawaii denied that there is a fundamental right to same-sex marriage,[107] the fundamental right to marry arguably should include the right to marry a same-sex partner.[108]

It might be suggested that individual interests militate against recognizing same-sex marriages in that according such rights might demean marriage in others' eyes. Thus, it might be suggested that allowing same-sex couples to marry would devalue the worth of marriage in the eyes of some opposite-sex couples, and that this is the reason that same-sex marriages should not be recognized. Yet, the speciousness of such an argument becomes apparent as soon as one considers other contexts in which such a claim might be made. Certainly, such an argument would not be given much weight were it offered to justify the refusal to recognize interracial or interreligious marriages. Yet, individuals might sincerely believe that the value of their marriages had been diminished by the state's recognizing interracial or interreligious unions.

THE COHERENCE MODEL

Some commentators seem to be offering a much different reason to believe that same-sex marriages should not be recognized by the state, namely, that recognizing such unions would allegedly not cohere with other state practices regarding marriage. This view might seem akin to a Law-as-Integrity theory.[109] However, close analysis yields the conclusion that the coherence model of law would support rather than undermine the state recognition of same-sex marriages.

Professor Finnis points out that sodomitical acts have not been recognized in law as consummating a marriage,[110] implying that the state should not recognize same-sex marriages because same-sex couples could not consummate them. Yet, such an argument is unpersuasive. Were same-sex unions legally recognized, the law would likely be changed so that sodomitical relations might in fact be viewed as consummating the marriage. Even were such a change not to occur, his observation still would not have the import that he suggests. For example, individuals who have married and who have only had sodomitical relations or who have never had sexual relations of any sort will remain married until the marriage is challenged and is held void by a court.[111] Thus, the ability or desire to have intercourse is neither necessary for getting married nor for having the marriage recognized by the state.

A separate point which undermines Professor Finnis's analysis is that, as various state supreme courts have recognized, marital sodomy is protected by the right to privacy.[112] Thus, his analysis notwithstanding, the law recognizes that sodomitical relations fall within the right to privacy for married individuals and thus there would be no lack of coherence in the law were the state to legally recognize same-sex unions.

That many states permit marriages to be annulled for nonconsummation does not suggest that the ability or desire to have sexual relations, much less a particular kind of sexual relations, is necessary for marriage, but merely that the state recognizes that sexual intimacy is an important element of marriage for many individuals. Individuals may reasonably expect that their marital partners will be willing to have sexual relations, although of course the courts will not be setting a standard with respect to how frequently such relations must take place (e.g., daily, weekly, monthly, annually, etc.).

Suppose that two individuals marry and unbeknown to one of the parties the other party is either unable or unwilling to have sexual relations. This might be viewed as a matter of fraud because, absent reason to think otherwise,[113] each of the parties might reasonably assume that the other would be willing to have sexual relations.[114] Yet, even in such a case in which there has been fraud, the marriage would have been made voidable rather than void.[115] If each member of the couple was satisfied with the marriage, lack of sexual relations notwithstanding, then the marriage would continue to be recognized by the state.[116] Thus, ironically, Professor Finnis's discussion of how the state treats marriage and sodomitical relations supports the state's recognizing same-sex marriages, since the state recognizes "nonconsummated" marriages as long as the parties themselves do not object.

THE PRODUCTION AND RAISING OF CHILDREN

Even if the law's treatment of sodomy and the conditions under which marriages will be viewed as valid would pose no difficulty for the state's recognizing same-sex marriages, it might seem that an obvious and important point has been omitted in the above analysis, since same-sex couples (allegedly) cannot fulfill the purpose of marriage. Consider the argument against same-sex marriage that has often been articulated and that seems to represent an instrumentalist natural law view of marriage, namely, that marriage is for the production of children and that same-sex couples should be precluded from marrying because they are unable to have children through their union.

One response is that same-sex couples do have children. However, suppose that were not so. Even if one brackets that same-sex couples are raising children, there is an additional difficulty posed by the purpose-of-marriage argument, namely, that theorists and courts offering this argument either ignore or downplay the importance of the state's not requiring either an ability or a willingness to have children when opposite-sex couples wish to marry.

One court addressing the "problem" posed by infertile, opposite-sex couples who nonetheless wished to marry suggested that the reason that it was permissible for them but not for same-sex couples to marry was that privacy issues would be implicated in the attempt to find out whether the opposite-sex couple could produce a child through their union, whereas no such issues would be involved when a same-sex couple was being considered.[117] Yet, two opposite-sex individuals who publicly volunteered that they were unable to procreate could not be precluded on that account from marrying, notwithstanding their having obviated the privacy issue alluded to by the court. Further, the current policies of some states with respect to the marriages of first cousins establishes that these states have rejected the instrumentalist natural law of marriage, since they will allow first cousins to marry only if they *cannot* reproduce through their union.[118] Not only is the privacy claim that allegedly obviates the need to find out whether opposite-sex couples can reproduce not an issue here, but these couples must affirmatively establish that they cannot produce a child through their union if they wish to marry. The claim that marriage is predicated on the ability and willingness of couples to procreate is not simply false as a theoretical matter but is directly contrary to existing state law.

The claim that natural law prohibits same-sex marriage is deceptive, if not false. The most that can be claimed is that some natural law moral theories condemn same-sex relations, although even those theories may include justifications that as readily support as undermine the moral permissibility of same-sex marriages.

The state clearly has an interest in providing a stable setting for the production and raising of children, and the institution of marriage may help to promote that interest. Yet, marriages have other purposes as well and, even were that the only purpose, recognizing same-sex marriages would promote rather than undermine that legitimate, significant state interest, because gay and lesbian couples do have and raise children.

Both the intrinsic and extrinsic natural law arguments against the state recognition of same-sex marriage are unconvincing. Further, the state has a variety of interests, not even addressed in those critiques, that would all be served by recognizing same-sex marriages. Finally, since many of the individual interests promoted in opposite-sex marriages are also promoted in same-sex marriages, there are overwhelming number of reasons for the state to recognize those unions.

IMPLICATIONS FOR NATURAL LAW AS A LEGAL THEORY

There is no small irony in the claim that natural law requires that same-sex marriages not be recognized, especially if one considers this a claim about what natural law as a legal theory requires. When Professor Lon Fuller offered reasons to think that it would be advantageous to require that law be connected to morality in an essential way, he suggested that such a requirement would be especially beneficial for minorities.[119] He offered a thought experiment to establish his point.

Professor Fuller imagined that he had been "transported to a country where . . . [his] beliefs were anathemas."[120] He suggested that there might be "reason to fear that the law might be covertly manipulated to . . . [his] disadvantage," although he doubted that he "would be apprehensive that its injunctions would be set aside by an appeal to a morality higher than law."[121] He was thus suggesting that moral claims would not be used to bolster unfair treatment of minorities.

Indeed, Professor Fuller was willing to take his argument a step further, since he was confident that if he as a member of a minority "felt that the law itself was . . . [his] safest refuge, . . . it . . . would be because even in the most perverted regimes there is a certain hesitancy about writing cruelties, intolerances, and inhumanities into law."[122] He believed that such a hesitancy would itself derive, "not from a separation of law and morals, but precisely from an identification of law with those demands of morality that are the most urgent and obviously justifiable."[123] He was thus suggesting that the allegedly necessary connection between law and morality would provide a bulwark against biased treatment of minorities.

Yet, some of the obvious demands of morality (e.g., that individuals should be treated equally and should have their fundamental interests respected absent countervailing, noninvidious, compelling state interests) are ignored in discussions of whether same-sex couples should be allowed to marry. Certainly, moral arguments are sometimes used to secure the law's treating minorities in a fairer way and, further, it is not hard to imagine other commentators using specious nonmoral reasons to establish, for example, that same-sex couples should be denied the right to marry. Thus, it is not suggested here that positing a necessary connection between law and morality will result in minorities receiving worse treatment. Rather, it is suggested that the natural law position provides no guarantee that minorities will be treated any more favorably than they would be treated in a legal positivist system.

There are numerous moral and legal reasons for states to recognize same-sex unions. That many if not most states will not recognize such unions, absent court order, has more to do with a current acceptance of second-class citizenship for a whole class of individuals than with the kinds of reasons traditionally offered to refuse to recognize such marriages.[124]

In 1996, Congress passed the Defense of Marriage Act, which ostensibly was intended to allow states to decide for themselves whether they wanted to recognize same-sex marriages. However, just as state refusals to recognize same-sex unions are appropriately characterized as attempts to stigmatize a particular group, so, too, is Congress's having passed the Defense of Marriage Act. As will be explained in the next chapter, that Act is unconstitutional, at least in part, precisely because it involved an attempt by Congress to impose a disability on a discrete, identifiable group.

NOTES

1. See Philip Soper, "Some Natural Confusions about Natural Law," 90 *Mich L. Rev.* 2393, 2395 (1992) (natural law as a legal theory "takes its shape from its explicit opposition to legal positivism: the legal positivist claims that no necessary connection exists between law and morality; the natural law legal theorist denies that a sharp separation of these concepts is possible").

2. See id.

3. See id. at 2400 ("To be a natural law legal theorist seems only to require that one determine legal validity by reference, not only to the positivist test of pedigree, but also by reference to morality—including conventional morality if that turns out to be the true theory of morality").

4. See Lon L. Fuller, "Positivism and Fidelity to Law—A Reply to Professor Hart," 71 *Harv. L. Rev.* 630, 644–45 (1958) (discussing the inner morality of law).

5. See Lon L. Fuller, *The Morality of Law*, 39 (New Haven, CT: Yale University Press, rev. ed. 1969) (discussing eight ways to fail to make a law); see also Daniel E. Wueste, Book Review, "Fuller's Processual Philosophy of Law," 71 *Cornell L. Rev.* 1205, 1213 (1986) (discussing Fuller's view).

6. See Soper, "Some Natural Confusions," 90 *Mich L. Rev.* at 2394 ("discussing one of the characteristics that makes a moral theory a natural law theory: namely, the insistence that moral principles are objectively valid and discoverable by reason"). See also Lloyd L. Weinreb, "The Moral Point of View," in Robert P. George ed., *Natural Law, Liberalism, and Morality*, 195, 196 (Oxford: Clarendon Press, 1996) (describing the common element of natural law theories as "simply the assertion of some moral principle [or set of principles] as certain and dispositive of the matter at hand").

7. See John Stuart Mill, *Utilitarianism*, in J. M. Robson ed., Vol. 10, *Collected Works of John Stuart Mill*, Chap. 1, 205 (Toronto: University of Toronto Press, 1969).

8. See id., Chap. 4, 234–39 (offering a kind of "proof" for the Principle of Utility).

9. See H. L. A. Hart, "Positivism and the Separation of Law and Morals," 71 *Harv. L. Rev.* 593, 596–97 (1958) (discussing Austin's reading of Blackstone to the effect that a law which conflicts with Divine Law is not a law).

10. See Scott Ruskay-Kidd, "The Defense of Marriage Act and the Over-

extension of Congressional Authority," 97 *Colum. L. Rev.* 1435, 1446 (1997) ("there are ample sources for the argument that gay and lesbian relationships contravene natural law"); Joseph W. Hovermill, "A Conflict of Laws and Morals: The Choice of Law Implications of Hawaii's Recognition of Same-Sex Marriages," 53 *Md. L. Rev.* 450, 482–83 (1994) (suggesting that same-sex marriages are contrary to natural law).

11. See Soper, "Some Natural Confusions," 90 *Mich L. Rev.* at 2395 ("Legal theory, in short, seems to address a question about the connection between two concepts, law and morality. Whatever the upshot of that conceptual inquiry, the question of which moral theory is true seems open to independent argument and determination").

12. See *Sniadach v. Family Finance Corp. of Bay View*, 395 U.S. 336, 351 (1969) (Black, J., dissenting) (suggesting that Natural Law "standards do not bind judges within any boundaries that can be precisely marked or defined by words for holding laws unconstitutional"). See also Lloyd L. Weinreb, *Natural Law and Justice*, 2 (Cambridge, Mass: Harvard University Press, 1987); Kathryn Dean Kendell, "Principles and Prejudice: Lesbian and Gay Civil Marriage and the Realization of Equality," 22 *J. Contemp. L.* 81, 92 (1996) ("natural law can be asserted for virtually any proposition on any side of an issue").

13. Cf. David A. J. Richards, *Women, Gays, and the Constitution: The Grounds for Feminism and Gay Rights in Culture and Law*, 246–49 (Chicago: University of Chicago Press, 1998).

14. Charles Rice suggests this. See generally Charles E. Rice, "Some Reasons for a Restoration of Natural Law Jurisprudence," 24 *Wake Forest L. Rev.* 539 (1989).

15. See, for example, Bruce A. Ackerman, *Social Justice in the Liberal State*, 45-49 (New Haven, CT: Yale University Press, 1980) (discussing the claim that utility comparisons cannot be made). See also Mark Strasser, *The Moral Philosophy of John Stuart Mill: Toward Modifications of Contemporary Utilitarianism*, 54–78 (Wakefield, N.H.: Longwood Academic, 1991) (discussing whether utilitarian calculations are possible).

16. See William N. Eskridge, Jr., *The Case for Same-Sex Marriage: From Sexual Liberty to Civilized Commitment*, 97 (New York: The Free Press, 1996) (discussing how the unitive goal of marriage would should induce natural law theorists to support same-sex marriage).

17. See *Kinney v. Commonwealth*, 71 Va. (30 Gratt.) 858, 869 (1878) (God and nature forbid interracial marriage); *State v. Gibson*, 36 Ind. 389, 402–5 (1871) (The state must be allowed to prohibit interracial marriage to effect God's wishes.); Rodney Patton, Student Work, "Queerly Unconstitutional?: South Carolina Bans Same-Sex Marriage," 48 *S.C. L. Rev.* 685, 703–4 (1997) ("South Carolina, like many other states, once prohibited interracial marriages because such unions were believed to violate natural law"); James Trosino, Note, "American Wedding: Same-Sex Marriage and the Miscegenation Analogy," 73 *B.U. L. Rev.* 93, 114 (1993) (discussing individuals "claiming that interracial marriage was against the will of God").

18. See *Naim v. Naim*, 87 S.E.2d 749 (Va. 1955). The Supreme Court of Appeals of Virginia made clear its belief that God prohibited interracial unions. See id. at 752. In *Loving v. Virginia*, 388 U.S. 1, 3 (1967), the United States Supreme Court discussed a lower court's opinion that God did not intend that the races marry.

19. See, for example, *Bob Jones University v. Simon*, 416 U.S. 725 (1974). The University subscribed to certain precepts, including that "God intended segregation of the races and that the Scriptures forbid interracial marriage." See id. at 735.

20. See John Finnis, *Natural Law and Natural Rights*, 44 (Oxford: Clarendon Press, 1980) (suggesting that rightness and wrongness depend upon the nature of things). Presumably, on this view, these moral qualities would be unchanging.

21. Francis Hutcheson, *A System of Moral Philosophy*, Bk. 1, Chap. 1, Art. 8, 30 (New York: A. M. Kelley, reprinted 1968). For a discussion of Hutcheson's moral views, see Mark Strasser, *Francis Hutcheson's Moral Theory: Its Form and Utility* (Wakefield, N.H.: Longwood Academic, 1990).

22. See Lynne Marie Kohm, "The Homosexual 'Union': Should Gay and Lesbian Partnerships Be Granted the Same Status as Marriage?" 22 *J. Contemp. L.* 51, 55–56 (1996).

23. See Rice, "Some Reasons for a Restoration," 24 *Wake Forest L. Rev.* at 560–562 (discussing the need for reason to be aided by revelation).

24. See *Lonas v. State*, 50 Tenn. (3 Heisk) 287, 310–11 (1871) ("A sound philanthropy, looking to the public peace and the happiness of both races, would regard any effort to intermerge the individuality of the races as a calamity full of the saddest and gloomiest portent to the generations that are to come after us").

25. See *Jones v. Commonwealth*, 79 Va. 213, 216 (1884).

26. See *Jones v. Commonwealth*, 80 Va. 538, 544–45 (1885).

27. *See Kinney*, 71 Va. at 869.

28. John Finnis, "Law, Morality, and 'Sexual Orientation,' " in John Corvino ed., *Same Sex: Debating the Ethics, Science, and Culture of Homosexuality*, 31, 37 (Lanham, Md: Rowman & Littlefield, 1997).

29. See id.

30. Id.

31. See, for example, Baehr v. Miike, 1996 WL 694235, at *20 (Hawaii Cir. Ct).

32. Cf. Finnis, "Law, Morality, and 'Sexual Orientation,' " in Corvino ed., *Same Sex* at 37.

33. See Toni M. Massaro, "Gay Rights, Thick and Thin," 49 *Stan. L. Rev.* 45, 100 (1996) (suggesting that Finnis's "claim that a particular action by government will have the effect of undermining companionate marriage is, at root, empirical and instrumental" and thus will be subject to disconfirmation). Finnis claims that marriages also have intrinsic worth. See John Finnis, "Is Natural Law Theory Compatible with Limited Government?" in George ed., *Natural Law, Liberalism, and Morality*, 1, 14.

34. See *Equality Foundation of Greater Cincinnati, Inc. v. City of Cincinnati*, 860 F. Supp. 417, 442 (S.D. Ohio, 1994) (heterosexual males are far more responsible for the breakdown of the family than gays), rev'd, 54 F.3d 261 (6th Cir. 1995), cert. granted, judgment vacated by 116 S. Ct. 2519 (1996), rev'd, judgment vacated by 128 F.3d 289 (6th Cir. 1997).

35. Cf. Finnis, "Is Natural Law Theory Compatible," in George ed., *Natural Law, Liberalism, and Morality* at 12 (discussing how silence about why gays and lesbians should be disadvantaged may raise the suspicion that such disabilities are "grounded in subrational motivations"). Yet, the same inference might be drawn when obviously specious arguments are offered.

36. *Bowers v. Harwick*, 478 U.S 186, 212 (1986) (Blackmun, J., dissenting).
37. Id. at 211–12 (Blackmun, J., dissenting).
38. *Commonwealth v. Wasson*, 842 S.W.2d 487, 501 (Ky. 1993).
39. Id.
40. See *Bowers*, 478 U.S. at 200 (Blackmun, J., dissenting).
41. See id. (Blackmun, J., dissenting) (suggesting that "the majority has distorted the question this case presents").
42. See *State v. Santos*, 413 A.2d 58, 68 (R.I. 1980) (right to privacy does not include the right to engage in nonmarital sodomy).
43. *Bowers*, 478 U.S. at 190.
44. See id. at 200 (Blackmun, J., dissenting) ("Unlike the Court, the Georgia Legislature has not proceeded on the assumption that homosexuals are so different from other citizens that their lives may be controlled in a way that would not be tolerated if it limited the choices of those other citizens").
45. *Perez v. Lippold*, 198 P.2d 17, 32 (Cal. 1948) (Carter, J., concurring).
46. See Lynn D. Wardle, "A Critical Analysis of Constitutional Claims for Same-Sex Marriage," 1996 *BYU L. Rev.* 1, 21 (charging that "opposition to same-sex marriage is treated as proof of narrow-mindedness, dangerous fundamentalism, or an unprofessional mixing of personal moral or religious preferences and law").
47. See id. at 75.
48. See id. at 79.
49. See *McLaughlin v. Florida*, 379 U.S. 184, 195 (1964).
50. See Mark Strasser, "Family, Definitions, and the Constitution: On the Antimiscegenation Analogy," 25 *Suffolk U. L. Rev.* 981, 1019–21 (1991) (discussing the hypocrisy involved in setting up a system of mutually reinforcing invidiously discriminatory laws and claiming such laws reasonable because they reinforced one another).
51. See *State v. Jackson*, 80 Mo. 175, 179 (1883) ("if the issue of a black man and a white woman, and a white man and a black woman, intermarry, they cannot possibly have any progeny, and such a fact sufficiently justifies those laws which forbid the intermarriage of blacks and whites").
52. See *Scott v. State*, 39 Ga. 321, 323 (1869). See also Trosino, "American Wedding," 73 *B.U. L. Rev.* at 101 (the popular belief that children of interrracial marriages were mentally and physically inferior to pure race children was offered as a justification to prevent interracial marriage).
53. See Eskridge, *The Case for Same-Sex Marriage*, 96–97.
54. See Finnis, "Is Natural Law Theory Compatible," in George ed., *Natural Law, Liberalism, and Morality* at 16.
55. Id. at 15.
56. John Finnis, "Law Morality, and 'Sexual Orientation,' " in Corvino ed., *Same Sex* at 34.
57. Id. at 35.
58. Id.
59. Id. at 35–36.
60. See Finnis, "Is Natural Law Theory Compatible," in George ed., *Natural Law, Liberalism, and Morality* at 16.
61. See Finnis, "Law Morality, and 'Sexual Orientation,' " in Corvino ed., *Same Sex* at 38 (describing intentionally sterilized intercourse as nonmarital).

62. For a discussion of act-individuation, see Mark Strasser, *Agency, Free Will, and Moral Responsibility*, 37–58 (Wakefield, N.H.: Hollowbrook Publishing, 1992).

63. See Stephen Macedo, "Homosexuality and the Conservative Mind," 84 *Geo. L.J.* 261, 280 (1995) (suggesting that heterosexual relations that cannot produce children are not appropriately included within the correct kind).

64. Some of the ideas expressed in this section are contained in Mark Strasser, *Legally Wed: Same-Sex Marriage and the Constitution* 54–55 (Ithaca, N.Y.: Cornell University Press, 1997).

65. See Finnis, "Is Natural Law Theory Compatible," in George ed., *Natural Law, Liberalism, and Morality* at 25–26 n.76.

66. Finnis, "Law Morality, and 'Sexual Orientation,' " in Corvino ed., *Same Sex* at 40.

67. See id. at 38.

68. Id. at 39.

69. Id.

70. Id. at 39–40.

71. Id. at 39.

72. Id.

73. See Finnis, "Is Natural Law Theory Compatible," in George ed., *Natural Law, Liberalism, and Morality* at 15.

74. Id.

75. See Mary Becker, "Problems with the Privatization of Heterosexuality," 73 *Denver U. L. Rev.* 1169, 1180–81 (1996) (discussing reasons people in marital relationships might have unwanted sex).

76. Finnis, "Law Morality, and 'Sexual Orientation,' " in Corvino ed., *Same Sex* at 37.

77. See Macedo, "Homosexuality and the Conservative Mind," 84 *Geo. L.J.* at 281 (questioning the "new Natural Law's cramped view of valuable sexual relations").

78. This might require artificial insemination of the husband's sperm.

79. Finnis, "Law Morality, and 'Sexual Orientation,' " in Corvino ed., *Same Sex* at 41.

80. Id.

81. The sibling of one partner might donate eggs or sperm to be combined with the genetic material of the other partner. That way, each would be biologically connected to the child.

82. It is not claimed here that one should only be faithful for the children's sake, but that is a separate matter.

83. Finnis, "Law Morality, and 'Sexual Orientation,' " in Corvino ed., *Same Sex* at 42.

84. See Robert P. George & Gerard V. Bradley, "Marriage and the Liberal Imagination," 84 *Geo. L.J.* 301, 302 (1995).

85. See id. at 304.

86. Id. at 305.

87. Id. at 307.

88. Id.

89. Id.

90. Bentham writes, "Prejudice apart, the game of push-pin is of equal value

with the arts and sciences of music and poetry. If the game of push-pin furnish more pleasure, it is more valuable than either." See "The Rationale of Reward," reprinted in John Bowring ed., *The Works of Jeremy Bentham*, vol. 2, 253 (New York: Russell & Russell, 1962).

91. Mill, in Robson ed., *Utilitarianism*, Chap. 2, p. 210.

92. Id.

93. Some of the points here are discussed in Strasser, *Legally Wed*, 55–56.

94. For an argument that same-sex relationships are morally preferable to opposite-sex relationships, see generally Mary Becker, "Problems with the Privatization of Heterosexuality," 73 *Denv. U. L. Rev.* 1169 (1996).

95. See Philip Soper, "Making Sense of Modern Jurisprudence: The Paradox of Positivism and the Challenge for Natural Law," 22 *Creighton L. Rev.* 67, 72 (1988) (suggesting that it is not surprising that there is no consensus about what natural law dictates).

96. See, for example, Vincent J. Samar, *Justifying Judgment: Practicing Law and Philosophy*, 188 (Lawrence: University Press of Kansas, 1998) (suggesting that natural law theory is compatible with same-sex marriage).

97. See *Berman v. Parker*, 348 U.S. 26, 32 (1954) (promotion of morality is part of the traditional police power of the state).

98. See Mark Strasser, "Suspect Classes and Suspect Classifications: On Discriminating, Unwittingly or Otherwise," 64 *Temp. L. Rev.* 937, 966–67 (1991) ("according to a variety of theories, homosexual behavior is morally permissible").

99. See Mark Strasser, "Judicial Good Faith and the *Baehr* Essentials: On Giving Credit Where It's Due," 28 *Rutgers L.J.* 313, 351 (1997) ("merely because Natural Law is *a* system of morality does not imply that it is the *only* system of morality").

100. *Bowers*, 478 U.S at 216 (1986) (Stevens J., dissenting). See also *Gryczan v. State*, 942 P.2d 112, 125 (Mont. 1997):

> it does not follow, however, that simply because the legislature has enacted as law what may be a moral choice of the majority, the courts are, thereafter, bound to simply acquiesce. Our Constitution . . . guarantee[s] to all persons, whether in the majority or in a minority, those certain basic freedoms and rights which are set forth in the Declaration of Rights, not the least of which is the right of individual privacy. Regardless that majoritarian morality may be expressed in the public policy pronouncements of the legislature, it remains the obligation of the courts—and of this Court in particular—to scrupulously support, protect and defend those rights and liberties guaranteed to all persons under our Constitution.

101. See Strasser, "Judicial Good Faith," 28 *Rutgers L.J.* at 361–63 (discussing states interests in marriage).

102. See *Adoption of Tammy*, 619 N.E.2d 315 (Mass. 1993); *In re Jacob*, 660 N.E.2d 397 (N.Y. 1995); *Adoptions of B.L.V.B. & E.L.V.B.*, 628 A.2d 1271 (Vt. 1993).

103. For further discussion of the societal interests implicated in recognizing same-sex marriages, see generally Mark Strasser, "Domestic Relations Jurisprudence and the Great, Slumbering *Baehr*: On Definitional Preclusion, Equal Protection, and Fundamental Interests," 64 *Fordham L. Rev.* 921, 976–980 (1995).

104. See generally *Baehr v. Miike*, 1996 WL 694235 (Haw Cir Ct.).

105. *Turner v. Safley*, 482 U.S. 78, 95 (1987).

106. Id. at 96.

107. See *Lewin*, 852 P.2d at 55.

108. See *Brause v. Bureau of Vital Statistics*, 1998 WL 88743, at *4 (Alaska Super.) (choice of same-sex life partner implicates fundamental right under Alaska Constitution). See also Strasser, *Legally Wed*, Chap. 3.

109. For a discussion of this theory, see generally Ronald Dworkin, *Law's Empire* (Cambridge, MA: Harvard University Press, 1986).

110. Finnis, "Law Morality, and 'Sexual Orientation,' " in Corvino ed., *Same Sex* at 36.

111. See *Woods v. Woods*, 638 S.W.2d 403 (Tenn. App. 1982) (lack of consummation made marriage voidable rather than void).

112. See *Christensen v. State*, 468 S.E.2d 188 (Ga. 1996); *State v. Santos*, 413 A.2d 58 (R.I. 1980).

113. See *Jarzem v. Bierhaus*, 415 So.2d 88, 90 (Fla. App. 1982) ("if the wife's claim for annulment or divorce had been based upon the fact that the husband was impotent, it would have been unavailing if she had knowledge of such a fact before the marriage").

114. See *In re Marriage of Liu (Liu v. Liu)*, 242 Cal. Rptr. 649, 656 (Ct. App. 1987) ("An annulment may be had for fraud where a wife harbors a secret intention at the time of the marriage not to engage in sexual relations with her husband") (citing *Handley v. Handley*, 3 Cal. Rptr. 910 [Ct. App. 1960]).

115. See *Tyson v. State*, 90 So. 622, 623 (Fla. 1922) ("The general rule, supported by the great weight of authority and which we regard as sound in principle, is to the effect that a marriage procured by fraud or while one of the parties thereto is actually under legal duress is voidable only, and therefore valid and binding upon the parties until annulled by a court of competent jurisdiction") (citing *Hawkins v. Hawkins*, 38 So. 640 [Ala. 1905]).

116. In *Jarzem v. Bierhaus*, 415 So.2d 88 (Fla. App. 1982), the marriage was dissolved, not because the husband and wife were not having sexual relations, but because he was having relations with someone else outside of the marriage. Had he been having sexual relations with no one, the marriage would not have been voidable. See id. at 90.

117. See *Adams v. Howerton*, 486 F. Supp. 1119, 1125 (C.D. Cal. 1980).

118. See Ariz. Rev. Stat. Ann. Sec. 25–101 (West 1991) (over 65 or one is unable to reproduce); 750 Ill. Comp. Stat. Ann. 5/212 (West 1997 Supp.) (over 50 or either party permanently and irreversibly sterile); Ind. Code Ann. 31–7-1–3 (West 1996 Supp.) (over 65); Utah Code Ann. § 30–1-1 (1995) (over 65 or both over 55 and one cannot reproduce); Wis. Stat. Ann. (West 1993) § 765.03 (female 55 or either submits affadavit permanently sterile).

119. See Fuller, "Positivism and Fidelity to Law," 71 *Harv. L. Rev.* at 637.

120. Id.

121. Id.

122. Id.

123. Id.

124. See Joseph Raz, "Liberty and Trust," in George ed., *Natural Law, Liberalism, and Morality*, 113, 126 (discussing various manifestations of bigotry that "condemn gay men and lesbians to second class status in their own society").

8

The Defense of Marriage Act

In 1996, Congress passed the Defense of Marriage Act (DOMA), which denied recognition of same-sex marriages for federal purposes and which purportedly gave each state the right not to recognize such marriages even if validly celebrated in another state.[1] The Act violates a number of constitutional provisions: the Due Process Clause, the Equal Protection Clause, the Bill of Attainder Clause, and the Privileges and Immunities Clause.[2] Further, it is terrible from a public policy standpoint, since it will undermine the unity that the Full Faith and Credit Clause was designed to secure, destabilize family relations, and disappoint the justified expectations of countless innocent individuals.

THE PRE-DOMA SETTING

The system involving interstate recognition of marriage and divorce that existed prior to DOMA's enactment involved a balancing of different state and individual interests, although as a general matter all parties concerned had, and continue to have, an interest in protecting the predictability of marriages[3] and the security and stability in marriages.[4] By recognizing those marriages validly celebrated in another state, even if prohibited in the domicile,[5] and by determining the validity of marriages by applying the laws of the states of celebration or domicile at the time of the marriage,[6] states promote the certainty and stability of marriage, thereby allowing individuals to feel secure in their marriages and to make future plans.

As a general matter, the reason that each state will recognize a marriage recognized in both the states of celebration and domicile is not that the Full Faith and Credit Clause requires that recognition. Rather, it is because each state as a matter of its own choice of law rules recognizes that the only states whose law might potentially be applicable to determine the validity of the marriage are the states of celebration and domicile at the time of the marriage.

Suppose that the system had been set up differently. Suppose that marriages validly celebrated in one state had to be recognized in each of the other states by virtue of the Full Faith and Credit Clause. That would mean that a domicile at the time of the marriage might be forced to recognize a marriage of its domiciliaries that contravened local law merely because some other state was willing to recognize that union. Although such a system would in fact increase the certainty and stability of marriage, this was thought to give each state too much power over the domestic relations law of sister states. Individuals domiciled in one state could evade local law by marrying elsewhere, all the while intending to live in the very state in which such unions had been declared contrary to an important public policy. In a sense, such a system would allow individuals to impose a fraud on their domicile, since at the very time that they were intending to live in that state they would be evading its law by marrying elsewhere.

Suppose that the different system described above was modified slightly—marriages validly celebrated in one state had to be recognized in each of the other states by virtue of the Full Faith and Credit Clause unless the marriage was obnoxious to an important public policy of the forum state. In such a system, the validity of any marriage would be at least potentially dependent upon its not being obnoxious to any state's law. Otherwise, someone who wanted to avoid the responsibilities of a marriage could simply move to a state where such marriages were considered obnoxious to an important public policy, confident that the state would refuse to recognize the marriage.

The current system is a compromise between these two possible systems. It does not force the domicile at the time of the marriage to recognize its domiciliaries' union merely because it was validly celebrated in another state. It also does not allow individuals to forum shop to defeat the responsibilities of marriage.[7] Thus, an individual who has tired of his marriage will not be permitted to go to another state to have a court declare that the marriage had never existed at all. While an individual can go to another state to get a divorce, he will not be able thereby to avoid his marital responsibilities, since the marriage still will have existed and there may be support to be awarded or property to be distributed.

THE DEFENSE OF MARRIAGE ACT

The Defense of Marriage Act has two sections, one specifying the Full Faith and Credit ramifications if a same-sex marriage is validly celebrated in one of the states, and the other specifying the definition of marriage for federal purposes. Each section of the Act is constitutionally infirm, although not entirely for the same reasons.

The part of the Act that affects Full Faith and Credit reads:

No state, territory or possession of the United States, or Indian tribe, shall be required to give effect to any public act, record, or judicial proceeding of any other State, territory, possession, or tribe respecting a relationship between persons of the the same sex that is treated as a marriage under the laws of such *other* State, territory, possession, or tribe, or a right or claim arising from such relationship.[8]

The very brevity of the provision makes it difficult to interpret. For example, it nowhere mentions choice of law rules, and it presumably does not entitle a state to ignore its own choice of law rules and refuse to recognize a same-sex marrage. Suppose, for example, that a state has adopted the *Second Restatement* with respect to the recognition of marriages. Suppose further that this state had no contacts with the parties or the marriage at the time that the marriage was contracted. According to its own law, the state must recognize the marriage if it was valid in the states of celebration and domicile at the time of the marriage.

If DOMA is neither intended to change state law[9] nor to permit states to ignore their own laws (including their own choice of law rules) with respect to whether a same-sex marriage will be recognized, it is unclear what effects the Act will have with respect to the interstate recognition of marriages. Those states "given" the option by DOMA to refuse to recognize same-sex marriages already have it and those states not having that option will not have suddenly acquired it through DOMA.[10] Indeed, some interpret DOMA not to be changing current law and, instead, merely to be reaffirming the right of the domicile to refuse to recognize a marriage validly celebrated elsewhere. Thus, the Act would have been adopted to make clear to courts that a domicile will be allowed to refuse to recognize its domiciliaries' same-sex marriages that have been validly celebrated in another state if, for example, the domicile had declared such marriages void. If this was the intention, the Act could have been written more felicitously to express that aim. As written, the Act simply is not clear with respect to its implications for choice of law, and it will serve as an open invitation for different courts to construe it in radically different ways.

CHOICE OF LAW

States have two different kinds of law that must be distinguished: (1) their substantive law, and (2) their choice of law rules. The substantive law will specify who may marry whom. The choice of law rules will specify which state's substantive law will apply to a marriage validly celebrated in another state.

State choice of law rules are double-edged, since they specify both when a particular state's law will apply and when it will not apply. If DOMA really merely "reaffirms current practice and policy,"[11] then same-sex marriages validly celebrated in one state will have to be recognized by all states unless the domiciliary state has (1) declared such marriages void or in some other way indicated that the marriage violates an important public policy of the State, or (2) passed an Evasion Statute. Further, a state that is not the domicile at the time of the marriage will be forced by its own law (as constrained by federal constitutional guarantees, as will be explained below) to recognize a marriage validly celebrated in another state as long as the domicile at the time of marriage recognized it.

CONGRESSIONAL INTENT AND CHOICE OF LAW RULES

It might be argued that Congress passed DOMA to allow states a wider range of choice of law options. However, an examination of the language of DOMA reveals that no choice of law rules are even suggested.[12] Further, the alleged problem that Congress was rectifying was that which would be posed by individuals marrying in Hawaii and then going back to their domiciles and demanding that their home states recognize the marriage.[13] Because Congress would have specified the range of choice of law rules had it been interested in doing so,[14] there is no reason to read them into the statute.

An additional difficulty posed by the wider range of choice of law rules interpretation is that it is simply unclear what this new range of choice of law rules would include. One possibility would be that any state that became the domicile of a same-sex couple would have the option of refusing to recognize their union. This would differ from the *First Restatement* approach in that the domicile would be permitted not only to refuse to recognize the incidents of marriage but also the marriage itself. Another possibility would be that a marriage would not have to be recognized in any state that made such unions void. This would allow even nondomiciles to refuse to recognize the marriage. Yet another possibility would be that such marriages would not have to be recognized in any state prohibiting such unions. Presumably, other possibilities might occur to a court. Of course, since Congress said nothing about the matter, a court would simply have to invent the new range of choice of law rules.

THE TWO FACES OF FEDERALISM

DOMA has been championed as an example of federalism at work.[15] However, DOMA is hardly that. Federalism has two faces. It protects state sovereignty in certain respects but also requires states to give up some of their sovereignty for the sake of the federal union. As the United States Supreme Court explained, "The Full Faith and Credit Clause . . . substituted a command for the earlier principles of comity and thus basically altered the status of the States as independent sovereigns."[16] DOMA does the exact opposite and substitutes the principles of comity for the earlier command to recognize sister state decrees. However, as the Court has already made clear, "For States of the Union, the constitutional limitation imposed by the full faith and credit clause abolished, in large measure, the general principle of international law by which local policy is permitted to dominate rules of comity."[17]

Actually, DOMA does not really alter the status of the states, since it allows them to use the principles of comity *only* when same-sex marriages are at issue. Congress has not enacted legislation that restores state sovereignty, but has merely authorized states to invidiously discriminate against lesbians and gays by treating same-sex marriages differently from any other marriage. Thus, suppose that one state treats first-cousin marriages as null and void but another state permits first cousins to marry. If two first cousins marry in the latter state while they are domiciled there, the former state would have to recognize the marriage should the couple move there a few years after the marriage was celebrated. The former state would not have been granted the right by Congress to assert its sovereignty and refuse to recognize the first-cousin marriage. On the contrary, because the marriage would have been valid in the states of celebration and domicile at the time of the marriage, the former state would have to recognize it.

Insofar as federalism requires states to give up some of the power they would have had as independent countries, DOMA undermines federalism by relieving states of the obligations they incurred by becoming members of the United States. The claim that Congress is protecting federalism by passing DOMA is as specious as the claim that Congress was preventing same-sex couples from enjoying "special rights." Only same-sex couples have been subjected to the possibility that their marriages may be treated as invalid, notwithstanding their having been valid in the states of celebration and domicile at the time of the marriage.

DUE PROCESS

The Supreme Court has suggested that a choice of law rule that grossly upsets justified expectations may violate Due Process.[18] As Justice Stevens has explained, a "choice-of-law decision that frustrates the justifiable expectations of the parties can be fundamentally unfair,"[19] and the prevention of unfairness "has been the central concern in this Court's review of choice-of-law decisions under the Due Process Clause."[20] It should be clear that individuals who marry in their domicile, having no plan to live elsewhere, would have the reasonable, justified expectation that their marriage would be valid.[21]

Ordinarily, the interest of the forum that justifies application of its own law must have existed at the time of the occurrence or transaction,[22] because application of the law of some other state would not be foreseeable and hence unfair.[23] In the case of marriage, the interested parties would include the domicile(s) of the parties, the state where the marriage takes place, and the state where the couple plans to live immediately after the marriage. A domicile acquired years after the marriage had taken place would simply have had no interest in the marriage at the time it was celebrated and thus application of its law would be fundamentally unfair. Use of a subsequent domicile's law to retroactively invalidate a marriage[24] would have all of the difficulties attendant on retrospective applications of law.[25]

Yet, DOMA has implications that are even more unfair than those suggested above. If indeed DOMA permits subsequent domiciles to invalidate marriages contracted years earlier, then it may also permit nondomiciles to invalidate marriages contracted years earlier, since there is no language in the Defense of Marriage Act which says that only future domiciles could invalidate a past marriage. If due process concerns are not implicated when a subsequent nondomicile retroactively nullifies a marriage celebrated twenty years earlier, it is not clear when those concerns would be implicated. The notions of reasonable expectations and unfair surprise have no meaning if they would not preclude this kind of case.

This point suggests that DOMA is unconstitutional but also that states could not of their own accord invalidate such marriages. Just as due process is violated by Congress's having accorded the states the power to invalidate marriages with which they had had no contacts at the time of celebration, due process would be violated by states appropriating that power for themselves. A subsequent domicile will lack the necessary contacts with a valid marriage at the time it was celebrated in a sister domiciliary state to be able to nullify it, say, twenty years later.

INTERSTATE RECOGNITION OF DIVORCE

Currently, the general rule is that if a court of general jurisdiction in one state issues a divorce decree, that decree will be unassailable in other states' courts absent fraud or lack of jurisdiction.[26] However, because DOMA states that no state shall be required to give effect to any judicial proceeding respecting a same-sex marriage under the laws of another state, DOMA would entitle a state to refuse to recognize a divorce decree of another state if it involved same-sex partners. This would mean, for example, that an individual would risk being charged with attempted bigamy should she attempt to remarry after having secured a divorce from her same-sex partner, because a forum might refuse to recognize the divorce that she had obtained, notwithstanding the absence of fraud and the decree-granting court having had both personal and subject matter jurisdiction.

It is by no means clear that Congress even has the power to create an exception with respect to which divorces shall be given full faith and credit. For example, the United States Supreme Court has pointed out that "the considerable interests involved and the substantial and far-reaching effects which the allowance of an exception [for divorce] would have on innocent persons indicate that the purpose of the full faith and credit clause" would be "thwarted to a substantial degree"[27] were such an exception made. Further, such an exception is especially suspicious when it is targeted to disadvantage a particular minority.

Late in the nineteenth century, the Court quoted with approval a decision by the Supreme Court of Connecticut in which the constitutionality of that state's divorce law was upheld.[28] The Connecticut court had worried that if it had struck down the law as unconstitutional, it could have caused "consequences easily conceived but not easily expressed, such as bastardizing the issue and subjecting the parties to punishment for adultery."[29] Thus, the court feared that striking the law would affect the status of children born in subsequent marriages (which might have been made bigamous and void had the divorce law been struck)[30] and would create the possibility that criminal charges of adultery (or bigamy) might be brought against the adults. DOMA creates the horrors that the United States Supreme Court recognized as unacceptable over a century ago.

CONGRESSIONAL POWER

Article 4 of the United States Constitution provides that "Full Faith and Credit shall be given in each State to the public Acts, Records, and judicial Proceedings of every other State."[31] The Article further provides that "Congress may by general Laws prescribe the Manner in which such Acts, Records, and Proceedings shall be proved, and the Effect thereof."[32] However, it is not clear how Article 4 should be interpreted, since the text specifies both that full faith and credit shall be given and that Congress may specify the effect of authenticated acts, records, and judgments. If possible, an interpretation of the text should be offered that nullifies the language of neither provision.

Regrettably, the United States Supreme Court has not made sufficiently clear what is encompassed by the congressional power to prescribe effects—whether, for example, it merely involves setting up the mechanism whereby the full faith and credit obligations will be enforced or whether, instead, it allows Congress to determine how much credit is due. The Court has noted, however, that the Constitution requires that " 'not some but full' faith and credit be given judgments of a state court."[33] As the Court has made clear, the "faith and credit given is not to be niggardly but generous, full."[34]

The Court has offered some guidance in how to interpret the Clause, explaining, "The authenticity of a judgment and its effect, depend upon the law made in pursuance of the Constitution; the faith and credit due to it as the judicial proceeding of a state, is given by the Constitution, independently of all legislation."[35] Here, the Court distinguished between the faith and credit due to a judgment, which is prescribed by the Constitution independent of congressional legislation, and the judgment's authenticity and effect, which are dependent upon the relevant congressional legislation. Yet, it is not immediately clear what distinction the Court was trying to capture, since the Court distinguished between the full faith and credit due to a judgment on the one hand and the effect of the judgment on the other.

First, it is important to establish what the Court was not doing. The Court was not distinguishing between the judgment's effect in the state in which it was issued and the judgment's effect in sister states. On the contrary, whether the Court was analyzing the faith and credit due to an authenticated judgment or, instead, the effect of such a judgment, the Court was discussing the obligations of one state when a sister state has already issued a judgment on the merits with respect to a particular controversy.

The Court has suggested that the Full Faith and Credit Clause itself made "judgments out of the state in which they are rendered . . . only evidence in a sister state."[36] Yet, it may be misleading to describe an authenticated judgment as *only* evidence in a sister state, since the issue at hand is, "Evidence as opposed to what?" Insofar as an authenticated judgment from a sister state would be conclusive evidence on the merits,[37] it might be quite misleading to describe a sister state's judgment as *mere* evidence.

DIFFERING INTERPRETATIONS OF THE EFFECTS CLAUSE

One interpretation of the Effects Clause is that the Constitution has given Congress the power to decide what kind rather than how much of an effect a sister state's judgment is to have. According to this interpretation, Congress is not to address whether the judgment will be given credit or how much credit it will be given but, rather, who will be required to make sure that the foreign judgment will be given its due. For example, Congress could set up some sort of registration system to preclude the need to have a new trial in a sister state in order for a foreign judgment to be given credit.[38] Such a system would be more efficient,[39] since "execution or other process under the law of the second state could issue directly upon the registered judgment, without necessity for new action with new service and all its attendant delays and disadvantages."[40]

The Supreme Court has suggested that the section of Article 4 referring to Congress "was intended to provide [Congress] the *means* of giving to . . . [sister state judgments] the conclusiveness of judgments upon the merits, when it is sought to carry them into judgments by suits in the tribunals of another state,"[41] thereby suggesting that Congress has been given the power to set up the mechanism whereby the Clause can be effectuated. On this interpretation of the Effects Clause, Congress would not have the power to lessen the faith and credit to be given to sister state judgments.

Another interpretation of the Effects Clause has been offered which also implies that Congress would lack the power to lessen full faith and credit. Some have interpreted the phrase "Congress may by general Laws prescribe the Manner in which such Acts, Records and Proceedings shall be proved, and the Effect thereof"[42] to mean that Congress can prescribe the manner and effect of the *proof* of sister state judgments.[43] Thus, Congress has been given the power to mandate the system by which judgments would be authenticated and the effect of that proof. (Presumably, the effect of the proof would be that the judgments would now be viewed as authenticated and therefore entitled to full faith and credit.)

Each of the competing interpretations of the Effects Clause has its weaknesses. The interpretation in which Congress is to prescribe the manner and effect of the proof of sister state judgments seems to involve a tortured reading of the text. When the phrase "the effect of" is used, the effect must be an effect of something. In the phrase "the Manner in which such Acts, Records and judicial Proceedings shall be proved and the Effect thereof," the effect presumably is either of the "Manner" or of the "Acts, Records, and judicial Proceedings." However, since neither of those corresponds to the "proof," this reading seems strained.

The interpretation in which Congress is empowered to set up the mechanism whereby sister state judgments will be given effect relies on a particular interpretation of the kind of procedural effect (manner) Congress is to prescribe. Congress is to regulate whether an individual will have to go to court in a state in order to have a judgment from a sister state enforced. However, Congress is not to regulate whether a sister state judgment is to be conclusive on the merits. Although this interpretation is possibly correct, it seems unlikely that Congress's powers would be delimited in this way.

The interpretation in which Congress can prescribe the effect of the acts, records, and judicial proceedings seems to involve the most natural reading of the text, since it would not seem necessary to have added that Congress has the power to prescribe the effect of the manner. For example, had "and the effect thereof" not been added, Congress presumably still would have had the power to say that only acts, records, and judgments proven in a particular manner would be subject to full faith and credit. Futher, as an historical matter, "thereof" was substituted for "which judgments obtained in one state shall have in another."[44] Thus, before the substitution, the phrase read "the effect which judgments obtained in one state shall have in another." This suggests that when making the change, Congress had in mind the effects of the judgments (and acts and records) rather than the effects of the manner. However, this interpretation also has its weaknesses. For example, insofar as it would allow Congress to lessen the full faith and credit that is due, it would contradict the textual requirement in the previous sentence that full faith and credit shall be given in each state to the judgments of the courts of sister states.[45]

PAST EXERCISES OF POWER UNDER THE EFFECTS CLAUSE

In deciding which interpretation is the most accurate, it may be helpful to consider how Congress has in fact exercised its power under the Full Faith and Credit Clause, especially insofar as those attempts have been endorsed by the Court. Congress first exercised this power by specifying that authenticated acts, records, and judicial proceedings "shall have the same full faith and credit in every court within the United States and its Territories and Possessions as they have by law or usage in the courts of such State, Territory, or Possession from which they are taken."[46] This has been interpreted to mean that each state must treat the judgment of a sister state as it would be treated in the state in which the judgment was rendered.[47] If the judgment is not subject to modification in the state rendering it, then the judgment is not subject to modification in other states either. However, if the judgment is subject to modification in the state rendering it, then it is subject to such modification elsewhere.[48]

Great difficulties can arise if sister states are permitted to modify judgments that were modifiable in the rendering state. Consider custody decrees, which generally are modifiable in the decree-granting state. Absent legislation to the contrary, such decrees are modifiable in sister states as well. As the United States Supreme Court explained, "Because courts entering custody orders generally retain the power to modify them, courts in other States were no less entitled to change the terms of custody according to their own views of the child's best interest."[49]

If sister states are permitted to modify custody decrees, parents who have lost a custody battle in one state will have an incentive to kidnap their children and relitigate the issue in a different forum.[50] To deter parents from kidnapping their children, states adopted their own versions of the Uniform Child Custody and Jurisdiction Act (UCCJA), which had been developed in an effort to avoid these jurisdictional conflicts.[51] However, even after states had adopted these acts, there was still too much confusion, both because some states had refused to enact their own version of the UCCJA[52] and because those enacting it had modified the Act,[53] thereby preserving the incentive for noncustodial parents to kidnap their children and go to certain states[54] to petition for a change in custody.[55] To remove the incentive for parents to take their children to a different jurisdiction and relitigate custody, Congress exercised its power under the Effects Clause to pass the Parental Kidnapping Prevention Act (PKPA) to limit the right of states to modify sister states' custody decrees.[56] Had Congress not acted, the Full Faith and Credit Clause would not have been a bar to sister states modifying the (modifiable) judgments of the original decree-granting states, because the Clause "obliges States only to accord the same force to judgments as would be accorded by the courts of the State in which the judgment was entered."[57]

Congress's having passed the PKPA has import for the appropriate interpretation of the congressional power under the Effects Clause. If Congress only has the power to prescribe whether a registration system will be set up, then it would seem that Congress would not have had the power to increase the full faith and credit due to a custody judgment by saying that a sister state will be precluded from modifying a judgment that is nonetheless modifiable by the decree-granting state.

At least two different responses might be made to the claim that Congress's having passed the PKPA strongly suggests which interpretation of the Effects Clause is correct: (1) Congress does *not* have the power to pass the PKPA under the Full Faith and Credit Clause, although it might have such a power under the Commerce Clause,[58] or (2) Congress does have the power to pass the PKPA under the Effects Clause, because it is seeking to increase rather than to decrease full faith and credit and thus does not run afoul of the constitutional provision that *full* faith and credit be given.

The first explanation might be accurate, although in a case addressing the PKPA, the Court gave no hint that there was any difficulty in Congress's having passed the PKPA under the Effects Clause.[59] While that could have been because the issue was not raised by the parties, the Court's language would seem to belie that analysis. For example, the Court described the PKPA as an "addendum to the full faith and credit statute"[60] without a hint that this was a constitutionally questionable exercise of congressional power. Further, the Court discussed the significance of "Congress' full faith and credit approach to the problem of child snatching,"[61] at least implicitly suggesting that this was a valid approach to solving the problem at hand.

There are additional reasons to believe that the second rather than the first explanation is correct. Consider Congress's first exercise of power under the Effects Clause.[62] There, Congress did not set up a registration system but, instead, prescribed that judgments will have the same effect in sister states that they have in the rendering state. The United States Supreme Court has spoken approvingly of that exercise of power. For example, the Court has described that Act of Congress as carrying the Full Faith and Credit Clause into effect[63] and, quite recently, endorsed the constitutionality of that Act of Congress, describing it as pursuant to the Full Faith and Credit Clause.[64] Thus, it seems at best implausible to claim that Congress does not have the power under the Full Faith and Credit Clause to increase the credit that is due to sister state judgments.

When interpreting the Effects Clause, a few different issues should be separated if headway is to be made in determining Congress's power under the Clause. One issue is whether Congress has merely been empowered to set up a registration system or, instead, also to regulate how much credit will be due to a sister state's judgment. If the latter, then an additional question is whether Congress has the power to decrease the amount of credit due, notwithstanding the explicit constitutional requirement that full faith and credit be given.

The Supreme Court has not yet had to decide whether Congress has the power to lessen full faith and credit,[65] because Congress has never before tried to do that. However, the Court has made comments that are suggestive of its position. For example, the Court suggested that Congress had "rightly interpreted the clause to mean not some but full credit,"[66] implying that a different interpretation would have been an incorrect interpretation of the Constitutional requirement. Further, the Court has suggested that Congress can exceed the requirements imposed by the Full Faith and Credit Clause and impose additional full faith and credit obligations,[67] for example, require that even judgments modifiable in the decree-granting state be given full faith and credit in sister states under certain conditions. However, it is not at all clear that the Court would hold that Congress can reduce the requirements imposed by the Clause,[68] especially given the explicit constitutional requirement that full faith and credit be given.

THE FEDERAL DEFINITION OF MARRIAGE

When Congress passed DOMA, it announced a definition of marriage that would now be used for federal purposes. This provision of the Act reads:

> In determining the meaning of any Act of Congress, or of any ruling, regulation, or interpretation of the various administrative bureaus and agencies of the United States, the word "marriage" means only a legal union between one man and one woman as husband and wife, and the word "spouse" refers only to a person of the opposite sex who is a husband or a wife.[69]

Unlike the other section, this one is rather straightforward. While the intent is clear, it is difficult to believe that this legislation has any legitimate justification at all, since the goal of disadvantaging a disfavored minority is not viewed as a legitimate purpose. The Supreme Court has already made quite clear that "if the constitutional conception of 'equal protection of the laws' means anything, it must at the very least mean that a bare . . . desire to harm a politically unpopular group cannot constitute a *legitimate* governmental interest."[70]

MAJOR DAMAGE TO FEDERAL INTERESTS

Chief Justice William Rehnquist has pointed out that family law is "a matter of peculiarly local concern and therefore governed by state and not federal law."[71] Deference is often accorded to state domestic relations law even when *federal* rights are at issue. The Supreme Court has suggested that state law should be applied especially "where a statute deals with a familial relationship."[72] This is because "there is no federal law of domestic relations, which is primarily a matter of state concern."[73] Thus, merely because a statute concerns federal benefits does not mean that state law is inappropriate to apply.

There are occasions, however, in which the federal government can supplant state domestic relations law—namely, when state law is doing " 'major damage' to 'clear and substantial' federal interests',"[74] for example, when national defense is at issue.[75] The important issue to be resolved is what qualifies as a sufficiently important interest for federal law to displace state law. The Court has made clear that it will not suffice to say that money will thereby be saved.[76] Otherwise, Congress could always justify its supplanting state law by claiming that doing so would save money.

DOMA supporters claim that DOMA not only saves money but helps confirm the tradition of marriage as a union between one man and one woman.[77] Yet, DOMA does not prevent states from recognizing same-sex marriages; it merely denies federal benefits to same-sex couples.

Congress has made clear that it does not believe that same-sex and opposite-sex unions are equally valuable. Yet, this does not suffice as a reason. Suppose, for example, that Congress decided that it did not believe that interracial and intraracial marriages were equally valuable. Presumably, no one would claim that Congress could withdraw federal benefits from interracial marriages because intraracial marriages were "preferred."[78] Or, suppose that Congress wanted to manifest its preference for marriages of individuals who had children through their union. Presumably, no one would claim that Congress could declare that couples who had no children biologically related to both of them "were not married for federal purposes."

EQUAL PROTECTION

When courts decide whether a state must recognize a marriage validly celebrated in another domiciliary state or, perhaps, whether a state must permit the enjoyment of the incidents of marriage within that state, they must keep in mind that the Equal Protection Clause constrains their decisions.[79] Thus, while states can recognize the validity of a marriage without allowing the enjoyment of certain incidents of that union,[80] it should not be thought that this can be done lightly.[81] Withholding the economic, social, or legal benefits of marriage[82] from only same-sex couples would implicate equal protection concerns. For example, if the only nonincestuous, nonpolygamous couples prohibited from cohabiting were those composed of same-sex partners, the classification would be difficult to justify and would invite close scrutiny.[83] The Supreme Court has made clear that it will not countenance a distinction that raises the "inevitable inference that the disadvantage imposed is born of animosity toward the class of persons affected."[84]

When faced with an unusual distinction in Florida's cohabitation law—namely, one that punished interracial cohabitation more severely than intraracial cohabitation—the United States Supreme Court wrote, "Judicial inquiry under the Equal Protection Clause . . . does not end with a showing of equal application among the members of the class defined by the legislation."[85] Thus, it did not suffice that both members of the interracial couple had the same disability imposed upon each of them. Nor would it suffice that a couple composed of a black man and a white woman would be treated in the same way as would a couple composed of a black woman and a white man. So, too, it will not suffice that both female and male same-sex couples have a disability imposed upon them. Rather, more must be shown. As the Court explained when considering the issues raised in the Florida case, the courts must determine whether the "classifications drawn in a statute are reasonable in light of its purpose—in this case, whether there is an arbitrary or invidious discrimination between those classes covered by Florida's cohabitation law and those excluded."[86] Just as Florida's having singled out interracial couples for special, adverse treatment in the state's cohabitation laws violated the Equal Protection Clause, a state's precluding same-sex married couples from cohabiting would also violate that clause. Indeed, the Florida case was decided before the Court had held interracial bans unconstitutional. Even if the Court were to hold that there was no fundamental right to same-sex marriage, that would not mean that states could invividously discriminate against same-sex couples by preventing them from cohabiting despite their having been validly married in another state.

The nineteenth century view that the state had almost unlimited discretion with respect to its marriage laws and thus, for example, could prevent individuals of different religions from marrying, is simply no longer good law.[87] Arguably, states are barred by the Fourteenth Amendment from prohibiting their own domiciliaries from marrying their same-sex partners.[88] In any event, that amendment certainly prevents states from refusing to recognize those nonpolygamous, nonincestuous, same-sex marriages recognized in the states of celebration and domicile at the time of the marriage.

When the citizens of Colorado passed an amendment to their state constitution withdrawing from "homosexuals but no others specific legal protection form the injuries caused by discrimination,"[89] the Court struck it down, holding that it violated the Equal Protection Clause of the United State Constitution. The Court worried about the amendment's "sheer breadth," that made it "inexplicable by anything but animus towards the class it affect[ed]."[90] So, too, the sheer breadth of the legislation depriving same-sex couples of all benefits accompanying federal recognition of marital status is only explicable by animus.[91] Should there by any doubt, one need only consult the *Congressional Record* for confirmation.

When examining the constitutionality of the Colorado amendment, the United Staes Supreme Court expressed concern about the Colorado electorate's having subjected one group to a disability that no other group had to bear. Rightly rejecting Colorado's contention that gays were seeking "special rights,"[92] the Court understood that the amendment would impose a special disability on lesbians, gays, and bisexuals.[93] Insofar as Congress has attempted to give states the right to refuse to recognize a same-sex marriage valid in the states of celebration and domicile at the time of the marriage, it has attempted to impose a disability on one group that no other group must bear.

PRIVILEGES AND IMMUNITIES

Perhaps it would seem that if individuals want to move to a new state, they should simply find out about the state's marriages laws and consider them before moving there. Yet, states are prevented from chilling the travel of citizens of the other states. The right to travel is included within the privileges and immunities protected by the Fourteenth Amendment.[94]

In the nineteenth century, courts considered whether the right to travel limited the rights of state to set up their own marriage laws.[95] In general, courts suggested that the Privileges and Immunities Clause did not affect that right.[96] However, those decisions rested, at least in part, on a conflation of several different issues that must be kept separate: (1) whether there must be a uniform standard of marriage, (2) whether the federal rather than the state legislature is to determine who may marry whom, and (3) whether states must recognize marriages recognized in previous domiciliary states. For example, the Tennessee Supreme Court suggested that the Privileges and Immunities Clause did not affect the right of each state to create its own marriage laws.[97] The Missouri Supreme Court suggested that the federal constitution did not confer "upon a citizen the right to marry any one who is willing to wed him,"[98] reasoning that were that so, "all our marriage acts forbidding intermarriages between persons within certain degrees of consanguinity are void, and the nephew may marry his aunt, the niece her uncle, and the son his mother or grandmother."[99] A Texas appellate court suggested that the Privileges and Immunities Clause "did not profess to control the power of the state governments over the rights of their own citizens."[100]

These courts addressed whether the United States Constitution wrested from the states and transferred to Congress the right to set up the marriage laws, correctly deciding that it did not. Congress does not decide who may marry whom;[101] rather, each state makes that decision for its own domicilaries. Further, states did not and do not have uniform marriage laws. Notwithstanding the state's right to determine the conditions under which its domiciliaries will marry, however, a separate question is whether the Privileges and Immunities Clause allows subsequent domiciles to refuse to recognize marriages validly celebrated in previous domiciliary states.

The Privileges and Immunities Clause is designed to foster national unity[102] by preventing unjustified discrimination against citizens of other states.[103] The Supreme Court has suggested that the "right of a United States citizen to travel from one State to another and to take up residence in the State of his choice is protected by the Federal Constitution."[104] Indeed, as Justice Sandra Day O'Connor has argued, "It is difficult to imagine a right more essential to the Nation as a whole than the right to establish residence in a new State."[105]

Perhaps it will be argued that the refusal to recognize a marriage valid in a previous domiciliary state does not prevent an individual from becoming a resident of a new state, but merely imposes a cost on the individual's moving there,[106] namely, that the person's marriage might not be recognized.[107] However, the Court has suggested that "even temporary deprivations of very important benefits and rights can operate to penalize migration" and thus be unconstitutional.[108] If a state's refusal to recognize a marriage recognized in a previous domiciliary state operates to penalize migration, the Privileges and Immunities Clause would be violated and the state's refusal would be unconstitutional.

Certainly, merely because something would deter an individual's moving to a new state would not mean that it was a penalty on migration. For example, state residency requirements for divorce do not constitute a penalty on migration,[109] although that is because a residency requirement delays rather than denies divorce.[110] At issue here is not merely some kind of temporary delay but, instead, a complete denial of the legal validity of one's marriage. A threatened nullification of one's marriage would operate as a clear penalty on migration.

Shortly after the Civil War, the Supreme Court considered whether a "tax upon persons residing in the State who may wish to get out of it, and upon persons not residing in it who may have occasion to pass through it" was constitutional.[111] The Court did not view "a tax of one dollar" as depriving a "citizen of any valuable right."[112] Nonetheless, the Court struck this as a violation of interstate travel.[113] More recently, the Court has ruled that a law imposing a one year waiting period for the receipt of government benefits was unconstitutional because the "purpose of inhibiting migration by needy persons into the State is constitutionally impermissible."[114] So, too, the purpose of deterring same-sex couples from migrating to a state would be constitutionally impermissible.

The claim here is not that states would be precluded from recognizing a marriage legally recognized *anywhere*.[115] It would matter whether the domicile in which the marriage was validly celebrated and legally recognized was a foreign country or instead a sister state. In the former case, the state might refuse to recognize the marriage. In the latter, however, the state could at best refuse to recognize some of the incidents of marriage, and even such a refusal would be subject to equal protection analysis.

The fact that DOMA was passed by Congress will not save it. The Supreme Court has already made clear that "Congress may not authorize the States to violate the Equal Protection Clause."[116] Further, where Congress acts unconstitutionally, "the departure from the constitutional plan cannot be ratified by the 'consent' of state officials."[117]

The right to travel includes both the right to *travel through* a state and also the right to *migrate to* a state. DOMA would have a chilling effect on both of these aspects of the right to travel. As written, the Act might allow future nondomiciles to rule that marriages validly contracted twenty years earlier are nonetheless void and of no legal effect. Thus, individuals who were tempted to vacation or do business in a state might be fearful that should something happen there such that the validity of their marriage would be important,[118] the state might choose not to recognize their marriage.

The Privileges and Immunities Clause is sometimes interpreted as a provision that assures that states will not disadvantage individuals who are residents of other states. It might seem, then that if a state can prevent its domiciliaries from contracting same-sex marriages, then it could of course refuse to recognize nondomiciliaries' same-sex marriages without imposing an undue burden on interstate travel. After all, the state would simply seem to be treating nondomiciliaries in the same way that it was treating its domiciliaries.

Yet, appearances notwithstanding, the state would not be treating domiciliaries and nondomiciliaries in the same way. When a state passes legislation declaring a particular marriage void, it prevents its domiciliaries from contracting a marriage of that type. A couple domiciled in a state where such marriages are void could not make plans and develop expectations based on the good faith belief that their marriage solemnized in another state would be treated as valid by the domicile. However, the situation is quite different where the domicile does recognize such a marriage, since couples living there would have a justified, good faith belief that they had a valid marriage. It would be both understandable and appropriate for them to make plans, develop expectations, and enter into binding legal agreements based on their being married.

Certainly, marriages are sometimes annulled or invalidated. However, that occurs when one of the parties asks for an annulment or, perhaps, when the marriage was never valid in the first place because the domicile considered such marriages void or, at least, voidable. Annulments do not occur in cases where the domicile at the time of the marriage considered the marriage valid (and not voidable) and neither of the married parties wishes the marriage to be dissolved.

Current domestic relations law does not allow states to invalidate a previously valid marriage without the consent of at least one of the parties. While a court can rule that a marriage was never valid, assuming that the relevant conditions have been met, a court cannot invalidate a marriage that the state itself previously recognized as valid if neither member of the couple wishes to have the marriage annulled. Thus, it is less surprising than might first appear that states are in a different position with respect to the recognition of marriages validly celebrated in another state if the celebrants are domiciliaries rather than nondomiciliaries. The state can refuse to recognize the marriage of domiciliaries celebrated elsewhere if that union is treated as void in the domicile. In that case, the marriage was never valid. However, the state cannot refuse to recognize the marriage of current domiciliaries if their marriage was recognized by their domicile at the time of the marriage.

The analog of a state's refusing to recognize a valid marriage of a couple domiciled in a different state at the time of their union would be the state's invalidating a marriage of its domiciliaries that the state had already recognized as valid without the consent of either party. Allowing states to invalidate previously valid marriages would be a public policy disaster: the justified and settled expectations of the parties would be disappointed,[119] the status of the children would be unclear, title to property would be clouded, and third party creditors would be in a tenuous position.[120]

BILLS OF ATTAINDER

Historically, the practice of passing bills of attainder can be traced back to England. Parliament would pass statutes in which one or more specific individuals were sentenced to death for allegedly having plotted against the government.[121] Sometimes, Parliament would pass statutes imposing less severe sanctions against specific individuals; such a statute would be called a bill of pains and penalties.[122] A bill of pains and penalties might include a variety of punishments (e.g., "imprisonment, banishment, and the punitive confiscation of property by the sovereign"[123]). While the practice of passing bills of attainder is associated with the British Parliament, it also occurred in the thirteen states during and immediately after the American Revolution.[124] Indeed, in this country, a new sanction was added to the list of possible bill of attainder punishments, namely, "a legislative enactment barring designated individuals or groups from participation in specified employments or vocations."[125] This particular sanction was often imposed "against those legislatively branded as disloyal."[126]

The United States Constitution prohibits Congress from passing bills of attainder.[127] However, bills of attainder involved an imposition of the sanction of death. Were the Bill of Attainder Clause limited in scope to a literal reading of its prohibition, Congress could pass statutes depriving identifiable individuals of a variety of civil rights as long as they did not deprive those individuals of their lives. However, the Court has declined to give the Bill of Attainder Clause "a narrow historical reading (which would exclude bills of pains and penalties),"[128] but has instead read it "in light of the evil the Framers had sought to bar: legislative punishment, of any form or severity, of specifically designated persons or groups."[129]

Persons or groups can of course be designated by name. However, bills of attainder and bills of pains and penalties did not always name the relevant parties but, instead, would sometimes describe the parties in a sufficiently detailed manner that they would be easily identified.[130] In England, acts of attainder would sometimes "inflict their deprivations upon relatively large groups of people, sometimes by description rather than name."[131]

WHAT IS A BILL OF ATTAINDER?

As a general matter, bills of attainder specifically identify persons or groups[132] who will be deprived of a right[133] as a kind of punishment.[134] Further, this punishment must be imposed legislatively rather than judicially.[135] As Justice Frankfurter explained, the "distinguishing characteristic of a bill of attainder is the substitution of legislative determination of guilt and legislative imposition of punishment for judicial finding and sentence."[136]

A sanction can involve "punishment," even if no one claims that the individual has broken a law. "Punishment presupposes an offense, not necessarily an act previously declared criminal, but an act for which retribution is exacted."[137]

Not all disabilities imposed by the government are viewed as punishments. Justice Frankfurter suggested that merely because "harm is inflicted by governmental authority does not make it punishment,"[138] suggesting that, in at least a manner of speaking, "all discomforting action may be deemed punishment because it deprives of what otherwise would be enjoyed."[139] Nonetheless, part of the test to determine whether a sanction is a punishment involves an examination of the allegedly nonpunitive purposes of the enactment. The Court will view the absence of a legitimate nonpunitive purpose as indicative that the sanction is indeed punitive. Where "legitimate legislative purposes do not appear, it is reasonable to conclude that punishment of individuals disadvantaged by the enactment was the purpose of the decisionmakers."[140] Even if legitimate purposes do appear, this will not end the analysis. The Court will then look to see whether less burdensome alternatives were possible before deciding whether a particular sanction was punitive.[141]

While the Court realizes that judicial "inquiries into Congressional motives are at best a hazardous matter,"[142] such inquiries are nonetheless necessary, especially when one of the important issues at hand is whether the legislature was attempting to impose punishment or act vindictively. The Court has explained that a "recognized test of punishment is strictly a motivational one: inquiring whether the legislative record evinces a congressional intent to punish."[143] For example, while the Court has denied that "a formal legislative announcement of moral blameworthiness or punishment is necessary to an unlawful bill of attainder,"[144] such a pronouncement would be probative, since a "major concern that prompted the bill of attainder prohibition"[145] was "the fear that the legislature, in seeking to pander to an inflamed popular constituency, will find it expedient openly to assume the mantle of judge or, worse still, lynch mob."[146] When the legislature adopts the wrong mantle, the enactments may well be struck down as bills of attainder.

THE PURPOSES OF THE BILL OF ATTAINDER CLAUSE

To understand the scope of the Bill of Attainder Clause, it is helpful to understand its purposes. The Supreme Court has explained that the "Bill of Attainder Clause was intended . . . as an implementation of the separation of powers, a general safeguard against legislative exercise of the judicial function, or more simply—trial by legislature."[147] Separation of powers is important to enforce,[148] especially because "the Legislative Branch is not so well suited as politically independent judges and juries to the task of ruling upon the blameworthiness of, and levying appropriate punishment upon, specific persons."[149] The clause is intended to limit "legislatures to the task of rule-making,"[150] and to leave judging to a different branch. Further, the Legislature will not be allowed to make rules that in effect announce guilt and impose a punishment.[151]

The Court has indicated that one of the concerns behind the Bill of Attainder Clause is to prevent the legislature's pandering to an "inflamed popular constituency."[152] It is thus also a purpose of the Clause not to allow the legislature to be vindictive or to allow the populace to be vindictive through their elected representatives.

SPECIFICITY

The Supreme Court has suggested that the Bill of Attainder Clause is only implicated if a punishment is being applied to named individuals or easily ascertainable members of a group.[153] The specificity requirement has caused great confusion.[154] Some have interpreted the easy ascertainability requirement to be a shorthand way of saying that the group must be "closed,"[155] that is, a class with a "membership that is permanently fixed when the class is defined, from which members can never exit and into which nonmembers can never enter, as a matter of law."[156]

It is easy to understand why one might make that assumption about the bill of attainder requirements, since some of the classic cases involved individuals who were being punished for past acts. Thus, if individuals are barred from the practice of law in federal courts because of something that they did in the past, they will never be able to escape that prohibition for as long as the law is on the books because they will never be able to change something that occurred in the past.[157] By the same token, individuals who are barred from preaching or teaching because of something that they have done in the past will never be able to do either of those for as long as the law is on the books.[158]

Yet, bill of attainder jurisprudence does not require that it is impossible to exit from the class.[159] Communists have been subject to bills of attainder, and it is clear that being a Communist is not a classification from which it is impossible to exit, since one can resign from the Party. For example, the Supreme Court struck down a statute that penalized individuals who were currently Communists or who had been Communists within the past five years.[160] An individual could have escaped the penalties at issue by resigning and then waiting five years. Nonetheless, despite the possibility of exiting from the class that would be disadvantaged, the Court characterized the statute as a bill of attainder. Indeed, the Court noted that historically some bills of attainder and bills of pains and penalties had "left the designated parties a way of escaping the penalty."[161]

A bill of attainder "may inflict punishment absolutely, or may inflict it conditionally."[162] For example, a bill of attainder might specify that all individuals of an easily identifiable class would be deprived of a particular civil right "provided they did not, by a day designated, do certain specified acts."[163] This too would be "within the inhibition of the Federal Constitution,"[164] provided that the other bill of attainder requirements had been met.

Certainly, the Court has sometimes denied that individuals were being subjected to a bill of attainder if they were able to avoid the penalty easily.[165] However, that is a far cry from a closed class requirement, and is quite compatible with saying that bill of attainder protections potentially apply to individuals who are penalized because of a characteristic that is difficult but not impossible to give up.

DOMA AS A BILL OF ATTAINDER

The Defense of Marriage Act deprives individuals of a civil right and numerous benefits as a kind of punishment.[166] The congressional enactment is a clear bill of attainder, if only because the members of Congress were quite willing to make clear what was motivating their votes.

Consider the refusal to extend federal recognition to same-sex marriages. This might seem to be motivated by a legitimate reason, namely, saving money.[167] However, as Justice Stevens has pointed out, legitimate reasons can be offered in at attempt to justify patently unconstitutional measures.[168] If the Congress were really interested in saving money, it would be surprising that the only valid marriages that it would choose not to recognize for federal purposes would involve those involving same-sex partners, since there would be no reason to think that such marriages would be more of a drain on the Treasury than other marriages. A more plausible reason is that the members of Congress and many of their constituents do not approve of such marriages and do not wish to have tax dollars used to support them.[169]

It is simply a misunderstanding of the Constitution to assume that Congress can extend or withdraw tax benefits as it sees fit. For example, it would clearly be impermissible for the Congress to deny recognition for federal purposes to interracial marriages, even if the public did not want its tax dollars spent to support such unions.[170]

It is clear that many members of Congress and many Americans do not approve of gays, lesbians, and bisexuals and wish to impose a disability upon them. One need look no farther than the *Congressional Record* to see this. For example, many members of Congress recognized that DOMA was "a mean-spirited form of . . . legislative gay-bashing."[171]

Yet, one need not look at the DOMA opponents' comments to see why this was a classic bill of attainder. Many of the proponents of the bill made clear that they were supporting DOMA as a way of serving God and preserving morality. Several members of Congress suggested that lesbians and gays were immoral, that same-sex marriages were immoral, and that somehow the entire moral fabric of our society would be destroyed were same-sex marriages recognized.[172]

Yet, same-sex relationships are not inherently immoral,[173] views to the contrary notwithstanding, just as interracial relationships are not inherently immoral, views to the contrary notwithstanding.[174] The morality of these relationships, like the morality of many others, is dependent upon how the individuals involved in the relationship treat each other.

As a separate matter, the Supreme Court has suggested that legislative announcements of moral blameworthiness are probative of punitive intentions.[175] Ironically, by so clearly pandering to their constituents,[176] many members of Congress made their punitive intent plain and made even clearer that the Defense of Marriage Act implicates Bill of Attainder protections.

An important issue is whether the loss of the right to marry or the loss of the various rights associated with marriage can properly be termed punishment. However, as Justice Stevens has pointed out, "The withdrawal of rights is itself among the most basic punishments that society can exact, for such a withdrawal qualifies the subject's citizenship and violates his dignity."[177] Indeed, the Court has already made clear that the "deprivation of any rights, civil or political, previously enjoyed, may be punishment, the circumstances attending and the causes of the deprivation determining this fact."[178] The Court has recognized what some in Congress seem to have forgotten, namely, that the "theory upon which our political institutions rest"[179] is that all citizens "have certain inalienable rights"[180] and that among these are "life, liberty, and the pursuit of happiness."[181]

It is clear that members of Congress passed DOMA as a way of expressing their disapproval of same-sex relationships and as a way of discouraging individuals from living with same-sex partners. Further, it seems clear that some members of Congress believed or hoped that by passing DOMA they would help dissuade children from becoming lesbian or gay.[182] Bracketing the etiological point that sexual orientation seems to be determined early in life so that these policies will not in fact act as a deterrent but will only make life more difficult for gays and lesbians,[183] there is the separate point that the legislation is clearly intended to act as a deterrent, one of the hallmarks of punishment.

Insofar as DOMA was designed to impose a particular moral point of view and to prevent the dissemination of ideas, it runs counter to the history and traditions of this country. As Justice Jackson pointed out, "Progress generally begins in skepticism about accepted truths."[184] Further, those who take intellectual freedom seriously must realize that such "freedom means the right to re-examine much that has been long taken for granted."[185] A free person "must dare to doubt what a legislative or electoral majority may most passionately assert."[186] Indeed, the idea that the Constitution "should protect individual nonconformity is essentially American,"[187] and it is at the very least ironic that the Congress should seek to undermine this most American of ideals. Indeed, there is a long history of using bills of attainder to chill speech.[188]

Numerous factors support that DOMA is a bill of attainder. The lack of legitimate nonpunitive reasons for the legislation, the public grandstanding about the alleged immorality of same-sex marriage in an attempt to please constituents at home, the intended deterrent effect, and the transparent attempt to impose a particular point of view all support that DOMA is a bill of attainder prohibited by the Constitution.

One of the disturbing features of bills of attainder is that they often impose penalties on individuals for things over which they have little if any control. Sexual orientation is, if not innate, established early in life. By preventing individuals from marrying their same-sex partners or by denying those individuals the benefits that other, similarly situated individuals have, the state imposes a heavy burden. Marital partners are not as interchangeable as trains.[189]

Were individuals told that they had no right to marry an opposite-sex partner or that in any event such marriages would not be given federal recognition, there would be a huge outcry about the injustice of such a position. No one would claim that those seeking to vindicate through the courts their right to marry an opposite-sex partner would somehow be doing something objectionable.[190] Further, the anger would not be averted were the state to point out that the marriage would be recognized and the accompanying benefits accorded as long as a same-sex partner was chosen as the spouse. The right to marry is simply too important to be denied on the basis of orientation.

Justice Frankfurter described the quality that gives a bill of attainder its significance as "a declaration of guilt under circumstances which made its determination grossly unfair."[191] Yet, gross unfairness is exactly what is implicated in DOMA.

When the right to marry a same-sex partner has been accorded, it cannot be taken away from an easily identifiable group as a punitive measure without offending constitutional guarantees. DOMA is a "classical bill of attainder which our Constitution in two places prohibits,"[192] for it is a legislative act that inflicts "pains, penalties and punishments in a number of ways without a judicial trial."[193] The Court must hold that DOMA is an unconstitutional violation of the Bill of Attainder Clauses. "Any lesser holding would ignore the constitutional mandate upon which our essential liberties depend."[194]

CONCLUSION

Commentators suggest that the state interests are not served by allowing lesbians and gays to marry their same-sex partners because such couples cannot produce children through their union. Yet, the state has an interest in having children raised in healthy environments even if they are not being raised by both of their biological parents. Further, the state has other interests that would be served by allowing same-sex couples to marry, since the individuals would then be happier and more productive members of society. As a separate but by no means insignificant matter, the important individual interests in marriage that are implicated for opposite-sex couples are also implicated for same-sex couples.

Commentators claim that if same-sex marriages are allowed, then incestous and polygamous marriages must also be allowed. Yet, this argument is specious, precisely because different interests and dangers are implicated in these different kinds of unions. So, too, adulterous relationships implicate different concerns than do same-sex unions, and there would be no inconsistency in protecting the latter without protecting the former.

Years ago, commentators claimed that if the Constitution required recognizing interracial marriages, it also required recognizing incestuous or polygamous marriages. The claim was specious then and the analogous argument is specious now.

The existence of same-sex sodomy laws is not incompatible with the existence of same-sex marriages, just as the existence of opposite-sex sodomy laws is not incompatible with the existence of opposite-sex marriage. Just as there is a marital exception to sodomy laws for opposite-sex couples, there would be one for same-sex couples. Thus, although sodomy laws themselves are probably unconstitutional because of due process guarantees, the analysis offered here is not dependent upon that.

The Hawaii Supreme Court was expected to affirm a lower court decision that the state's same-sex marriage ban violated state constitutional equal protection guarantees, at least in part, because the state constitution existing at the time of the decision imposed a very difficult standard for the state to meet. An Alaska trial court suggested that the state constitution protected the right to marry a same-sex partner. The Hawaii and Alaska electorates voted to modify their state constitutions to prevent same-sex partners from marrying. However, same-sex marriage bans violate federal equal protection guarantees and, thus, such marriage bans are still unconstitutional. Same-sex marriage bans discriminate facially on the basis of sex and also discriminate on the basis of gender by reinforcing inaccurate stereotypes about the sexes. Further, such bans discriminate on the basis of orientation without a legitimate reason.

The referenda themselves raise constitutional questions, since the Court has struck down other state constitutional amendment attempts to disadvantage particular minorities. Such amendments can only be understood as attempts to abridge the rights of a disfavored group. Further, should another state attempt to pass a referendum that in addition would nullify existing same-sex marriages, that referendum would be unconstitutional for the additional reason that such unions cannot be retroactively nullified by a legislature without violating constitutional guarantees.

While the Full Faith and Credit Clause does not have an obnoxiousness exception for other states' judgments, it has never been understood to require domiciles at the time of the marriage to recognize their domiciliaries' marriages validly celebrated elsewhere if those marriages violated an important public policy. Yet, domiciles at the time of the marriage must be distinguished from subsequent domiciles and from nondomiciles. Even when states were viewed as having much more sovereignty than they are viewed as having today, they usually felt obligated to recognize those marriages valid in the states of celebration and domicile at the time of the marriage unless those unions fell within a very narrow exception and were polygamous or involved certain kinds of incestuous unions. This exception was not understood to involve all marriages that were deemed as offensive as polygamous marriages, because such an exception would simply swallow the rule, since subsequent domiciles would be permitted to refuse to recognize any marriage of which they disapproved by simply saying that they found it too offensive. It goes without saying that subsequent nondomiciles could not invalidate marriages recognized in the states of celebration and domicile at the time of the marriage.

The natural law exception within domestic relations jurisprudence has a very narrowly defined meaning and thus cannot be used to justify a refusal to recognize same-sex marriages. Even natural law more broadly understood does not offer a compelling justification for such a refusal for at least two reasons. First, the reasons offered by natural law theorists to justify refusing to recognize same-sex marriages can just as readily be used to support recognizing them. Second, the existing state practices regarding marriage simply do not incorporate these theories, instead recognizing marriages that the natural law theorists imply should not be recognized.

The Defense of Marriage Act violates numerous constitutional provisions. Congress did not even try to hide its animus when enacting that legislation. Suppose, however, that Congress had passed a much more general law that allowed states to refuse to recognize any marriage that violated local public policy. Bracketing that the public would never stand for such a rule, a whole host of important individual and state interests would be undermined. Individuals might have their marriages dissolved against their will merely because they crossed state lines. Title to property would be in doubt. Custody and support awards might be open to revision to the detriment of the parties involved.

Congress has enacted legislation to assure that individuals will be unable to evade their marital responsibilities by crossing state lines. It has recognized the difficulties that can be created by allowing states to second-guess their sister states' judgments with respect to custody arrangements. It is simply ridiculous to suggest that Congress wants to promote federalism in the domestic relations context when it has been doing the exact opposite *except when same-sex families are involved.*

The Full Faith and Credit Clause was designed to make the states parts of a single nation. By agreeing to form a Union, states gave up some of their own sovereignty to promote interstate harmony and cooperation. To allow states to pick and choose when they can act like sovereign countries would undermine our nation as a whole, since some states would choose to act like sovereign states in certain contexts and others would act like sovereigns in other contexts.

DOMA is unconstitutional because it is invidiously discriminatory. However, it is also bad public policy because it invites states or particular interest groups to petition for other exceptions to Full Faith and Credit, whether in family law (e.g., giving states the option not to recognize no-fault divorces issued in other states) or other areas of law (e.g., giving states the option not to enforce judgments if such a judgment could not be awarded in the forum state).

Commentators sometimes imply that a state which recognizes same-sex marriages would be foisting its own marriage laws on the rest of the country. Yet, this is false for a variety of reasons. First, in order for a marriage to be valid, it must not be contrary to an important public policy of the domicile. If indeed individuals were flying to a particular state to marry, their marriages would not be valid unless their home states would recognize the marriage, too. Currently, the laws of several states imply that those states will recognize a same-sex marriage if validly celebrated in another state.

When some states recognized interracial marriages, they were not accused of subverting the United States or of infringing upon the rights of those states wishing to invidiously discriminate. Such accusations are similarly inappropriate in the same-sex marriage context.

States that refused to recognize interracial marriages were not claiming a right to violate constitutional guarantees; instead, they were merely claiming to uphold morality. However, just as the refusal to recognize interracial marriages involved invidious discrimination, claims of upholding morality notwithstanding, the refusal to recognize same-sex marriages involves invidious discrimination, claims of upholding morality notwithstanding.

Same-sex marriages should be recognized in every state because of the Fourteenth Amendment to the United States Constitution, not the Full Faith and Credit Clause. The latter merely imposes minimal requirements on the states with respect to choice of law, and more stringent requirements with respect to giving full faith and credit to sister state judgments. Nonetheless, even these minimal requirements are not met by DOMA and by those states claiming the right not to recognize a marriage valid in the states of celebration and domicile at the time of the marriage. To say that the Constitution can be suspended when the rights of same-sex couples are at issue so that fundamental interests can be ignored if these couples dare to move to or, perhaps, even visit another state is to destroy the pillars of liberty, equality, and respect upon which this country is based. Not even a conservative, "moral" Congress could claim to want that.

NOTES

1. Pub. L. No. 104–199, 110 Stat. 2419 (1996).

2. For additional arguments suggesting that Congress exceeded its powers under the Full Faith and Credit Clause, see Mark Strasser, *Legally Wed: Same-Sex Marriage and the Constitution,* Chap. 6 (Ithaca, N.Y.: Cornell University Press, 1997).

3. *Vandever v. Industrial Commission of Arizona*, 714 P.2d 866, 869 (Ariz. App. 1985).

4. See Thomas Keane, Note, "Aloha, Marriage? Constitutional and Choice of Law Arguments for Recognition of Same-Sex Marriages," 47 *Stan L. Rev.* 499, 516 (1995) ("Clarity of marital status gives the married couple security in their relationship and also benefits third parties, notably children and creditors"). See also Joseph W. Hovermill, "A Conflict of Laws and Morals: The Choice of Law Implications of Hawaii's Recognition of Same-Sex Marriages," 53 *Md. L. Rev.* 450, 455 (1994) ("A choice of law rule that validates out-of-state marriages provides stability and predictability in questions of marriage, ensures the legitimization of children, protects party expectations, and promotes interstate comity").

5. See *In re Marriage of Kinkead*, 57 N.W.2d 628, 632 (Minn. 1953).

6. See, for example, American Law Institute, *Restatement (Second) of the Conflict of Laws*, § 283 (St. Paul, Minn.: American Law Institute Publishers, 1971).

7. See *Black's Law Dictionary*, 655 (6th ed. 1990) (Forum shopping—"Such occurs when a party attempts to have his action tried in a particular court or jurisdiction where he feels he will receive the most favorable judgment or verdict").

8. See 28 U.S.C.A. sec. 1738C (1998) (italics added).

9. See 142 *Cong. Rec.* S4870 (Sen. Nickles) (5/8/96) ("This bill does not change State law, but allows each state to decide for itself with respect to same-sex marriage").

10. Cf. id. ("This effort hardly seems to be news as it reaffirms current practice and policy").

11. Cf. id.

12. See 1996 WL 10829470 (statement of Mr. Wardle before the Senate Judiciary Comm. on S. 1740, the Defense of Marriage Act) (7/11/96) ("A state may have or may create conflict of laws rules that would recognize same-sex marriages if legal in other states").

13. See 1996 WL 10829443 (statement of Sen. Hatch before the Senate Judiciary Comm. on S. 1740, the Defense of Marriage Act) (7/11/96) ("Thus, it would not be surprising that persons who want to invoke the legitimacy of 'marriage' for same-sex unions will travel to Hawaii to become 'married'. Then, they will return to their home states where it would be expected that the state recognize, as valid, a Hawaii marriage certificate"); 1996 WL 10829445 (statement of Rep. Largent before the Senate Judiciary Comm. on S. 1740, the Defense of Marriage Act) (7/11/96) ("If the state court in Hawaii legalizes same-sex marriage, homosexual couples from other states around the country will fly to Hawaii to 'marry'. These same couples will then go back to their respective states and argue that the Full Faith and Credit Clause of the U.S. Constitution requires their home state to recognize their union as a 'marriage' ").

14. Ironically, when Congress passed the Full Faith and Credit for Child Support Orders Act, it did include a provision regarding choice of law. See 28 U.S.C.A. sec. 1738B(h).

15. See 1996 WL 256695 (written statement of Mr. Wardle before the House of Rep. Judiciary Comm. on H. 3396, the Defense of Marriage Act) (5/15/96) (a main principle underlying DOMA is a "respect for federalism").

16. *Estin v. Estin*, 334 U.S. 541, 545–46 (1948).

17. See *Broderick v. Rosner*, 294 U.S. 629, 643 (1935).

18. *Phillips Petroleum Co. v. Shutts*, 472 U.S. 797, 822 (1985) (expectations of the parties are important considerations when determining fairness); *Kulko v. Superior Court*, 436 U.S. 84, 97–98 (1978) (basic considerations of fairness key consideration); Gary J. Simson, "State Autonomy in Choice of Law: A Suggested Approach," 52 *S. Cal. L. Rev.* 61, 65 (1978) ("a choice of law that grossly upsets a party's justified expectations violates the due process clause despite the fact that the selected law is supported by a governmental interest in its application under the particular circumstances"); Gene R. Shreve, "Choice of Law and the Forgiving Constitution," 71 *Ind. L.J.* 271, 281 (1996) ("courts and commentators periodically express concern that chosen law not unreasonably disturb the expectations of a party"). Cf. *Williams v. North Carolina*, 317 U.S. 287, 302–3 (1942) ("*Williams I*") ("So when a court of one state acting in accord with the requirements of procedural due process alters the marital status of one domiciled in that state by granting him a divorce from his absent spouse, we cannot say its decree should be excepted from the full faith

and credit clause merely because its enforcement or recognition in another state would conflict with the policy of the latter").

19. *Allstate Insurance Co. v. Hague*, 449 U.S. 302, 327 (1981) (Stevens, J., concurring in the judgment).

20. Id. (Stevens, J., concurring in the judgment). See also id. at 333 (1980) (Powell, J., dissenting) (describing the touchstone of choice of law as "the reasonable expectation of the parties").

21. Anthony Dominic D'Amato, Note, "Conflict of Laws Rules and the Interstate Recognition of Same-Sex Marriages," 1995 *U. Ill. L. Rev.* 911, 942 ("if a same-sex couple from Hawaii married in that state but later moved to Illinois, Illinois probably would have to recognize the marriage. . . . During this period, no state other than Hawaii had any interest in the marriage, and under the laws of Hawaii, the couple, as well as Hawaii, rightfully developed an expectation that a valid marriage existed").

22. Brainerd Currie, "Full Faith and Credit, Chiefly to Judgments: A Role for Congress," 1964 *Sup. Ct. Rev.* 89, 96 ("ordinarily the interest of the forum that justifies the application of domestic law must have existed at the time of the transaction").

23. See *Allstate Insurance Co.*, 449 U.S. at 326 (Stevens, J., concurring in the judgment) ("It may be assumed that a choice-of-law decision would violate the Due Process Clause if it were totally arbitrary or if it were fundamentally unfair to either litigant"); Currie, "Full Faith and Credit," 1964 *Sup. Ct. Rev.* at 97–98 ("There is a definite concern with the foreseeability of the possible application of a law different from that which originally determined the rights of the parties—in other words, with fairness"); Russell Weintraub, "Due Process and Full Faith and Credit Limitations on a State's Choice of Law," 44 *Iowa L. Rev.* 449, 457 (1959) ("a state may have a significant contact with the parties or with the occurrences, but may have acquired that contact so late in the history of the transaction in dispute, that to apply its law would result in a serious disregard of the justifiable expectations of one of the parties. If this is the case, if use of a state's law will inject an element of unfair surprise, such use will violate due process").

24. Cf. *Allstate Insurance Co.*, 449 U.S. at 319 (The Court has "held that a postoccurrence change of residence to the forum State was insufficient in and of itself to confer power on the forum State to choose its law") (citing *John Hancock Mutual Life Ins. Co. v. Yates*, 299 U.S. 178 [1936]).

25. Currie, "Full Faith and Credit," 1964 *Sup. Ct. Rev.* at 93 ("To apply domestic law when the forum state had no interest in the application of its policy at that time raises problems similar to those raised by the retrospective application of laws"). For a discussion of retroactive legislation, see generally Charles B. Hochman, "The Supreme Court and the Constitutionality of Retroactive Legislation," 73 *Harv. L. Rev.* 692 (1960).

26. See *Treines v. Sunshine Mining Co.*, 308 U.S. 66, 77 (1940).

27. *Williams I*, 317 U.S. at 303–4.

28. See *Maynard v. Hill*, 125 U.S. 190, 207–8 (1888) (quoting *Starr v. Pease*, 8 Conn. 541 (1831)).

29. Id. at 208.

30. Compare *Harvey v. Harvey*, 298 S.E.2d 467 (W.V. 1982) (bigamous mar-

riage voidable rather than void) with *Toler v. Oakwood Smokeless Coal Corp.*, 173 Va. 425 (Va. 1939) (bigamous marriage void ab initio).

31. U.S. Const. art. 4, § 1.

32. Id.

33. *Williams I*, 317 U.S. at 294 (quoting *Davis v. Davis*, 305 U.S. 32, 40 [1938]).

34. *Johnson v. Muelberger*, 340 U.S. 581, 584 (1951).

35. *M'Elmoyle ex rel. Bailey v. Cohen*, 38 U.S. 312, 324–325 (1839).

36. Id. at 325. See also *Baker v. General Motors Corp.*, 118 S. Ct. 657, 668 (1998) (Scalia, J., concurring).

37. See Joseph Story, *Commentaries on the Constitution of the United States*, Vol. 2, 2nd ed., § 1312 (Boston: C. C. Little and J. Brown, 1851) (discussing controversy whether the evidence should be viewed as conclusive or prima facie).

38. See Robert A. Leflar, *American Conflicts Law*, rev. ed. § 79 (Indianapolis, Ind.: Bobbs-Merrill Co., 1968):

> The last sentence of the full faith and credit clause, authorizing the Congress to prescribe by general law "the effect" of sister state judgments, permits that body to provide by statute for a general registration of judgments procedure to be administered in state courts, whereby a judgment in one state, upon registration in another state (without new action or new service of process) would be at once enforceable by execution or otherwise on the same basis as judgments of the second state.

See also Rex Glensy, Note, "The Extent of Congress' Power under the Full Faith and Credit Clause," 71 *S. Cal. L. Rev.* 137, 164 (1997) ("To avoid the confusing, intricate, and somewhat contorted way of enforcing sister state judgments, the enabling provision was meant for Congress to enact a statute providing for registration of state judgments").

39. See Leflar, *American Conflicts Law*, § 76 ("The procedure of bringing a new action in a second state on a judgment previously rendered, after full litigation of issues or opportunity therefor, is slow, clumsy, and sometimes ineffectual").

40. Id.

41. *M'Elmoyle*, 38 U.S. at 324 (emphasis added).

42. U.S. Const., art. 4, § 1.

43. See Story, *Commentaries on the Constitution*,Vol. 2, § 1303.

44. See James M. Patten, Comment, "The Defense of Marriage Act: How Congress Said 'No' to Full Faith and Credit and the Constitution," 38 *Santa Clara L. Rev.* 939, 946–47 (1998) (citing William M. Meigs, *The Growth of the Constitution in the Federal Convention of 1787*, 255 [Littleton, Colo.: F. B. Rothman Publishing Co., 1987]); Scott Ruskay-Kidd, Note, "The Defense of Marriage Act and the Overextension of Congressional Authority," 97 *Colum. L. Rev.* 1435, 1454–55 (1997).

45. Prof. Whitten has offered an interpretation of the Full Faith and Credit Clause that would allow Congress to lessen the effect of judgments in sister states without violating constitutional guarantees. See generally Ralph U. Whitten, "The Original Understanding of the Full Faith and Credit Clause and DOMA," 32 *Creighton L. Rev.* 255 (1998). However, the Court has not accepted his interpretation of the Full Faith and Credit Clause. See Jeffrey L. Rensberger, "Same-Sex Marriage

and the Defense of Marriage Act: A Deviant View of an Experiment in Full Faith and Credit," 32 *Creighton L. Rev.* 409, 414 (1998) (suggesting that Professor Whitten's view does not account for the case law interpreting the Full Faith and Credit Clause).

46. See *Baker*, 118 S. Ct. at 663 (quoting 28 U.S.C. § 1738).

47. See *Morris v. Jones*, 329 U.S. 545, 547 (1947).

48. See Leflar, *American Conflicts Law*, § 73 ("if a judgment lacks conclusive effect in the state where it was rendered, it will not be conclusive elsewhere either").

49. *Thompson v. Thompson*, 484 U.S. 174, 180 (1988).

50. See id.

51. See id. at 181.

52. See Melanie Togman Sloan, "No More Baby Jessicas: Proposing Revisions to the Parental Kidnapping Prevention Act," 12 *Yale L. & Pol'y Rev.* 355, 357 (1994) (discussing states that had not adopted the Act).

53. See *Thompson*, 484 U.S. at 181.

54. See Sloan, "No More Baby Jessicas," 12 *Yale L. & Pol'y Rev.* at 357 (By 1979, the eleven states that had not adopted the UCCJA "had become sanctuaries in which kidnappers could live with their kidnapped children").

55. See *Thompson*, 484 U.S. at 181.

56. See *Murphy v. Woerner*, 748 P.2d 749, 750 (Alaska 1988) ("When the UCCJA proved an imperfect remedy for the staggering national problem of parental child-snatching and forum shopping in interstate custody disputes, Congress enacted the PKPA to provide a uniform federal standard to ascertain the one state with jurisdiction to modify an existing child custody order").

57. *Thompson*, 484 U.S. at 180.

58. See U.S. Const. art 1, § 8.

59. See *Thompson*, 484 U.S. at 177, 180–81.

60. See id. at 183.

61. Id. at 182.

62. See Act of May 26, 1790, 1 Stat. 122.

63. *Thompson v. Whitman*, 85 U.S. (18 Wall.) 457, 461 (1873).

64. See *Baker*, 118 S. Ct. at 663.

65. See Paige E. Chabora, "Congress' Power under the Full Faith and Credit Clause and the Defense of Marriage Act of 1996," 76 *Neb. L. Rev.* 604, 635 (1997).

66. *Davis*, 305 U.S. at 40.

67. See *Davis*, 448 U.S. at 272 n.18 ("Congress clearly has the power to increase the measure of faith and credit that a State must accord to the laws or judgments of another state").

68. See *Thomas v. Washington Gas Light Co.*, 448 U.S. at 261, 272 n.18 (1980) (there is "some question whether Congress may cut back on the measure of faith and credit required by a decision of this Court").

69. See 1 U.S.C.A. Sec. 7 (1998).

70. *United States Dept. of Agriculture v. Moreno*, 413 U.S. 528, 534 (1973).

71. *McCarty v. McCarty*, 453 U.S. 210, 237 (1981) (Rehnquist, J., dissenting) (citations omitted). See also *United States v. Lopez*, 514 U.S. 549, 564 (1995) (casting doubt on the appropriateness of Congress's regulating family law).

72. *De Sylva v. Ballentine*, 351 U.S. 570, 580 (1956).

73. Id.

74. *Rose v. Rose*, 481 U.S. 619, 625 (1987) (citing *Hisquierdo v. Hisquierdo*, 439 U.S. 572, 581 [1979], quoting *United States v. Yazell*, 382 U.S. 341, 352 [1966]).

75. See *Wissner v. Wissner*, 338 U.S. 655, 660–61 (1950) (upholding serviceman's right to make insurance benefit "payable to the relative of his choice" as legitimate because it "might well directly enhance the morale of the serviceman." The exemption involved an end that was "a legitimate one within the congressional powers over national defense"). See also *Mansell v. Mansell*, 490 U.S. 581, 583 (1989) (state courts may not "treat as property divisible upon divorce military retirement pay waived by the retiree in order to receive veterans' disability benefits"); *Ridgway v. Ridgway*, 454 U.S. 46, 55 (1981) (upholding Servicemen's Group Life Insurance Act under which the "insured service member possesses the right freely to designate the beneficiary and to alter that choice at any time by communicating the decision in writing to the proper office"); *McCarty v. McCarty*, 453 U.S. 210 (1981) (upholding right to Congress not to have "application of community property principles to military retired pay").

76. See *Yazell*, 382 U.S. at 348 (not allowing government to ignore state rule of coverture, while recognizing "there is always a federal interest to collect moneys which the Government lends").

77. See 142 Cong. Rec. H7277 (Rep. McInnis) (7/11/96); id. at 7275 (Rep. Barr) (7/11/96).

78. For a more general discussion comparing the former prohibition of interracial marriage and the current prohibition of same-sex marriage, see Mark Strasser, "Family, Definitions, and the Constitution: On the Antimiscegenation Analogy," 25 *Suffolk U. L. Rev.* 981 (1991).

79. Brainerd Currie & Herma Hill Schreter, "Unconstitutional Discrimination in the Conflict of Laws: Privileges and Immunities," 69 *Yale L.J.* 1323, 1325 (1960) ("The pursuit of domestic interests must yield whenever it comes into conflict with the constitutional prohibitions against discrimination").

80. *Garrett v. Chapman*, 449 P.2d 856, 859 (Or. 1969) ("The courts of this state may refuse to give a particular effect to a marriage contracted in another state or nation if to do so would be contrary to a strong public policy of this state").

81. C. W. Taintor II, "What Law Governs the Ceremony, Incidents and Status of Marriage," 19 *B.U. L. Rev.* 353, 358–59 (1939) ("denial of an incident of a valid marriage is a harsh measure").

82. See *Baehr v. Miike*, 1996 WL 694235, *18 (Hawai'i Cir.Ct.) ("people marry for a variety of reasons including, but not limited to the following: (1) having or raising children; (2) stability and commitment; (3) emotional closeness; (4) intimacy and monogamy; (5) the establishment of a framework for a long-term relationship; (6) personal significance; (7) recognition by society; and (8) certain legal and economic protections, benefits and obligations").

83. Professor Koppelman writes, "If a [same-sex] couple is domiciled within a state, wholesale denial of benefits may make sense." See Andrew Koppelman, "Same-Sex Marriage, Choice of Law, and Public Policy," 76 *Texas L. Rev.* 921, 988 (1998). Yet, federal constitutional guarantees would presumably be implicated were a state to try to do this.

84. *Romer v. Evans*, 517 U.S. 620, 632 (1996).

85. *McLaughlin v. Florida*, 379 U.S. 184, 191 (1964).

86. Id. at 191.

87. See *Ex parte Francois*, 9 F. Cas. 699, 700 (Case No. 5,047) (W.D. Tex. 1879) ("If a state thought proper to do so, I am not satisfied that she would be prohibited by any express provision of the federal constitution, or of the civil rights bill, from passing a law forbidding a marriage . . . between a Christian and a Jew").

88. See generally Mark Strasser, *Legally Wed: Same-Sex Marriage and the Constitution* (Ithaca, N.Y.: Cornell University Press, 1997).

89. *Romer*, 517 U.S. at 627.

90. Id. at 632.

91. For a listing of some of those benefits, see Barbara A. Rabb, "The Constitutionality of the Defense of Marriage Act in the Wake of *Romer v. Evans*," 32 *New. Eng. L. Rev.* 263, 301–4 (1997).

92. *Romer*, 517 U.S. at 626.

93. Id. at 627.

94. *The Slaughter-House Cases*, 83 U.S. (16 Wall.) 36, 80 (1872) ("One of these privileges is . . . that a citizen of the United States can, of his own volition, become a citizen of any State of the Union by a bona fide residence therein, with the same rights as other citizens of that State."); *Dred Scott v. Sandford*, 60 U.S. (19 How.) 393, 417 (1856) (describing privileges and immunities as including "the right to enter every other State whenever they pleased, singly or in companies, without pass or passport, and without obstruction, to sojourn there as long as they pleased, to go where they pleased at every hour of the day or night without molestation, unless they committed some violation of law"); *In re Hobbs*, 12 F. Cas. 262, 264 (Case No. 6550) (N.D. Ga. 1871) (Privileges and Immunities Clause applies to travel).

95. *Hobbs*, 12 F. Cas. at 264; *Lonas v. State*, 50 Tenn. (3 Heisk.) 287, 306–7 (1871); *State v. Jackson*, 80 Mo. 175, 177 (1883); *Frasher v. State*, 30 Am. Rep. 131, 134–35 (Tex. Ct. App. 1877).

96. *Lonas*, 50 Tenn. at 306–7; *Jackson*, 80 Mo. at 177; *Frasher*, 30 Am. Rep. at 135.

97. *Lonas*, 50 Tenn. at 310 ("These police powers of the state extend to every conceivable subject, where the good order, the domestic peace, the private happiness or public welfare of the people demand legislation. Unless that legislation is inhibited in the fundamental law, no State has acquitted itself of the duties of government without it. We hold that such legislation is not, never has been, and never should be, prohibited to the States, in reference to the intermarriage of the races").

98. *Jackson*, 80 Mo. at 177.

99. Id.

100. *Frasher*, 30 Am. Rep. at 135.

101. For a discussion of why Congress overstepped its bounds by attempting to regulate marriage for federal purposes in the Defense of Marriage Act, see Mark Strasser, "*Loving* the *Romer* Out for *Baehr*: On Acts in Defense of Marriage and the Constitution," 58 *U. Pitt. L. Rev.* 279, 314–21 (1997).

102. Seth F. Kreimer, " 'But Whoever Treasures Freedom . . .': The Right to Travel and Extraterritorial Abortions," 91 *Mich. L. Rev.* 907, 920 (1993) ("the equality that the Privileges and Immunities Clause seeks to foster is one that affirmatively advances national unity"); id. ("the Privileges and Immunities Clause not only fosters national unity and inhibits parochial discrimination, but also imparts to individual American citizens the freedom that accompanies national citizenship").

103. Douglas Laycock, "Equal Citizens of Equal and Territorial States: The Constitutional Foundations of Choice of Law," 92 *Colum. L. Rev.* 249, 265 (1992) ("Each unjustified discrimination against a citizen of a sister state is a constitutional wrong to that citizen, regardless of the impact on national unity").

104. *Jones v. Helms*, 452 U.S. 412, 417–18 (1981).

105. *Zobel v. Williams*, 457 U.S. 55, 76–77 (1982) (O'Connor, J., concurring).

106. This might also be a benefit, since individuals might thereby be relieved of their marital responsibilities.

107. See Seth F. Kreimer, "Territoriality and Moral Dissensus: Thoughts on Abortion, Slavery, Gay Marriage and Family Values," 16 *QLR* 161, 182 (1996) ("The price of obtaining the benefits of a new state citizenship is leaving behind the benefits of the old. Even for visitors from other states, the Privileges and Immunities Clause of Article IV has long been interpreted only 'to insure to a citizen of State A who ventures into State B the same privileges which the citizens of State B enjoy' ").

108. See *Attorney General of New York v. Soto-Lopez*, 476 U.S. 898, 907 (1986).

109. *Sosna v. Iowa*, 419 U.S. 393 (1975).

110. Id. at 406 ("Iowa's requirement delayed her access to the courts, but, by fulfilling it, she could ultimately have obtained the same opportunity for adjudication which she asserts ought to have been hers at an earlier point in time").

111. *Crandall v. Nevada*, 73 U.S. (6 Wall.) 35, 39 (1867).

112. Id. at 46.

113. Id.

114. *Shapiro v. Thompson*, 394 U.S. 618, 629 (1969).

115. Peter D. Isakoff, Note, "Unconstitutional Discrimination in Choice of Law," 77 *Colum. L. Rev.* 272, 283 (1977) ("The privileges and immunities clause has uniformly been interpreted as protecting citizens of other states from the discriminatory application of the forum state's laws. Only an individual who is a citizen of a sister state of the United states has standing to invoke the clause").

116. *Shapiro*, 394 U.S. at 641.

117. *New York v. United States*, 505 U.S. 144, 182 (1992).

118. For example, were there an accident, a spouse might be able to authorize a medical procedure in time of need. If the relationship were not recognized, the individual would stand in no closer legal relation to the life-partner than would any other third party.

119. See *Second Restatement*, § 283, cmt. b ("Protection of the justified expectations of the parties is a basic policy underlying the field of marriage").

120. A fuller version of this argument can be found in Strasser, *Legally Wed*, 141-147.

121. *United States v. Brown*, 381 U.S. 437, 441 (1965) ("The bill of attainder [involved] a parliamentary act sentencing to death one or more specific persons . . . who had attempted, or threatened to attempt, to overthrow the government"). See also Jane Welsh, Note, "The Bill of Attainder Clause: An Unqualified Guarantee of Process," 50 *Brook. L. Rev.* 77, 83 (1983) ("Originally, a bill of attainder was an enactment of the English Parliament, typically proclaiming a condemnation of death directed against a particular group. It was most often used to punish political activities that Parliament or the sovereign found threatening or treasonous").

122. *Brown*, 381 U.S. at 441–42 ("The 'bill of pains and penalties' was identical to the bill of attainder, except that it prescribed a penalty short of death, e.g., ban-

ishment, deprivation of the right to vote, or exclusion of the designated party's sons from Parliament") (footnote omitted).

123. *Nixon v. Administrator of General Services*, 433 U.S. 425, 474 (1977).

124. *Brown*, 381 U.S. at 442 ("The use of bills of attainder and bills of pains and penalties was not limited to England. During the American Revolution, the legislatures of all thirteen States passed statutes directed against the Tories; among these statutes were a large number of bills of attainder and bills of pains and penalties"). See also Thomas B. Griffith, Note, "Beyond Process: A Substantive Rationale for the Bill of Attainder Clause," 70 *Va. L. Rev.* 475, 477 (1984) ("one can reasonably infer that the Framers were at the very least proscribing a legislative practice used in England since the sixteenth century and in the colonies until 1787").

125. *Nixon*, 433 U.S. at 474.

126. Id.

127. See U.S. Const., Art. I, § 9 ("No bill of Attainder . . . shall be passed.")

128. *Brown*, 381 U.S. at 447. See also Griffith, "Beyond Process," 70 *Va. L. Rev.* at 478 ("The distinction between common-law bills of attainder and bills of pains and penalties has never been of much import in constitutional adjudication").

129. *Brown*, 381 U.S. at 447 (citing *Fletcher v. Peck*, 10 U.S. [6 Cranch] 87, 138 [1810]).

130. Id. at 442 ("Most bills of attainder and bills of pains and penalties named the parties to whom they were to apply; a few, however, simply described them").

131. Id. at 461.

132. See *Nixon*, 433 U.S. at 538 (Burger, C.J., dissenting).

133. Id. (Burger, C.J., dissenting).

134. See Michael P. Lehmann, "The Bill of Attainder Doctrine: A Survey of the Decisional Law," 5 *Hastings Const. L.Q.* 767, 790–91 (1978) ("the modern definition of a bill of attainder has four distinct components: it is (1) a legislative act (2) imposing punishment (3) upon a designated person or class of persons (4) without benefit of judicial trial"). See also Glenn Willett Clark, "How the Superfund Congress Crafted a Bill of Attainder: Misappropriation of the Judicial Power of the United States—Of Unbounded Civil Liabilities, Retroactive Taxes, and Legislative Adjudication," 4 *Seton Hall Const. L.J.* 3, 29 (1993) (pointing out these requirements).

135. See *Garner v. Bd. of Public Works*, 341 U.S. 716, 722 (1951).

136. *United States v. Lovett*, 328 U.S. 303, 321–22 (1946) (Frankfurter, J., concurring).

137. Id. at 324 (Frankfurter, J., concurring).

138. Id. (Frankfurter, J., concurring).

139. Id. (Frankfurter, J., concurring).

140. *Nixon*, 433 U.S. at 476. See also David P. Restaino, Comment, "Conditioning Financial Aid on Draft Registration: A Bill of Attainder and Fifth Amendment Analysis," 84 *Colum. L. Rev.* 775, 788 (1984) ("the retribution-deterrence distinction is irrelevant in bill of attainder analysis. The bill of attainder clause can prohibit legislation of both deterrent and retributive natures").

141. *Nixon*, 433 U.S. at 482 ("In determining whether a legislature sought to inflict punishment on an individual, it is often useful to inquire into the existence of less burdensome alternatives by which that legislature . . . could have achieved its legitimate nonpunitive objectives").

142. *Flemming v. Nestor*, 363 U.S. 603, 617 (1960).

143. *Nixon*, 433 U.S. at 478.

144. Id. at 480 (citing *Lovett*, 328 U.S. at 316).

145. Id.

146. Id. (citation omitted).

147. *Brown*, 381 U.S. at 442.

148. Id. at 445 ("the Bill of Attainder Clause . . . was intended as one implementation of the general principle of fractionalized power"). See also id. at 442–43 (discussing separation of powers as one of the purposes of the clause); Note, "The Bounds of Legislative Specification: A Suggested Approach to the Bill of Attainder Clause," 72 *Yale L.J.* 330, 345 (1962) (discussing separation of powers rationale).

149. *Brown*, 381 U.S. at 445.

150. Id. at 446.

151. Cf. id. at 455 (striking down "general rule" that pronounced guilt and imposed punishment).

152. *Nixon*, 433 U.S. at 480.

153. See *Lovett*, 328 U.S. at 315.

154. See David Kairys, Note, "The Bill of Attainder Clauses and Legislative and Administrative Suppression of 'Subversives'," 67 *Colum. L. Rev.* 1490, 1492 (1967) (specificity requirement has created controversy and confusion).

155. See Roderick M. Hills, Jr., Correspondence, "Is Amendment 2 Really a Bill of Attainder? Some Questions About Professor Amar's Analysis of *Romer*," 95 *Mich. L. Rev.* 236, 240 (1996).

156. Id.

157. See *Ex parte Garland*, 71 U.S. 333 (1866).

158. See *Cummings v. Missouri*, 71 U.S. 277 (1866).

159. Note, "The Bounds of Legislative Specification," 72 *Yale L.J.* at 340 (history indicates that there is no "inescapable class" requirement).

160. *United States v. Brown*, 81 U.S. 437 (1965).

161. Id. at 442.

162. *Cummings*, 71 U.S. at 324.

163. Id. at 325.

164. Id.

165. See *Selective Service System v. Minnesota Public Interest Research Group*, 468 U.S. 841, 851 (1984) (student who wants public assistance can simply register for the draft and then qualify).

166. It is clear that the Bill of Attainder Clause prohibits punishments involving the denial of either rights or privileges. See Lehmann, "The Bill of Attainder Doctrine," 5 *Hastings Const. L.Q.* at 846 (discussing a "pernicious . . . spurious distinction [which] is based on the putative dichotomy between rights and privileges"); Charles H. Wilson, Jr., Comment, "The Supreme Court's Bill of Attainder Doctrine: A Need for Clarification," 54 *Calif. L. Rev.* 212, 238–239 (1966) (no distinction for bill of attainder purposes between the denial of a right and the denial of a privilege).

167. See 142 Cong. Rec. S10111 (Sen. Byrd) (discussing costs of the recognition); 142 Cong. Rec. H7495 (Cong. Lipinski) (same).

168. See *Bell v. Wolfish*, 441 U.S. 520, 585 (1979) (Stevens, J., dissenting) (any restriction reducing costs "could not be characterized as 'arbitrary or purposeless' ").

169. See 142 Cong. Rec. H7487 (Rep. Funderburk) (discussing outrage over paying for benefits based on recognition of same-sex marriages).

170. For a discussion of some of the respects in which current laws banning same-sex marriages are analogous to former laws banning interracial marriages, see Mark Strasser, "Family, Definitions, and the Constitution: On the Antimiscegenation Analogy," 25 *Suffolk U. L. Rev.* 981 (1991).

171. See 142 Cong. Rec. S10101 (Sen. Kennedy). See also 142 Cong. Rec. E1320 (Rep. Collins) (describing DOMA as "blatant homophobic gay-bashing"); 142 Cong. Rec. E1299 (Rep. Velaquez) (describing DOMA as "legitimizing hate and discrimination"); 142 Cong. Rec. E1299 (Rep. Waxman) (discussing the espousal of "official bigotry").

172. See 142 Cong. Rec. H7486 (Rep. Buyer) (upholding God's Will and Morality); 142 Cong. Rec. H7487 (Rep. Delay) (need to protect morality); 142 Cong. Rec. H7487 (suggesting that homosexuality is inherently wrong and harmful); 142 Cong. Rec. H7491 (Rep. Canady) (suggesting that gay relationships are immoral); 142 Cong Rec. H7494 (Rep. Smith) (suggesting that gays engage in unnatural and immoral behavior); 142 Cong. Rec. H7495 (Rep. Lipinski) (suggesting that all know that the issue of gay marriage is a moral one); 142 Cong. Rec. H7277 (Rep. Hoke) (comparing gay marriage to theft, burglary, rape, and murder); 142 Cong. Rec. S4947 (Sen. Coats) (suggesting that gay marriages are immoral); 142 Cong. Rec. S10111 (suggesting that gay marriage violates Judaeo-Christian precepts); 142 Cong. Rec. S10067 (Sen. Helms) (suggesting that recognizing gay marriage would destroy the moral fabric of the country).

173. See Mark Strasser, "Suspect Classes and Suspect Classification: On Discriminating, Unwittingly or Otherwise," 64 *Temple L. Rev.* 937, 960–65 (1991).

174. See Strasser, "Family, Definitions, and the Constitution," 25 *Suffolk U. L. Rev.* at 1008 (suggesting that neither relationship is immoral, views to the contrary notwithstanding).

175. *Nixon*, 433 U.S. at 480.

176. See 142 Cong. Rec. S10101 (Sen. Kennedy) (noting this transparent electoral strategy).

177. *Bell*, 441 U.S. at 589–90 (Stevens, J., dissenting).

178. *Cummings*, 71 U.S. at 320.

179. Id. at 321.

180. Id.

181. Id.

182. See 1996 WL 10829445 (Congressional testimony of Rep. Largent) (discussing his wish to model children's behavior).

183. Theorists tend to agree that sexual orientation is set early in life so it is doubtful that this would be an effective deterrent. See Troy R. Holyroyd, Commentary, "Homosexuals and the Military: Integration or Discrimination?" 8 *J. Contemp. Health L. & Pol'y* 429, 447 (1992).

184. *American Communications Ass'n v. Douds*, 339 U.S. 382, 442 (Jackson, J., concurring and dissenting, each in part). (1950)

185. Id. (Jackson, J., concurring and dissenting, each in part).

186. Id. (Jackson, J., concurring and dissenting, each in part).

187. Id. at 443 (Jackson, J., concurring and dissenting, each in part).

188. See Griffith, "Beyond Process," 70 *Va. L. Rev.* at 500–501 (discussing the use of bills of attainder to suppress speech).

189. See *Perez v. Lippold*, 198 P.2d 17, 25 (Cal. 1948).

190. See 142 Cong. Rec. H7487 (Rep. Funderburk) (suggesting that the attempt to secure the right to marry a same-sex partner is somehow objectionable).

191. *Lovett*, 328 U.S. at 315, 326–27 (Frankfurter, J., concurring).

192. *Communist Party v. Subversive Activities Control Board*, 367 U.S. 1, 146 (1961) (Black, J., dissenting).

193. Id. (Black, J., dissenting).

194. *Kennedy v. Mendoza-Martinez*, 372 U.S. 144, 186 (1963).

Selected Bibliography

FEDERAL COURTS

Supreme Court

Alaska Packers Association v. Industrial Accident Commission of California, 294 U.S. 532 (1935)
Allied Structural Steel Company v. Spannaus, 438 U.S. 234 (1978)
Allstate Insurance Company v. Hague, 449 U.S. 302 (1981)
American Communications Association v. Douds, 339 U.S. 382 (1950)
American Land Company v. Zeiss, 219 U.S. 47 (1911)
Attorney General of New York v. Soto-Lopez, 476 U.S. 898 (1986)
BMW of North America, Incorporated v. Gore, 517 U.S. 559 (1996)
Baker v. General Motors Corporation, 118 S. Ct. 657 (1998)
Barbier v. Connolly, 113 U.S. 27 (1884)
Bell v. Wolfish, 441 U.S. 520 (1979)
Berman v. Parker, 348 U.S. 26 (1954)
Blount v. Windley, 95 U.S. 173 (1877)
Bob Jones University v. Simon, 416 U.S. 725 (1974)
Bowen v. Georgetown University Hospital, 488 U.S. 204 (1988)
Bowers v. Harwick, 478 U.S 186 (1986)
Bradford Electric Light Company, Incorporated v. Clapper, 286 U.S. 145 (1932)
Bradley v. School Board of City of Richmond, 416 U.S. 696 (1974)
Broderick v. Rosner, 294 U.S. 629 (1935)
Brown v. Board of Education, 347 U.S. 483 (1954)
Brown, United States v., 381 U.S. 437 (1965)
Burrus, Ex parte, 136 U.S. 586 (1890)
Caban v. Mohammed, 441 U.S. 380 (1979)
Carlton, United States v., 512 U.S. 26 (1994)

Chapman v. California, 386 U.S. 18 (1967)
Chase Securities Corporation v. Donaldson, 325 U.S. 304 (1945)
Chicago & A. R. Company v. Wiggens Ferry Company, 119 U.S. 615 (1887)
Chicago, Burlington, & Quincy Railroad Company v. McGuire, 219 U.S. 549 (1911)
Cohen v. Beneficial Industrial Loan Corporation, 337 U.S. 541 (1949)
Communist Party v. Subversive Activities Control Board, 367 U.S. 1 (1961)
Craig v. Boren, 429 U.S. 190 (1976)
Crandall v. Nevada, 73 U.S. (6 Wallace) 35 (1867)
Crane v. Hahlo, 258 U.S. 142 (1922)
Crawford v. Board of Education, 458 U.S. 527 (1982)
Cummings v. Missouri, 71 U.S. 277 (1866)
Dartmouth College v. Woodward, 17 U.S. (4 Wheaton) 518 (1819)
Davis v. Beason, 133 U.S. 333 (1890)
Davis v. Davis, 305 U.S. 32 (1938)
De Sylva v. Ballentine, 351 U.S. 570 (1956)
Dred Scott v. Sandford, 60 U.S. (19 Howard) 393 (1856)
Dunn v. Blumstein, 405 U.S. 330 (1972)
Eisenstadt v. Baird, 405 U.S. 438 (1972)
El Paso v. Simmons, 379 U.S. 497 (1964)
Elmendorf v. Taylor, 23 U.S. 152 (1825)
Energy Reserves Group, Incorporated v. Kansas Power & Light Company, 459 U.S. 400 (1983)
Estin v. Estin, 334 U.S. 541 (1948)
Fauntleroy v. Lum, 210 U.S. 230 (1908)
Flemming v. Nestor, 363 U.S. 603 (1960)
Fletcher v. Peck, 10 U.S. (6 Cranch) 87 (1810)
Garland, Ex parte, 71 U.S. 333 (1866)
Garner v. Board of Public Works, 341 U.S. 716 (1951)
General Motors Corporation v. Romein, 503 U.S. 181 (1992)
Gooding v. Wilson, 405 U.S. 518 (1972)
Gordon v. Lance, 403 U.S. 1 (1971)
Gray v. Sanders, 372 U.S. 368 (1963)
Great Northern Railway Company v. Sunburst Oil & Refining Company, 287 U.S. 358 (1932)
Griswold v. Connecticut, 381 U.S. 479 (1965)
Groppi v. Wisconsin, 400 U.S. 505 (1971)
Grover & Baker Sewing Machine Company v. Radcliffe, 137 U.S. 287 (1890)
Groves v. Slaughter, 40 U.S. 449 (1841)
Haddock v. Haddock, 201 U.S. 562 (1906)
Hague v. Committee for Industrial Organization, 307 U.S. 496 (1939)
Hall v. United States, 92 U.S. 27 (1875)
Hardware Dealers' Mutual Fire Insurance Company v. Glidden Company, 284 U.S. 151 (1931)
Harper v. Virginia State Board of Elections, 383 U.S. 663 (1966)
Hartford Accident & Indemnity Company v. Delta & Pine Land Company, 292 U.S. 143 (1934)
Hilton v. Guyot, 159 U.S. 113 (1895)
Hisquierdo v. Hisquierdo, 439 U.S. 572 (1979)

Home Building and Loan Association v. Blaisdell, 290 U.S. 398 (1934)
Hunter v. Erickson, 393 U.S. 385 (1969)
Indiana ex rel. Anderson v. Brand, 303 U.S. 95 (1938)
Irving Trust Company v. Day, 314 U.S. 556 (1942)
J.E.B. v. Alabama ex rel. T.B., 511 U.S. 127 (1994)
James v. Valtierra, 402 U.S. 137 (1971)
John Hancock Mutual Life Insurance Company v. Yates, 299 U.S. 178 (1936)
Johnson v. Muelberger, 340 U.S. 581 (1951)
Jones v. Helms, 452 U.S. 412 (1981)
Kaiser Aluminum & Chemical Corporation v. Bonjourno, 494 U.S. 827 (1990)
Kennedy v. Mendoza-Martinez, 372 U.S. 144 (1963)
Kingsley International Pictures Corporation v. Regents of the University of the State of New York, 360 U.S. 684 (1959)
Kotch v. Board. of River Port Pilot Commissioners, 330 U.S. 552 (1947)
Kramer v. Union Free School District, 395 U.S. 621 (1969)
Kulko v. Superior Court, 436 U.S. 84 (1978)
Landgraf v. USI Film Products, 511 U.S. 244 (1994)
Late Corporation of the Church of Jesus Christ of Latter-Day Saints v. United States, 136 U.S. 1 (1890)
Leffingwell v. Warren, 67 U.S. 599 (1862)
Lochner v. New York, 198 U.S. 45 (1905)
Lopez, United States v., 514 U.S. 549 (1995)
Loughran v. Loughran, 292 U.S. 216 (1934)
Louisville Gas and Electric Company v. Coleman, 277 U.S. 32 (1928)
Lovett, United States v., 328 U.S. 303 (1946)
Loving v. Virginia, 388 U.S. 1 (1967)
Lucas v. Forty-Fourth General Assembly of State of Colorado, 377 U.S. 713 (1964)
Lucas v. South Carolina Coastal Council, 505 U.S. 1003 (1992)
Magnolia Petroleum Company v. Hunt, 320 U.S. 430 (1943)
Mansell v. Mansell, 490 U.S. 581 (1989)
Massachusetts Board of Retirement v. Murgia, 427 U.S. 307 (1976)
Maynard v. Hill, 125 U.S. 190 (1888)
McCarty v. McCarty, 453 U.S. 210 (1981)
McLaughlin v. Florida, 379 U.S. 184 (1964)
M'Elmoyle ex rel. Bailey v. Cohen, 38 U.S. 312 (1839)
Michael H. v. Gerald D., 491 U.S. 110 (1989) (plurality opinion)
Michael M. v. Superior Court, 450 U.S. 464 (1981)
Milliken v. Meyer, 311 U.S. 457 (1940)
Mills v. Duryee, 11 U.S. (7 Cranch) 481 (1813)
Milwaukee County v. M. E. White Company, 296 U.S. 268 (1935)
Mississippi University for Women v. Hogan, 458 U.S. 718 (1982)
Morris v. Jones, 329 U.S. 545 (1947)
Murphy v. Ramsey, 114 U.S. 15 (1885)
Naim v. Naim, 350 U.S. 891 (1955)
Naim v. Naim, 350 U.S. 985 (1956)
Nesmith v. Sheldon, 48 U.S. 812 (1849)
Nevada v. Hall, 440 U.S. 410 (1979)
New York v. United States, 505 U.S. 144 (1992)

Nixon v. Administrator of General Services, 433 U.S. 425 (1977)
O'Brien v. Skinner, 414 U.S. 524 (1974)
Ogden v. Saunders, 25 U.S. 213 (1827)
Pace v. Alabama, 106 U.S. 583 (1883)
Pacific Employers Insurance Company v. Industrial Accident Commission, 306 U.S. 493 (1939)
Palmore v. Sidoti, 466 U.S. 429 (1984)
Paul v. Virginia, 75 U.S. (8 Wallace) 168 (1868)
Personnel Administrator of Massachusetts v. Feeney, 442 U.S. 256 (1979)
Phillips Petroleum Company v. Shutts, 472 U.S. 797 (1985)
Pink v. A.A.A. Highway Express, Incorporated, 314 U.S. 201 (1941)
Planned Parenthood of Southeastern Pennsylvania v. Casey, 505 U.S. 833 (1992)
Poe v. Ullman, 367 U.S. 497 (1961)
Railroad Company v. Grant, 98 U.S. 398 (1878)
Reed v. Reed, 404 U.S. 71 (1971)
Reitman v. Mulkey, 387 U.S. 369 (1967)
Reynolds v. Sims, 377 U.S. 533 (1964)
Reynolds v. United States, 98 U.S. 145 (1878)
Ridgway v. Ridgway, 454 U.S. 46 (1981)
Rochin v. California, 342 U.S. 165 (1952)
Roe v. Wade, 410 U.S. 113 (1973)
Romer v. Evans, 517 U.S. 620 (1996)
Rose v. Rose, 481 U.S. 619 (1987)
Rowan v. Runnels, 46 U.S. 134 (1847)
San Antonio School District v. Rodriguez, 411 U.S. 1 (1973)
Santosky v. Kramer, 455 U.S. 745 (1982)
Selective Service System v. Minnesota Public Interest Research Group, 468 U.S. 841 (1984)
Shapiro v. Thompson, 394 U.S. 618 (1969)
Sherrer v. Sherrer, 334 U.S. 343 (1948)
Sniadach v. Family Finance Corporation of Bay View, 395 U.S. 336 (1969)
Sosna v. Iowa, 419 U.S. 393 (1975)
South-Eastern Underwriters Association, United States v., 322 U.S. 533 (1944)
St. Louis Southwestern Railway Company v. Arkansas ex rel. Norwood, 235 U.S. 350 (1914)
Storaasli v. Minnesota, 283 U.S. 57 (1931)
Strauder v. West Virginia, 100 U.S. 303 (1879)
Sturges v. Crowninshield, 17 U.S. (4 Wheaton) 197 (1819)
Sun Oil Company v. Wortman, 486 U.S. 717 (1988)
Supreme Lodge, K. P. v. Meyer, 265 U.S. 30 (1924)
Texas v. Florida, 306 U.S. 398 (1939)
The Slaughter-House Cases, 83 U.S. (16 Wallace) 36 (1872)
Thirty-seven (37) Photographs, United States v., 402 U.S. 363 (1971)
Thomas v. Washington Gas Light Company, 448 U.S. 261 (1980)
Thompson v. Thompson, 484 U.S. 174 (1988)
Thompson v. Whitman, 85 U.S. (18 Wallace) 457 (1873)
Treigle v. Acme Homestead Association, 297 U.S. 189 (1936)
Treines v. Sunshine Mining Company, 308 U.S. 66 (1940)

Turner v. Safley, 482 U.S. 78 (1987)
Union National Bank v. Lamb, 337 U.S. 38 (1949)
United States v. ——— (see opposing party)
United States Department of Agriculture v. Moreno, 413 U.S. 528 (1973)
United States Trust Company v. New Jersey, 431 U.S. 1 (1976)
Usery v. Turner Elkhorn Mining Company, 428 U.S. 1 (1976)
Vanderbilt v. Vanderbilt, 354 U.S. 416 (1957)
Virginia, United States v., 518 U.S. 515 (1996)
W. B. Worthen Co. v. Thomas, 292 U.S. 426 (1934)
Washington v. Davis, 426 U.S. 229 (1976)
Washington v. Seattle School District No. 1, 458 U.S. 457 (1982)
Webster v. Cooper, 55 U.S. 488 (1852)
West Virginia State Board of Education v. Barnette, 319 U.S. 624 (1943)
Williams v. North Carolina, 317 U.S. 287 (1942) ("*Williams I*")
Williams v. North Carolina, 325 U.S. 226 (1945) ("*Williams II*")
Winfree v. Northern Pacific Railway Company, 227 U.S. 296 (1913)
Wissner v. Wissner, 338 U.S. 655 (1950)
Worcester County Trust Company v. Riley, 302 U.S. 292 (1937)
Yazell, United States v., 382 U.S. 341 (1966)
Yick Wo v. Hopkins, 118 U.S. 356 (1886)
Zablocki v. Redhail, 434 U.S. 374 (1978)
Zobel v. Williams, 457 U.S. 55 (1982)

Courts of Appeal

Cotner v. Henry, 394 F.2d 873 (7th Cir. 1968)
Fagg, United States v., 34 M.J. 179 (1992)
Francois, Ex parte, 9 F. Cas. 699 (Case No. 5,047) (W.D. Tex. 1879)
George v. Sullivan, 909 F.2d 857 (6th Cir. 1990)
Hobbs, In re, 12 F. Cas. 262 (Case No. 6550) (N.D. Ga. 1871)
Kinney, Ex parte, 14 F. Cas. 602 (Case No. 7,825) (E.D. Va. 1879)
Lovisi v. Slayton, 539 F.2d 349 (4th Cir. 1976)
Moe v. Dinkins, 669 F.2d 67 (2nd Cir.), cert. denied, 459 U.S. 827 (1982)
Shahar v. Bowers, 114 F.3d 1097 (11th Cir. 1997), cert. denied, 118 S. Ct. 693 (1998)
The Slaughter-House Cases, 83 U.S. (16 Wall.) 36 (1872).
State v. ——— (see opposing party)
Tutty, State v., 41 F. 753 (S.D. Ga. 1890)

District Courts

Adams v. Howerton, 486 F. Supp. 1119 (C.D. Cal. 1980), aff'd, 673 F.2d 1036 (9th Cir.), cert. denied, 458 U.S. 1111 (1982)
Chlystek v. Kane, 412 F. Supp. 20 (W.D.Pa 1976)
Devine v. Rodgers, United States ex rel., 109 F. 886 (E.D. Pa. 1901)

Equality Foundation of Greater Cincinnati, Incorporated v. City of Cincinnati, 838 F.Supp. 1235 (S.D. Ohio 1993)
Equality Foundation of Greater Cincinnati, Incorporated v. City of Cincinnati, 860 F. Supp. 417 (S.D. Ohio 1994); rev'd, 54 F.3d 261 (6th Cir. 1995), cert. granted, judgment vacated by 116 S.Ct. 2519 (1996), rev'd, judgment vacated by 128 F.3d 289 (6th Cir. 1997)
Oliverson v. West Valley City, 875 F. Supp. 1465 (D. Utah 1995)

STATE COURTS

Abelt v. Zeman, 179 N.E.2d 176 (Ohio Ct. Common Pleas 1962)
Adams (Adams v. Adams), In re Marriage of, 604 P.2d 332 (Mont. 1979)
Addison v. Addison, 399 P.2d 897 (Cal. 1965)
Adoption of Tammy, 619 N.E.2d 315 (Mass. 1993)
Adoptions of B.L.V.B. & E.L.V.B., 628 A.2d 1271 (Vt. 1993)
Arnelle v. Fisher, 647 So.2d 1047 (Fla. App. 1994)
Arnold v. Department of Health of City of New York, 571 N.Y.S.2d 14 (App. Div. 1991)
Baehr v. Lewin, 852 P.2d 44 (Haw.), reconsideration granted in part, 875 P.2d 225 (Haw. 1993)
Baehr v. Miike, CIV. No. 91–1394, 1996 WL 694235 (Haw. Cir. Ct. Dec. 3, 1996)
Bagnardi v. Hartnett, 366 N.Y.S.2d 89 (1975)
Baker v. Nelson, 191 N.W.2d 185 (Minn. 1971)
Baker, People v., 442 P.2d 675 (Cal. 1968) (in bank)
Banks, In re Estate of, 629 N.E.2d 1223 (Ill. App. 1994)
Barnes (Barnes v. Barnes), In re Marriage of, 743 P.2d 915 (Cal. 1987)
Barquin v. Flores, 459 So.2d 436 (Fla. App. 1984)
Barrington v. Barrington, 200 Ala. 315 (1917)
Bell, State v., 66 Tenn. (7 Baxt.) 9 (1872)
Benton v. State, 461 S.E.2d 202 (Ga. 1995)
Bernstein v. Bernstein, 201 A.2d 660 (Conn. Super. 1964)
Bingham v. Miller, 17 Ohio 445 (1848)
Black, In re Interest of, 283 P.2d 887 (Utah 1955)
Bobala v. Bobala, 33 N.E.2d 845 (Ohio App. 1940)
Bockemehl v. Bockemehl, 604 S.W.2d 466 (Tex. Civ. App. 1980)
Bouquet (Bouquet v. Bouquet), In re Marriage of, 546 P.2d 1371 (Cal. 1976) (in bank)
Bowen, Ex parte, 247 S.W.2d 379 (Ky. 1952)
Brause v. Bureau of Vital Statistics, 1998 WL 88743 (Alaska Super.)
Brinson v. Brinson, 96 So.2d 653 (La. 1957)
Brown, State v., 23 N.E. 747 (Ohio 1890)
Bruce v. Bruce, 296 P.2d 310 (Wash. 1956)
Bucca v. State, 128 A.2d 506 (N.J. Super. Ct. Ch. Div. 1957)
Buck, State v., 757 P.2d 861 (Or. App. 1988)
Buol, In re Marriage of, 705 P.2d 354 (Cal. 1985) (in bank)
Burns v. State, 48 Ala. 195 (1872)
Byrne v. Bercker, 501 N.W.2d 402 (Wis. 1993)

Caballero, Succession of, v. Executor, 24 La. Ann. 573 (1872)
Calma v. Calma, 128 S.E.2d 440 (Va. 1962)
Campbell v. Sundquist, 926 S.W.2d 250 (Tenn. App. 1996)
Campione v. Campione, 107 N.Y.S.2d 170 (1951)
Cantelou v. Doe, ex dem. Hood, 56 Ala. 519 (1876)
Caribe Hilton Hotel v. Toland, 307 A.2d 85 (N.J. 1973)
Casanova Club v. Bisharat, 458 A.2d 1 (Conn. 1983)
Catalano v. Catalano, 170 A.2d 726 (Conn. 1961)
Cheryl D. v. Estate of Robert D.B., 559 N.W.2d 272 (Wis. App. 1996)
Christensen v. State, 468 S.E.2d 188 (Ga. 1996)
Citizens for Responsible Behavior v. Superior Court, 2 Cal.Rptr.2d 648 (Ct. App. 1991)
City of Sherman v. Henry, 910 S.W.2d 542 (Tex. App. 1995), rev'd by 928 S.W.2d 464 (Tex. 1996)
Clark vs. Clark, 10 N.H. 380 (1839)
Coghill v. Boardwalk Regency Corporation, 396 S.E.2d 838 (Va. 1990)
Commonwealth v.———(see opposing party)
Cornell v. Cornell, 164 N.E.2d 395 (N.Y. 1959)
Coulter v. Melody, 489 S.W.2d 156 (Tex. App. 1972)
Custody of (see name of party)
Danza, In re, 591 N.Y.S.2d 197 (App. Div. 1992)
Dauderman v. Dauderman, 263 N.E.2d 708 (Ill. App. 1970)
Davidson v. Davidson, 151 N.W.2d 53 (Wis. 1967)
Demorest v. DiPentima, 324 N.W.2d 634 (Mich. App. 1982).
Demoss v. Demoss, 195 N.E.2d 496 (Ind. App. 1964)
Dibble v. Meyer, 278 P.2d 901 (Or. 1955)
Dickson v. Dickson, 9 Tenn. (I Yerger) 110 (Tenn. 1826)
Don v. Don, 114 A.2d 203 (Conn. 1955)
Dubish, State v., 675 P.2d 877 (Kan. 1984)
Dupre v. Executor, 10 La. Ann. 411 (1855)
Edmondson v. State, 464 S.E.2d 839 (Ga. App. 1995)
Eggers v. Olson, 231 P. 483 (Okla. 1924)
Ellis v. State, 42 Ala. 525 (1868)
Enderle Marriage License, In re, 1 Pa. D. & C.2d 114 (1954)
Estate of (see name of party)
Ex rel. (see name of party)
Evans v. Romer, 854 P.2d 1270 (Colo. 1993)
Evans v. Romer, 882 P.2d 1335 (Colo. 1994) (en banc)
Ezeonu, People v., 588 N.Y.S.2d 117 (1992)
Fabian (Fabian v. Fabian), In re Marriage of, 715 P.2d 253 (Cal. 1986) (in bank)
Fensterwald v. Burk, 129 Md. 131 (1916)
Fergusson v. Fergusson, 149 N.Y.S.2d 836 (1956)
Fetters, In re Marriage of, 584 P.2d 104 (Colo. App. 1978)
Findlen v. Findlen, 695 A.2d 1216 (Me. 1997)
FMS Management Systems Inc. v. Thomas, 309 S.E.2d 697 (N.C. App. 1984)
Forgan v. Bainbridge, 274 P. 155 (Ariz. 1928)
Francis v. Tazewell, 120 Va. 319 (1917)
Franks, In re Marriage of, 542 P.2d 845 (Colo. 1975) (en banc)

Frasher v. State, 30 Am. Rep. 131 (Tex. Ct. App. 1877)
Fuqua v. Fuqua, 268 Ala. 127 (1958)
Gabisso, Succession of, 44 So. 438 (La. 1907)
Garcia v. Garcia, 127 N.W. 586 (S.D. 1910)
Garrett v. Chapman, 449 P.2d 856 (Or. 1969)
Gassman v. Gassman, 296 N.W.2d 518 (S.D. 1980)
Geile, State ex. rel. Miesner v., 747 S.W.2d 757 (Mo. App. 1988)
Georgina G. v. Terry M. (In re Angel Lace M.), 516 N.W.2d 678 (Wis. 1994)
Gessner v. Gessner, 614 So.2d 307 (La. App. 1993)
Gibson, State v., 36 Ind. 389 (1871)
Giroux, In re Marriage of, 704 P.2d 160 (Wash. App. 1985)
Golden v. Golden, 68 P.2d 928 (N.M. 1937)
Green v. State, 58 Ala. 190 (1877)
Greenhow v. James' Ex'or, 80 Va. (6 Hansbrough) 636 (1885)
Gryczan v. State, 942 P.2d 112 (Mont. 1997)
H.S.H.-K., In re Custody of, 533 N.W.2d 419 (Wis. 1995)
Hairston, State v., 63 N.C. 439 (1869)
Hamlet v. Hamlet, 242 Ala. 70 (1941)
Handley v. Handley, 3 Cal. Rptr. 910 (Ct. App. 1960)
Harvey v. Harvey, 298 S.E.2d 467 (W.V. 1982)
Hawkins v. Hawkins, 38 So. 640 (Ala. 1905)
Heikes, In re Marriage of, 899 P.2d 1349 (Cal. 1995)
Henley v. Foster, 125 So. 662 (Ala. 1930)
Hernandez, Succession of, 46 La. Ann. 962 (1894)
Hinson v. Hinson, 356 So.2d 372 (Fla. App. 1978)
Hobson v. Dempsey Const. Co., 7 N.W.2d 896 (Iowa 1943)
Hood v. State, 56 Ind. 263 (1877)
In re (see name of party)
Intercontinental Hotels Corporation v. Golden, 254 N.Y.S.2d 527 (N.Y. 1964)
Interest of (see name of party)
Jackson, State v., 80 Mo. 175 (1883)
Jackson v. State, 682 N.E.2d 564 (Ind. App. 1997)
Jacob, In re, 660 N.E.2d 397 (N.Y. 1995)
Jarzem v. Bierhaus, 415 So.2d 88 (Fla. App. 1982)
Johnson v. Branson, 319 S.E.2d 735 (Va. 1984)
Johnson v. Shepherd, 143 Ala. 325 (1904)
Jones v. Hallahan, 501 S.W.2d 588 (Ky. 1973)
Jones v. Commonwealth, 79 Va. 213 (1884)
Jones v. Commonwealth, 80 Va. 18 (1885)
Jones v. Commonwealth, 80 Va. 538 (1885)
Karin T. v. Michael T., 484 N.Y.S.2d 780 (Fam. Ct. 1985)
Kay v. Kay, 252 N.Y.S. 518 (1931)
Keith v. Commonwealth, 181 S.E. 283 (Va. 1935)
Kennedy, State v., 76 N.C. 251 (1877)
King, Commonwealth v., 372 N.E.2d 196 (Mass. 1977)
Kinkead, In re Marriage of, 57 N.W.2d 628 (Minn. 1953)
Kinney v. Commonwealth, 71 Va. (30 Grattan) 858 (1878)
Kleinfield v. Veruki, 372 S.E.2d 407 (Va. App. 1988)

Ladd v. Ladd, 640 A.2d 29 (Vt. 1994)
Laikola v. Engineered Concrete, 277 N.W.2d 653 (Minn. 1979)
Lair, State v., 301 A.2d 748 (N.J. 1973)
Lane, Commonwealth v., 113 Mass. 458 (1873)
Lang v. Reetz-Lang, 488 N.E.2d 929 (Ohio App. 1985)
Lanham v. Lanham, 117 N.W. 787 (Wis. 1908)
Leland v. Leland, 847 P.2d 518 (Wash. App. 1993)
Lenherr, In re Estate of, 314 A.2d 255 (Penn. 1974)
Liu (Liu v. Liu), In re Marriage of, 242 Cal. Rptr. 649 (Ct. App. 1987)
Lonas v. State, 50 Tenn. (3 Heisk.) 287 (1871)
Loughmiller, Estate of, 629 P.2d 156 (Kan. 1981)
M & R Investments, Company, Incorporated v. Hacker, 511 So.2d 1099 (Fla. App. 1987)
Mahan v. Mahan, 88 So.2d 545 (Fla. 1956)
Malott v. Malott, 703 P.2d 531 (Ariz. App. 1985)
Mangrum v. Mangrum, 220 S.W.2d 406 (Ky. 1949)
May's Estate, In re, 114 N.E.2d 4 (N.Y. 1953)
McCown v. Quillin, 344 S.W.2d 576 (Tenn. App. 1960)
McGinley v. McGinley, 295 S.W.2d 913 (Tex. Civ. App. 1956)
McPherson v. Commonwealth, 69 Va. (28 Grattan) 939 (1877)
McQuiston, State v., 922 P.2d 519 (Mont. 1996)
Medway v. Needham, 16 Mass. 157 (1819)
Merrick v. Merrick, 194 N.E. 55 (N.Y. 1934)
Miller's Estate, In re, 214 N.W. 428 (Mich. 1927)
Minvielle (Domec v. Barjac), Succession of, 15 La. Ann. 342 (1860)
Morgan v. M'Ghee, 24 Tenn. (5 Humphreys) 13 (1844)
Murphy v. Woerner, 748 P.2d 749 (Alaska 1988)
Musser, State v., 175 P.2d 724 (Utah 1946), vacated and remanded by 333 U.S. 95 (1948)
Naim v. Naim, 87 S.E.2d 749 (Va. 1955)
Nakashima, State v., 114 P. 894 (Wash. 1911)
Needham v. Needham, 33 S.E.2d 288 (Va. 1945)
Nelson, State v., 271 N.W. 114 (Minn. 1937)
Noel v. Ewing, 9 Ind. 37 (1857)
Osoinach v. Watkins, 180 So. 577 (Ala. 1938)
Patterson v. Bingham, 101 Va. 372 (1903)
Payne v. Payne, 214 P.2d 495 (Colo. 1950)
Pennegar v. State, 10 S.W. 305 (Tenn. 1889)
People v. ——— (see name of party)
Perdew v. Perdew, 64 P.2d 602 (Colo. 1936)
Perez v. Lippold, 198 P.2d 17 (Cal. 1948)
Peters v. Narick, 270 S.E.2d 760 (W.V. 1980)
Phillips v. Consolidated Supply Company, 895 P.2d 574 (Idaho 1995)
Powers (Powers III v. Powers), In re Marriage of, 267 Cal. Rptr. 350 (Ct. App. 1990)
Putnam v. Putnam, 25 Mass. (8 Pickering) 433 (1829)
Rabie (Rabie v. Rabie), In re Marriage of, 115 Cal.Rptr. 594 (Ct. App. 1974)
Raia v. Raia, 214 Ala. 391 (1926)
Rickard v. Trousdale, 508 So.2d 260 (Ala. 1987)

Robert D.B. (Cheryl D. v. Estate of Robert D.B.), In re Estate of, 559 N.W.2d 272 (Wis. App. 1996)
Ross, State v., 76 N.C. 242 (1877)
Ryan v. Ryan, 277 So.2d 266 (Fla. 1973)
S.I., In re Interest of, 173 A.2d 457 (N.J. Super. Ct. 1961)
Santos, State v., 413 A.2d 58 (R.I. 1980)
Schmit, State v., 139 N.W.2d 800 (Minn. 1966)
Scott v. Raub, 88 Va. 721 (1892)
Scott v. State, 39 Ga. 321 (1869)
Seeley v. Erringer, 57 N.W.2d 628 (Minn. 1953)
Semmler, In re Marriage of, 481 N.E.2d 716 (Ill. 1985)
Shattuck, State v., 69 Vt. 403 (1897)
Singer v. Hara, 522 P.2d 1187 (Wash. Ct. App. 1974)
Slivka (Slivka v. Slivka), In re Marriage of, 228 Cal. Rptr. 76 (Ct. App. 1986)
Smith v. Goldsmith, 223 Ala. 155 (1931)
Smith v. Smith, 486 S.E.2d 516 (S.C. Ct. App. 1997)
Smith v. Winder (In re Winder's Estate), 219 P.2d 18 (Cal. Ct. App. 1950)
Starr v. Pease, 8 Conn. 541 (1831)
State v. ——— (see opposing party)
Steele v. Campbell, 82 N.E.2d 273 (Ind. App. 1948)
Stevenson v. Gray, 56 Ky. 154 (17 Ben Monroe 193) (1856)
Stewart, In re, 721 P.2d 405 (N.M. 1986)
Stiles, In re Estate of, 391 N.E.2d 1026 (Ohio 1979)
Stowell, Commonwealth v., 449 N.E.2d 357 (Mass. 1983)
Stull, Estate of, 183 Pa. 625 (1898)
Succession of (see name of party)
Superior Court, State ex rel. Tufton v., 90 P. 258 (Wash. 1907)
Sutton v. Warren, 51 Mass. 451 (1845)
Takahashi's Estate, In re, 129 P.2d 217 (Mont. 1942)
Taylor v. Taylor, 31 So.2d 579 (Ala. 1947)
Thurman v. State, 18 Ala. 276 (1850)
Toler v. Oakwood Smokeless Coal Corporation, 173 Va. 425 (1939)
Tyson v. State, 90 So. 622 (Fla. 1922)
Tyson v. Tyson, 727 P.2d 226 (Wash. 1986) (en banc)
Union Securities Company v. Adams, 236 P. 513 (Wyo. 1925)
United States Steel Credit Union v. Knight, 204 N.E.2d 4 (Ill. 1965)
Van Storch v. Griffin, 71 Pa. 240 (1872)
Van Voorhis v. Brintnall, 86 N.Y. 18 (1881)
Vandever v. Industrial Commission of Arizona, 714 P.2d 866 (Ariz. App. 1985)
Wall v. Wall, 534 A.2d 465 (Pa. 1987)
Walton (Walton v. Walton), In re Marriage of, 104 Cal. Rptr. 472 (Ct. App. 1972)
Warner v. Warner, 256 S.W.2d 734 (Ark. 1953)
Washington v. Washington, 69 Ala. 281 (1881)
Wasson, Commonwealth v., 842 S.W.2d 487 (Ky. 1993)
Weaver v. State, 116 So. 893 (Ala. Ct. App. 1928)
West Cambridge v. Lexington, 18 Mass. (1 Pickering) 506 (1823)
Wilkins v. Zelichowski, 129 A.2d 459 (N.J. Super. Ct. App. Div. 1957), rev'd 140 A.2d 65 (N.J. 1958)

Williams v. State, 494 So.2d 819 (Ala. App. 1986)
Wilson v. Cook, 100 N.E. 222 (Ill. 1912)
Woods v. Woods, 638 S.W.2d 403 (Tenn. App. 1982)
Woods v. Moten, 129 Ala. 228 (1900)
Zizzo v. Zizzo, 247 N.Y.S.2d 38 (1964)

SECONDARY LITERATURE

Ackerman, Bruce A. *Social Justice in the Liberal State.* New Haven, Conn.: Yale University Press, 1980.

Adams, William E., Jr. "Whose Family Is It Anyway? The Continuing Struggle for Lesbians and Gay Men Seeking to Adopt Children." 30 *New England Law Review* 579 (1996).

Allen, Beth A. Comment. "Same-Sex Marriage: A Conflict-of-Laws Analysis for Oregon." 32 *Willamette Law Review* 619 (1996).

American Law Institute. *Restatement of the Law of the Conflict of Laws.* St. Paul, MN: American Law Institute Publishers, 1934. (*Restatement (First) of the Conflict of Laws*)

———. *Restatement (Second) of the Conflict of Laws.* St. Paul, Minn.: American Law Institute Publishers, 1971.

———. *Restatement (Second) of Contracts.* St. Paul, Minn.: American Law Institute Publishers, 1981.

Applebaum, Harvey M. "Miscegenation Statutes: A Constitutional and Social Problem." 53 *Georgetown Law Journal* 49 (1964).

Arkes, Hadley. "The Closet Straight." In Andrew Sullivan ed., *Same-Sex Marriage: Pro and Con: A Reader.* New York: Vintage Books, 1997.

———. "The Role of Nature." In Andrew Sullivan ed., *Same-Sex Marriage: Pro and Con: A Reader.* New York: Vintage Books, 1997.

Avins, Alfred. "Anti-Miscegenation Laws and the Fourteenth Amendment: The Original Intent." 52 *Virginia Law Review* 1224 (1966).

Baird, Robert M. & Stuart E. Rosenbaum eds. *Same-Sex Marriage: The Moral and Legal Debate.* New York: Prometheus Books, 1997.

Balian, Habib A. Note. " 'Til Death Do Us Part: Granting Full Faith and Credit to Marital Status." 68 *Southern California Law Review* 397 (1995).

Ball, Carlos A. "Moral Foundations for a Discourse on Same-Sex Marriage: Looking Beyond Political Liberalism." 85 *Georgetown Law Journal* 1871 (1997).

Bank, Steven A. "Anti-Miscegenation Laws and the Dilemma of Symmetry: The Understanding of Equality in the Civil Rights Act of 1875." 2 *University of Chicago Law School Roundtable* 303 (1995).

Beale, Joseph H. "Marriage and the Domicil." 44 *Harvard Law Review* 501 (1931).

Becker, Mary. "Problems with the Privatization of Heterosexuality." 73 *Denver University Law Review* 1169 (1996).

Bennett, William. "Leave Marriage Alone." In Andrew Sullivan ed., *Same-Sex Marriage: Pro and Con: A Reader.* New York: Vintage Books, 1997.

Bentham, Jeremy. "The Rationale of Reward." Reprinted in John Bowring ed., *The Works of Jeremy Bentham.* Vol. 2. New York: Russell & Russell, 1962.

Beschle, Donald L. "Defining the Scope of the Constitutional Right to Marry: More than Tradition, Less than Unlimited Autonomy." 70 *Notre Dame Law Review* 39 (1994).

Bowman, Craig A. & Blake M. Cornish. Note. "A More Perfect Union: A Legal and Social Analysis of Domestic Partnership Ordinances." 92 *Columbia Law Review* 1164 (1992).

Bradford, Laura. Note. "The Counterrevolution: A Critique of Recent Proposals to Reform No-Fault Divorce Laws." 49 *Stanford Law Review* 607 (1997).

Bradley, Craig M. "The Right Not to Endorse Gay Rights: A Reply to Sunstein." 70 *Indiana Law Journal* 29 (1994).

Brandes, Joel R. & Carole L. Weidman. "Same-Sex Marriage." 217 *New York Law Journal* 3 (1/28/97).

Brilmayer, Lea. "Credit Due Judgments and Credit Due Laws: The Respective Roles of Due Process and Full Faith and Credit in the Interstate Context." 70 *Iowa Law Review* 95 (1984).

Bruce, Teresa M. Note. "Neither Liberty Nor Justice: Anti-Gay Initiatives, Political Participation, and the Rule of Law." 5 *Cornell Journal of Law & Public Policy* 431 (1996).

Calamari, John D. & Joseph M. Perillo. *The Law of Contracts.* 3rd ed. St. Paul, Minn.: West Publishing Co., 1987.

Chabora, Paige E. "Congress' Power under the Full Faith and Credit Clause and the Defense of Marriage Act of 1996." 76 *Nebraska Law Review* 604 (1997)

Chambers, David L. "What If? The Legal Consequences of Marriage and the Legal Needs of Lesbian and Gay Male Couples." 95 *Michigan Law Review* 447 (1996).

———. "Polygamy and Same-Sex Marriage." 26 *Hofstra Law Review* 53 (1997).

Christensen, Craig W. "Legal Ordering of Family Values: The Case of Gay and Lesbian Families." 18 *Cardozo Law Review* 1299 (1997).

———. "If Not Marriage: On Securing Gay and Lesbian Family Values by a 'Simulacrum of Marriage.' " 65 *Fordham Law Review* 1699 (1998).

Clark, Glenn Willett. "How the Superfund Congress Crafted a Bill of Attainder: Misappropriation of the Judicial Power of the United States—Of Unbounded Civil Liabilities, Retroactive Taxes, and Legislative Adjudication." 4 *Seton Hall Constitutional Law Journal* 3 (1993).

Clark, Homer H. *The Law of Domestic Relations in the United States.* 2nd ed. St. Paul, Minn.: West Publishing Co., 1988.

Closen, Michael L. & Carol R. Heise. "HIV-AIDS and the Non-Traditional Family: The Argument for State and Federal Judicial Recognition of Danish Same-Sex Marriages." 16 *Nova Law Review* 809 (1992).

Cordell, Robert II. "Same-Sex Marriage: The Fundamental Right of Marriage and an Examination of Conflict of Laws and the Full Faith and Credit Clause." 26 *Columbia Human Rights Law Review* 247 (1994).

Cox, Barbara. "A (Personal) Essay on Same-Sex Marriage." In Robert M. Baird & Stuart E. Rosenbaum eds., *Same-Sex Marriage: The Moral and Legal Debate.* New York: Prometheus Books, 1997.

Currie, Brainerd. "Full Faith and Credit, Chiefly to Judgments: A Role for Congress." 1964 *Supreme Court Review* 89.

Currie, Brainerd & Herma Hill Schreter. "Unconstitutional Discrimination in the

Conflict of Laws: Privileges and Immunities." 69 *Yale Law Journal* 1323 (1960).

Currie, David P. "The Constitution in the Supreme Court: State and Congressional Powers, 1801–1835." 49 *University of Chicago Law Review* 887 (1982).

———. "Full Faith and Credit to Marriages." 1 *Green Bag* 7 (1997).

D'Amato, Anthony Dominic. Note. "Conflict of Laws Rules and the Interstate Recognition of Same-Sex Marriages." 1995 *University of Illinois Law Review* 911.

Davidson, Donald. *Essays on Actions and Events.* Oxford: Clarendon Press, 1980.

———. "Intending." In Donald Davidson ed., *Essays on Actions and Events.* Oxford: Clarendon Press, 1980.

Davis, Peggy Cooper. *Neglected Stories: The Constitution and Family Values.* New York: Hill and Wang, 1997.

Dillon, Judith Lillian. Note. "A Proposal to Ban Sexual Orientation Discrimination in Private Employment in Vermont." 15 *Vermont Law Review* 435 (1991).

Duncan, Richard F. "Wigstock and the Kulturkampf: Supreme Court Storytelling, the Culture War, and *Romer v. Evans.*" 72 *Notre Dame Law Review* 345 (1997).

Dworkin, Ronald. *Law's Empire.* Cambridge, Mass.: Harvard University Press, 1986.

Editors, The. "Let Them Wed." In Andrew Sullivan ed., *Same-Sex Marriage: Pro and Con A Reader.* New York: Vintage Books, 1997.

Elovitz, Marc. "Adoption by Lesbian and Gay People: The Use and Mis-use of Social Science Research." 2 *Duke Journal of Gender, Law, & Policy* 207 (1995).

Ely, John Hart. "Choice of Law and the State's Interest in Protecting Its Own." 23 *William & Mary Law Review* 173 (1981).

Eskridge, William N. Jr. "Reneging on History? Playing the Court/Congress/President Civil Rights Game." 79 *California Law Review* 613 (1991).

———. Essay. "Gaylegal Narratives." 46 *Stanford Law Review* 607 (1994).

———. *The Case for Same-Sex Marriage: From Sexual Liberty to Civilized Commitment.* New York: The Free Press, 1996.

Estrin, Michele A. Note. "Retroactive Application of the Civil Rights Act of 1991 to Pending Cases." 90 *Michigan Law Review* 2035 (1992).

Ettelbrick, Paula L. "Since When Is Marriage a Path to Liberation." In Robert M. Baird & Stuart E. Rosenbaum eds., *Same-Sex Marriage: The Moral and Legal Debate.* New York: Prometheus Books, 1997.

Fajer, Marc A. "Can Two Real Men Eat Quiche Together? Storytelling, Gender-Role Stereotypes, and Legal Protection for Lesbians and Gay Men." 46 *University of Miami Law Review* 511 (1992).

Farnsworth, E. Allan. *Farnsworth on Contracts,* Vol. 2. Boston: Little, Brown, and Co., 1990.

Finkelman, Paul. "The Crime of Color." 67 *Tulane Law Review* 2063 (1993).

Finnis, John. *Natural Law and Natural Rights.* Oxford: Clarendon Press, 1980.

———. "Is Natural Law Theory Compatible with Limited Government?" In Robert P. George ed., *Natural Law, Liberalism, and Morality.* Oxford: Clarendon Press, 1996.

———. "Law, Morality, and 'Sexual Orientation.'" In John Corvino ed., *Same Sex: Debating the Ethics, Science, and Culture of Homosexuality.* Lanham, Md.: Rowman & Littlefield, 1997.

Friedman, Andrew H. "Same-Sex Marriage and the Right of Privacy: Abandoning

Scriptural, Canonical, and Natural Law Based Definitions of Marriage." 35 *Howard Law Journal* 173 (1992).

Fuller, Lon L. "Positivism and Fidelity to Law—A Reply to Professor Hart." 71 *Harvard Law Review* 630 (1958).

———. *The Morality of Law*. Rev. ed. New Haven, CT: Yale University Press, rev. ed., 1969.

Gardner, Mary F. Note. "*Braschi v. Stahl Associates Co.*: Much Ado About Nothing?" 35 *Villanova Law Review* 361 (1990).

George, Robert P. & Gerard V. Bradley. "Marriage and the Liberal Imagination." 84 *Georgetown Law Journal* 301 (1995).

George Robert P., ed. *Natural Law, Liberalism, and Morality*. Oxford: Clarendon Press, 1996.

Gerhardt, Michael J. "The Pressure of Precedent: A Critique of the Conservative Approaches to Stare Decisis in Abortion Cases." 10 *Constitutional Commentary* 67 (1993).

Glensy, Rex. Note. "The Extent of Congress' Power under the Full Faith and Credit Clause." 71 *Southern California Law Review* 137 (1997).

Goldberg, Suzanne B. "Gay Rights through the Looking Glass: Politics, Morality and the Trial of Colorado's Amendment 2." 21 *Fordham Urban Law Journal* 1057 (1994).

Goldman, Alvin. *A Theory of Human Action*. Princeton, NJ: Princeton University Press, 1970.

Goodrich, Herbert F. "Foreign Facts and Local Fancies." 25 *Virginia Law Review* 26 (1938).

Green, Vincent C. "Same-Sex Adoption: An Alternative Approach to Gay Marriage in New York." 62 *Brooklyn Law Review* 399 (1996).

Grey, Thomas C. "*Bowers v. Hardwick* Diminished."68 *University of Colorado Law Review* 373 (1997).

Griffith, Thomas B. Note. "Beyond Process: A Substantive Rationale for the Bill of Attainder Clause." 70 *Virginia Law Review* 475 (1984).

Hart, H. L. A. "Positivism and the Separation of Law and Morals." 71 *Harvard Law Review* 593 (1958).

Henson, Deborah M. "Will Same-Sex Marriages Be Recognized in Sister States?: Full Faith and Credit and Due Process Limitations on States' Choice of Law Regarding the Status and Incidents of Homosexual Marriages Following Hawaii's *Baehr v. Lewin*." 32 *University of Louisville Journal of Family Law* 551 (1994).

Hills, Jr., Roderick M. Correspondence. "Is Amendment 2 Really a Bill of Attainder? Some Questions about Professor Amar's Analysis of *Romer*." 95 *Michigan Law Review* 236 (1996).

Hillyard, Carrie. "The History of Suffrage and Equal Rights Provisions in State Constitutions." 10 *Brigham Young University Journal of Public Law* 117 (1996).

Hochman, Charles B. "The Supreme Court and the Constitutionality of Retroactive Legislation." 73 *Harvard Law Review* 692 (1960).

Holland, Maurice J. "The Modest Usefulness of DOMA Section 2." 32 *Creighton Law Review* 395 (1998).

Holyroyd, Troy R. Commentary. "Homosexuals and the Military: Integration or

Discrimination?" 8 *Journal of Contemporary Health Law & Policy* 429 (1992).

Horsburgh, Beverly. "Schrdegreesodinger's Cat, Eugenics, and the Compulsory Sterilization of Welfare Mothers: Deconstructing the Old/New Rhetoric and Constructing the Reproductive Right to Natality for Low-Income Women of Color." 17 *Cardozo Law Review* 531 (1996).

Hovermill, Joseph W. "A Conflict of Laws and Morals: The Choice of Law Implications of Hawaii's Recognition of Same-Sex Marriages." 53 *Maryland Law Review* 450 (1994).

Hutcheson, Francis. *A System of Moral Philosophy*. New York: A. M. Kelley, reprinted 1968.

Hutchison, Darren Lenard. "Out Yet Unseen: A Racial Critique of Gay and Lesbian Legal Theory and Political Discourse." 29 *Connecticut Law Review* 561 (1997).

Isakoff, Peter D. Note. "Unconstitutional Discrimination in Choice of Law." 77 *Columbia Law Review* 272 (1977).

Jaasma, Keith. Note. "The Religious Freedom Restoration Act: Responding to *Smith*; Reconsidering *Reynolds*." 16 *Whittier Law Review* 211 (1995).

Jackson, Robert H. "Full Faith and Credit—The Lawyer's Clause of the Constitution." 45 *Columbia Law Review* 1 (1945).

Johnson, J. Phillip. "The Validity of a Marriage under the Conflict of Laws." 38 *North Dakota Law Review* 442 (1962).

Johnson, Julie L. B. Comment. "The Meaning of 'General Laws': The Extent of Congress's Power under the Full Faith and Credit Clause and the Constitutionality of the Defense of Marriage Act." 145 *University of Pennsylvania Law Review* 1611 (1997).

Kairys, David. Note. "The Bill of Attainder Clauses and Legislative and Administrative Suppression of 'Subversives.' " 67 *Columbia Law Review* 1490 (1967).

Karst, Kenneth. "The Freedom of Intimate Association." 89 *Yale Law Journal* 624 (1980).

Keane, Thomas. Note. "Aloha, Marriage? Constitutional and Choice of Law Arguments for Recognition of Same-Sex Marriages." 47 *Stanford Law Review* 499 (1995).

Keller, Christopher J. "Divining the Priest: A Case Comment on *Baehr v. Lewin*." 12 *Law & Inequality* 483 (1994).

Kelly, Jon-Peter. Note. "Act of Infidelity: Why the Defense of Marriage Act Is Unfaithful to the Constitution." 7 *Cornell Journal of Law & Public Policy* 203 (1997).

Kendell, Kathryn Dean. "Principles and Prejudice: Lesbian and Gay Civil Marriage and the Realization of Equality." 22 *Journal of Contemporary Law* 81 (1996).

King, Sondrea Joy. "Ya'll Cain't Do That Here: Will Texas Recognize Same-Sex Marriages Validly Contracted in Other States?" 2 *Texas Wesleyan Law Review* 515 (1996).

Klingeman, Nancy & Kenneth May. Recent Development. "For Better or Worse, in Sickness and in Health, until Death Do Us Part: A Look at Same-Sex Marriage in Hawaii." 16 *University of Hawaii Law Review* 447 (1994).

Kohm, Lynne Marie. "The Homosexual 'Union': Should Gay and Lesbian Partnerships Be Granted the Same Status as Marriage?" 22 *Journal of Contemporary Law* 51 (1996).

———. "A Reply to 'Principles and Prejudice': Marriage and the Realization That Principles Win over Political Will." 22 *Journal of Contemporary Law* 293 (1996).

Koppelman, Andrew. "Why Discrimination Against Lesbians and Gay Men Is Sex Discrimination." 69 *New York University Law Review* 197 (1994).

———. "Dumb and DOMA: Why the Defense of Marriage Act Is Unconstitutional." 83 *Iowa Law Review* 1 (1997).

———. "Same-Sex Marriage, Choice of Law, and Public Policy." 76 *Texas Law Review* 921 (1998).

Kramer, Larry. "Return of the Renvoi." 66 *New York University Law Review* 979 (1991).

———. "The Public Policy Exception and the Problem of Extra-Territorial Recognition of Same-Sex Marriage." 16 *Quinnipiac Law Review* 153 (1996).

Krauthammer, Charles. "When John and Jim Say 'I Do.' " In Andrew Sullivan ed., *Same-Sex Marriage: Pro and Con: A Reader.* New York: Vintage Books, 1997.

Kreimer, Seth F. " 'But Whoever Treasures Freedom . . . ': The Right to Travel and Extraterritorial Abortions." 91 *Michigan Law Review* 907 (1993).

———. "Territoriality and Moral Dissensus: Thoughts on Abortion, Slavery, Gay Marriage and Family Values." 16 *Quinnipiac Law Review* 161 (1996).

Lamm, Jocelyn B. Note. "Easing Access to the Courts for Incest Victims: Toward an Equitable Application of the Delayed Discovery Rule." 100 *Yale Law Journal* 2189 (1991).

Laycock, Douglas. "Equal Citizens of Equal and Territorial States: The Constitutional Foundations of Choice of Law." 92 *Columbia Law Review* 249 (1992).

Leflar, Robert A. "Conflicts Law: More on Choice-Influencing Considerations." 54 *California Law Review* 1584 (1966).

———. *American Conflicts Law.* Rev. ed. Indianapolis, Ind.: Bobbs-Merrill Co., 1968.

Lehmann, Michael P. "The Bill of Attainder Doctrine: A Survey of the Decisional Law." 5 *Hastings Constitutional Law Quarterly* 767 (1978).

Lorenzen, Ernest G. "Territoriality, Public Policy and the Conflict of Laws." 33 *Yale Law Journal* 736 (1924).

Lund, Nelson. "Retroactivity, Institutional Incentives, and the Politics of Civil Rights." 1995 *Public International Law Review* 87.

Lythcott-Maims, Julie C. Note. "Where Do Mixed Babies Belong? Racial Classification in America and Its Implications for Transracial Adoption." 29 *Harvard Civil Rights-Civil Liberties Law Review* 531 (1994).

Macedo, Stephen. "Homosexuality and the Conservative Mind." 84 *Georgetown Law Journal* 261 (1995).

Maguire, Daniel. "The Morality of Homosexual Marriage." In Robert M. Baird & Stuart E. Rosenbaum eds., *Same-Sex Marriage: The Moral and Legal Debate.* New York: Prometheus Books, 1997.

Mahoney, Margaret M. "A Legal Definition of the Stepfamily: The Example of Incest Regulation." 8 *Brigham Young University Journal of Public Law* 21 (1993).

Massaro, Toni M. "Gay Rights, Thick and Thin." 49 *Stanford Law Review* 45 (1996).

McClain, Linda C. " 'Irresponsible' Reproduction." 47 *Hastings Law Journal* 339 (1996).

McConnell, Michael W. "Contract Rights and Property Rights: A Case Study in the Relationship between Individual Liberties and Constitutional Structure." 76 *California Law Review* 267 (1988).

Mendicino, Thomas R. Note. "Characterization and Disease: Homosexuals and the Threat of AIDS." 66 *North Carolina Law Review* 226 (1987).

Mill, John Stuart. *Utilitarianism*. In J. M. Robson ed., *Collected Works of John Stuart Mill*. Vol. 10. Toronto: University of Toronto Press, 1969.

Mishra, Devjani. "The Road to Concord: Resolving the Conflict of Law over Adoption by Gays and Lesbians." 30 *Columbia Journal of Law & Social Problems* 91 (1996).

Mohr, Richard D. "The Case for Gay Marriage." 9 *Notre Dame Journal of Law, Ethics, & Public Policy* 215 (1995).

Mortland, Jean A. "Interstate Federalism: Effect of Full Faith and Credit to Judgments." 16 *University of Dayton Law Review* 47 (1990).

Nedrow, G. Keith. "Polygamy and the Right to Marry: New Life for an Old Lifestyle." 11 *Memphis State University Law Review* 303 (1981).

Neff, Brian. Comment. "Retroactivity and the Civil Rights Act of 1991: An Opportunity for Reform." 1993 *Utah Law Review* 475.

Note. "The Bounds of Legislative Specification: A Suggested Approach to the Bill of Attainder Clause." 72 *Yale Law Journal* 330 (1962).

Nutting, Charles B. "Suggested Limitations on the Public Policy Doctrine." 19 *Minnesota Law Review* 196 (1935).

Paige, Rebecca S. Comment. "Wagging the Dog—If the State of Hawaii Accepts Same-Sex Marriage Will Other States Have To?: An Examination of Conflict of Laws and Escape Devices." 47 *American University Law Review* 165 (1997).

Patten, James M. Comment. "The Defense of Marriage Act: How Congress Said 'No' to Full Faith and Credit and the Constitution." 38 *Santa Clara Law Review* 939 (1998).

Patton, Rodney. Student Work. "Queerly Unconstitutional?: South Carolina Bans Same-Sex Marriage." 48 *South Carolina Law Review* 685 (1997).

Paulsen, Monrad G. & Michael I. Covern. " 'Public Policy' in the Conflict of Laws." 56 *Columbia Law Review* 969 (1956).

Penas, Dwight J. "Bless the Tie That Binds: A Puritan-Covenant Case for Same-Sex Marriage." In Robert M. Baird & Stuart E. Rosenbaum eds., *Same-Sex Marriage: The Moral and Legal Debate*. New York: Prometheus Books, 1997.

Phillips, Robert M. Comment. "Good Faith and Fair Dealing under the Revised Uniform Partnership Act." 64 *University of Colorado Law Review* 1179 (1993).

Posner, Richard A. *Sex and Reason*. Cambridge, MA: Harvard University Press, 1992.

Prager, Dennis. "Homosexuality, the Bible, and Us—A Jewish Perspective." In Andrew Sullivan ed., *Same-Sex Marriage: Pro and Con: A Reader*. New York: Vintage Books, 1997.

Rabb, Barbara A. "The Constitutionality of the Defense of Marriage Act in the Wake of *Romer v. Evans*." 32 *New England Law Review* 263 (1997).

Rauch, Jonathan. "For Better or Worse." In Andrew Sullivan ed., *Same-Sex Marriage: Pro and Con: A Reader*. New York: Vintage Books, 1997.

Raz, Joseph. "Liberty and Trust." In Robert P. George ed., *Natural Law, Liberalism, and Morality*. Oxford: Clarendon Press, 1996.

Reese, Willis L. M. "Marriage in American Conflicts of Laws." 26 *International & Comparative Law Quarterly* 952 (1977).

Rensberger, Jeffrey L. "Same-Sex Marriage and the Defense of Marriage Act: A Deviant View of an Experiment in Full Faith and Credit," 32 *Creighton Law Review* 409 (1998).

Restaino, David P. Comment. "Conditioning Financial Aid on Draft Registration: A Bill of Attainder and Fifth Amendment Analysis." 84 *Columbia Law Review* 775 (1984).

Reynolds, William L. "The Iron Law of Full Faith and Credit." 53 *Maryland Law Review* 412 (1994).

Ricciardi, Laura. Comment. "The Aftermath of *United States v. Carlton*: Taxpayers Will Have to Pay for Congress's Mistakes." 40 *New York Law School Law Review* 599 (1996).

Ricciardi, Laura & Michael B.W. Sinclair. "Retroactive Civil Legislation." 27 *University of Toledo Law Review* 301 (1996).

Rice, Charles E. "Some Reasons for a Restoration of Natural Law Jurisprudence." 24 *Wake Forest Law Review* 539 (1989).

Richards, David A. J. *Women, Gays, and the Constitution: The Grounds for Feminism and Gay Rights in Culture and Law*. Chicago: University of Chicago Press, 1998.

Rosenblum, Darren. "Queer Intersectionality and the Failure of Recent Lesbian and Gay 'Victories'." 4 *Law & Sexuality* 83 (1994).

Rubenfeld, Jed. "The Right of Privacy." 102 *Harvard Law Review* 737 (1989).

Ruskay-Kidd, Scott. Note. "The Defense of Marriage Act and the Overextension of Congressional Authority." 97 *Columbia Law Review* 1435 (1997).

Sage, Candace L. Note. "Sister-State Recognition of Valid Same-Sex Marriages: *Baehr v. Lewin*—How Will It Play in Peoria." 28 *Indiana Law Review* 115 (1994).

Salten, Melissa G. "Statutes of Limitations in Civil Incest Suits: Preserving the Victim's Remedy." 7 *Harvard Women's Law Journal* 189 (1984).

Samar, Vincent J. *Justifying Judgment: Practicing Law and Philosophy*. Lawrence: University Press of Kansas, 1998.

Seidelson, David E. "Resolving Choice of Law Problems through Interest Analysis in Personal Injury Actions: A Suggested Order of Priority among Competing State Interests and among Available Techniques for Weighing Those Interests." 30 *Duquesne Law Review* 869 (1992).

Shreve, Gene R. "Choice of Law and the Forgiving Constitution." 71 *Indiana Law Journal* 271 (1996).

Simson, Gary J. "State Autonomy in Choice of Law: A Suggested Approach." 52 *Southern California Law Review* 61 (1978).

Sloan, Melanie Togman. "No More Baby Jessicas: Proposing Revisions to the Parental Kidnapping Prevention Act." 12 *Yale Law & Policy Review* 355 (1994).

Smead, Elmer E. "The Rule against Retroactive Legislation: A Basic Principle of Jurisprudence." 20 *Minnesota Law Review* 775 (1936).

Smith, Bryant. "Retroactive Laws and Vested Rights." 6 *Texas Law Review* 409 (1928).

Soper, Philip. "Making Sense of Modern Jurisprudence: The Paradox of Positivism and the Challenge for Natural Law." 22 *Creighton Law Review* 67 (1988).

———. "Some Natural Confusions about Natural Law." 90 *Michigan Law Review* 2393 (1992).

Sterk, Stewart. "The Marginal Relevance of Choice of Law Theory." 142 *University of Pennsylvania Law Review* 949 (1994).

Story, Joseph. *Commentaries on the Constitution of the United States.* 2nd ed. Vol. 2. Boston: C. C. Little and J. Brown, 1851.

Strassberg, Maura I. "Distinctions of Form or Substance: Monogamy, Polygamy and Same-Sex Marriage." 75 *North Carolina Law Review* 1501 (1997).

Strasser, Mark. "Family, Definitions, and the Constitution: On the Antimiscegenation Analogy. 25 *Suffolk University Law Review* 981 (1991).

———. "Suspect Classes and Suspect Classifications: On Discriminating, Unwittingly or Otherwise." 64 *Temple Law Review* 937 (1991).

———. "Domestic Relations Jurisprudence and the Great, Slumbering *Baehr*: On Definitional Preclusion, Equal Protection, and Fundamental Interests." 64 *Fordham Law Review* 921 (1995).

———. "Unconstitutional? Don't As; If It Is, Don't Tell: On Deference, Rationality, and the Constitution." 66 *University of Colorado Law Review* 375 (1995).

———. "Legislative Presumptions and Judicial Assumptions: On Parenting, Adoption, and the Best Interest of the Child." 45 *University of Kansas Law Review* 49 (1996).

———. "Judicial Good Faith and the *Baehr* Essentials: On Giving Credit Where It's Due." 28 *Rutgers Law Journal* 313 (1997).

———. *Legally Wed: Same-Sex Marriage and the Constitution.* Ithaca, NY: Cornell University Press, 1997.

———. "*Loving* the *Romer* Out for *Baehr*: On Acts in Defense of Marriage and the Constitution." 58 *University of Pittsburgh Law Review* 279 (1997).

———. "For Whom *Bell* Tolls: On Subsequent Domiciles' Refusing to Recognize Same-Sex Marriages." 66 *University of Cincinnati Law Review* 339 (1998).

Sullivan, Andrew ed. *Same-Sex Marriage: Pro and Con: A Reader.* New York: Vintage Books, 1997.

Susoeff, Steve. Comment. "Assessing Children's Best Interests When a Parent Is Gay or Lesbian: Toward a Rational Custody Standard." 32 *University of California at Los Angeles Law Review* 852 (1985).

Taintor, C. W. II, "What Law Governs the Ceremony, Incidents and Status of Marriage." 19 *Boston University Law Review* 353 (1939).

Thomas, Cal. "Marriage From God, Not Courts." In Robert M. Baird & Stuart E. Rosenbaum eds., *Same-Sex Marriage: The Moral and Legal Debate.* New York: Prometheus Books, 1997.

Toulon, Erik J. "Call the Caterer: Hawaii to Host First Same-Sex Marriage." 3 *Southern California Review of Law & Women's Studies* 109 (1993).

Trosino, James. Note. "American Wedding: Same-Sex Marriage and the Miscegenation Analogy." 73 *Boston Univerity Law Review* 93 (1993).

V., P. H., Annotation. "Marriage Valid Where Celebrated." 127 *American Law Reports* 437 (1940).

Wadlington, Walter. "The *Loving* Case: Virginia's Anti-Miscegenation Statute in Historical Perspective." 52 *Virginia Law Review* 1189 (1966).

Wardle, Lynn D. "A Critical Analysis of Constitutional Claims for Same-Sex Marriage." 1996 *Brigham Young University Law Review* 1.

Weiler, Andrew C. Note. "Has Due Process Struck Out? The Judicial Rubberstamping of Retroactive Economic Laws." 42 *Duke Law Journal* 1069 (1993).

Weinberg, Louise. "Choosing Law: The Limitations Debates." 1991 *University of Illinois Law Review* 683.

Weinreb, Lloyd L. *Natural Law and Justice*. Cambridge, MA: Harvard University Press, 1987.

———. "The Moral Point of View." In Robert P. George ed., *Natural Law, Liberalism, and Morality*. Oxford: Clarendon Press, 1996.

Weintraub, Russell. "Due Process and Full Faith and Credit Limitations on a State's Choice of Law." 44 *Iowa Law Review* 449 (1959).

Welsh, Jane. Note. "The Bill of Attainder Clause: An Unqualified Guarantee of Process." 50 *Brooklyn Law Review* 77 (1983).

Whitten, Ralph U. "The Original Understanding of the Full Faith and Credit Clause and DOMA." 32 *Creighton Law Review* 255 (1998).

Wilkinson, J. Harvie III & G. Edward White. "Constitutional Protection for Personal Lifestyles." 62 *Cornell Law Review* 563 (1977).

Wilson, Charles H. Jr. Comment. "The Supreme Court's Bill of Attainder Doctrine: A Need for Clarification." 54 *California Law Review* 212 (1966).

Wilson, James Q. "Against Homosexual Marriage." In Andrew Sullivan ed., *Same-Sex Marriage: Pro and Con: A Reader*. New York: Vintage Books, 1997.

Woodruff, Michael Joseph. "Lawyers and Sacred Gold." 27 *Texas Tech Law Review* 1411 (1996).

Wueste, Daniel E. Book Review. "Fuller's Processual Philosophy of Law." 71 *Cornell Law Review* 1205 (1986).

Index

About the Author

MARK STRASSER is Professor of Law at Capital University. His research interests include constitutional law, jurisprudence, bioethics, and gay and lesbian legal issues. This is his second book on the issues surrounding same-sex marriage.

www.ingramcontent.com/pod-product-compliance
Lightning Source LLC
LaVergne TN
LVHW011754200926
848484LV00003B/698
9780275966249